Up Sterling Creek Without a Paddle

CONFESSIONS OF A RECOVERING JOURNALIST

PAUL FATTIG

HELLGATE PRESS   ASHLAND, OREGON

UP STERLING CREEK WITHOUT A PADDLE
©2017 PAUL FATTIG

Published by Hellgate Press

(An imprint of L&R Publishing, LLC)

Hellgate Press
PO Box 3531
Ashland, OR 97520
email: sales@hellgatepress.com

Cover & Interior Design: L. Redding

Library of Congress Cataloging-in-Publication Data available from the publisher on request

ISBN: 978-1-55571-847-3

Printed and bound in the United States of America
First edition 10 9 8 7 6 5 4 3 2 1

Contents

DEDICATION

Placing the Blame

W RITING THE DEDICATION WAS THE MOST difficult challenge in completing
this book because there were so many to blame and those left standing
scurried for cover. But we'll give it the old college try.

Foremost is my late father whose passion for books instilled in me a
lifelong love with the printed word. Although he left the classroom after
the eighth grade, Paul R. Fattig, Sr. was an avid reader who was self taught
well beyond his formal education. He left an indelible imprint.

I also had many fine teachers in my formative years. Two of my favorites
were Don and Eileen Orton, talented pedagogues at Kerby Elementary
School who both strived—with varying degrees of success—to teach me
the fundamentals of our mother tongue. Another was science teacher Bill
Bryant, an easy-going fellow who made the hard sciences come alive.

Nor can I forget Bob Grant, the curmudgeonly editor of the weekly
Illinois Valley News in Cave Junction who, against his better judgment,
gave me a part-time job as a printer's devil while I was a high school
sophomore in 1967. He whetted my appetite for journalism.

But my greatest Fourth Estate mentor was a fine fellow named Joe
Cannon, an editor and publisher who hired me to edit a new weekly
newspaper he was launching. Never mind that I was still a student at the

University of Oregon. Joe was a terrific boss and adviser who gave me a chance when I sorely needed one. Nor can I forget the excellent professors at Duck U, including the inimitable Duncan McDonald and peerless Ralph Salisbury.

There are so many editors who have saved me from utter ruin over the years: Cathy Noah and Bob Hunter in Oregon; Carmen Dybdahl, Carol Murkowski and Duncan Frazier in Alaska; and Gene Bisbee in California, to name a few.

Our children—Sara, Rick, Amy, Derra and Sheena—contributed significantly by becoming fine humanoids, despite being part of a melded family. Like Lake Woebegone offspring, our grand children are all above average, of course.

Finally, without my wife, Maureen, at my side, no book would have been forthcoming. With apologies to the poet William Ernest Henley, she is the mistress of my soul.

An Awakening

A PPROACHING THE BIRTH OF 2014, I AWOKE TO AN epiphany that changed my life. After more than thirty years as a newspaper journalist, it dawned on me: The hand that fed me was dying. Although I am usually buoyantly optimistic, at times to the point of being slow on the uptake, I couldn't help but notice a few liver spots developing on the ink-stained appendage. However, I happily ignored the obvious signs of old age along with frequent whispered warnings by fellow toilers in the Fourth Estate that the end of print journalism as we knew it was at hand. Deep down, even I had an inkling that papers were evolving into an electronic format that would turn them into permanent denizens of the digital universe. Newspapers were dinosaurs.

Of course, this is no revelation if you are a member of the millennial generation or just reached the point of being able to decipher the printed word. After all, raised as a cyberspace cadet, you only have a vague notion of what constitutes a newspaper. Your grandparents, those old geezers from the Baby Boom generation, could tell you about them, if you could just get the decrepit wheezers to look up from their smart phones for a moment. God, I loathe old people my age who are computer whizzes. For your edification, newspapers consisted of large sheets of paper covered with news and featured articles, photographs and advertising. Neanderthals and their troglodyte pals found them handy to line their cave floors while conducting the messy business of painting bison and mastodons on the walls. In the 20th Century, owners of canaries found a similar use for newspapers as did folks who had a successful day at the fishing hole.

Yet I obliviously kept plugging along, trying to forget Ralph Waldo Emerson's admonition that a foolish consistency is the hobgoblin of little minds. I've never been precisely sure what a goblin is, let alone the hob edition. Moreover, Mr. Emerson lived long before humankind ever dipped a timid toe into the digital waters. What the heck did he know?

I prefer to believe I wasn't a Luddite. I was simply hoping print journalism would get a second wind in its long run of more than three centuries. Yet its coughing and wheezing became more pronounced each year. If you listened carefully, you could sometimes hear the raspy gasp of a death rattle in the newsroom. Still, no one jumped out the office windows. I chock that up to the fact we were on the second floor. Smacking onto the parking lot below would have only broken multiple bones, followed by a painful medical bill. Not a good scenario since our once healthy health insurance package had been gutted like a mackerel and was in intensive care. Sadly, it was not expected to recover. Greedy corporate relatives were already fighting over its last will and testament.

The more astute scribes had read the hand writing on the newsroom wall. One fellow writer was surreptitiously studying to get his realtor's license while another took a managerial job with a non-profit dedicated to improving the lives of abused children. Our crime reporter, a talented fellow who previously taught writing at Oregon State University, followed his felonious muse by snagging a job counseling habitual criminals. The published poet among us hung on by his fingernails until he could drop safely into a retirement nest festooned with iambic pentameter.

I didn't want to be the only one left to attend the wake. I needed to take the leap. Preferably not out the news room windows, having already broken several bones over the years. I was hoping for something that didn't involve a hard landing, followed by a long and painful recovery. I don't mind a few lumps, bumps and bruises. It's just that I get woozy when I see a compound fracture with its telltale splintered bone jutting out and copious amounts of blood spurting forth, particularly when it's my blood. What I hoped to find was another adventure involving playing with words.

With those parameters in mind, my wife, Maureen, and I pored over our finances. After a long weekend which included walking barefoot on the soothing sands of the glorious Oregon coast, we decided I should take early retirement from my newspaper job and try my hand at writing books. Our kids were somewhat potty trained and had largely fledged. Our pets had completed their advanced schooling. By tightening belts and eating every other day, we could survive. OK, maybe we wouldn't be skipping meals. But we hoped dinner wouldn't involve slicing smelly cold cuts from furry creatures found dead along Oregon highways.

Despite the trepidation, I was excited about making a dramatic lifestyle change. My longtime goal has been to become a recovering journalist writing books focusing on subjects of my own choosing. I longed to wax eloquently about the people, places and things on our strange little planet, just knowing that hordes of eager readers are waiting to hang onto every amazing detail and astounding insight. Yeah, I know, all the world needs is another over-the-hill journalist writing endless prattle. You correctly suspect that, as a seasoned reporter who knows a little about a lot of things but a lot about nothing, I am a past master at prattling. Whether it is worth reading you decide. This marks the first offering. So be kind. At the outset of this endeavor, I figured writing a book would be as easy as pulling words out of the air like so many daisy petals. But apparently some persnickety readers like to see the words in a rational order which at least makes a wild stab at coherency. Go figure.

While I don't profess to recall everything I learned at university, I do remember writing professors urging writers to focus on what they know. These were professors of creative writing, not journalism instructors. There is a difference between fiction and journalism. Honestly. For my first book, I decided to write about the partially-burned log house we bought and restored along Sterling Creek in southwest Oregon. As you shall soon discover, living with Maureen is a hoot.

But I must offer a sincere apology to fans of Peter Mayle whose brilliant

A Year in Provence book inspired this tome. The Mayles restored a 200-year-old stone house in rural France while we were patching back together a wood house half that age. Unlike the grand stones of France, our humble home was built of logs and lumber. And the original builders were apparently not particular when it came to the chore. But we love the place which we fondly refer to as a cabin.

I freely admit this book lacks Mayle's remarkable writing style, incredible wit and wonderful segues into French cuisine which would leave literary buffs hungry for more of that 1989 best seller. Nor did we find two Napoleonic gold coins as they did during their restoration in Provence, albeit we uncovered a 1907 Indian head copper penny. But our pets are smarter. And the wine from the Applegate Valley vineyards isn't too shabby. Moreover, you do get nearly fifteen years in our rustic cabin that remains a work in progress. I know. It seems longer.

Before we proceed further, you need to get acquainted with the two principals inhabiting the following pages. In truth, I could correctly be described as the antagonist since I frequently make comments that cause my significant other to look to the heavens for strength. Her keel is always even, always steady. Mine wanders all over the place, particularly when I'm ranting and raving. But I like to think I keep her life interesting.

Maureen is a hair stylist who has a salon on commercial property we bought in Medford, the regional hub for Southern Oregon and far Northern California. She has owned similar hairy establishments in Montana, Idaho and California. As a testament to her talent, several of her former clients from California's Bay Area traveled to Medford for years to have her coiffeur their pigmented filaments. She even had clients with relatives in Germany who scheduled appointments with her while visiting Oregon relatives. *Danke shoen.*

No readers or their attorneys, thankfully ever followed me anywhere. At least they weren't successful in their efforts to track me down to pursue threatened legal action.

At the time of my decision to pursue my dream of writing books, I was a columnist and reporter for the *Mail Tribune* newspaper out of Medford. It had been a good job with talented coworkers. We also got free doughnuts every other Wednesday. Hey, take it from me; those beignets—one of the few words I remember from my college French—were a big deal in newspaperdom where perks are notoriously scant. The doughnuts, coupled with an interesting and fun job whose perks included working alongside competent and congenial journalists, kept me there for more than two decades.

The *Medford Mail Tribune* lined a few cave floors over the years, becoming the fourth largest paper in Oregon. It even earned a Pulitzer Prize nearly a century ago, back in those distant decades when people actually got their news from newspapers and not on TV or the internet. That was a little while before I came along, of course.

I had written for more than a dozen papers on the West Coast, principally in Oregon but included stints in California and Alaska. While I was not a particularly gifted practitioner of my chosen profession, I managed to muddle along well enough to have had an interesting career, traveling a bit and meet a lot of fascinating folks, including one U.S. president—George W. Bush. Think what you will but he did sit in the Oval Office and pondered a bit. He also flew around the globe on Air Force One. So he fits the presidential profile. Thus, I can honestly say I had a very short conversation with the most powerful person on the planet.

Granted, it is true many political pundits on both sides of the aisle considered the forty-third U.S. president a diminutive one at best. But I found him an interesting fellow nonetheless. As I grow long of tooth, I have come to understand that none of us, save for Mr. Hitler and his evil ilk, are all bad. Or all good, for that matter. Best we can do is treat each other with respect and kindness, knowing full well we will periodically fall short. Vengeance at the hands of mortals may be frowned upon by godly beings, but I've noticed many religious zealots think they can get by with it if they bellow loud and long and get to church on time.

Strangely, my presidential encounter—I also had a short chat with the man who would be White House inhabitant No. 41 in the form of George H.W. Bush when he was a mere vice president—occurred roughly a mile as the crow flies from the rustic cabin we had just purchased. At the time, there was an old toilet sitting innocently in the cabin's back yard. I'll leave it to you to decide what symbolism to attach to the commode vis a vis the presidential visit. We will get to that odd but true tale in due time. Be patient. As you shall see, the old cabin seems to trigger rather bizarre events and attract unusual humanoids and other odd mammals. True, it could be something in the water. Either that or the peculiar human inmates suffering cabin fever in the dwelling are magnets for the wacky and weird.

The Bush incident reflects an observation made by a U.S. Attorney I came to know while covering a trial. In his opening statement to me, he noted that I seemed to lead a Forrest Gump life. However, unlike Mr. Gump who accidentally ends up in historical events, I bump into people who have left their mark on history, he correctly concluded in his closing argument. I like to think it was a compliment but I am harassed by doubt, knowing I am sometimes as hapless as the Gumpster.

Armed with the realization that I could finally take my book-writing plunge, I took a deep breath and leapt. I quit my day job at the end of 2013 to plunge into what for me was uncharted waters. A friend who has written several books—and had them published—advised that the trick is not to be intimidated by your magnum opus: you write it one page at a time. But you treat it like a job and go to work daily, he stressed.

So I took his advice. Now, each morning before dawn, I climb upstairs to my writing loft. I'm usually carrying a hot cup of tea, although I do fire up a pot of coffee when Earl Grey fails to provide sufficient stimulation. I write for a couple of hours, then wake Maureen and make her a cup of hot mocha. We engage in a pleasant morning chat over a light breakfast of toast, muffins and bananas. No *beignets*. Our two large pooches invariably mooch a piece of toast or a bit of muffin to tide them over until I serve them a hearty breakfast.

After Maureen goes to work, I tidy up a bit. When I feel particularly frisky, I even shave and brush my teeth. But I only floss the ones I want to keep. That lame joke is one I like to tell our dentist, a bright but beefy fellow who played football at Oregon State University. He grimaces at my sophomoric humor, apparently accepting it as the price to pay for having a patient who graduated from a ducky university south of Corvallis.

Prepared for the day, I feed our mooching mutts and ten assorted cats

Maureen has collected. An assorted cat is one which hasn't been sorted out when it comes to pedigree, by the way. With the wildebeests having gorged, I then take the dogs out to our dog park to let them conduct their business and stretch their legs. They also do a thorough reconnaissance, sniffing out any nocturnal activities that may have occurred overnight. This, of course, requires watering down numerous bushes and trees. Later, after refilling their tanks, they will take me for a short walk up the valley to irrigate yet more vegetation. The dogs drag me along by their leashes as they visit attractive points of interest such as a bush where a coyote urinated the night before or to a fascinating little pile of poop left by some nocturnal creature. A large mound of fresh bear scat, particularly if it is still steaming, causes a quick retreat to the cabin, despite the protestations from my furry comrades who fear no bear. There is no bar to the door to bar bears, but I securely lock the dead bolt should the bruin come sniffing around. At that point I would take the sage advice of Ogden Nash who wrote the great line, "If called by a panther don't anther." Now there was a fellow with a way with words.

Unfortunately, my domestic duties also include house work, a job that I don't find all that inspiring. That ultimately means chasing after dust bunnies that are larger than your average house cat. The scraggly hares make the fat felines jittery. Even the dogs get a little jumpy when a rather large dust bunny hops silently up from the floor. My job is to hunt them down and kill them, something this reformed hunter doesn't particularly enjoy. I let them live as long as possible. But the dishes are generally properly washed. Rarely does Maureen, who is much more fastidious than her husband, discover a dead dust bunny in a bowl or glass; not that often, anyway. When she saw a bunny peeping out from under the couch recently, she reminded me of a line from a poet I've loved since childhood.

"As you often say, Robert Service wrote that, 'A promise made is a debt unpaid,'" she said. "And you promised to keep the house clean if you were able to write at home. Now is your chance to make good on that promise. Did I mention that we do have a perfectly good vacuum?"

"You know perfectly well he was referring to cremating Sam McGee and not about firing up the Hoover," I countered. "Besides, cremating someone has to be much more pleasant than vacuuming. Aside from the sizzling sound and greasy odor at the outset, I'm sure it is a rather pleasant business, particularly on a barge on frozen Lake LaBarge."

Such was my appreciation for the poet that I once made a detour while driving the Alaska-Canada Highway to spend a night on the shores of Lake Laberge in the Yukon Territory. It was on that very real body of water that the fictitious cremation occurred. Service changed the name to Lake Labarge in the poem, apparently so he would have a rhyme for "marge," otherwise known as the lake's edge. It isn't really a lake but a three-mile wide section of the Yukon River. It's a beautiful spot should you ever seek a respite from the piercing scream of vacuum cleaners.

"Unlike a cremation, vacuuming is hideous from beginning to end," I said to Maureen, resuming my rant. "Deservedly so, the guy who invented the vacuum cleaner was cremated while he was still alive by a mob of angry people driven mad by the sound of vacuums. They figured it was a light punishment for the madman who created the vile machine that makes such an odious racket."

When I launch into a flight of fancy in an attempt to change the subject, I like to wander into a forest of non sequiturs. Segues—and Mr. Mayle—be damned. If it works as intended, I find it a good way to lead the victim off the beaten path. I prefer to believe that the whimsical wanderings keep Maureen on her toes while allowing me to take my pent-up restless imagination for a short walk. On a leash, of course. Never mind it has occurred to me that I may be wrong on both counts.

No matter. Maureen has grown wise to my methods. She invariably stays on point.

"You made a solemn promise," she reiterated. "Perhaps you might think about cremating some of these dust bunnies before they take over. They're reproducing faster than you can get rid of them."

She is right about my housekeeping responsibilities, of course. I do rev up the shrill scream machine when gangs of dust bunnies roam the cabin, spoiling for a fight. Unfortunately, just like their live counterparts, the dusty hair balls are masters of reproduction. Yes, it may very well be a family values thing but I refuse to hop into the politics of rabbits.

When I finish all my chores, including the detestable one that really sucks, I retreat up stairs to resume writing. Maureen refers to my writing space as the "man cave." But it is more aptly the lair of the beasts. I usually wade through a furry crowd of snoozing cats and dogs in able to reach my desk. Once there, I am in my element. The sound of snoring dogs and purring cats adds a beastly atmosphere that prompts a periodic grunt of approval from this caveman.

As a rehabilitating journalist, I have weaned myself from incessantly reading about the news or listening to it on the radio. We don't watch television so that isn't a problem. I'm now at the place where I concur with the old song by Simon and Garfunkel, the one including the line, "I get all the news I need from the weather report." Maureen is pleased but some old newsies I know are gob smacked at my journalistic heresy of wandering off the Fourth Estate into sublime pastures of cheat grass along Sterling Creek.

I now subscribe to "slow journalism," a term I first saw penned by Paul Salopek, a very talented journalist. He used the phrase to describe his anticipated seven-year Out of Eden walk to retrace the migratory steps of our Stone Age ancestors, starting in the birthplace of humankind in Africa all the way to the tip of South America. As I write this, he is walking through the Middle East. It is a journalistic excursion well worth following.

With that, I must offer a few words of caution about this tome. Some of us writers are like people who fish: our stories tend to grow over the years. Consider the six-pound German brown trout I caught in the Deschutes River a dozen years ago in central Oregon. That already hefty trout has grown nearly ten pounds, having gained a pound or so with each telling of the story. If I live to be 100, the trout will exceed twenty pounds, attaining lunker status.

But I'll endeavor to keep this slippery fish within legal literary limits, whatever that may be.

I shall also try to rein in tangents which have been known to lure me off the path, leaving the reader bewildered and lost deep in an untrammeled wilderness of words. As you have dubiously discovered, we've already wandered into the world of dust bunnies, Yukon-style crematoria, and canine "marking" habits. Future digressions, poor things, will be tethered so they can't ramble too far afield and unable to find their way back home.

But I digress. You are wondering why on earth Maureen and I ever bought an old cabin. That strange tale skulks in chapter one, waiting to pounce on those brave readers who have survived thus far.

ONE

Cabin Fever

F OR NORMAL PEOPLE LOOKING FOR THAT DREAM HOME, the toilet squatting in what passed for a yard would have prompted a hasty retreat back to the civilized world.

Indeed, anyone with even a tentative grip on real estate reality would jump back in the car, lock the doors and roar back down the long driveway in a cloud of dust. The expletives they were likely to yell out the side windows would have be lost in the sound of flying gravel, followed by smoking, squealing tires upon reaching the pavement. Later, in telling the tale, they would guffaw at the hapless saps ending up with the disaster waiting to befall them.

However, Maureen and I were not your average saps in search of new digs in our native southern Oregon in the fall of 2001. Very peculiar but largely mentally sound, our friends would tell you. They are extremely charitable, considering how high we score on the wackiness scale.

"We may want to give some thought about moving that toilet," I observed as we surveyed the yard debris. "On the other hand, we could just leave it there and wave at passersby while doing our business. Wouldn't want them to think we were antisocial."

"Sometimes I wonder about your sense of decorum, sweetie," Maureen countered. "I realize you came from rural Oregon but you need to remember you now live in civilized society. Of course we don't have to move it. We'll just build a little frame and put curtains around it. Something pea green with a flowery design would be nice."

With that, we both started giggling and snorting. They are right, our friends. We plead guilty of being peculiar, maybe even a tad eccentric. I'll leave it to you the jury to decide which one of us is more reality challenged.

There is no denying we were long past slap happy when it came to looking at potential new homes. For more than two years, we had been property hunting in search of a place closer to our jobs. We wanted acreage in the country but relatively close to town. Not too far, not too close. Anything outside the city limits but within twenty minutes of town was in our Goldilocks zone.

We were also seeking a fixer upper, an old place chock full of history. As a result, we had waded through some real down-in-the-dumps dumps that would have scared the bejabbers out of a veteran EPA field worker. So a few imperfections didn't faze us at that point. What's more, we figured the blemishes came with the territory, given our financial limitations. Anything short of discovering mummified remains in a closet would be taken in stride.

The place we had come to check out during our extended lunch break was about a half dozen miles south of the historic mining boom town of Jacksonville in Jackson County. The property itself included a nearly century old largely log cabin with two bedrooms and two baths nestled in a little valley on nearly forty-five acres along Sterling Creek. It was ripe with both potential and pitfalls. There was a substantial forest of evergreens, including cedar, pine and fir. It was also thick with deciduous trees like laurel, oak and maple. The southern exposure on the north side of the little valley also had a stand of giant manzanita more than a foot in diameter at the base. It was the picturesque kind of place you would envision your forefathers and foremothers settling in after arriving from the old country, wherever the heck that was.

But the cabin had been gutted by fire more than a decade earlier. It was largely a skeletal shell, protected from the elements by a barn-red metal roof. It seemed to be waiting for the right people to stumble upon it.

The immediate area was also steeped in history which was a big draw for us. The property was little more than a gold nugget's throw from the long defunct mining boom town of Sterlingville, one of many tiny towns that mushroomed up in the headlong scramble for precious metal in the West. Like a forest fungi which ultimately fades back in the earth from whence it came, Sterlingville died away a century ago.

Without getting too deep into the weeds, you need to get to know the two principal personalities you will be living with in the coming pages. Not to worry. We are mostly user friendly. We even have lucid moments at times.

You will soon realize that I can be a starry-eyed Don Quixote; Maureen is the Sancho Panza with earthy wit, although she has more common sense than the windmill challenger's sidekick. However, unlike Cervante's Sancho, she is neither anyone's servant nor a bit of a slow poke whose ideas ride in on a plodding donkey. Her bursts of excitation and energy upon having hatched a new idea would have dazzled Tesla.

I am loathe to admit it but she is also the brainier one in the outfit. She invariably comes up with sound ideas to solve whatever dilemma we encounter. While I am prone to endless mulling, often leading to far-flung forays into God knows what, she zeros in on the problem. Her brain seldom switches off. The prudent thing to do is to sit back and wait, something I am still working on since I am the impatient type. Yet her ideas invariably prove educational, although they can be a tad bit scary or downright hilarious. Sometimes both. I find it best to keep one eye open when awake.

Like all of us, she is not perfect, although it took me a few years to discover her one flaw. She has yet to meet an animal she did not want to turn into a pet, a genetic disorder inherited from her father. Thus we have always lived with a hairy harem that includes a couple of dogs and numerous cats. Given the pets, our new home and land had to be able to accommodate them. Did I mention that pet hair is a condiment in our house? The cool thing about it is you rarely have to floss. But it is no fun coughing up a hair ball.

Don't get me wrong. I love our furry brothers and sisters. But I can get restless and cranky when my feeding and watering comes after all the beasts have been made comfy. Comes from a survivalist mentality acquired during childhood , I suppose. Truth be told, I can be a little slow when it comes to doing the right thing. Although I don't have cloven hooves, I sometimes need to be poked and prodded to follow Maureen's kindly footsteps. I like to think it doesn't take as much cajoling as it once did for me to be a halfway decent humanoid.

But I was ready to fight when a journalistic friend described me as uxorious. While I was willing to make allowances for his having been born in England, he had obviously stepped over the line.

"In my native Josephine County, you had better be ready to brawl when you throw a word like that at someone," I told him. "I've been accused of a lot of things in my life but I believe I have never been called something that foul sounding. Would you like to apologize before things turn ugly?"

"Sorry," he replied. "I forgot you are from Kerby. Being uxorious simply means you dote on your wife, albeit a bit excessively."

I informed him that people from Kerby are decent folk, not the type who would wildly launch words like "uxorious" and "albeit" in one sentence, let alone utter such words in a lifetime. But I accepted his apology, what with English being a second language for the English.

Besides, I do adore my wife. Not only is she easy on the eyes, but she is bright, likable and has an infectious laugh. To put it in the vernacular spoken when the cabin was young, she's the bee's knees, although I'm not precisely sure what a bee's knee looks like. Me, I am not something an optometrist would recommend staring at for too long a period. I'm also something of a bookworm and taciturn at times to the point of being misanthropic. When I am asked to speak at a public gathering, my knees tend to buckle. However, thanks to having made a public ass of myself enough times and lived to tell about it, I'm starting to realize public elocution and public executions are not synonymous. At least the incontinence problems are drying up.

As noted, we were both born with webs between our toes, figuratively speaking, although the skin between my big toes and the fellow next in line looks a little froggish. We have a deep affection for the webfoot state which has been celebrating its birthday every Valentine's Day since 1859. Arizona was also officially born on Valentine's Day. But Oregon is half a century older, doubtlessly making its biped beavers wiser than the two-footed desert rats. Not to be snooty, of course.

"We're like the salmon we came home to die," Maureen loves to tell people when they ask why we left California to return to rustic southern Oregon. The quip is usually met with nervous laughter, followed by discreet inquiries about our physical and mental health. "Oh, we're fine," she'll reply with a sweet smile. "We are just spawned out like a couple of soreback salmon."

At that point, folks unfamiliar with the life cycle of those Pacific Northwest waterborne inhabitants appear as though they are about to hurl. They look around for a place to quickly wash the hand that just shook Maureen's little but powerful pinky. I hastily inform them that we really don't have a communicable disease, at least none whose symptoms include disgusting sores on our backs. I explain soreback refers to salmon that are starting to die naturally after having completed their reproduction cycle. Their skin loses its healthy sheen, becomes mottled and starts sloughing off here and there, making them resemble river-dwelling zombies. They die, their discarded flesh providing protein for their offspring and for hungry bears as part of the circle of life.

Incidentally, I do have a periodic itchy spot between my shoulder blades. "Nothing to worry about," my wife concluded after a cursory inspection, "probably just the heartbreak of psoriasis. Either that or the onset of leprosy. Don't hug me for the next six months."

I should mention that, in addition to being as cute as a bug's ear, she is also the funny one.

We hail from blue-collar families in the relatively poor region of this rural state. But it would be wrong to categorize us as dirt poor: our families didn't own much dirt to speak of. Even in Kerby, where being well off often meant the head of the household only sought unemployment relief during the winter months, my family was down and out. Our mom was a jobless widow with five young children and a mutt named Willy living in a shack largely held together by termites. The insects were doubtlessly considered by their woodworm relatives to be lowbred louts living in a dismal dwelling not fit for habitation by high-toned termites. While roadkill was never on our scant menu, we may have looked wistfully at a road side meal a time or two. Still, we never knowingly ate termites. That was mostly out of respect for their job of holding the house together. We also suspected termite stew lacked a satisfying piquant.

Maureen likes to say she is from the poor side of the tracks in the relative metropolis of Grants Pass. Yet she was reared in a two-parent working household with a likable but sassy sister and a largely purebred pooch named Dusty. I figured she was high class. Still do, after all these years.

While we ought not to get too deep into the weeds, you need to at least part the poison oak and blackberries to gain further insight into our unorthodox journey through life. We met when we were 16, went together in high school, then one of us got a wild hair and joined the Marine Corps in 1969.

I can tell you I served with Sgt. Richard Eubank in the 4th Marine Division, that I have been to Vietnam, spent most of 1971 in the Veterans Hospital in Portland and walk with a pronounced limp. Members of the Veterans of Foreign Wars will recognize the still gungho Richard, now a retired master sergeant, as the VFW's 2010-11 national commander. As I write this, he is now serving as the commander of the state VFW chapter in Oregon, having retired to the Beaver state from his native California.

About now you have concluded that I was wounded in Vietnam but your conclusion would have jumped far beyond the facts. My friendship with Richard can be chalked up to yet another Forrest Gump episode in my life. Like many in the military and unlike Richard, the only battles I ever experienced in the military were fighting hangovers. I lost every time, incidentally. I was stateside throughout my tour. Richard arrived at the division headquarters at Camp Pendleton in California where I was stationed after he completed a tour in Vietnam. I broke my neck in a car wreck—I bought the 1964 Volkswagen I was driving at the time from Richard—while foolishly celebrating with buddies shortly after completing my hitch. Rendered a quadriplegic, I learned how to walk again in the VA hospital, albeit I never regained full dexterity on my right side, hence a hitch in my gait. I went to Vietnam as a journalist years after I left the Corps. As a marine, I did absolutely nothing more than occasionally play war games with reservists who lacked any enthusiasm for what they clearly felt were pointless endeavors. They may have been on to something.

I bring this up because too many wrongfully conclude that anyone who served in uniform is a hero. That myth does a disservice to those who were in combat, particularly those who gave either a limb or their all. For instance, of my three brothers who all served in Vietnam while in the Army, only my twin was in combat. Even in the Corps, many of the fellows I served with had never been in the heat of battle. Yet we were all ready and willing. Of course, there was also a few what we called non hackers, also known by coarser language as shit birds. But they were only a few foul feathers in an otherwise fine flock.

Suffice it to say my joining the military resulted in both Maureen and I going our separate ways, eventually getting married to folks with whom we had little in common other than walking upright and having opposing thumbs. This is not meant as a pejorative to the others involved, although I'm not convinced one individual had a fully developed brain stem. No names, given our litigious society.

The bottom line is we now know we should have stayed together from the outset, cutting out the middle men and women. It took two decades for us to reunite, becoming a blended allAmerican family with five kids bound together by love and laughter with intermittent debates and disagreements. We found that duct tape helps. Baling wire is also an excellent fall back in the event the tape doesn't stick. One doesn't want a family member wriggling loose and terrorizing society. Actually, Maureen and I have Lake Woebegone children: they are all above average. The girls are frighteningly strong. But there is nary a felon in the bunch.

Let us get back to what led us to the yard toilet which, by the way, was not hooked up to any plumbing. It was just sitting there, no doubt pondering the state of the world. Or it could be it was waiting for some kind of movement, real estate wise.

Our decision to move from a house we owned in the little hamlet of

Williams in southeastern Josephine County was driven by our need to live closer to our jobs in Jackson County. But it was more than a simple desire to reduce mileage. We wanted land where we had more elbow room, a place to put down permanent roots from which our activities and discoveries would become fond memories. Our offspring had all fledged and were doing well.

Nor had we just fallen off the potato truck when it came to buying property. We had bought and sold homes as new jobs required over the years. We knew what we wanted. But we had yet to find our fantasy property, the place where we would live out the remainder of our years. This would be our last stand.

The land we sought was already forming an image in our minds: it would be a restorable cottage or cabin in a little valley a few miles from the nearest town. Ideally, the town would be a historic hamlet, a quaint little place with friendly folks who didn't drool incessantly, cool old buildings filled with history and decent restaurants that didn't serve mystery meals. Cheerful tourists with fat wallets would stroll along the streets, marveling at the beauty of the place and the intelligence of its sophisticated inhabitants.

When those tourists took a short drive into the nearby countryside, they would see our impressive little country home nestled on land that would take their breath away. There would be big trees with open fields here and there where deer were browsing, looking up periodically to pause and chew their cud while evaluating the gawkers. On a spring day, you would see a fawn gamboling about on a carpet of multicolored wild flowers. Come winter, a beautiful blanket of snow would coat the land. A wisp of smoke would drift up out of the chimney, indicating a cheerful fire was crackling away in the wood stove. There would be tracks left by forest creatures we knew were there but seldom seen. Sasquatch? Sure, he would be welcome, providing he behaved himself. He would not be allowed to bellow late at night, couldn't eat us or our pets and had to bury his scat. Deep.

Regardless of the nature of the furry forest dwellers, acreage was paramount. We didn't want neighbors breathing down our necks, particularly if they had a penchant for garlic. More to the point, we wanted to be able to take our dogs or an occasional cat on short hikes, stopping to sniff the wild roses along the way. We also wanted to raise a vegetable garden, taking advantage of Maureen's green thumbs. Our table would be filled with fresh bounty from the garden. There would be a hammock strung between two shade trees where I could comfortably watch Maureen toil in the soil. Life would be good.

This would be our final stopping place. With both of us half a century old, we wanted a home to which we would be forever wed. Yessiree Bob, it was to be the place we would love and cherish until death do us part.

Given our limited budget, it stood to reason the house would not be luxurious. Indeed, it would most certainly be a fixer upper. However, since we have basic carpentry skills and all of our digits, despite a couple of close encounters with a table saw, we figured we were up to most challenges. But we prefer our toilets inside.

Still, we weren't quite prepared for some of the hovels we encountered during our long hunt for the land of our day dreams. Some were nightmares that would have scared the daylights out of Stephen King.

Take the chicken coop that the featherbrained owner who, with a straight face, tried to pass off as a house. A work in progress, he called it. Please. Any chicken with a beak's worth of common sense would have squawked at the mere thought of having to spend the night there. There were rafters with feathers still clinging to them, apparently glued on by what comes out the south end of a northbound hen. A retirement nest it was not.

Chicken had been on the menu in another fixer upper we checked out. The inhabitants had left the remnants of the foul fowl dinner with all the trimmings on the table, disappearing like the crew and passengers on the Mary Celeste. The mashed potatoes, still in the bowl, had an interesting yellowish tan which an archaeologist would have called a rind. The once green salad had long turned brown. The skin on one chicken leg looked like it could have belonged to King Tut some 3,000 years dead. You wouldn't have had to be a cannibal to have preferred a pharaoh leg over the shriveled chicken appendage. Maybe the thigh of a mummified Egyptian king tastes like chicken jerky.

Unused napkins had been carefully placed next to the plates. Glasses were half full or half empty, depending on your perspective. The surface of what appeared to have been a glass of milk was coagulated. I'm only surmising it was liquid from a bovine, mind you. We didn't sample to verify its contents.

Had they received a call in mid-meal informing them that a loved one had died? Did they suddenly decide to flee creditors? Or was there a murder most foul, triggered by one too many debates over real estate? Whatever the story we weren't buying it, the house, that is.

Then there was the rustic A-frame home in which I climbed to the top loft where I was told I would have a great view of the nearby forest. The view was terrific but it was hard to appreciate it, what with the terrifying prospect of having to climb back down the rickety ladder which rose nearly thirty feet above a concrete floor. It was reminiscent of a boarding ladder used to climb up the side of an English battleship in centuries past, back when losing a sailor or two over the side was no big deal.

Maureen will tell you she had to pry my hands off the top railing while trying to talk me down from the precarious perch. That's a slight exaggeration, of course. I wasn't really panicking. My hands were simply locked up by a little arthritis. But it is true I get a touch of vertigo every time I look down at my imminent death caused by falling from great heights. In any case, I couldn't hear her words of encouragement, what with all the whimpering and whining coming from the top rung.

You get the gist. We had seen it all. Nothing would shock us, certainly not a mere toilet perched innocently in the yard. For us, it was nothing more than a curiosity, a trifle. Nope, we would not quibble over a decorative toilet.

We had employed the services of a realtor friend who we shall call Pat since she answers to that moniker. Having been selling real estate in the area for some twentyyears, she knew the lay of the land. She is also an excellent representative of the interesting people who come to the region. Born in Canada, she is a world traveler with a degree in English from the University of Colorado. Her partner in life is a smart fellow named Bud who, like yours truly, was born and reared in rural southern Oregon. He is one of those rare guys who can do a lot of different things well when it comes to hands-on work. They came from different backgrounds yet are attracted to each other by the things they have in common, including reaching out to help others.

For more than a year, Pat had been patiently taking us to rustic homes that were on the market. But nothing caught our fancy.

"We'll just keep looking at anything with land on it until we find the one," Maureen reiterated for the umpteenth time after we left one place whose land did not measure up to our expectations.

"Most of which should be above water," I added helpfully.

They wisely ignored my oft-repeated attempt at real estate humor.

"There is this one place out past Jacksonville you might be interested in," Pat said. "I haven't seen it but it does have 44 acres with trees on it. It sounds like the old house could use a lot of work. Apparently there was a fire a couple of years ago. Nobody lives out there now. I haven't seen the property but it may be worth a look."

We agreed such a place offered possibilities, albeit the $145,000 asking price was a little higher than what we wanted to pay. It doesn't sound like much now but this was just before land prices ballooned up, mind you. However, our nest egg did not come from the golden goose. Our egg was small, fractured and oozing a bit of the yoke. If the property included land that wasn't completely submerged, we wanted to take a look.

We took a long lunch break one day in early October of 2001 and met Pat at the property which is off a winding but picturesque county highway called Sterling Creek Road. We had driven through the area several times in the recent past in search of land. We were already fans of the beautiful Little Applegate River watershed.

"Hey, this is that place we really liked!" I told Maureen as we turned into the driveway. "Remember, we drove by it last spring and we both agreed we wanted something like this. Look at that setting."

Nestled cozily in a little valley, the cabin with its red metal alpine roof stood about 300 feet west of the road. Some old-growth fruit trees heavy with apples and pears could be seen in a field across from the dwelling. Orchard grass grew thick and deep. Beyond the cabin was a forest with big trees on the north slope and the hoped for open spaces on the south side where deer would graze.

From the road, it looked like a place where grand parents would make their last stand. You could almost smell the fresh coffee brewing in the kitchen and grandma's hot apple pie cooling on the wood stove. There would be grandpa with a twinkle in his eyes as he lit up his old smelly pipe before spinning a yarn. OK, tobacco smoke makes me gag but I am known for sometimes telling tales. And Maureen does bake an apple pie to die for. In any case, this could be it, the land where we would build our future.

"You're right it's the place I said would be perfect for our grand kids to visit," she said. "But I don't remember seeing a 'For Sale' sign. It also looked like someone was living here. There are a couple of cars up by the house."

Pat explained it had been on the market for six months, and there had apparently been no offers. The owner was motivated to sell, she added.

That's when we began to notice a few blemishes. The wooden gate at the end of the driveway looked like it was suffering from a major hangover. A sailor coming in after a wild weekend of imbibing wouldn't have listed as badly as the gate. Sagging in the middle, the gate resembled an old swayback horse. One hinge had only one nail keeping it attached to the post. A strong breeze could bring about its demise. We also became aware of the weeds three feet tall in the center of the driveway. No tires had rolled across the driveway in recent months. Given the fact it had been a dry fall with fire danger still lingering, we parked our vehicles at the end of the long driveway and began walking up the slight incline to the cabin.

I picked my way carefully through the weeds. It was still warm and dry so there could be a rattlesnake underfoot, impatient and cranky from being underfed and underwatered. Buzzworms give me the willies. Fortunately, they were not in the biting mood that day. Or perhaps they were taking a midday nap, snoozing while the meaty calves strode past.

Pat was right about the cars. What we had assumed were the owner's cars parked by the cabin were deader than Henry Ford. But we could blame Henry for only the Ford Mercury and the Ford van. There was also an old Chevrolet pickup truck with a camper attached. Every vehicle had broken windows and flat tires. Later we would discover two other discarded cars up the valley.

After commenting on the beauty of the area while taking note of the debris field outside the cabin, we walked up on the attached deck whose redwood boards were gray with age. Pat stepped halfway inside the doorway of the cabin whose windows had been broken. Whether they were shattered from the fire or vandalism we knew not.

"Oh, my God!" she exclaimed. "It's really gross in there. I can't show this place to you."

Or words to that effect. She had already turned heel, walking out the door. Maureen and I peeked through the doorway. Pat had been diplomatic: to call it gross was like saying Hurricane Katrina dinged up New Orleans a little. The interior had been blackened by the fire. Scorched sheetrock hung from the open ceiling. Where it was wasn't covered by burned rubbish and ashes, the slate green concrete floor was stained by all manner of objects that had melted onto it. Log rafters overhead were charred. No one had bothered to clean up after the fire.

"Well, since we are here, we might as well see everything," Maureen said as she waded farther into the rubbish. "It does look kind of interesting. It has possibilities."

"Should have brought a pith helmet," I muttered as we picked our way through the clutter.

Actually, the living room floor wasn't a complete debris field. A small area in the center of the living room floor had been partially cleared. Someone, probably local urchins, had sprayed a pentagram on the floor with a can of red spray paint. Doubtlessly, they were trying to conjure beelzebub or some specter from beyond the veil. All they did was add another stain to the floor, one we would have a devil of a time removing. Several of the slower vandals had even signed their names. Does Jack still love Sandra or was it just a passing juvenile fancy?

Beyond it sat a wood stove, a huge one that would have devoured short logs as the homeowner tried to keep the drafty cabin warm on a cold winter's night. Just behind it was a vertical wooden ladder attached to the wall and used to access the loft above the kitchen. You could see blue sky where the fire had eaten through the loft's west wall.

Stepping into what had been the kitchen, we could see where an electric cooking stove and refrigerator once stood. Both had left telltale footprints on the fire-stained floor. Whatever cupboards there had been were gone, razed by the flames. The kitchen had been thoroughly cooked.

The ravenous fire had also exposed the interior of the log walls built by someone who obviously did not have a Lincoln Logs set as a kid to perfect his craftsmanship. The old cabin had been erected with vertical fir logs, each one roughly a foot in diameter. Conceivably, they were logged from the property when the cabin was built. The exposed logs gave the old place a look of a rustic fort from the days when Oregon was still a territory.

An old codger who was a sapling when log cabins were still the mainstay told me that vertical log walls enabled settlers to replace a wall fairly easily in the event of a fire. But he may have been full of happy horse hockey. Either that or just having fun with a youngster too thick to know the difference.

The small bedroom off the kitchen had also borne the brunt of the fire. Even the upright logs were charred. Yet the master bedroom had escaped intact, albeit the walls and ceiling were smoke stained. A small woodstove stood in one corner of that bedroom. The master bedroom had originally been another cabin which was connected to the main cabin by a short hallway. It had a fir floor which seemed sound. The two bathrooms both had toilets in place, leaving us to wonder about the purpose of the orphan toilet out in the yard. We paused for a moment at the burned doorway where the back door once stood, and studied the porcelain throne.

It wasn't attached to anything. It was just there, a conversation piece. Perhaps it was used for contemplating life. It was the large kind popular back in the mid1900s before dainty low-flow commodes were fashionable. This water closet could have been employed by those gargantuan people you read about who get caught in a bathroom and have to be hoisted out by a crane.

Yet the toilet with its smoke stains I preferred to assume they were smoke stains didn't stand out all that much in the debris field that included everything from charred timbers to fire-ravaged household appliances, even the kitchen sink. Think firebombed Dresden, World War II.

Towering above the toilet was an old-fashioned hot water tank decorated with what was undeniably an immense rust stain, one which resembled South America all the way down to Terra del Fuego. But the southern tip had a bit of a curly cue. It brought back happy memories of the crude map I had drawn in Kerby Elementary School. I had given the southern tip of the continent a bit of a hook with Patagonia pointing north toward Florida. I thought it was a nice whimsical touch but the teacher was not impressed with my geographically challenged rendition of the New World. Still, I received a C for the creative effort, reflecting the fact the kind pedagogue saw me as a charity case with a wild imagination. I was pleased, given the grade gave my GPA a much needed boost.

Surrounding the hot water tank were various fascinating items, chief among them another old wood stove which likely first began heating the old place when Model A's bounced along what was then an old dirt road out front.

Rising from the ground were several rusting water pipes, writhing in frozen agony over the disastrous fire. Two of the pipes reached about 12 feet in the air, indicating that another old structure that was next to the cabin had been leveled by the fire. That structure apparently had a second story.

With the odd toilet, the pipes jutting up, the old wood stove and the weird hodge podge of charred remains of other household items, it would have prompted normal home buyers to give an amazingly accurate rendition of Edvard Munch's The Scream, complete with sound effects. That would, of course, be the famous painting of a poor fellow frozen in a scream, his contorted face filled with agonizing anxiety and deep despair. Munch was certainly an impressionist who made a lasting impression.

But, as noted earlier, Maureen and I are a little shy of normal. Nor are we in a hurry to get there. Moreover, we are made of stern stuff. Despite the fire-gutted interior, the junk in the yard and the dead vehicles, we agreed the old place had a certain charm. But so did our jobs. We headed back to work.

That evening as we were driving home together, Maureen nonchalantly asked how I liked the Sterling Creek property.

"I like the land really well that little valley has a wonderful feeling about it ," I replied. "I even like the old cabin. But it would take a lot of work. It would have to be gutted, of course. And we would have to haul away a lot of crap."

Maureen was quiet for a moment as I drove along. I knew something was brewing. But I was patient for once and let her thoughts percolate.

"I like it, too," she said. "I know we only saw it for about a half hour but you know that old saying that you need to strike while the iron is hot."

"Perhaps we need to strike," I said, my eyes on the road ahead as I negotiated a turn.

"We struck," she said. "Pat suggested we offer way under what the owners wanted. Since there have been no offers she thought the owners might be motivated to drop their price and counter our bid."

"And?" I asked.

"We offered them $116,000," she said.

"So what was their counter offer?" I pressed.

"They didn't counter," she said. "They . . ."

"Rats!" I interrupted. "The more I think about it, the more I like that place. It has tons of potential. I loved that forest and the little valley. The cabin has a nice Alpine look. And the deck was kind of cool, even if it was placed over the septic tank. Maybe we should offer a little more. You know, grease the skids a bit."

At that point, Maureen broke into that Cheshire cat grin she always gets when she is about to let a writhing feline out of the bag.

"They didn't counter because they accepted our offer," she said. "We are now the proud owners of 45 acres on Sterling Creek, buddy boy."

I was silent for a moment, stunned by the news. I felt like the car-chasing dog who, upon finally catching a mechanical prey, is perplexed about what to do next, other than watering down one tire while giving it a think.

"Well, we really ought to remove that toilet," I finally said. "It is the epitome of butt ugly."

She groaned at the sophomoric play on words but concurred with the conclusion.

"Yes, the toilet needs to go," she agreed.

For a dream home, it was a very inauspicious beginning.

TWO

Southern Oregon History 101

B EFORE BEING INTRODUCED TO BARBARIC TOOLS such as a drawknife, the weapon masochists in pioneer times employed to peel slabs of skin from their knuckles while inadvertently removing bark from logs, you need to be become familiar with the region and its interesting inhabitants. They are a likable lot, the mosaic of folks from all walks of life who call the Applegate Valley their home. And the land beckoning these bipeds is easy on the eyes.

I love southern Oregon, warts and all. As a product of both the land and its people, I freely acknowledge accentuating the positive when it comes to assessing its intrinsic value. It's kind of like judging your own child: a parent tends to brag on the little tykes, unwilling to acknowledge the anti-social tendencies even after little Freddy or Freda ends up doing ten to fifteen in the Big House for repeated felonious behavior. However, other than one of the nation's top ten most wanted fugitives discovered living in the valley in the late 1990s, there isn't much major criminal activity in our little part of the world. Our man in the top ten wasn't an ax murderer. He was involved in some sort of high finances white collar crime. In fact, a friend who goes by the initials J.D. used to go fishing with him. J.D. was mighty surprised to find his fishing buddy was a nationally-known criminal. He was a good man to ride the Rogue River with, J.D. noted. About the only other local major crime I know about is someone professing to be a writer hacking out a book. But I'm proud to say he is the only fraud in the family.

My paternal grandparents came to the region from the Midwest at the tail end of the 1800s. By then, my maternal ancestors were already in the Northwest, having arrived in the early 1850s via the Oregon Trail from back East. Those who contributed to the maternal gene pool were settlers in the truest sense of the word while my paternal forefathers and foremothers were pseudo pioneers. But at least they had the good sense to eventually land in the valley named after the pioneering Applegate family.

Of course, they arrived yesterday compared to the indigenous people whose generations go back more than 10,000 years in this region. If you consider the average generation being about thirty years, then the indigenous folk have stacked up more than 3,333 generations, although you would have to factor in bears and cougars pouncing in to thin the gene pool periodically. In comparison, my ancestors just fell off the potato truck. Several landed on their heads and remained a little daft the remainder of their days. Very sad.

But the fact my maternal side of my ancestry goes back to before Oregon became the 33rd state gives us some bragging rights with the provincially-minded dwellers of the Beaver state. Never mind the justifiable smirking among our indigenous friends with their regional ancestry reaching back to the dawn of time. I like to tell them my ancestors thought about taking the land bridge leading to present-day Alaska but decided to wait for a boat before heading off to the New World. They figured the boats would be more tourist friendly than the hungry polar bears waiting on the icy land bridge, I add. Our Native American friends don't buy it, of course. At any rate, we are all related if you go back far enough. Undeniably, we are certainly in the same boat as we voyage onward into an uncertain future.

An odd thing is that many Oregonians purport to despise folks from California. Never mind the lion's share of Oregon residents or their ancestors hail from the Golden State. As one of the most populous states in the Union, it's understandable many would migrate north for more elbow room.

I recall a local gas station owner named Pete who used to constantly bad mouth Californians. "Pete, where are you from?" I asked him after he made a snide comment about folks hailing from south of the state line, knowing full well from whence he came. "I'm from California but that was 14 years ago," he replied in a huff. "I just don't want any more of them up here. They aren't like us."

I didn't ask him what he meant by that, concerned it was something I didn't want to hear. But I figure most Californians have broadened our state's diversity base, making an improvement, providing they treat others with respect, even those from the Golden state.

It is true that serious scholars of past events don't place Oregon as high as California when it comes to making its mark on our nation's history. Yet you'll find Oregon does have some historic heft, providing you nose around a bit and aren't too persnickety. Mssers. Lewis and Clarke seemed to like the place.

Most people don't realize that President Thomas Jefferson specifically told Lewis and Clark to check out the Applegate River Valley when he instructed them to explore the far western part of the continent during their trip of discovery back in 1804-6. OK, I made that up. But there is little doubt Mr. Jefferson knew in his gut there was some wonderful country to be found out West. His instinct was spot on, of course. Unfortunately, the captains of exploration spent the winter of 1805 near present-day Astoria. I believe they would have had a better time of it in the Rogue Valley where the weather is more dweller friendly. But they probably wanted some good seafood after munching on dog much of the trip. Mutt meat must get old real quick, although Clark apparently developed a fondness for it. Too bad about the Clark family pooch coming up missing shortly after the hungry man of the house returned to civilization. But the adventurer enjoyed the home coming dinner, particularly the roast.

Anyway, a bunch of settlers figured the place needed a name if they were going to live here. Someone suggested Oregon, although no one seems to know with certainty who came up with the moniker. One story an old timer named Johnny Valen told me when I was a kid in Kerby was that the name came from early explorers sailing along the coast who came up with it after spotting a church organ floating off shore. Wanting to give it a little Western gravitas, what with its gun culture and all, they called it "Ory-gun." The name stuck. Mr. Valen never explained how a church organ came to be floating along the coast off what was then a wilderness. Perhaps angry sailors tipped it over the side after missionaries aboard refused to share their wine. In truth, I doubt a church organ would float, not even one that is heaven bound. But there it is. Mr. Valen, a kindly old fellow born late in the 1800s who often wore garters on his sleeves, did have a mischievous twinkle in his eyes when he told what I realized in later years was a very tall tale.

After acquiring a name, Oregonians had to get Uncle Sam to go along with their scheme to create the Beaver state. Not many people know this but their covert goal was to establish a place for the Portland Trailblazers basketball team to play. They were eagerly anticipating that Dr. James Naismith's invention of the game of basketball when he got bored and started dribbling in Springfield, Mass back in 1891.

They were also thinking big, real big. They created what became the humongous Oregon Territory which was incorporated into the United States in 1848. The area included the current states of Oregon, Washington, and Idaho, as well as parts of Montana and Wyoming. Eleven years after the territory was established we achieved statehood, the territory's southwest portion, that is.

Sadly, it would take 91 long years after statehood that my alma mater, the University of Oregon, won the national collegiate basketball championship. Sure, that is a milestone most stuffy historians ignore, but they do so at the peril of their profession, creating yet another reason for our youth not to read history. Although I could never walk and dribble a ball at the same time, I've always found the game of basketball fascinating, a sort of microcosmic reflection of life's game. Instead, I wrestled in high school, finding some success in that sport. Now I grapple with words, albeit with limited success. I frequently take on a word or phrase that has me on the mat gasping for breath as I struggle to escape with a little dignity intact. The sad truth of it is a white-haired grammar teacher who uses a walker to get around can still best me in two out of three rounds. But I'm still practicing, hoping one day for at least a take down on that aged but feisty old biddy.

Granted, most folks probably don't think about grammar when they look for a place in the country. But it is important, especially the nouns. You are going to be living with the people, places and things. Best to learn about their care and feeding.

The people populating the region hard against the Oregon/California state line are, by and large, an interesting bunch, particularly those who walk up right. You have an abundance of easy-going retirees from throughout the continent happily content in living out the autumn of their lives here in this valley named after pioneers. But there are also maddog conservatives whose politics are three steps to the right of John Wayne, frothing liberals who look at FDR as a tax-cutting industrialist and a host of other colorful characters, including miners, loggers, ranchers, vintners and goat cheese makers. The drainage houses a veritable people potpourri.

The smarter ones in this human stew of meat eaters and vegetarians have one thing in common: they largely follow the creed of the old West of live and let live. The rare exceptions are former Californians who hate former Californians. Fortunately, none of them shave with a straight razor. But most rural folks know you never can tell when you are going to be in a pinch and might need a little help from someone who may not share your political or religious beliefs. As one who has evacuated in the face of both fire and flood in southern Oregon, I can attest to the fact rescuers have neither time nor interest in hearing a rant about politics or religion. And Mother Nature certainly doesn't give a whit about your personal doctrine.

The Applegate Valley is smack dab in the mythical State of Jefferson. That's the region of far northern California and southern Oregon where a fair share of residents often feel their opinions are ignored by the folks in the respective state capitols of Sacramento and Salem. However, aside from a few raving extremists who periodically create a flash in the political pan, the movement has generally been tongue in cheek.

There is no question the region has a rich history of housing some feisty folks itching for a fight. Perhaps that is because many back in the day came here in search of precious yellow metal. Gold miners can be a spirited lot, particularly if they've dug in the dirt all day and have nothing to show for it except a broken pick and an aching back. That tends to make anyone cranky.

Jacksonville and Sterlingville in Jackson County and Kerby in neighboring Josephine County all got their start in the gold rush which began in the early 1850s in the Oregon Territory. Jacksonville and Kerby vie for the bragging rights of being the place in the territory where the gleaming yellow metal was first discovered in 1851. The precious metal was first found in Sterling Creek in 1854, resulting in the boom town of Sterlingville. At its zenith, the bustling hamlet reportedly had two general stores, two saloons, a bakery, at least one dance hall, a blacksmith shop and a barber shop, not to mention cabins whose architecture would have made Li'l Abner feel right at home.

Gold had been found earlier in other places in the territory but for various reasons did not trigger the 1851 stampede of miners seeking instant riches by digging what amounts to raw money out of the ground. The problem, of course, is the ground is immense and the money well hidden. Unless you are incredibly lucky, there is a lot of digging with nary a nugget to show for it.

Jacksonville was the county seat before it was transferred to Medford, now the regional hub. In fact, Jacksonvillians in the mid-1800s could have truthfully boasted they lived in the largest inland hub between Sacramento and Seattle. This was before Portland emerged out of a dank little burg originally dubbed Stumptown. While Jacksonville is no longer the seat of power, it continues to shine as one of the Pacific Northwest's finest historical nuggets.

Like Jacksonville, Kerby still survives, although it is but a shadow of its former self. Shortly after gold was discovered on nearby Josephine Creek, Kerby sprang up, quickly becoming the Josephine County seat. But it wasn't long before Grants Pass on the Rogue River stole the title from Kerby. Some of us Kerby expatriates still hold a grudge against that upstart town more than a century later. A grudge is not necessarily considered a bad thing in the goldmining mountains of southern Oregon. The drive to get even keeps us motivated. But it is considered bad form to involve gun play in a grudge match, particularly if the other fellow is armed with only a pick ax.

Kerby is now an unincorporated little burg, a mere wide spot on old state Highway 199 leading from Oregon's southwestern interior to the coast. Not much there. No yard toilets to speak of. Some write it off as inconsequential but I would submit Kerby has memories as well as the capacity to one day spring back to its glory days. It's patiently biding its time. Then it won't be a town to be trifled with. Just you wait.

There are also those who are inclined to view such hamlets as areas where children all look like the banjo-playing kid in the 1972 movie *Deliverance.* But that is a bit harsh, although life could be challenging to Kerby kids back in the day. My childhood goal was to become a goodfornothing bon vivant whose only job is to rub elbows with the hoi polloi. I'm still working on that.

During my uneventful hitch in the Corps, I initially would tell other jarheads inquiring about my hometown that I was from Kerby, Oregon. "Where the hell is that?" asked one sergeant from Texas. "Down in southern Oregon," I replied. "No," he cut me off, "where the hell is Oregon?" Smart ass. But I empathized. Having been to Texas, I understand why the sergeant would be envious of any green place outside the dusty environs of the Lone Star state. Actually, we became good friends, despite his Beaver state challenged ways and my reluctance to admit Texas to the Union. Besides, in weak moments, I have been known to accept that Texas may even have a few attributes. Hey, the chili is mighty tasty.

Texas does have the Big Bend country but it does not have the Applegate Valley. When it comes to beautiful river valleys, the Applegate watershed is the Mona Lisa of little river systems in my book.

The watershed stretches some sixty miles from 7,000 feet above sea level in the Siskiyou Mountain peaks of far northern California to its confluence with the mighty Rogue River in Oregon. Including the rich bottom land and forested mountain sides, the valley covers about half a million acres. The land was forged by volcanic upheaval at the sunrise of time, later carved by glaciers, and fine tuned by Mother Nature's floods and forest fires over the eons.

Of course, well before the European Americans discovered the valley in the early 1800s, it had been home for thousands of years to aboriginal people. Historians tell us the three tribes of Indians known to have inhabited the region each had a different name for the Applegate region. Takelma Indians called the river "S'bink" after the beavers they found along its banks. The Shasta Indians knew it as "Iskatawayeki," a word whose meaning has faded away over time. The Athapascans called it "Ta'khoo-pe" which apparently meant "pretty place." Given the region's natural beauty, I prefer the latter, although my enunciation of it sounds like I'm trying to get a hair off the end of my tongue.

The first people in the valley fished the river and its tributaries, but were mindful to hold an annual late spring ceremony honoring the salmon which provided them with much of their subsistence. Hunters and gatherers all, the Indians made short migrations into the Siskiyou Mountains on a seasonal basis. They would kill game, pick berries and gather bear grass and hazel sticks for weaving baskets. These were resourceful folks who didn't need to nip into the freezer section of the super market to grab something for dinner.

They also practiced rudimentary forest management, using wildfires as a tool to remove underbrush and small trees to create grassy areas among towering trees to make prime habitat for deer and elk. If done at the right time of year, it would leave the fire- resistant old growth. While it is not an exact science, sometimes burning too much or too little, periodically lighting a low-intensity fires helps Mother Nature create a healthy ecosystem for flora and fauna. Of course, that approach would be problematic today, what with homes now dotting the valley.

Interestingly, the valley is now home to one of a half dozen major forest restoration pilot projects in the Pacific Northwest which could change timber management on federal forest land. Led by University of Washington forest scientist Jerry Franklin and Norm Johnson, his counterpart at Oregon State University, the point of the 80,000-acre project in the Applegate is to keep the spotlight on what is going to be left in the forest, not what is cut.

"Our focus is on the old trees," Johnson told me back in 2012 when I was still a working journalist. "Where the old trees exist, the strategy anchors on nurturing them and opening up the stand around them, removing the competition."

If the strategy by the well-respected scientists works, forest management in the valley will have come full circle to a practice not unlike that used by the first people in this pretty place.

Not many of the people coming into the valley in the mid to late 19th Century were interested in learning from those who came before. Most came to farm the land, cut the big trees to make lumber for homes and dig up the earth in search of metals precious to the new arrivals. They came with the same ambitions and dreams that had brought their ancestors to the New World. They were carving out a living for their families in this fertile valley of green grass and deep forests.

In fact, my paternal grandparents Jonas and Harriett Viola Fattig would homestead in the valley in 1907, after living for a few years in Ashland in southeastern Jackson County. The Midwesterners arrived too late to settle the rich river bottom land but they created a family farm in the foothills a half dozen miles as the crow flies from our Sterling Creek cabin. In essence, we would become neighbors, albeit six air miles and a century apart.

Jonas and Harriett, both of whom died before I was born, arrived in the greater Rogue River basin long after the short-lived Rogue River Indian War in the mid-1850s. Following the hostilities, most Indians living in the basin, including the Applegate drainage, were rounded up in 1856 and force marched to the Siletz and Grand Ronde reservations east of Salem. It was not the Oregon Territory's finest hour.

With most of the native people gone, Caucasians comprised the majority of regional residents. But there were also Chinese laborers hired to work the mines, although they were forbidden by law from owning property. Yet a few, like a remarkable fellow named Gin Lin, were able to circumvent that rule. He owned and operated a mine on the Little Applegate River near the confluence of Sterling Creek, employing Chinese laborers.

There were only a few blacks, including a blacksmith whose surname has been buried by the dust of time. Yet his first name is forever attached to Negro Ben Mountain overlooking the middle Applegate Valley. Old maps refer to the mountain with the pejorative form of his race.

With people of different backgrounds and philosophies drawn to the valley, political differences inevitably surfaced. During the Civil War, some local southern sympathizers supposedly demonstrated their colors by hoisting the Confederate flag in Jacksonville. The flag was quickly pulled down by no-nonsense woman who was a staunch Union supporter, so the story goes. A settlement mushrooming up during the war near where the Little Applegate River joins the main Applegate was dubbed Union Town, reflecting sentiment for the North. My father spent the only eight grades he was formally educated studying at Union Town School. He was one of those rare individuals who could self-educate, and didn't have to rely on lessons being spooned out. After losing a leg in a logging accident, he became a self-taught botanist, and could tell you the Latin names for many of the indigenous plants in southern Oregon. He most certainly did not learn Latin in Union Town School where he began his tutelage nearly half a century after the Civil War ended. The conflict's name was a bit of a misnomer since there was nothing civil about it. But the skirmishes in the Applegate appear to have been verbal, and likely followed the uncorking of a bottle of spirits.

Still, those who became what has fondly became known as an "Applegater," whether they are early-day descendants or arrived last week, all share a strong common bond: a love affair with the picturesque watershed.

Flowing south into the Little Applegate, Sterling Creek is in the upper reaches of the Applegate watershed. From start to finish, the stream is only half a dozen miles long. Yet it is firmly part of the valley structure, attached to the main Applegate like a branch to a tree trunk.

There is an urban myth that folks living in the country all know each other and their business. That's what a university professor of mine would have called a lot of happy horse hockey, at least when it comes to modern-day country living. It may have been true back in horse and buggy days when one's world didn't extend much beyond his neighbors. Our society is mobile now, making us largely independent of each other. The exception, of course, is the aforementioned natural disasters.

I suspect country living draws more independent types who prefer to live in peace and quiet. They just figure out a way to survive in regions where jobs are about as scarce as hens' teeth. Now, I've never actually pried open a hen's beak to look for teeth. I'm relying on the wisdom of those who created the maxim way back when.

While writing a feature article a decade ago about folks who lived locally but worked out of state, I interviewed an Applegate Valley resident who worked as a plastic surgeon in Southern California. He would spend a month or so lifting sagging jowls, tucking tummies and the like, then match that time back on his Applegate spread. He was as content as a purring cat, at least when he was back in the valley. Granted, he may hiss a bit during those longs days on the job.

Some folks in Hollywood like to imply that many of those living in the country are uneducated rubes. Yet within half a dozen miles of the cabin are two doctors, two registered nurses, a teacher, two retired college professors, not to mention several ivy-league educated folks. There are also loggers, miners, ranchers and farmers, none of whom I would consider rubes.

For instance, both Applegate Valley carpenters we hired to help restore the cabin were college educated. They simply prefer working with their hands over a desk job. Thanks to the cabin, I would also meet a well driller who, after some twenty years, grew weary of lawyering and threw his law practice in for a drilling rig. To keep the world in balance, there must be an attorney out there who is a former well driller. I do know one attorney who is a former journalist. One day I hope to meet former well-drilling attorney who became a journalist but I suppose that is reaching for the stars. After all, there are levels to which a well driller will not sink. But I'm acquainted with a logger who freely admits he did time as a college-educated journalist. A logger is made of stout stuff, and doesn't mind sullying his reputation by being a resident of the Fourth Estate. But only for a short time, mind you. Loggers, too, have their limits.

Hollywood also delights in painting country dwellers as misanthropes. There are certainly rural residents who dislike people, avoiding them whenever possible. Yet when I've done time in cities I've also found urban inhabitants who have little time for other bipeds, snapping at their approach. Maureen thrives in either city or country. I can do cities for a while before misanthropic symptoms begin to emerge like the fangs of a werewolf under a full moon. Maureen tells me the signs include snarling, snapping and general crankiness. On the other hand, I periodically need the rejuvenating energy of a city to keep everything in balance.

Enough of Oregon history, its people and my philosophic balderdash. We need to figure out how we are going to restore an old cabin badly burned by fire, beaten up by vandals and left to the wild beasts.

THREE

General Contractors: Do the Good Guys Wear White Hard Hats?

H ENRY DAVID THOREAU OBSERVED THAT MOST men live lives of quiet desperation. This coming from a fellow who built a small cabin overlooking Walden Pond where he pondered in peace and quiet for a few years. With all due respect to that remarkable contemplator of the human belly button, I suspect Mr. Thoreau had no more than a passing acquaintance with the life of a desperate man, quiet or otherwise. Much of his energy was spent pondering the grand mysteries of life while picking lint out of his navel.

After all, he built the cabin with the help of friends, although it is true he did a lot of the work himself, including trimming logs with a borrowed ax. He also had the freedom to work from the ground up with his vivid imagination serving as his guide. He was not restricted to a floor plan laid out by a concrete foundation already in place. He most certainly did not have to put up with a toilet in the yard, mocking his efforts. Nor did he have a herd of hairy pets waiting impatiently to move into their new digs. There was no flock of college kids eager to roost at home between semesters. No, and he didn't work full time, balancing bills and bosses. Mr. Desperation was a total stranger to the man who helped bring transcendentalism to the fore.

Henry David kept it simple, building a rustic cabin that was ten feet wide and fifteen feet long. He used timber, stone and sand from the local land on which he was but a guest since his friend Ralph Waldo Emerson owned the property. History books didn't record whether any hobgoblins were lurking about. Thoreau also cheated a bit by purchasing a nearby shanty for its lumber. All told, he reported his building cost was $28.12 ½. The latter referred to a half-cent piece minted back in those days. In contrast, we would pay $116,000 for our property and spend nearly $60,000 in restoration, figures that would have stunned that day-dreaming pond dweller. Yet, in today's prices, we probably did nearly as well as that philosophic cabin builder back in 1845, give or take.

Incidentally, our property came with a Walden Pond of sorts. However, unlike the roughly sixty-acre pond near Concord, Massachusetts, apparently carved out by a glacier more than 10,000 years ago, ours is a half-acre puddle created up the valley by the previous property owner with a bulldozer. Being a seasonal pond, it isn't much of a place to ponder life. But a springtime transcendentalist could use it in a pinch.

Although I never developed the nervous twitch of a truly desperate man, there was some hand ringing and whimpering after we acquired the old cabin. After all, we intend it to be our home until leaving this mortal coil. In addition to the weighty issue of deciding where I would hang my hammock or place the ice chest bulging with cold beer, there were myriad problems to be solved. The very fact we weren't given any keys spoke volumes. Keys would have been superfluous. The west wall where a door had been was largely burned away, leaving only a few charred logs. On the other side of the cabin, the door leading to the deck was swinging in the wind whistling through the structure. All of the windows were broken out. Where to start?

The reconstruction challenge was like standing at the base of a very large mountain you are about to ascend. You can see the sunlit peak in the distance, but you know you face an arduous climb. After hacking your way through the jungle at the base, you face sheer cliffs, treacherous pitfalls and dangerous crevices. And you can expect fields of crumbly rock, the kind where you slide back half a step with each step forward.

Thinking about the uphill climb ahead, I could not keep Mr. Desperation in check.

"We are about to step into a whole world of schist," I warned Maureen.

"There is really no need for coarse language, little mister," she replied with a rare frown. "It makes you sound like a bumpkin. We'll get through it. Just take it one step at a time. And why are you suddenly talking with a lisp? "

You should know that "Goofus" or "Sparky" are terms of endearment. When she calls me "Little Mister," I duck for cover. A storm is brewing. There is lightning in her eyes; thunder in her voice. She may be petite but, like Saint Paul, she does not suffer fools gladly.

Not being the sainted one, I quickly explained that I was talking about a crystalline rock called schist. I got a blank stare.

"It can be flaky—I read about it in a geology book," I continued, trying in vain to clear the air concerning my misguided metaphor. Or was that a simile? It was all getting very confusing, this cabin-restoration business.

"There is also likely going to be some falling rock so we'll have to keep our eyes out for them," I added, fully aware I had just built a full-scale mountain out of a mole hill.

Maureen studied me for a moment the way a teacher does when trying to connect with a dullard who doesn't comprehend the subject at hand.

"Sometimes I don't have the foggiest idea what you are talking about," she said. "We are not going to be climbing any mountains. We are just rebuilding an old cabin."

She changed her tact, picking up and dusting off the metaphor approach I had mangled and left dying on the mountainside. But she shrewdly chose a different mode of conveyance.

"We are going to develop a game plan and carry it out," Maureen said. "It'll be a fun challenge."

"Sure thing, coach," I said. "But, just out of curiosity, I'd like to know the rules before you send me in."

Like a coach calling for time out to try to regain control of her team,

Maureen held up her hands in the t-formation. In this case, her team consisted of a player who couldn't dribble, unless he was babbling.

"Perhaps I could read a book about restoring old homes," I suggested.

"You read a book," she said as she walked away, massaging both her temples.

While we did not know precisely what lay ahead, one thing we knew for sure was that we would see it through. We could, of course, give up our $1,000 earnest money but that was a lot of money in our book. Besides, we had already fallen in love with both the unusual cabin and the picturesque property. We were determined to somehow get to the mountaintop.

Before I began poring over yet another book, Maureen suggested we sit down at the kitchen table where all major decisions are made and study our situation. Financially, we were shipshape with only a few little holes to plug to keep us afloat. We had already sold our home in Williams so we would have the cash needed to make a sizable down on the Sterling Creek property. We were then paying rent to the new owners who had yet to move north from their home in California. We were both working full time. The kids had fledged. The time was ripe to make our move since they wouldn't know our new address. They may be blood hounds but they wouldn't be able to pick up our scent for awhile. Just joshing. They would be there for us as we were there for them. Good people, our kids.

Maureen began gently tapping her pencil against her nose, a sign that trouble may be afoot.

"Don't panic but there is one little hitch we'll have to work out regarding a loan," she said.

Maureen who knows her stuff when it comes to banks, a world I find frustratingly bothersome, particularly when I have a checkbook in hand. She took over the bills after discovering I could bounce a check much better than a basketball.

"Is this a give-away-our-first-born-male-child kind of hitch?" I asked.

"No, goofus," she said, indicating I was back in her good graces. "It's actually no real big deal. But, because the fire took out the entire kitchen, we will have to obtain a construction loan. That will be something new for us. That means we will also be the general contractors, subcontracting out for some of the work. We will directly hire the carpenters, electricians, plumbers and whoever else we may need to help us restore the place."

Given her rules and regulation knowledge and my lack thereof, I had to take her word that we needed a construction loan to rebuild a home sans a kitchen. But it seemed like an arbitrary regulation to me. I could understand requiring a construction loan if there were no bathrooms since potty breaks are inevitable. You could set up a makeshift kitchen with a cooler, a card table and a jug of water. However, a bathroom fix is not so accommodating, unless you acquire one of those portable outhouses. You can stave off a meal but the call of nature will not be staved.

"I guess the toilet in the yard wouldn't answer, anyway," I grumbled to myself.

A committee somewhere apparently cooked up the kitchen regulation, no doubt after quaffing a few brewskis. But the more I thought about being a general contractor, the more I liked it.

"If Dick Cheney can do it, so can we," I told Maureen.

"What are you talking about?" she asked.

"When Dick Cheney was asked by Bush the second to head a committee to select a vice president candidate, Cheney chose himself," I said. "So a precedent has been set. It's OK if we choose ourselves as general contractors who are, in essence, vice presidents to the owners who are the presidents."

"Sometimes it must be very frightening to be in that head of yours," she said, laughing.

"Hey, being general contractors will give us a lot of clout," I continued. "I believe that will make us the top dogs at the job site. When a subcontractor wants to know something, we can talk in circles like Donald Rumsfeld. And I quote, 'There are known knowns. There are known unknowns. There are things that we know we don't know. But there are also unknown unknowns. There are things we don't know we don't know.' Who knew Donald would be there for us? The workers will be mystified."

"As am I already," Maureen said of my attempted witticism, adding as she looked skyward, "Give me strength."

In my defense, the former Secretary of Defense had just uttered that infamous comment at a news conference while trying to explain what was known about the supposed weapons of mass destruction in Iraq. It was just before the start of the Iraq War early in 2002. Maureen quickly disabused me of the notion I could begin speaking Rumsfeldian. She correctly note you can get away with talking like that when you are about to unleash the dogs of war but it is not safe for a general contractor working up close with claw hammer-carrying carpenters. Makes subcontractors want to lash out with whatever tool they have at hand, she observed.

In the coming months, I would discover it was the height of naiveté to believe that trades people, folks who have spent years perfecting their professional skills, would pay any attention to the views of an obviously know-nothing general contractor. They know they know their stuff. They also know you don't know anything about the job they have been hired to do or else you would be doing the work. They are their own bosses who will humor your input only so far before reaching for the hammer. A sharp chisel waved in an aggressive manner would do in a pinch, I would learn.

However, for reasons I never quite understood, they accepted Maureen's common sense suggestions more readily than my proposals. Go figure.

The trick, of course, is to hire a competent person to do the job at the outset. We relied largely on word of mouth and gut instinct. In hindsight, we chose well. We were never unsatisfied with the work, albeit the plumbing crew did leave half a case of empty beer cans behind. The imbibing apparently didn't affect their work since it was approved by the county building inspectors. Yes, I suppose the beer cans could have been left by the inspectors but they probably would have gone for more expensive micro brews.

There is no question the building inspectors are the top dogs in the pack since they had the final word whether the work was up to snuff when it came to meeting county building codes. In essence, general contractors such as ourselves would be stuck in the middle like referees trying to keep both teams happy. Our job could be a hazardous one, what with the armament of dangerous power tools at the job site, all fueled by high levels of testosterone. Fortunately, Maureen is a very good facilitator who made sure her hubby didn't throw gas on the fire when a little smoke periodically began rising from the friction.

As already mentioned, we are capable of doing a lot of rudimentary carpentry and other work, although we certainly couldn't be described as accomplished carpenters. For the skilled jobs, we would have to hire contractors who knew their stuff. Or, as Donald would have said, those who knew they knew their stuff.

Because of our jobs, both Maureen and I are acquainted with a lot of people who do different kinds of work. Not in the sense that translates into any monetary shortcuts or anything shady, mind you. But it meant we knew who to trust to do a good, honest job.

For restoration carpentry, I called Chris Bratt, a longtime acquaintance who, with his business partner, Richard Goodnough, specialized in restoring old homes. Both live in the Applegate Valley. I didn't know Richard at the time but figured he was a high-caliber fellow if he was Chris' work mate. He would not disappoint. Richard turned out to be a skilled worker with a can-do attitude which also serves him well as a longtime volunteer fire department officer.

Chris listened patiently as I told him about the property we had just acquired, noting we wanted to restore the old cabin rather than build a new house from the ground up. We knew it would be cheaper but we also liked the old cabin, I said.

"It's really a cool place," I said. "It has character. But we need to know if it can be salvaged as well as how much is salvageable."

Noting they were just finishing up a job at the time, Chris allowed the Sterling Creek cabin sounded like an interesting project. Naturally, he needed to see the cabin before making a commitment. Chris was then in his early seventies, but had the energy of someone a generation younger. His age and knowledge was not something I was worried about. My main concern was whether I could keep up with him, both intellectually and physically.

Chris is one of those Applegate Valley residents whose pedigree never ceases to amaze. His father was George Bratt who acted opposite James Cagney and Myrna Loy on Broadway. His nephew is noted actor Benjamin

Bratt. I toss that out just to drop a few names, of course. We were hoping the nephew would drop in to see his uncle at work. I wouldn't have minded showing actress Julia Roberts around the cabin, but apparently her relationship with Chris' nephew was already on the skids at that point. Perhaps their relations would have endured a little longer had they been able to soak in the peace and quiet of Sterling Creek. No doubt the short-lived adoration doled out to Hollywood stars is rough on long-term commitments.

Benjamin's uncle became known throughout the Northwest for his strong environmental stance and helping launch the Applegate Partnership in the early 1990s. The group consisted of environmentalists, timber industry representatives and others trying to reach a peaceful agreement on how to best manage our federal timberlands. They are still working on the solution. Incidentally, as one who hails from a logging family, I also have friends in that community. My father lost his leg in a logging accident; I used to set chokers in the logging woods in another life. I figure there is room on this planet for both a healthy environment and responsible logging. How you balance the two is the question.

When Chris and I arrived for his inspection, the cabin had more of a "O' Brother, where art thou?" look than I had remembered. It seemed a little shabbier, causing me to wonder just what we had gotten ourselves into. Shabby chic may have been in vogue at the time but this was more like dilapidated decay, I recall thinking. I began to have doubts about bringing Chris out to the cabin with its dead cars, burned walls and trash decor.

A photojournalism friend who fancies himself as a bit of a wag would dub it Kaminski's cabin. It was funny, in a smarting sort of way. But he was wrong, of course. The Unabomber would have been mortified at the thought of spending one night in our crude cabin.

As we pulled up to the old place, Chris took it all in, including the burned walls and the toilet.

"Nice," he said as he stepped out of my pickup truck.

You are thinking he was being snide. Far from it. He was impressed with the potential. Like Maureen and I, he saw what could be done with the place, not what had been done to it. That four-letter word brought me instant relief from my nagging second thoughts.

"Beautiful little valley—love those trees," he said. "And the cabin is very interesting. The metal roof helped preserve the wood that wasn't burned. Some of it will still be usable. Let's have a look inside."

With that, he fished out a pocket knife and began testing the wood for soundness as he inspected the interior. Like a doctor checking out an ailing patient, he periodically let out a "hmmmm" or an "ah." I followed him from room to room, nervously waiting for his prognosis on our patient with the third-degree burns.

"Sure, we can restore this place," the wood doctor concluded as he closed his pocket knife with a snap. "It'll take some work but it can be done fairly easily. This is quite a house. Some of the carpentry work was done very well."

However, he cautioned that he wanted Richard to have a chance to weigh in on whether they took it on as a project. A few days later the restoration partners were checking the place out together. Like Chris, Richard poked and prodded the cabin, looking for dry rot as well as areas where the fire had weakened the structure.

"Not a problem," he concluded after making his inspection. "This is definitely salvageable."

But he was curious about electrical power since they would need it when they began their work. There was a power pole at the end of the driveway but no lines running to the cabin which obviously had power at one time.

Assuming it was underground, we looked for a connection to the structure to no avail. What Richard did find was a spot in a blackberry jungle near the cabin where a power pole had been cut level to the ground, indicating that electricity had been delivered in typical fashion via poles. But the poles and wires were long gone. After establishing there was no electrical power to the cabin, we added another priority item to our must-do list: reconnect the cabin to the grid.

Within that blackberry jungle we also discovered an old farm implement with metal tires. It turned out to be an antique McCormick Deering bar sickle mower with thirty-four-inch metal wheels that could drawn either by horse or early-day tractor. A Big 6 MB1475 series, the machine was built sometime from 1915 to 1934. No, I am not that much of a nerd that I would have known the information off hand. I looked it up.

"That old piece of farm machinery is worth what you paid for the place," said Chris, an aficionado of heavy metal farm antiques. But he may have been exaggerating a mite about the value.

"I'll let you have that old machine for $116,000," I said. He grinned but didn't reach for his check book.

I would later tow it with our four-wheel drive pickup down to the end of the driveway, taking advantage of a heavy fall frost to skid it along since its iron tires were frozen in place. It was an ignoble way for the old machine to be dragged along. Yet it held up fine for its final move to a place of honor overlooking Sterling Creek Road.

Maureen and I also found an old scatter rake near the upper seasonal pond on the property. It has a ten-foot wide swath with four-and-a-half-foot light metal wheels. There is no readily recognizable writing on it to trace its origins, although it likely of similar vintage as the sickle mower. The scatter rake was light enough for us to wheel it down the valley to the end of the driveway were it will spend the rest of its days across from the old sickle mower. We placed them there as a way to honor those who came before, helping in a small way to tell their story.

Chris and Richard agreed they would participate in the cabin salvage project. But the general contractors were informed by the subcontractors that the former had work to do before any carpentry work could begin later that spring.

"We'll need everything removed so we can get down to the wooden skeleton," Chris said. "All the sheet rock has to be torn out. Any of the obviously burned boards will have to be removed. We'll also need all the ash and other debris swept out. And the junk will have to be taken out of the yard so we can get to the cabin."

In other words, clean up this dump, including the toilet.

"Now the real fun is about to start," Maureen said after the carpenters completed their inspection.

But there was one niggling question that was still pestering my troubled mind.

"Where are we going to live while all this is going on?" I asked. "We will have to pay for rent as well as our mortgage. Financially, that is going to be real tough."

"Got that all figured out," my other half replied. "You are going to like this one."

I took a deep breath, bracing myself like a wounded man gulping a shot of whiskey before the battlefield surgeon begins sawing off a limb.

"Oh, schist," I whispered to myself.

FOUR

Trailer House Blues

T HE PROBLEM WITH BUYING ONE HOME WHILE you are living in another
is that you can end up paying two mortgages simultaneously. Some
folks may have the financial wherewithal of having one or both the homes
paid off. Best we could manage at the time was one mortgage, albeit we
would later buy some commercial property in Medford.

"This idea I have will solve everything for us," Maureen said. "And it
won't cost us a dime, at least in the end it won't. In essence, we will live
rent free. It's practically a no brainer."

"OK, let's have it," I said as one eyebrow dipped low to show I was
dubious from the outset. It does that on its own volition, by the way.
Honest. It's like having an eyebrow with Tourette's syndrome.

"What we'll do is buy a used trailer, live in it while we are reconstructing
that place, then sell it when we are ready to move into the cabin," she said.
"We won't have to pay rent, and we will be reimbursed for our investment.
Before you start puckering out that lower lip, remember this will save us a
year's rent or however long it takes to make the cabin livable."

My wife likes to tell people that I'm a world-class pouter but that's laying
it on a little thick. Best I can do is pout for four or five hours. That's farm
team talent at best, well short of major league status.

My lower lip started to protrude at her suggestion. A used trailer? I was gob smacked.

Now it is true I had been born to poverty, even had an outhouse as a wee lad. I knew what it was like to not have a winter coat. As kids, we had worn what my sister Delores dubbed "talking shoes," the kind whose sole had separated from the toe of your footwear and appeared to be talking when you walked. All our socks had holes at both ends. You would stick your foot in one end and your toes out the other. Down and out living had been a faithful companion through childhood. Yet my widowed mom and her five young children never lived in a used trailer house. We had our pride.

Besides, here I was a college educated adult with a career. Admittedly, it was as a newspaper scribe which never paid a lot. One of my Forrest Gump connections, Ann Curry, a college classmate who was much more savvy and talented, had gone into television and fortune and fame. She became a nationally-known fixture on the Today Show where high salaries were the norm. She was also extremely talented. I remember hiking along a muddy Oregon logging road with Ann in the early 1980s while she was still with a relatively small-town television TV station. The story we were both tracking down was an environmental protest against logging old-growth trees—trees older than Methuselah—in a remote area of a national forest. All of the other half dozen journalists covering the regional event refused to hike in several miles to where the loggers and enviros were butting heads. We made the muddy hike and got the real story. I was impressed with Ann's willingness to go the extra mile in ankle-deep mud and her thoughtful questions to loggers and protesters alike. That she would become an award-winning television journalist on the national stage was no surprise.

Now Maureen was asking me to go the extra mile to achieve a dream of a lifetime, a goal which was nearly as important to me as getting a story. I had to admit her plan had a sound financial attribute in the form of a low-cost place to sleep at night. Yet the thought of intentionally buying a used trailer went against the grain. It was one thing if a practical jokester of a bachelor uncle had died and left you his moldy old trailer in his will as one last gag from the great beyond.

"You are telling me we have to live in a broken-down tin house on wheels before we can move into an old log cabin," I said, finding it difficult to enunciate because of my jutting lower lip. "Does that mean we have to eat TV dinners, the kind where the vegetables are sludge of different colors? I want you to know right now that I refuse to take up smoking. It's a nasty habit. I won't do it. And don't talk to me about getting a tattoo."

I took a deep breath, then continued my rant which, I had to agree, was sounding more than a bit bizarre.

"Aren't you supposed to get into drunken squabbles in used trailers every weekend?" I asked. "How can we do that? You don't drink. And a glass of wine or a beer instantly puts me asleep? We don't even measure up as non hackers when it comes to booze. We'll be the laughing stock of the trailer park. We would also have to learn how to squabble."

"Oh, my God. Where on earth does that come from?" she asked, shaking her head. "On the weird meter, you just went off the chart."

Then she burst out laughing, letting me know she knew I was letting off a little exaggerated steam.

"OK, first of all you know full well that plenty of very fine people live in trailers as well as the parks that house them," she said. "There is absolutely nothing wrong with living in a trailer park if that is your preference. So you know that's just plain goofy.

"That aside, we will not be living in a park but on our property," she added. "As for the cabin, we can't move into it until it is restored. And we can't afford to rent another place until the cabin is livable. Think about it. If you come up with a better plan, let me know."

With that, she left the room, leaving me to stew for awhile. She knows me well. After a bit of mulling, I accepted the obviously practical solution she had proposed. There was really no other answer. However, to save face, I obviously couldn't immediately embrace her plan.

"OK, fine, but I'm not going to like it," I told her an hour later, having completed a short pout. The lower lip had retreated to its proper place but the one eyebrow was still hanging low.

"You, sir, are going to have the time of your life," she said. "Consider it an adventurous challenge. It'll be fun."

That's not a word I would have used, but she was right about the adventure, beginning with the search for a previously-owned mobile dwelling—the phrase one salesman liked to throw out there—that would not have caused a rat to scurry away in terror. The worst previously-owned stick houses we had seen were McMansions compared to the old trailers. In one, you could actually see the ground between your feet.

"All you need is a throw rug," said the smiling salesman who had a tattoo of naked lady on his hairy right forearm. She was also hairy and rather well endowed on one side when he flexed his forearm. "Besides, you folks just need it for a little while. You won't be in it very long. We're talking win-win here."

He was correct about not being in it very long. We exited before he could show us the rest of the previously-owned mobile dwelling from hell.

Another trailer had a smell wafting out of the bathroom shower whose stench was reminiscent of a slaughter house I had once visited as a journalist. This was not your usual butcher shop house with fresh beef and hog cadavers hanging on hooks in refrigerated rooms. This slaughter house targeted roadkill from which it rendered fat and ground the bones into fertilizer. It was never fully explained what happened to the flesh of deer and other poor creatures which were hauled to the odorous establishment. I remember the stair well in the building was slippery because the lard had somehow spread throughout the facility, attaching itself to every surface. It took weeks to get the smell out of my mustache.

"I think there was a murder in this trailer," I whispered to Maureen as we walked through it. "I bet it was a knifing. Remember Hitchcock's movie Psycho? I could never take a shower in here."

"I think you are right," she replied in mock *sotto voce*. "I remember reading about it. The wife grabbed a butcher knife after she couldn't take any more wacky comments from her nutty hubby while they were looking for a used trailer. After the deed was done, the jury found him guilty of being terribly annoying, posthumously of course. They said he deserved it."

But she agreed there was a smell that she found hard to stomach. She also informed her hubby that he was not to accompany her on any more trail house searches. If he were to do so, she warned, there could be an unfortunate butcher knife incident. Not trusting the jury system, I concurred.

Although handicapped by my absence, she found a trailer which she felt would meet our needs during the reconstruction process. To her credit, I have to admit it had the basics, including a bathroom with a shower, a gas stove and refrigerator, even a closet of sorts and room to sleep six. The latter was needed for the furry contingent. Of course, none of the pets slept in their appointed places. Most slept on the floor, making it possible to walk on solid fur at night from what served as a master bedroom at one end to the bathroom. The fur growled, hissed and yowled at every step.

The trailer was a twenty-eight-footer which had not been treated well in its younger years. Several stickers on the rear bumper indicated the owner had spent some time in Arizona, possibly a snow bird migrating to that warmer clime during the winter months. One sticker indicated he was an Air Force veteran while another identified him as a member of an experimental aircraft group. The trailer looked like it had crash landed with no survivors. One end appears to have been sand blasted by a desert storm. The door had also been pried open at one time, causing it to jam every time it was closed tightly. Either he lost his keys and had to break in or the trailer had been burgled. Naturally, I suspected the latter.

The interior had also been roughly abused. A couple of the cupboard doors were constantly askew. No amount of tinkering with them would set them right. Every time you closed a cupboard door, it would pop open the moment you walked away. I blamed it on trailer ghosts. These poltergeists no doubt had tattoos of naked ladies.

But what really bothered me was the lack of space to move about. I could barely turn around without bumping into something.

"There isn't enough room in here to swing a cat, particularly one with a long tail," I observed. "Perhaps we ought to get one with a bob tail. Actually, we could just grab a bobcat passing by. Of course, a short tail would be hard to grip. Maybe we could attach Velcro to it. Wouldn't want the little fellow to fly out a window."

Maureen was not amused by my fling at feline humor.

"You will just have to live with it," she said. "I have looked all over for a trailer. This is the best of the lot. At $4,000, we got a very good deal. If you don't like it, you can sleep in the car, little mister."

I was going to correct her that the actual price, according to the paperwork, was $3,999 but a look in her eyes told me not to go there.

"Sorry, Yodin, you are absolutely right," I said. "We will make do. Besides, it will only be for a couple of months."

I retreat to the "Y" word when I need to get back into her good graces. One of the children had believed as a youngster that "Y," the first letter in her middle name, stood for "Yodin" instead of her christened middle moniker of "Yvonne." That innocent observation cracked me up. Still does. Actually, I like the name, preferring it over Maureen's given middle moniker. I think of Yodin as the female answer to Odin, the powerful god in Norse mythology. In my mind, Maureen has always been a goddess in her own right and a mighty powerful one at that.

As it turned out, I would be the first one to spend a night in our shaky house on wheels. We had moved half of the stuff we would need to survive to the cabin, storing it in the large bedroom where no major restoration work was planned. I drove the moving truck over while Maureen and Sheena, a daughter visiting from college, followed me in the car. The trailer was delivered that afternoon by a fellow who sped up the driveway and yelled out the window, "Where ya want it?" I pointed to a flat spot about fifty feet behind the cabin. He backed it into place, jumped out and unhooked it with the efficiency of a Daytona 500 mechanic, then raced back down the driveway. He either had a very tight schedule or didn't like the looks of rural ruffians who kept a toilet as yard decor.

We finished unloading the boxes into the bedroom just before dark. Before heading back to our warm and well lit house where they would spend a comfortable night, the wife and daughter wished me good luck.

"It's kind of creepy around here at night," Sheena observed as darkness closed in on the little valley. "That old cabin looks really scary in the dark, like it's haunted or something. Do we know if anybody was ever murdered here? And what kind of monstrous creatures prowl these woods at night? Geez, I would be afraid to stay here alone. Of course, you aren't afraid of the dark so that won't bother you."

I am definitely not scared of darkness. Believing the dark can hurt you is just plain dumb. But I certainly have misgivings about things that I cannot see, particularly those hairy creatures that growl or go bump in the night as they drag a bloody carcass into the deep woods for a little feast. If she hadn't mentioned the possible presence of ghosts or creatures moving in closer as darkness descended I probably wouldn't have given either much thought. Remember when President Richard M. Nixon said he was not a crook? What sticks with you is the crook part.

Thanks to an over-active imagination, I could already see ax murderers sharpening their bloody tools. At the very least, ghouls were dusting off their shrouds and powdering their decaying faces. God knows what other foul creatures lurking in the nearby trees were lining up for a pound of my flesh.

So I did what comes naturally.

"Pshaw, a walk in the park," I blustered. "Remember, I am the pater familia. Fearless. Besides, any creatures intent on sinking their fangs into me will have to get past Ally."

At the time, we had a grand dog named Alyeska who was part Akita and German shepherd. Every ounce of her ninety pounds was filled with a fearsome woof. Looking up at us with her loving big brown eyes, she was faithful unto death. Although getting a little long of tooth, she remained as regal as a queen, one who took seriously her responsibilities as the head of the realm.

The first night I spent in the trailer was March 9, 2002. In Afghanistan, our nation was in the early months of its longest war. I was about to embark on one of the longest nights of my life. Ever.

There was no electricity, no propane. When Maureen and Sheena left with the car's red tail lights bouncing down the driveway, the dog and I were completely in the dark.

"OK, it looks like it's just you and me, kid," I told the pooch. She curled up on the floor, let out a sigh and fell fast asleep. Some guard dog, that one.

A flashlight? Hey, I'm not that dense. In fact, I had a new one just purchased for the occasion. A very good one, the kind police officers use when venturing out into the dark of night looking for doers of bad deeds.

The fact the box of batteries were buried somewhere in the mountain of boxes proved to be a bit of a drawback. The only available light was from my illuminated wrist watch. But I was exhausted from the long day of moving so I was happy to hit the sack early, hunkering down in my sleeping bag in the master bedroom. Actually, it was the only bedroom, apart from the bunks that supposedly slept four people. They would have fit, providing they were no larger than the smaller Munchkins from the land of Oz. Turns out they did sleep more than half a dozen cats quite nicely.

I could have used a couple of the warm and fuzzy cats that night. My sleeping bag was not the plush kind I had in Alaska. It was made for the namby-pamby residents of the Lower 48. Unfortunately, the temperature that night felt reminiscent of the Far North, albeit did not drop below zero. But temperatures are relative. It froze hard, plummeting into the teens in the little valley whose elevation is some 2,600 feet. I felt as cold as I ever had in Alaska. It was like trying to sleep in a freezer.

I shivered in the sleeping bag, periodically rolling over to thaw the side that was freezing. Calls for Alyeska to join me were ignored. The heartless pooch refused to share her furry warmth. Of course, she wasn't cold. Her fur coat was thick, making her impervious to the bone-numbing temperatures. She may have even been too warm, poor thing.

I could have stepped outside to warm up but I didn't know what monstrous creature was out there. Waiting. It was as dark as the proverbial tomb. There was no moon. You quite literally could not see your hand in front of your face. The stars glittered like frozen crystals overhead.

After what seemed like several hours, I glanced at my watch.

"Wow, almost nine o'clock," I muttered to myself. "Only nine more hours to go before I can get up. Time crawls like a slug when you are miserable."

Actually, mere misery would have been an improvement. And time wasn't the only thing that was glacial. I reached over to touch the window. There was a thin film of frost on the inside.

Around midnight I had to take a whiz. Really, really bad. It was a stop-the-car-now emergency. I didn't want to use the trailer bathroom because it wasn't ready for business, having yet to be plumbed. Besides, I couldn't see anything. Confusing a closet with the bathroom would have been bad form, even in a used trailer. Nor was I going to use the yard toilet, providing I were to find it in the impenetrable darkness.

The only option was to step outside onto the frozen grass, whiz really fast and jump back inside before being slain by a fearsome creature. The damned jammed door wouldn't budge, of course. I put my shoulder into it, forcing it open. Like the blind man I was, I stepped down with my bare right foot, trying to find the first step. That's when I remembered the steps were not there, that I had climbed aboard without them because I couldn't get them to slide out from underneath the carriage. So I grabbed the outside handle and swung to the ground. I closed the door tightly out of fear that Alyeska, unfamiliar with the area, would wander off. Finding a lost dog in the dark was beyond my ability.

Quickly taking care of business, I found the door handle and pulled. It didn't budge. The door was jammed tight.

I yanked hard. Perhaps the previous owners had been the Stamper family from Ken Kesey's best book, *Sometimes a Great Notion*. Like the Stampers, it never gave an inch. But I wasn't thinking about my Gump days back when I met the most famous Oregon writer when I was covering high school wrestling in the Eugene area where his son was a star wrestler. After seeing him at several matches, I struck up a conversation. He had wrestled for the University of Oregon and knew the sport. I had wrestled in high school, although I wasn't the same caliber athlete. We talked wrestling, not literature. I figured it wasn't the place to ask about his writing.

Just as standing outside the trailer after midnight wasn't the place to reminisce. By this time, I had totally lost it, yanking on the door and screaming curses at the former owner, the manufacturer and the fellow who invented the tin house on wheels.

"You rotten piece of crap!" I snarled, or words to that effect. My verbiage was much worse, trust me.

The door still didn't move, but I did manage to awaken the faithful guard dog. She began growling and barking, apparently under the impression a burglar was trying to break in.

"It's me, you worthless mutt," I yelled.

I finally got her to realize the fellow trying to get into the trailer was also the one who feeds her. She still let out an occasionally woof to let me know she was displeased about being rudely awakened.

After more tugging, aided by begging and cursing, I finally got the door unjammed. I crawled back into my sleeping bag, grumbling more profanities.

Maureen arrived with the new day, bringing us breakfast. Her smile was as warm as the morning sun.

"You look a little haggard, sweetie," she said. "Did you have a bad night?"

"Words cannot express the utter misery of the last twelve hours," I replied. "If you spent a lot of time and money on this trailer, making drastic improvements, you would still have a mobile house from hell. The pioneers had it easy. They just had to carve a house out of the woods with their bare hands. They didn't have to endure life in a trailer with a bifurcated tail."

"The pioneers had trailers—they were called 'covered wagons,' " Maureen replied. "And they weren't grumps like some people today. Nor did they gibber about beelzebub."

That coming from someone who didn't have to spend the worst night in the trailer during the time we had the cursed thing. Actually, I'm glad Maureen didn't have to share that miserable night with me. Of course, she would have had the forethought to have a flashlight with batteries, not to mention a thermos of hot chocolate or tea and some fresh cookies to help us get through the night. Moreover, Alyeska would have leaped onto the bed, sharing her warm and fuzzy self.

Unlike Darwin's finches who adapted to the Galapagos Islands, I never did adjust to our tin-shelled habitat. No doubt there are trailers in which I could live happily. Ours was just not one of them. It had been too roughly used. Not only did none of the cabinets close properly but the awning, which the salesman had promised worked fine, didn't awn. At first, it refused to budge from its roll. Finally, after relenting to our tugs and yanks, it unrolled to reveal a long tear down its middle. We were awningless.

To be fair, there were times when life in the trailer bordered on pleasant, particularly when a summer thunderstorm would bring a shower. These are those storms which arrive with big, splashy raindrops after the lightning and thunder has shaken everything up.

Pling! Pling-plong! The rain brought a musical drum beat to our world as well as a sweet smell that is unique to a refreshing summer shower.

But the trailer had one more devious little trick up its tin sleeve, thanks to the aid of our medical doctor. A friendly fellow who also happens to live near us on the opposite side of what was Sterlingville, Dr. Chris decided that both of us needed to have a colonoscopy, having reached the half century milestone. At least his stated reason was our age, although he does have a keen sense of humor and had just learned we had temporarily moved into the little trailer with a single bathroom smaller than those portable toilets you see at construction sites.

But, as is always the case, his professional reasoning was sound.

"At your age, a colonoscopy is highly recommended as a screening exam to check for any signs of colorectal cancer, commonly called colon cancer," he explained in his grave medical voice. "With the exam, they can detect polyps before they become cancerous."

You will notice he said "they," not "I." He referred us to a local specialist regionally known for his expertise in exploring the nether regions.

A little dubious about the need for the invasive medical maneuver, I asked Chris if there was a medical alternative to the procedure.

"I'm afraid not," he said. "A lot of people have a misplaced sense of modesty when it comes to having a colonoscopy but it is important you have a screening test at your age. With colon cancer, it's essential it is caught early."

I've never entertained any daydreams about becoming a film star but if I had, I'm sure it wasn't about a screen test with my colon starring in a dark little film. The flick wouldn't fare well in the Cannes film festival but apparently proctologists find them very entertaining.

Chris explained that a colonoscope, a thin flexible, lighted tube with a tiny video camera on the end, is inserted in your posterior to explore all the nooks and crannies for signs of something that ought not to be there. The little video camera then broadcasts big pictures of its expedition to a television screen where medical specialists become film critics. I could just see them munching on popcorn and guzzling sodas while chortling at the sight of that site which is not spoken of in polite company.

"Uh, I am one of those people with a misplaced sense of modesty," I said. "Please tell me I won't be awake for this."

"You will sleep through it like a baby," Chris said, noting that the victim—he jokingly referred to him or her as the patient—is put to sleep before the procedure. "You won't even know it was done. It's quite simple, really."

He paused for a moment to scan our charts, checking to make sure he hadn't forgotten anything.

"Of course, you will need to fully evacuate your bowels thoroughly the day before you have the test," he continued. "You can only have Jell-O that day. We need everything cleared out. But it's not really as bad as it sounds. I'll prescribe a laxative that will do the job nicely. They have improved the taste. You drink it with ginger ale. You will need to take the day off when you are drinking the laxative and the following morning for the procedure."

I wondered aloud how we would manage, what with us acting as a laxative-induced tag team making emergency pit stops in the trailer's one tiny restroom. He suggested it may be wise for us to do the procedure on different days but Maureen insisted it would be easier with our schedules to have them done on the same day. It may be best for one of us to begin the laxative consumption a little before the other in an effort to offset the demand for toilet time, Chris said.

"Perhaps you could work out a schedule that way," he said, then looked down at the charts again. It seemed he had suddenly developed a nervous twitch in the corner of his mouth, the way someone does when they are trying to stifle laughter. Either that or he was suffering a petit mal.

"Yes, you will certainly want to coordinate the bathroom visits," he said after regaining his doctor decorum. "With two of you, there won't have much time between visits toward the end of it."

By then, he had crossed both arms across his chest, and brought one hand up to cradle his chin. His mouth was beginning to twitch again.

"Well, I'm sure you'll do just fine," he said, clearly fighting the onset of another seizure. In the years we've known him, it was the only time he seemed to have such attacks, poor fellow.

"If I didn't know better, I think the good doctor was about to burst out laughing at the thought of our upcoming predicament in the tiny trailer," I said after we drove away. "He looked like he was about to lose his professional propriety. I have a nagging suspicion that he may be chortling all the way home tonight."

"I don't know how he managed to control himself—I would have collapsed laughing," she replied with a giggle. "It would have been wiser to schedule two different days for this but I don't see how we could do it with our jobs. We'll just have to make this work out."

We both knew that we—and our tiny bathroom—were about to be sorely tested. We carefully followed his medical advice on the morning we began taking the liquid laxative. If researchers had improved the taste, it must have been truly horrible because it was still downright disgusting. And the ginger ale chaser did little to remove the foul after taste.

"Holy moly!" I gasped after the first swallow. "That stuff is really nasty. Arghhh!"

Maureen, whose strong stomach would make cast iron seem frail, was equally revolted.

"Oh, my God!" she said after taking a slug of the laxative. "I don't know if I can do this."

But do it we did. Our breakfast was Jell-O, followed by a lunch of Jell-O. By then, I wasn't looking forward to a Jell-O dinner.

"You know, this doesn't seem to be working," I told Maureen after consuming more of the foul liquid. "I wonder if we got a weak batch."

Five minutes later there was a rumble down below.

"Mother of God!" I yelled as I leaped over cats and dogs. Actually, I lurched. But quite swiftly.

That set the pattern for the rest of the day. Moments of calm were punctuated by periods of panic and racing to the bathroom end of the trailer. More than once one of us was doubled over in front of the closed bathroom door, pleading for the other to complete his or her business as quickly as possible.

"Yow!" I would yell. "There gates of hell are about to be unleashed!"

"Calm down," Maureen would respond as she opened the door. "You are going to scare the animals."

They looked amused as they watched our antics. They were no doubt disappointed when morning came and our bathroom sprints were over. Our medical mission had been accomplished. All that remained was getting a ride to the facility where the professionals would perform what was for them a routine test. Fortunately, we weren't aware when they went south. We were fast asleep.

We both came through the tests with no ugly surprises. But there was a long lasting aftermath. For months, the mere sight of ginger ale in a store invariably made us recoil and search frantically for a restroom. Fortunately, that also passed, so to speak.

FIVE

Used Car Lot

BEFORE WE COULD MOVE THE TRAILER ON SITE, four dead vehicles behind the cabin had to be removed. The yard toilet may have been butt ugly but the vehicles were not only ghastly eye sores but in the way of progress. Better they be recycled into vacuum cleaners than continue to suck up the beauty of the little valley. The neighbors certainly wouldn't be sorry to see their rusting bumpers disappearing down the road.

The vehicle owners apparently had a penchant for the eclectic. Each deceased vehicle was a different model and color. But the owners were patriotic consumers. Every vehicle was American made, and most had the Henry Ford stamp of approval. Not a funny-talking foreigner in the bunch.

"We have enough vehicles here to start our own used car lot," I told Maureen as we looked them over. "We could tell people they are classic road warriors whose value increases every year. As a sales pitch, we could suggest that Kim Novak may have ridden in one. After all, she does live in the Rogue Valley."

"First, they don't call them 'used' anymore," Maureen countered. "Now they are 'pre-owned.' Second, Kim Novak wouldn't have been caught dead in one of these. She is a classy lady. Third, these junkers are not classics. They are going to be hauled off."

Although she rightfully suspected I was joking, she wasn't taking any chances and headed me off at the pass before my zany idea took root. Sensing my window of opportunity for gibbering was quickly closing, I hurriedly pitched out a little more horse hooey.

"OK, perhaps Kim Novak is a little too sophisticated for our purposes," I said. "But we have other actors to turn to. Kirstie Alley had a ranch in the Little Applegate Valley for several years. Patrick Duffy has a home in Eagle Point. And Jack Elam and Ginger Rogers were Rogue Valley residents. They all had to drive at one point. One of these could have been theirs. I can see Jack Elam driving that old pickup, squinting through the cracked windshield with his one good eye. We can call it 'Sterling Creek's Already Broken In Cars.'"

"More like the 'Already Broken Down Cars,'" she quipped. "But, no matter what you call it, it is not going to happen, goofus."

I wasn't seriously quibbling with her logical protest, of course. I knew my tongue-in-cheek proposal as a seller of used and abused cars was a nonstarter.

As a journalistic Gumpster, I had interviewed the late Elam when he lived in Ashland. A friendly fellow with a quick wit, he told me how he lost the sight of his left eye through a childhood incident. But he didn't let it get in the way of a hugely successful Hollywood career, largely as a lovable bad guy in Westerns. He was also a smart fellow who wouldn't have tolerated any nonsense about him having driven the old truck. Nor would have Fred Astaire's dance partner been caught dead in any of the junk heaps. Like Novak, Rogers, who had a home along the Rogue for decades, was an uptown lady. As for Alley and Duffy, they surely would have also found the idea repugnant.

Maureen was right about getting rid of the vehicles. The mechanical geezers looked haggard. Save for one. That was the oldest, a 1958 Chevrolet pickup truck with a camper. It was one of those unique models with a dump bed, the kind that tipped up to dump its load, making it somewhat of a rarity. The fellow we bought the property from assured me the old truck still ran, although he admitted it may take a little tinkering. I suspect starting it would have called for a major overhaul. Perhaps it did run when he last lived on the property a decade earlier. But it appeared spent, like a marathon runner who had run into the wall. And it was the only one with inflated tires. Two, anyway.

The other three vehicles included a Ford van, a Maverick and a Cougar, all of the early-to-mid-1960s vintage. The van was white while the Maverick was what my twin would have indelicately called a baby-poop green. The Cougar was a light blue.

With the exception of the van, all of them sat with their hoods up. It was as though a backyard mechanic, the kind who dangles a cigarette from one lip while squinting at you through the smoke, had just stepped away to find the right wrench but instead went for a beer. Think James Dean in a torn t-shirt.

As it turned out, finding someone interested in restoring the pickup truck was a simple matter. It didn't event require resorting to erecting the "Already Broke In Cars" sign. It merely took a call to the local rural fire department chief, asking him to drop in to give us a few pointers on how to make the home more resistant to fires.

"You have quite a challenge ahead," he said when he arrived on a Saturday morning to check out our place. "But it'll look nice when you're done. Beautiful piece of land."

I had told him we wouldn't be building a new house but restoring the cabin. He walked around the cabin, looking at it from a structure firefighter's perspective.

"Well, the metal roof will help if there is a wildfire but you will need to keep the gutters clear," he observed. "Leaves and other debris can build up in gutters during the summer. A spark can ignite the leaves, leading to a house fire."

We would be replacing the section of the roof that had burned, and installing new gutters throughout, I told him.

"The gutters will be kept tidy," I promised.

"The big thing you need to do is remove the ladder fuel growing around the structure," he said, explaining the brush and low-lying limbs feeds a fire, allowing it to climb the trees. "You don't want any wood—firewood, lumber—stacked near the house. That just provides more fuel for a fire.

Obviously, you want to keep the flames away from the house so it doesn't catch fire."

We continued walking around the side of the house, reaching the backyard with its debris field and dead vehicles.

"Yeah, you've got quite a job ahead of you," he repeated. "You'll need to remove all of this so we can get a fire truck back here if we need to. Right now, we would be unable to get any kind of firefighting rig in here."

He stopped talking to gaze at the outdoor toilet.

"That does make quite an ornament, though," he said with a chuckle.

That's when I told him we were removing all the junk, including the uncouth commode. A tow truck was coming out to remove all the dead vehicles in a few days, I added.

"They'll all be recycled," I said. "Meanwhile, everything, including the antique toilet, is available at very reasonable prices. We do take checks."

"That's kind of a cool old truck," he said as he went over to inspect it. "Does it run?"

"I was told it did when it was parked there, but I'm a little skeptical," I said. "It looks to me like it would take a lot of work but could be a fun project for the right person."

He peered under the hood at the straight six-cylinder engine and stuck his head inside the cab.

"I might be interested in taking this off your hands," he said. "What do you want for it?"

Unlike any other used car dealer on the planet, I was struck dumb for a moment. Earlier, I had nearly asked him what he thought it would cost to have someone tow away the junkers.

"Er, uh, it's yours for hauling it away," I blurted out, then managed to salvage a little sales decorum with the caveat the camper had to go with it. "They can't bear to be separated. There's a magnetic attraction there. Childhood romance, you know."

He ignored my attempted used-car humor.

"I've always wanted to fix up an old vehicle," he said. "And the department can use the camper in a burn-to-learn exercise."

Sure enough, he returned the next morning with a large flat-bed trailer to haul the old Chevy away, camper and all. It's removal took a sizable bite out of the junk yard behind the cabin. What's more, getting rid of what was arguably the most difficult vehicle to haul off turned out to be surprisingly easy. However, I made a mental note to avoid the fire chief for a year or two in case he had receiver's remorse. I didn't want to give him the opportunity to return the mobile junk pile, camper and all.

Buoyed by the experience, I began calling around and quickly found a junk dealer/recycler who would haul the rest of the vehicles off for $25 each. By this time I was mentally patting myself on the back and thinking how easy it was going to be to clean up the debris and restore the cabin.

"Yep, got it made in the shade," I told Maureen.

Little did I know the gods of cabin restorations were just toying with us. If I had listened carefully, I would have heard muffled giggles somewhere in the ether over Sterling Creek. They were about to throw a wrench into what I assumed would be a well-oiled dead vehicle removal machine. Things quickly gummed up.

On the Monday I was to meet the tow truck man on the property, it began pouring. We're talking the kind of rain that tests a good waterproof watch. I had gone to work early so I could steal away for a long break to be at the cabin while the vehicles were removed. As I waited in the car for the tow truck, periodically turning on the windshield wipers to see outside, I wondered if we were of sound mind, taking on the cabin project. It wouldn't be the last time the disquieting notion popped into my head.

I checked my cell phone, noticing for the first time there was no service. Turns out we were in a dead zone, one which radiated out several miles in all directions from our property. That was probably the result of the mountain range, albeit a troubled mind would chock it up to unnatural forces emanating from the cabin. On some days, I blame mountain interference.

Whatever the cause, this meant I would be unable to call my office or my wife, both capable of wringing their hands should I disappear for a few hours. I had told my handlers it would take about two hours to rid the property of the dead cars. Tops. My time estimate fell short of reality, of course.

The tow truck man turned out to be a likable bear-like man guy with one pace that ignored my timetable. Nothing seemed to bother him, not even the downpour. His world was slow and deliberate.

"We need this rain," he said as he pulled on an extra-large green slicker over his one-piece dark gray coveralls. The rain gear was superfluous, given the grease stains providing waterproofing on ninety percent of the coveralls.

"The rain we get now will help when the forest fires start this summer," he continued. "More water in the trees, you understand. Slows the fire down so the firefighters can catch it."

The rain was running off the bill of his old baseball hat, forming a miniature waterfall. Like the overalls, it was waterproofed by grease stains, apparently the result of having been repeatedly grabbed by thick greasy fingers. Water dripped from the curly gray-white hair poking out over his temples.

Based on his comments, I figured he was an old-time Oregonian who hailed from a time when they were called "forest fires." Those were the Smokey the Bear years, before the term "wild fires" was adopted and before "the" was dropped from the bear's moniker, leaving the poor mascot without a middle name. The tow truck driver was right about water-soaked trees being more resistant to being torched. But despite the rain that day, the woods would be mighty dry come July of that year, prompting us to evacuate our trailer ahead of a threatening forest fire. Sorry, wild fire.

But fires in the woods were not on my mind that wet day. I was fighting a losing battle to stay dry while helping the tow truck operator rid the property of unclassic dead vehicles.

Removing the van and the Maverick proved to be simple chores. Both were easily accessible since the pickup truck had already been hauled off. With the van and the Maverick, it was merely a case of hooking the cable to the undercarriage and pulling each vehicle up piggyback. The back wheels rested on a massive dolly. It took all of fifteen minutes to load each vehicle. I'd like to say I was helpful but I mostly just offered small talk while he methodically went about his job.

Nor did I want to distract him. Time was moving swiftly and he was not. With the time it took him to haul each vehicle off to the junk yard and return for the other one, two hours quickly elapsed. Maureen would be getting worried. I didn't want to think about the finger-tapping clock watchers back in the news room.

Finally, the tow truck man returned to retrieve the last vehicle. The Cougar was parked about 300 feet up the valley from the cabin. It had been treated badly during its life, what with numerous dents and dings. It was also lodged against a young pine tree that was about four inches in diameter. A scar in the base of the tree indicated it had been scraped when the car was pulled to that location. I doubt if the Cougar had been driven to the spot. It was apparently already dead when it arrived.

"I'd like to save that pine if we can," I yelled through the rain to my slickered friend. "But it's kind of wedged up against the car."

"We can do 'er," he replied. "It'll just take a little tugging this way and that."

He hooked the cable to the front driver's side, careful to keep from crinkling the fender. Some of the parts may be sold to collectors so he didn't want to damage them, he explained. The winch slowly pulled the cable tighter. He was guiding the cable with one hand when his calloused index finger, about the size of a sausage, got caught between the cable and the car. It must have hurt like hell but all that appeared on his craggy face was a slight grimace.

"Could you pull that handle back a bit?" he asked, using his free hand to point to the leaver on the truck which he had been using to control the winch.

His request was nonchalant. He might have been asking me to pass the ketchup. Never mind that blood was streaming from his hand and running down the fender. I reached over and yanked the handle back the other way, hoping it was the right direction. Slicing off the finger and seeing it twitching on top of the fender would have left me retching in the rain. That was one bony finger of indignation I didn't want pointing at me. There was also the distinct possibility the large fellow would have been a mite peeved at me for lopping off his digit. I'm guessing it was the one thing that might have hastened his pace, causing him to lunge at me with a tire iron waving wildly in his good hand. I hoped to avoid either scenario.

Fortunately, the cable immediately slacked off, freeing his hand.

"Now that smarts a little," he said in his unhurried way as he inspected the digital damage. He fished into a deep pocked with his blood-free right hand, pulling out a badly stained handkerchief. He wrapped it around the finger dripping with rain-diluted blood. "That'll hold 'er," he said.

"Good God! You had better have someone look at that," I said. "It looks like a deep cut. It might get infected."

"Naw, it's fine," he said.

The scene was reminiscent of the Black Knight in the 1975 movie, *Monty Python and the Holy Grail.* After the knight had both arms hacked off in a sword fight, he challenged his opponent to resume the fight. "Just a flesh wound," observed the double amputee of his blood-spouting stumps. "'Tis' but a scratch," he insisted as he egged his opponent to be a man and continue the contest.

The tow trucker operator still had one good hand to continue his car combat in the steady downpour. Instructing me where to hook the cable under the rear of the car, he expertly guided the Cougar up onto the dolly. Apparently no worse for wear, he drove leisurely back down the valley and onto the road, waving goodbye with his left arm out the window. The last I saw of him was the red bandage of his hand, fluttering like a battle flag. The Black Knight would have been impressed.

I walked slowly back down to my car parked near the cabin, my socks squishing inside my shoes at each step. My hair was plastered to my head. But the rain no longer bothered me. I was soaked, not to mention totally spent.

Having been gone more than four hours, I knew there was no way to salvage the afternoon. Best I could do was go back to the office and see if I was still gainfully employed. After sopping up the water dripping off me, using nearly all the available paper towels in the newsroom bathroom, I checked in with the city desk. For once, nothing had popped up on my beat that I had to worry about.

"You realize the wet head is dead?" offered my lanky cubicle mate next door when I squished over to my desk.

"I intend to be in style when it makes a come back," I grumbled.

The red message light was flashing on my desk phone. Two were from a frantic wife. Amidst all the bedlam, I had forgotten to call Maureen when I got back into cell phone range to let her know I was safe and somewhat sound.

"Oh, my God, I thought something bad happened to you," she said when I called from my desk. "I called the sheriff's department. You were out there all afternoon. Do you realize it is getting dark?"

"You called who?"

"I called the sheriff because I was worried about you," she said. "You didn't call and it's getting dark. I just talked to them a few minutes ago. They were sending someone out to check on you."

"That's crazy," I said. "Please call them back and tell them I'm OK. There is no cell phone service out there."

She contacted the department to report her wet-headed husband had reported back for duty. Fortunately, my name was not broadcast over the newsroom scanner. The heckling would have been merciless. Journalists are notorious for tormenting their own kind. The razing would have followed me to the grave.

While the removal of the four vehicles was a milestone, we were not yet out of the automobile wrecking yard business. There was the matter of the old tires scattered about the property with the lion's share in the old garage near the cabin. Built of lightweight cedar boards, the ancient garage had not stood up well under the weight of time. It was careening to one side like a Saturday night drunk on Sunday morning. One of the former property owners more than half a century earlier had apparently been reluctant to part with old tires. While some were from the 1960s, others were of the narrow vintage, rolling back to the time when cars were young.

In all, we had collected ninety-six old tires, most of them as smooth as billiard balls. Gathering old tires together is one thing. Finding a place that will take them without demanding the equivalent of a mortgage payment is quite another. But we finally located a dealer in tired tires who would accept them for a mere $3 each. Although it is always dangerous for a journalist to do math, that added up to $288, a hefty sum for bald tires. They would be used to power an energy plant in Southern California, according to the bored fellow helping us load them onto an eighteen-wheeler.

It seemed like an ignoble end for the veteran road warriors but it was better than letting them continue to serve as mosquito luxury homes and spas. After the tires fill with rainwater, they become incubators for the little bloodsuckers. Few things can ruin an otherwise pleasant June evening more than squadrons of the tiny winged vampires rising from water- filled tires. Once they get a fix on your location, the bloody sorties continue nonstop until dark or until you are a quart low.

While the bloodletting is vexing, the bugs the bugs carry is more worrisome. I may have thought Egypt's Nile River was an interesting waterway when I saw it during a journalistic excursion in 2001 but my appreciation stops well short of the West Nile virus which originated in the drainage. Thanks to our modern mobile world, that dastardly bug is now carried by some mosquitoes lurking in our neck of the woods. So we wage war on their habitats, including the old tires that cradle their nasty little offspring.

At this juncture I was feeling smug about having removed all the old vehicles and their round rubber shoes from our property. Sure, there had been a couple of setbacks, including a nearly severed finger. But the scar would hardly be noticeable. In the end, it 'twas but a scratch. Things were once again moving along rather nicely.

Until I had a chat with the neighbor's teenage son, that is. We had hired him to give us a hand in digging a 350-foot narrow ditch to bury an electrical line that would link the cabin to the power grid.

"Did you know there is a 1957 Chevy buried on your property up the valley?" he asked during a break in the hard labor.

"Are you serious?" I replied. "You mean to tell me there we have another dead car?"

"Yep, it's right up there," he said, pointing to a spot where the valley narrows to a ravine. "All you can see is the back end. It's buried in an old dump up there."

"Great, that's the last thing we need," I said. "Well, we'll definitely check it out."

Later, as I trudged up the valley toward the area where he indicated, I was a little doubtful. Surely it wouldn't be a whole car. Not in a garbage pit. Maybe it was just a rear fender.

As a product of rural Oregon, I knew that country residents routinely buried their garbage prior to the creation of a garbage collection service or before people could take their trash to the county transfer site. It was practical back in the day, albeit not particularly friendly to the soil that sustains us. Early in Oregon history, there was little concern for those who would follow after, no niggling little worries about eventual ground water contamination and the like. But our garbage production had not reached today's output. We had yet to become the throw-away society that futurist Alvin Toffler wrote about in his 1970 book, *Future Shock.*

Now there is no excuse for us to trash our beautiful state, leaving future generations to clean up our mess. We know better. Besides, unless you are the product of Uncle Dad and Aunt Mom, you don't shove an entire car into a dump site. It is not done. Today, we country bumpkins have a sense of propriety.

So I was confident as I pushed my way through a thicket of trees and brush lining the ravine that I would only find a part of a car. A fender could easily be removed from the site. All it would take is winch it out, load it onto a flatbed truck and sell it. A fender in good shape from a 1957 Chevy would no doubt fetch a handsome price. As for the rest of the dump, a couple of big garbage bags would surely clean it up.

But when I finally reached the point where I could part the branches and look down into the ravine, there was no mere fender. There was a whole car there, all right. Only it wasn't a 1957 Chevy with its telltale extended fenders. Just what it was I hadn't a clue. The car was half buried and turned on its right side with only the rear end sticking out.

Whatever it was, I was sure it wasn't a classic. But it was time to call in an expert. That would be John Decker, a longtime friend who happens to be an ace automobile mechanic as well as an old car aficionado. He has owned and operated his own shop in the Medford area for decades, earning an outstanding reputation for competence and honesty. Consider this: John received a University of Oregon alumnus t-shirt for his birthday a few years ago but figured it wouldn't be right to wear it because he didn't graduate from the university. So he gave it to me. If John hadn't been such a stickler for integrity, he would have made a fine journalist.

Like me, John spent much of his child hood on the mean streets, er, street, of Kerby. We also happen to share the same birthday. A stout fellow, he had been a standout running back on the high school football team.

"I just found another old car on our property," I told John when I called him about the latest find. "But I don't know what the heck it is. We need a car sleuth for this one."

"Sounds interesting," he replied in his usual casual approach to life. "We could stop by next week and check it out."

He and his son, Jesse, are the only known descendants of royalty to have stepped inside our cabin. John is the great, great grandson of Princess Winema, the Modoc Indian woman also known as Toby Riddle. She served as an interpreter between the Modoc tribe and the Uncle Sam's Army during the Modoc War in the early 1870s. Like her local descendent, she was apparently big on integrity. When she learned that a peace commission was going to be attacked in 1873, she warned members in advance, saving the life of the commission leader. Given the fact she was first cousin to Captain Jack, the Modoc tribal leader during the war, it was a dangerous move on her part. For her heroic action, congress awarded her a military pension in 1891, making her one of the few Native American women during that era to receive such an honor.

Although she was given a different Indian name at birth, she later earned the name Winema. The native word means "woman chief," one she was honored with after rescuing some young friends whose canoe had capsized in dangerous rapids. In other words, John and Jesse chose their ancestors wisely.

Rescuing canoes and their contents is apparently a family trait. John saved our canoe during an ill-fated canoe trip down the Wood River in southern Oregon a couple of years ago during one of numerous water voyages together.

On this particular spring trip, snow was falling on the Cascade Range to our west when we launched that spring morning. When the wind picked up, you could feel the chill deep in your bones. However, unless we did something silly like flip the canoe, we would be fine. And we were fine until about halfway through the six-hour trip.

The Wood is a small river with virtually no rapids. You would have to work at it to drown in this stream. But its waters are fed spring and summer by runoff from the deep snow blanketing the 7,000-foot rim above Crater Lake. As you would expect, the water is very, very cold. You certainly don't want to take a dip during that early June morning we were on the river.

Just what happened remains a mystery to me. I had just cast into a promising pool, one where I was sure lurked a lunker German brown or rainbow trout. It is a catch-and-release stream for the most part. As a concession to that niggling little voice which always asks me why I would torture fish by catching and releasing them, I crimped the barbs on my hooks so it's easy to unhook them. It's a small thing but it eases my conscience somewhat.

I was anticipating the strong tug of a big trout from deep in the swirling water when the canoe suddenly flipped over, pitching us into the drink. Since we were coming alongside a tree that had fallen halfway into the stream, it's possible the canoe struck an unseen submerged limb.

We executed a rather nice Eskimo roll. Half of it, anyway. I came up, involuntarily gasping at the sheer cold. I grabbed a limb and hung on. John popped up and grabbed the canoe as it drifted past. One of those rare folks who keeps his cool during an emergency, he flipped over the waterfilled craft and saved our gear. He salvaged everything save for the fishing rods, which sank to the bottom.

Stuart and Jim, two other friends following us in another canoe, paddled up so I could grab the stern of their craft. They towed me over to the opposite bank where I was able to crawl up on the grassy bank. We returned to the site about a month later on a rod-salvage expedition. Braving the cold water, John dove in and retrieved his rod. But we were unable to spot mine in the watery depths. Good thing, that. There was no way I was going to take the plunge for my rod, much as I was fond of it. The thought of that cold water still gives me the shivers.

Although walking up to investigate the old car with John and Jesse wasn't as adventurous as canoeing a river, I intended to be prepared for all eventualities. I grabbed a hefty walking stick, one they would call a "shillelagh" in Ireland. I wasn't expecting to take on a couple of brigands, at least not those who walk upright. In addition to using it as a walking aid, I wanted to be able to defend myself against buzz worms that sometimes lurk in the tall grass. It was early fall but still toasty enough for vipers to be about. We did notice a couple of their airborne cousins in the form of a couple of yellow jackets flying around.

After fighting through the tall grass, brush and low-lying limbs, we finally reached the ravine. John chose to come down from an embankment while Jesse and I worked our way up the ravine from the bottom.

"It's a Dodge," John observed after one glance. "But I am not really into old Dodges as far as knowing the year. I do know they used to put the date it was made on the tail light."

Unfortunately, the tail lights were not on the car. As Jesse and I moved in closer to see if one was buried nearby in the debris, we did see a "Dodge" emblem on the trunk, confirming John's assessment.

"Let's look around a little for tail lights," Jesse said. "Maybe one is buried in this garbage."

Several bullet holes in the trunk indicated the car had been used for target practice. There were also three bullet holes in a tight group around the keyhole. They appeared to have been from a high-powered weapon, likely a 30-caliber.

"Looks like someone was trying to break in," John said. "Either that or they put were putting bullet holes in the trunk to enable their captive to breathe. I believe those are known as mafia breathing holes."

"Or perhaps they were patriots exercising their God-given 2nd Amendment rights," I offered.

John continued looking down at the car from above, trying to get a fix on its age.

"It's too bad—kids with guns, shooting at anything and everything," he said. "If someone was interested in this model, it might be worth trying to get it out. But the bullet holes aren't encouraging."

Jesse was moving closer in to inspect the trunk when he let out a yell and began swatting the air. I started to laugh at his antics when something stung my forehead. Another stung my left calf. I joined the swatting and yelling choir. A swarm of yellow jackets came boiling up out of the debris under my feet. It may not be wise to anthropomorphize the behavior of creatures, but these guys seemed very, very mad.

It was an angry airborne mob. One stung my right cheek while another stabbed a stinger into the back of my left hand. Two others decided to investigate under my t-shirt and began drilling about an inch apart near my backbone just above my belt. Other members of the flying swat team stung my wrists, forearms and neck. A fly swatter would have served me better than my shillelagh.

But I wasn't keeping a close count. Both Jesse and I were making our way through the debris and underbrush, fleeing the attacking swarm in slow motion. Being much faster than me, Jesse was able to make his escape with only a couple of stings. The little monsters jabbed me at least a dozen times. Unlike honey bees, yellow jackets can sting multiple times. The fact the stings were simultaneous indicated there were multiple culprits joining in the fun.

"I guess that's true about what they say: you don't have to be fast, just faster than the other guy," observed a grinning John who was literally above the fray. He wasn't stung once.

Both Jesse and I continued swatting and yelling as we retreated down the ravine. We finally calmed down, although we were still a little jumpy. We decided to join John in the yellow jacket-free zone.

"No need to bring your little friends up here," John said. "I'm doing fine without them, thank you."

Although still smarting from the yellow jacket attack, we checked out the car from the safety of our new position. The top of the ravine also provided a better vantage point of the entire garbage pit. It appeared that someone had used a bulldozer to dig a trench for the purpose of creating a dump site. It was not a pretty sight. A quick survey revealed all the trash humanoids could throw at Mother Nature: an old bathtub, an ancient vacuum cleaner—I was glad to see a dead one—washer and dryer, wine bottles, oil cans, jars of every shape and size, bicycles. There were even several old wooden window frames and doors, apparently from an old cabin that had been dismembered.

"Everything, including the kitchen sink," John observed. Sure enough, there was an old kitchen sink floating in the flotsam.

The trench is roughly forty feet long, a dozen feet wide and perhaps 15 feet at the deep end. Painted an ivory color, the car is at the bottom end, its rear fenders sticking out like the pale tail of Moby Dick.

"I think it is a two-door," John said. "You can tell that by the roof. It's too bad they shoved it over into that pit. It's probably rusted pretty bad underneath."

By then, Jesse and I were ready to return to the cabin to recuperate from our aerial attack. We decided to go back to the car after the weather had turned frosty, a time when the guardians of the garbage had succumbed to the cold.

On our second trip to the Dodge in the dump, John brought a civilian version of a military entrenching tool, the kind soldiers use to dig fox holes. It is basically a small folding shovel which you can pack along on a long march. John began scraping off dirt and debris to inspect the rear quarter panel on the passenger side.

"I believe this is a 1960," he said when he paused for a break. "From the information I've dug up on this, there were three different editions that year. The Pioneer was the middle of the line for Dodge that year. You had your base model which was the Senica. That was basically the standard model. Next was the Pioneer, the middle of the line for Dodge that year. The top one was the Phoenix. That was the top tier, the one with all the bells and whistles. It was kind of the sporty version.

"We should know which of the three versions it is in a few minutes," he added. "They put the name on the side of the back fender."

He continued digging, careful not to scrape the paint should someone decide the vehicle is worth restoring. Fortunately, most of the debris was needles shed from nearby pine trees.

"Ah, here it is," he said, brushing the last of the material aside. "This is very rare. It's an 'ioneer.' "

The "P" was no longer attached, creating the abridged name. He stopped talking for a moment to remove several branches from the top of the car.

"This is a two-door hardtop," he said. "It wasn't a bad looking car back in its day."

He was quick to observe the 1960 Dodge could not compete against the Chevrolets and Fords of that era. Back then, the Dodge was considered too stodgy for anyone who didn't have gray hair.

John reached down and picked up a piece of plastic.

"Here is your speedometer," he said, tossing it to me. The speedometer indicated the car could have reached speeds of 120 miles per hour. Climbing down to the rear bumper, he removed a little more debris.

"There is a small door here which still opens," he said. "It's for the gas tank. Like I said, it's an interesting model."

The hood appeared to be missing, although we did find another hood nearby, one which had apparently belonged to the pea green Maverick which had been hauled off by the tow truck driver with the bloody digit.

Strangely enough, we found what appears to be the hood to the Dodge in an older and smaller dump site higher on the hillside about 300 yards to the south. John also discovered what he believes was a left headlight frame for the Dodge at the smaller dump.

Given the fact the hood was intact; albeit at the other dump site on the hill, there is a chance the car doesn't have a wrecked front end. But it is also likely it didn't fare well in the garbage pit.

"The Dodge could be a collector's item for someone," John said. "Because of the circumstances, I don't know if it would be worth it to a collector to get it out of here. The part that is sticking out doesn't look that bad. But you would need to find someone who is really interested in this particular model."

If you are interested in a 1960 Dodge Pioneer, a deal awaits at Sterling Creek's Already Broken In Cars. A shady salesman there may suggest Kim Novak once drove that very car. Or one very much like it.

UP STERLING CREEK WITHOUT A PADDLE

SIX

Batting Clean-Up

WITH THE OLD VEHICLES NEAR THE CABIN GONE to their reward, I figured the old place would look a little spiffier, perhaps even attractive. But the vacancy left by the departure of the old truck and its dilapidated brethren only focused the attention on that lovely yard toilet and the rest of the flotsam floating amid the ash and dirt of the back yard. Beyond the strewn garbage loomed the partially-burned abode we intended to make into our permanent home. At that point, the charred structure looked even more like it had received a direct hit from an incendiary bomb. Anyone with a touch of mysophobia—that nasty old dread of dirt or filth—would run screaming down the road after a peek inside the cabin.

The sight brought to mind the Stephen Foster song about hard times in a hardscrabble cabin. Written in 1854, the same year James Sterling discovered gold in Sterling Creek, it tells of a downtrodden cabin where life was barren and bleak.

"Hard times, hard times, come again no more, many days you have lingered around my cabin door," Foster wrote, adding the refrain, "Oh, hard times come again no more."

Indeed, our future home had suffered exceedingly hard times. It sorely needed a little tender loving care. Actually, it desperately required intensive care, including reconstructive surgery and a major facelift. Even then we would still be roughing it. I was beginning to worry that our dream for the cabin was about to morph into a nightmare.

And Maureen? She couldn't have been more ebullient as we surveyed the mess.

"It's going to look so comfy and cozy, the way all grandparent homes are supposed to be," she said as she reached over to hold my hand. "Our kids and grandkids are going to love it."

"Yep, it is going to be very homespun," I observed. "All you will need is a prairie and Laura Wilder's great, great, great grandkids would be envious of our little house."

My wife was too enthused with envisioning the future cabin to bother with my attempted sarcastic witticism. As usual, her enthusiasm was contagious. As she talked about special features our home would have, including a loft where I could someday stay home and write, I couldn't help but be lifted by her buoyant spirit. My worries began to fade like mist before the morning sun.

Both being Oregon born and bred, we preferred a little valley with trees and mountain meadows to a windswept plain where the Wilders settled. We also liked the fact we were restoring an old cabin in a region ripe with history. We were ready to roll up our sleeves and get to work.

"We are going to love being here," Maureen said. "Just think, your grandparents probably came by here in their buggy more than a hundred years ago."

"Yeah, I'm sure they did," I replied. "And I bet Grandpa Jonas reined in their two horses, Old Jake and Captain Jack, looked up this little valley for a moment and said, 'Now there is a place grandparents ought to live.'"

Hand in hand, we walked around, talking about how we would tackle the work ahead. When Maureen's fingers entwined in mine, I felt confident we could overcome any challenge. After all, I was with my confidant. I freely acknowledge I am not a touchy-feely person who likes to hug other humanoids. But that barrier dropped the first moment I saw her. When her hand touches mine, the sun comes out. I suspect when you truly fall in love, it is with the person you most want to emulate. She is the one with whom I can let my guard down. What does she see in me? Damned if I know, although a friend says the fact she loves to rescue lost little puppies may provide a helpful clue.

We had done some renovation over the years, including installing an oak floor, remodeling a kitchen and extending a deck in a previous home. We had built up an arsenal of tools with lethal weapons such as a table saw and a circular saw as well as other sharp implements capable of slicing off body parts. Yet we also retained the fingers and thumbs we were born with, no mean feat when it comes to working with power tools. I have great respect for their digital removal ability. As a child, I was there the day my dad lopped off the end of his left thumb, including the entire nail, with a table saw. The stump of his thumb was a grim reminder of that hideous accident. But it helped balance his body since he had lost his right leg in a logging accident a few years earlier.

To keep us sharp, so to speak, Maureen and I had been faithful fans of "This Old House" on PBS back when we watched television. With our rudimentary carpentry skills, we were like two high school bench sitters watching professional basketball players doing slam dunks. But it inspired us to believe we could do some of the restoration work demonstrated by Tom, Norm and the boys. Once we moved onto the job site and no longer watched television, we would subscribe to *This Old House* magazine to keep up with the carpentry lads latest fixer-upper techniques.

Yet we couldn't help feel a little overwhelmed by the enormity of the task ahead. We knew that Chris, Richard and the other talented subcontractors— our answer to the "This Old House" gang—would be doing the work that required the skills of a journeyman carpenter, plumber or other specialty. But we were unsure if we would be able to hold up our end, elementary as it was.

Fortunately, Chris has an easy way about him of patiently boiling everything down to make it sound simple.

"Right now, you just need to remove all the charred material from the house that is not supporting the frame," he stressed at the outset. "That includes taking out all the debris inside the house, especially the sheet rock. You have to strip it all down to the bones so we can begin restoring it."

For a second, his comments reminded me of the Vietnam war in which the goal of the U.S. military appeared to be to destroy a village in order to save it. But I had the good sense not to crack wise.

"Think of it this way," the veteran carpenter said. "You will be saving us a couple of week's worth of work. You don't want to pay us to strip the house and haul off all the debris. So you'll be saving yourself a lot of money."

Chris and Richard had another job that would take them some two months to complete. Our mission was to have the cabin and the yard cleaned up so they could start working on day one. Actually, we had to have it spruced up sooner than that so it could be inspected by an appraiser from the bank, an inspection which would decide whether the place qualified for the construction loan we needed. The county had already approved our plan to rebuild the old structure but we required the loan to hire the experts for the work we lacked the skills to do. Without the loan, our future would include living in a dismal trailer house beside a partially burned cabin. At this point, the trailer had yet to arrive. We had sold our house in Josephine County and were temporarily renting from the new owner until we got the trailer. I wanted to make sure we had the construction loan before we got the metal house on wheels. The loan would ensure the mobile visitor didn't set down roots. We had no time to dally.

With Chris' encouragement, we knew where we wanted to start. We flushed the yard toilet, removing it from the yard, that is. I hastened the porcelain potty's departure one morning by sitting on it and waving at Maureen when she came walking around the cabin. No, I hadn't dropped my trousers. Geez, that's disgusting. But the unsettling sight spurred Maureen to place getting rid of the toilet tops on our priority list. While hauling it to the dump may not have been a huge step forward, it felt like we were finally going on the offensive. Despite our on-going jokes about it, having to look at that stained toilet really, well, stunk.

With the toilet now history, we waded into the rest of the yard debris, eagerly tossing garbage into the back of our pickup truck and becoming familiar faces at the county dump. We mined yards and yards of debris from our back yard. In addition to the toilet, other big items included a hot water tank and a small wood stove. The metal we hauled to a recycling center. But much of the debris was remnants of burned material whose original purpose forever remained a mystery.

When it came to cleaning up the back yard, it would have been helpful to know what had stood there before the fire. We had only a short conversation with the previous owner so we never were able to get a proper handle on what that area looked like before it was razed by flames. The folks we bought the property from had moved off of it a decade earlier.

But it was obvious what was becoming our back yard had been no yard before the fire. Two rusting water pipes jutting up out of the ground a dozen feet in the air behind the main cabin appears to have delivered water to the upstairs of an adjacent structure that had burned to the ground in the blaze. The pipes had not been warped by the heat, causing them to twist upwards. They definitely had been plumbed for the vertical delivery of water to a second story.

Not knowing what the structure looked like before the fire, we dubbed it Cabin Incognito. The square nails we found in pieces of partially buried wood confirmed there had once been a very old structure there. But Cabin Incognito's purpose remained a puzzle to us. The section which would have been the north side of the structure was either a storeroom or someone's bedroom, judging from items we found in debris left by the fire. That included a dozen ear rings, a couple of coins from half a century ago and other bric-a-brac that included countless shards of glazed pottery. Some of the glass items had been melted by the fire but others survived the heat intact, including an antique eye washer. Strangely, the south side of the cabin area gave up countless old tools, several which had been forged by a blacksmith, indicating that side had been a shop or a place where tools were stored. The structure was doubtlessly not something you would have found in a glamour magazine, unless it had a piece on taking shabby chic beyond the limits of propriety.

The small artifacts we uncovered after we removed the bigger pieces intrigued me. That curiosity triggered one of my episodes of compulsive behavior, an idiosyncrasy I blame on the family gene pool. When it is triggered, I tend to get carried away in the way a gambler does when entering a Reno casino. Kiss the money goodbye. In this case, I was only spending time, albeit valuable. I obtained some fine wire mesh which would trap anything slightly smaller than a pea, set up a makeshift rocker in the form of a wheelbarrow to sift the material and began screening scoop shovel loads of yard dirt. The search was for artifacts which would escape the naked eye. This was all done, of course, after Maureen had dashed into town on several errands. She is a multi tasker while her husband frequently looks for ways to turn work into play unless he is properly supervised.

In my defense, we were largely done with cleaning up the yard. Sifting through the material was also done in the interest of learning more about Cabin Incognito. As a fan of all things related to digging into the past, I had been to a lot of archaeological digs over the years while a working journalist. I knew how the experts sifted through what they call the inhabited zone in search of clues to the past.

When Maureen returned from town, I was happily sorting through the dirt, well into my long recess in my newly discovered playground.

"So what are we up to now, dearie?" she asked as she stepped out of the car. "I leave you for a few hours and you start playing in the dirt."

"Please remove that little smirk, young lady," I replied smugly. "We are now archaeologists willing to get our hands dirty for a little ground truthing. While someone else was gadding about town, one of us has been working hard to advance Sterling Creek history."

I showed her a shoe box of loot that included old buttons, a few fire-scorched coins whose dates were illegible, an old Christmas ornament in the form of a tiny glass angel, several ear rings, two dozen square nails and other historic items. Just as I expected, she was curious yet well short of astounded by the treasure.

"These are interesting," she agreed as she checked out the items. "That little angel is adorable. Those buttons look like they came off an old coat, the kind women wore in the 1920s or '30s."

Maureen continued inspecting the material for a moment before putting them back in the box. She pursed her lips the way a teacher does before gently telling a stubborn child reluctant to return to the class room that recess is over.

"You know we have to get back to cleaning up this mess," she said. "We don't have much time before the bank appraiser pays a visit. We've already found a lot of old stuff like this. Don't you think our time would be better spent cleaning inside the cabin now instead of playing around out here?"

I was beginning to profoundly dislike the cursed appraiser from the equally annoying bank. I hadn't even met the appraiser yet but his threatened visit was already blocking out my sun. I started to remind my wife that she had been irresponsible for the physical digression by leaving me unsupervised, a point she had voiced concern about before leaving for town. But I had a surprise that I knew would catch her rapt attention.

Of course, you don't just throw out little wonderments nonchalantly, like potatoes tossed into the back of a farm truck. You reveal them slowly, tantalizingly.

"Do you honestly think Indiana Jones was playing around when he discovered the Holy Grail?" I asked. "Was Hiram Bingham out on recess when he found Machu Picchu? What if Howard Carter's mom made him stop playing archaeologist when he was a kid? King Tut's treasures may have never been found."

"OK, you lost me with Hiram what's his face and his macho something," she said. "But let's skip all that. You get like this when you are up to something. What did you find?"

She was grinning now, knowing full well that I had found something that would pique her interest. But she also knew I would try to prolong the revelation with windy verbiage about Hiram what's his face and other finders of lost stuff.

"Hiram Bingham was the guy who discovered the Inca stronghold of Machu Picchu in Peru more than a century ago," I said. "In truth, he just rediscovered it since it was already known to the locals..."

"Oh, for heaven's sakes, just tell me what you found!" she exclaimed.

"I was merely trying to put it in context for you," I sniffed.

While talking, I reached into my pocket to pull out a small aspirin bottle. There were no white pills inside. Yet something rattled around in the bottle when I held it up and shook it.

"Do you recall my promise that one day I would give you a diamond?" I asked with my trademark meadow-muffin eating grin.

"You found a diamond?" she asked. "Are you kidding me?"

"I kid you not—I found a diamond."

It took me a moment to get the lid off the bottle, the kind you have to fight with because it is child proof and adults need the skills of a safe cracker to get to the contents. Maureen was about to grab it out of my hand by the time I poured a glistening pea-size diamond into her palm.

"That's really cool," she said, reverting back to late 1960's vernacular. "It's so beautiful."

"Indeed, it is," I said. "I found it about an hour ago in the area where we think the bedroom was. It was probably from a ring. Of course, it's probably not a real diamond. I'm sure it's a piece of glass cut perfectly to look like the real thing.

"But it really sparkled in the sun when I saw it on the screen," I added. "I got a little excited for a minute there. I knew you'd like it."

Maureen carefully put the diamond back into the bottle, sealed it and handed it back to me. She was smiling when she picked up the screen.

"Are you ready to get serious?" she asked. "We need to do this in a grid fashion, section by section. You've probably missed a lot of jewelry and coins already. We've only got a couple of hours of daylight left. Let's get moving."

For a second, I wanted to sternly remind her we had no time for playing in the dirt, that we had real work to do. But my silly grin would have given me away as a verbal fraud.

"I was hoping you might see it my way," I said. "You bet. I'm ready to get down and dirty, homey."

We spent the rest of the afternoon blissfully playing in the dirt, joking and chatting away as we sifted shovels full of dirt with the mesh screen. We didn't find much of consequence but enough square nails and other little items to keep us interested. It was a pleasant break from the mundane task of hauling garbage to the dump. We are both history buffs, whether it is found in books or in soil. But it is fun to play dirt detective sometimes, if for no other reason than serving as an excellent bonding experience for partners in life. You might want to try it the next time you have a spousal tiff.

As for the faux diamond, one day we will have it checked out by a jeweler. While we are assuming it is cut glass, the kind of bauble folks wore a century ago, we wondered aloud why it didn't melt during the fire. Perhaps it was shielded in some way from the intense heat. On the other hand, real diamonds don't readily melt, I reminded Maureen. That prompted jokes about the Sterling Creek gem being worth a mint. Never mind that mint may be the kind you buy in a candy store for a few cents.

The bottom line is Maureen has her diamond, one that in her mind is priceless. Her dirt detective of a husband couldn't agree more.

But we both knew that pleasant afternoon was a temporary respite from the task at hand. We had to leave Cabin Incognito and get back to cleaning debris from the cabin that was still standing if we were ever to make it inhabitable again. There was fire-blackened sheet rock hanging from the walls and ceiling. Ashes, six inches deep in places, covered the concrete floor. In other areas there were piles of charred wood and other debris. The west wall was nothing more than blackened logs. When you looked back down at the cabin from farther up the valley, it looked like it was grinning at you with rotting teeth.

"Maybe we ought to call it 'Joe Bob,'" I told Maureen.

"Don't even think about it," she replied. "You are not going to put a hillbilly curse on our cabin."

As we did with the yard, we began removing the large debris and worked down to the finer material ion the cabin. Some of the partially burned wood from the cabin was hauled up the valley and piled to burn along with brush we had cut around the cabin. Slowly, the old place began to lose its spitting image of the county dump. And I do mean spitting.

All of the sheet rock in the cabin had been stained by the fire and smoke. But we found it had also served as a fire inhibitor since it does not burn, just as Chris had predicted. Where we could, we peeled entire sheets off the walls and vaulted ceiling. Carting off large pieces was easier than shoveling the bits and pieces.

It took more than a week to remove and haul off all the sheet rock, most of which crumpled when we grabbed it. When we weren't working our day jobs in Medford, we became close friends with scoop shovels at the cabin. We're talking first name basis here.

"I'm christening mine 'Ruth,'" Maureen announced one evening. "It does such a nice job of cleaning up. Of course, it's all about knowing how to handle it."

"I didn't know you had an ancestor by that name," I said. "Was that on your dad's side?"

"No, dummy, I'm talking about Babe Ruth, the Sultan of Swat," she said. "He always cleaned up the bases when he came to bat. You really need to become more familiar with sports legends as well as your shovel."

"I know what a shovel is for," I responded. "You lean on the handle while you watch your wife work. Any dummy knows that."

She was right about my ignorance when it came to professional sports, although I did know about the Bambino. Well, I knew he had a candy bar named after him. But it surprised me that she knew George Herman Ruth Jr. from first base.

"Sometimes you shock me with your knowledge of random things," I said. "I didn't know you knew anything about the baseball legend. It's a little scary."

"I like to keep you guessing, sweetie," she replied before wheeling the barrow to the pickup to unload the debris.

What did I name my shovel? It's a moniker not fit for print, but a word the famous slugger uttered from time to time when he encountered an umpire whose call he didn't appreciate. I understand he believed most umpires didn't know the names of their fathers.

In the cabin-stripping phase, one of the most difficult challenges was cleaning out the attic above the kitchen and guest bedroom. The attic is now my writing loft which is accessible by a very solid and comfortable stairs. Back then, you had to climb a ninety-degree makeshift ladder nailed to the wall to reach the area. For me, it was a scary climb, what with not having full dexterity on my right side. Moreover, once you made the ascent, the soundness of the loft's plank floor was questionable. The fire had eaten away the top of the log wall, leaving the entire outer west wall unattached to the roof ridge. Standing up there was dicey at best. Smacking into the concrete floor some ten feet below was not my idea of a good time.

But it was the only way to reach the burned debris in that section of the cabin. Noting the top of the west wall had burned to the point it was not supporting the roof, Chris had suggested we could easily push the wall away from the cabin.

"It isn't supporting anything—removing it won't affect the roof," he had told us when he was walking us through the cabin to advise us what to strip. "If you can push it down, you can then haul it away in sections. We need to get it out of there since we be replacing it with a new supporting wall."

Sure enough, when we pushed the wall from the top, utilizing rakes to provide reach, it neatly fell away from the cabin. We were able to break it up and add it to a burn pile.

Once we had removed the larger burned material and debris, we still had to clean the cabin of ash and dirt to make it presentable for inspection by the bank appraiser. We didn't want it to look like a fire-bomb house when he came to check it out.

"I've got a bad feeling in my gut about this inspector," I warned Maureen.

"It's probably that junk food you had for lunch," she said. "Besides, I don't want to know about your strange thoughts concerning the inspector. He is part of our future whether you like it or not."

Of course, she was dying to know my analysis of the bank appraiser we had yet to meet. She can be such a tease sometimes.

"No doubt he is going to be a pencil pusher, a bureaucrat's bureaucrat," I told her. "He will be a real stickler for rules and regulations. He will probably have beady little eyes and a ferret face, the kind you want to slap. And his voice will be shrill and whiney."

"Oh puhleez!" she said. "Why don't we give him a chance? You really need to control that wild imagination of yours, little mister."

But she agreed we had a few major hurdles to clear before his arrival. Since the ugly trailer was not yet parked in the back yard, we had no way to efficiently heat water to scrub the floors or wash the walls in the bathrooms. As usual, she had a solution.

"It's simple," she said. "You know those big plastic tubs we use for holding dry dog food? The ones with the thick plastic lids? We can get a couple of them, put them in the back of the pickup and fill them with hot water. The water should still be nice and warm when we get to the cabin."

"That has to be the craziest idea you have ever come up with, and there have been some real doozies," I wailed. "There is no way I will ever be part of such a wacky scheme."

I was still grousing about it when I backed the pickup truck up to the house we had just sold and were renting from the new owners. I jerryrigged a hose to attach it to a hot water faucet and began filling the tubs Maureen had bought for the purpose. Part of my agitation came from the fact I would be using the last of my vacation scrubbing bathrooms and the concrete floor of the cabin. My wife wouldn't be there, of course. She would be working in her comfortable shop, far from the misery. Once again, Alyeska, was accompanying me as the appointed watchdog. That is, her job was to watch over me to make sure I didn't wander off or slip a fishing rod into the pickup.

"This is the nuttiest thing Mo has ever talked me into," I growled to the big dog. "This is beyond goofy. It won't work. The water will be cold by the time we get there. Besides, I'm sure we must be breaking some kind of law, transporting hot water between counties. Never mind common sense is taking a serious beating."

Alyeska scratched behind her ear as though she was mulling over what I had just said. But I didn't bite her gambit. I knew it was just a flea. Man's best friend wasn't living up to the old maxim.

While I wasn't willingly buying into Maureen's plan, I did drive the roughly 12 miles to the cabin fairly fast. Since I was going to be using the water and it was cold in the cabin, I was hoping the water would be at least luke warm for the job. I was almost looking forward to informing my wife that her plan was an abysmal failure.

Turns out the water was nearly too hot for me to dip my hand in when we got there. What's more, the hot water, soap and a bit of scrubbing on my part did the job. Maureen's weird plan worked. For several days, I hauled hot water and scrubbed away in the cabin. I didn't exactly enjoy myself but it wasn't half bad. With a thermos of hot coffee and a hefty lunch, Alyeska and I fared well. Fortunately, the mutt didn't much care for coffee, although she did insist I share my sandwiches and cookies with her.

Naturally, I didn't want to tell Maureen that she was right. Again.

"It was hard but I was able to make it work," I said. "The water was just above freezing, of course. And babysitting that spoiled dog was no fun. It was a miserable couple of days but I pulled it off. Mission accomplished."

Alyeska woofed at me, letting me know she didn't appreciate the tall tale of misery. Fortunately, the woof alert from the hairy snitch didn't register with Maureen. Her mind was already on the bank appraiser's visit scheduled for the next day.

"The bank just wants to make sure the cabin is what we say it is in terms of being restorable," she said. "The appraiser will check out what he needs to. It's all fairly routine so don't let your imagination run wild again."

I readily agreed there was no need to let a vivid imagination stampede rational thought. But the two old maid sisters, Fussy and Fret, insisted that I speak out. The two siblings are the ones with their hairs in buns and wearing long black dresses, standing with their arms akimbo in the back of your mind. The old biddies invariably refuse to disappear until your worries are aired.

"I'm just telling you these bank inspectors don't know anything about living in the country," I said. "He will be real finicky, saying things like 'ick' and 'yow.' I'll bet you he will be wearing both a belt and suspenders. He'll be carrying a little clipboard so he can keep track of the demerits. Then, after he puts the kibosh on our dream cabin, I will have to say I told you so."

"Fine," she said. "But we are going to treat him with respect."

It was snowing lightly the day the appraiser arrived in a two-wheel-drive cream-colored sedan that fishtailed down Sterling Creek Road and careened like a drunken sailor up our driveway. Out stepped a short, gray-haired fellow wearing a shirt and tie, slacks and dress shoes. Inside his jacket you could see suspenders. And under that? A belt. To cap it off, he reached back into the car to pick up a clipboard. Our fate was sealed. I groaned.

"Shush," Maureen whispered as we walked over to greet him.

"How you folks doing?" he asked as he shook our hands. "You've got a beautiful place here. This is a very pretty little spot."

The gregarious fellow told us his ancestors were farmers who settled the west end of the Applegate Valley, arriving prior to statehood. Unfortunately, the farm house the family built in the late 1800s had just been torn down by a new owner, he added.

"I always feel bad when an old home can't be restored," he said. "When that happens, a lot of history is lost. We need to do what we can to save these old places."

The bank appraiser—my new best friend—continued talking cheerfully as he inspected the old cabin. He checked a few boxes and scribbled a few notes during his short tour of the place.

Although cautioning the ultimate decision wasn't his to make, he indicated the value of the cabin appeared to be more than adequate to obtain the construction loan we wanted.

"You have a lot of work ahead of you but it will be worth it," he said as he shook our hands again before leaving. "I'd love to see it when it is finished."

"Nice guy," I said to Maureen as he headed down the driveway. "You had absolutely nothing to worry about."

"Oh, my God!" she said with a laugh. "You just can't admit it when you're wrong, can you? But you know what? We are going to get that construction loan."

She was right on both counts.

SEVEN

Education of
a Greenhorn

W ITH THE CONSTRUCTION LOAN IN HAND AND THE trailer pulled into place behind the cabin, we were ready to move forward. The old cabin was now down to its skeletal structure in the areas where it had burned. All of the charred wood had been removed; the debris hauled to the dump. The time had come to reverse the process, restoring it to its former glory. Short of that, we wanted to at least make it livable.

We knew the rattletrap plastic and metal house on wheels would be our home during the restoration process which could last up to a year. While the thought was depressing, it was also a helpful motivator, prompting us to spend every spare moment working in the cabin.

As unsightly as it was, I found the burned wooden shell more attractive than our trailer.

"It's sad when what has all the appearances of a trash dump has more appeal than the place where we will be living," I grouched to Maureen shortly after moving into the trailer. "Once we make the cabin inhabitable, this metal abomination is going to hit the road."

"I'm with you there, honey, but you had better get used to living here for a while because we do have a lot of work ahead of us," she said. "This isn't going to happen overnight."

As usual, she was spot on. We began referring to the cabin as the job site, warning visitors that our place was a work in progress. We are still using the same cautionary words, come to think of it.

As one of the general contractors, I was ready to shoulder weighty responsibilities. After all, there were important decisions to be made. Finally, after being a lowly corporal in the Corps, I was now a general. It mattered not one whit that our restoration project was of no consequence to the rest of the world. Our future hinged on it. I could almost feel the weight of the shiny silver stars on my shoulders. Decisions awaited that could decide our very fate. This was not a responsibility to be taken lightly. I was determined not to let anyone down.

When the carpenters arrived for work on day one, Chris pulled me aside. I knew I was about to face my first big decision as a general contractor, one which would clearly establish my ability to be a leader among men and a woman.

"If you don't mind, it would help us a lot to have you sweep up after we leave late in the afternoon," Chris said. "Otherwise we will have to do it. And I doubt that you want to pay us to sweep up the sawdust. You can save yourself a little money. In any case, it will have to be done before we can begin work the next morning."

It wasn't working like a full-fledged carpenter as anticipated but I figured he was just testing me to see if I would be worker friendly.

"That I can do," I said.

"It's important it be done," he continued. "A lot of owners say they are going to do it but they don't follow through. When we get to the job site in the morning and it hasn't been cleaned up, it messes up our schedule. So we need to know we can count on you to do the job."

"Scout's honor," I promised, neglecting to mention my scouting days were limited to a few months as a cub scout in Kerby. My scouting career ended with the scout leader suggesting a new merit badge would have to be created for me, one earned for having the decency to leave the troop which met at her house. I honestly wasn't aiming at her snoozing cat when I let fly one of those silly little airplanes powered by rubber bands we had just made. If memory serves, our scout leader was a little high strung from the get go. But her hissy fit was mild compared to her cat's spitting tantrum.

As the general contractor, I was disappointed the sweeping job was a bit below my station. But I did not want to get into a kerfuffle with the subcontractors. Besides, I was able to tell those who asked that I had to drop by the job site each day after my work at the newspaper to "clean up the mess" the subcontractors left behind. As long as they didn't press for details, it sounded like an impressive supervisory role. Even my jumpy scout leader would have been impressed.

Like you, I was thinking there would be a bit of sawdust on the floor, barely enough to fill a dustpan. Wrong. These guys were like giant termites creating foot-deep piles of sawdust in their wake. With a table saw, sanders, routers and various other implements whining or growling away, they churned out sawdust. You could have driven a four-wheeler over their sawdust dunes.

But I found a handy use for it, spreading the sawdust on the ashes left by the structure that burned to the ground adjacent to the main cabin. During the hot dry days that typify our Mediterranean-like summers, the ashes were stirred up each time you stepped into them. The dust would float in the air until dissipated by a breeze. When it rained, the ash mimicked wet flour dough, creating a glop that clung to your shoes. Mixing the sawdust with the ashes formed a material which did not glom on when wet or rise up on hot days like phantasmagoric wisps following your footsteps into the cabin.

I was immensely proud of my sawdust-ash solution. Naturally, I was quick to share it with Chris and Richard, looking at them the way a first grader looks at a teacher after handing in a homework assignment he was proud of.

"Hey, that's not a bad idea," Chris said as he checked out the sawdust spread on the ashes.

"Works for me," Richard echoed.

The first grader beamed.

Coming from journeymen carpenters, I considered it high praise. Now there are those who assume that most folks living in the southern Oregon mountain valleys are spitting images of the Washington B. Hogwallop character from the classic movie, "O' Brother Where Art Thou." Backwoods hayseeds spawned by generations of unbiblical sex. Chris and Richard must have been academically challenged rubes or they wouldn't be swinging hammers, they would further conclude. Nothing could be further from the truth. Both are college graduates who continually tested this well-traveled journalist's experience and intellect. And I usually came up short.

On my days off from offending newspaper readers, I was ready to tackle whatever duties they asked of me. My main goal was to reduce the construction costs but I also wanted to demonstrate my carpentry skills, albeit rudimentary. Lest you think sweeping sawdust as a drudge was the extent of my general contractor duties, know that I was responsible for other tasks which required a special skill not involving a broom.

One job actually included wielding a hammer, although it would include far more prying than pounding. Richard explained my weighty responsibilities.

"When we do a restoration, we like to recycle all the boards we can," he said. "A lot of these old boards are in very good shape. The problem is they are usually full of nails which have to be removed. Your job, should you elect to do it, is to remove the old nails."

"That I can do," I said again.

There was already a growing pile of used lumber which they had already taken from the cabin. While logs were used to build the outer walls of the cabin, sawed boards were employed for the remainder of the structure. Those that had not burned were in remarkably good shape.

Little did Richard know that he was in the presence of a nail-pulling phenom. As a youngster in Kerby, I learned to pull nails from boards when we needed nails because we had no others. A visit to the hardware store was not in the cards. I had heard wondrous tales of shiny new and perfectly straight nails but never saw a sack of these astonishing creatures until I was an adult. Those shiny straight pieces of metal remain a marvel to this day.

Armed with a hammer and a short crow bar, I attacked the pile of old boards. Some had nails driven into them shortly after round nails replaced the old square ones. The boards were also tighter grained, meaning the wood was denser, making it more difficult to remove a nail than it would be from a board cut from a younger tree with wider grains.

Back when the cabin was built, if a nail was longer than the board, the carpenter simply pounded the protruding end over. That meant the nail remover coming along nearly a century later had to pry the tip of the nail straight, then carefully pound it back from whence it was driven until the head popped up, giving the crowbar or claw hammer something to grab. Sometimes the head would break, forcing me to use a straight nail to drive the old nail out of the wood. The old wood was also full of brittle slivers eager to embed themselves into gloveless fingers. For reasons I've never understood, slivers from old boards smart more than those from newly cut wood. Letting fly a few well-placed cuss words helped reduce the pain.

Many of the boards were sawn back in the days when a two-by-four was full size, not the wannabies of today. But there were also boards of odd sizes, apparently manufactured from a local sawmill somewhere in the Applegate country when lumber wasn't as uniform as now. As a result, the carpenters ran them through the table saw or planer so they would conform to the other boards being used. It all added to my sawdust piles.

Of course, nothing could be ripped or planed until I had removed the old nails. Before long I had a bucket full. I was getting deep into the recycling effort.

"You know, I could straighten these nails out for you," I told the carpenters. "But some of them are a little rusty. They may not hold up too well."

"Uh, that's taking recycling a bit further than we are prepared to go," Chris said. "Where are you from anyway? Kerby."

In retrospect, that may have been extreme recycling, although I have often thought of trying out our growing collection of square nails we have gathered to build something. Some of them would no doubt stand up well to the hammer. Others would perform like poor boxers, collapsing from the first hard blow.

When it came to recycling wood, Chris and Richard were passionate. They used boards salvaged from a late 1800s era house they renovated in Jacksonville to form what I learned were the balusters in the stairway railing to the loft where I now write. As I climb the stairs every morning, I can't help but wonder about the lives of the people who had cut the lumber back in the 1800s, and those whose home the lumber once helped support. It reminds me that we are all here but a short period. Sadly, we bipeds are not recyclable as a general rule. The exception would be members of a cannibalistic society. But theirs is a finite group whose members are probably always nervous about who is on the menu.

I learned all I know about stairs from a fellow named Paul—not me—who Chris and Richard called in to build the stairway. Like them, the fellow Applegater was congenial and very talented. He hailed from Gettysburg, Pa. where he roamed the famous Civil War battlefield as a youngster. Coincidentally, he would fight as a U.S. Army infantryman in a real war between the north and the south, albeit a century after our civil war in a distant country called Vietnam. In their homeland, the Vietnamese rightfully refer to it as the American War.

Having left his battlefields behind, he is now an expert at many phases of home restoration, including the complicated task of building a stairwell. It was fascinating to watch him install what I called the vertical sticks in the handrail system on the stairs.

"Some people call them spindles or uprights," he explained as he worked. "Collectively, they form what is called the balustrade that helps support the handrail and the parapet."

I nodded, although I barely got the gist of his explanation. When someone tosses out a word like "balustrade," it tends to gum up the works in my cranium. But he obviously knew what he was talking about. The fact I didn't quite get it was immaterial.

"I want you to know I really appreciate these stairs," I told him. "Before, they had a hand-made ladder nailed to the wall. I climbed it once. Scared the hell out of me. Took me an hour to muster up the courage to climb down."

"I hope these stairs won't be too steep for you," said the stair master.

"The landing had to be in the center of the cabin. The total rise is eight feet, matching the total run. That's not beyond the norm."

"Sounds good to me," I said, again hoping my total bafflement wasn't too obvious. My mind had been reeling ever since he hit me with the "B" word.

Although the journeymen carpenters claimed to be red-blooded Americans, their parlance was suspect. They tended to speak in code while on the job. They probably even had a secret handshake when gathering to meet in some clandestine location to plot against this great republic of ours.

Of course, they wouldn't speak their secret language all the time. Probably because I was still a working journalist and keeping notes, they seemed to reserve cryptic conversations for those moments when I was around. It was as if I had parachuted into Provence out of the blue to communicate with the locals with my college French. Only out of the extreme kindness did my foreign language professor give me passing grades. His fear that I would simply take the classes again probably tilted a passing grade in my favor. What I did learn from those classes is that I should stick to mangling the King's English. At the risk of sounding like a braggart, I like to think I mangle it rather well.

Despite having little success with foreign language, I was able to average out some of the carpenters' cryptic words, particularly those which were self defining.

For instance, I knew what Richard was referring to when he announced he would need his "MacGyver" to take care of a trifling problem he encountered. He simply needed his combination knife-pliers-screwdriver to right the carpentry wrong. Back when I watched TV, there was a show by that name about a fellow who could use a tool like that to dismantle an atom bomb or build a rocket ship. Of course, he did cheat a little by using duct tape.

Other words I understood were those which were self defining. I could understand why they referred to the cabin as a "stick" house since it was constructed of wood. Obviously, a load-bearing wall is one which supports weight while non load-bearing walls, sometimes called curtain walls, do not. The difference between rough carpentry and finish carpentry was also self evident. I could even understand "on center," a term referring to measuring from one structural member to another.

Of course, I was already on fairly sound footing when they talked about the floor, walls, rafters and roof. These were things that many of us had or at least heard about in our childhood homes back in Kerby. But things got a little baffling beyond those solid boundaries. Their carpentry speak may as just as well been Greek.

Oddly enough, Maureen, despite having never been to the Mediterranean, had no problems understanding them. She became quite fluent in the use of their idioms.

But if I am ever called to testify before the congressional committee that investigates un-American activities, I will be able to say with some confidence that she never learned the secret handshake. But I'm afraid I won't be able to state it categorically. Congressional witness always state things categorically, you understand. Then again, they do speak a secret code in congress.

"We need to check the hypotenuse of that rafter," Maureen declared one evening when we were surveying the renovation progress after our day jobs were done.

"Well, it's certainly a lot skinnier than the big fat one we saw at the San Francisco zoo," I offered. "That was one big hippo."

"Very funny, goofus," she said. "We need to know the length of the rafter to see if the fascia board is long enough to go over the cornice."

Et tu, Brutus, I thought to myself as I ran the cryptic words through the planer in my brain. So I soldiered on with the real general contractor leading the verbal way.

"That one will obviously take a header," she observed as she studied the roughed out doorway into the guest bedroom .

This time I knew precisely what she was talking about, although for the life of me I couldn't figure out why it was necessary. Thanks to my gimpy right leg, I was a past master at tripping and taking headers. Frankly, despite my expertise at falling down, I never particularly enjoyed the process.

"Are you sure?" I asked. "It seems to me we can avoid all that."

"You always need a support beam above the door in order to help reenforce the structural components above the doorway," she said. "Why? What are you talking about now?"

"Sorry, I seemed to be developing a hearing problem—all those power tools and sawdust," I mumbled, sticking a finger into my ear in what I hoped would look like an attempt to clean it out. "I thought you said 'chedder.'"

I quickly moved on, leaving her to wonder if the other general contractor on the jobsite had suddenly started drinking on the job.

Later, after a consulting a book on basic carpentry I bought, I discovered she was referring to the stout board that goes above the doorway. In time I did learn to speak a little of the coded language, although it was just enough to get me into trouble.

I was excited when I found an interesting little number called the "head jamb yoke," a creature which apparently inhabits the top of a door or window frame. As far as I know, I've never actually seen one. But the mere knowledge that one lurks above a door or window gives one pause. It sounds positively medieval.

I couldn't wait to toss it out in a casual conversation back at the cabin. But I didn't want to bash Chris or Richard over the head with it. I decided to try it out on a stranger first. As it happened, one of the county building inspectors dropped shortly after I acquired the carpentry bible. The inspectors dropped in periodically to make sure everything was being built according to Hoyle, the guy who wrote the rules for five-card stud as well as the county building codes when it came to all things studly.

Unfortunately, I couldn't remember the exact nomenclature for the complicated thing above the window frame the inspector was checking out. But here was a chance to take my new language for a test drive. So I winged it.

"I wanted to tell you about the head damn joke," I told him. "But it's too bad it isn't double hung. Of course, you would need a bigger set of dadoes for that."

The building inspector had that same look of bewildering fear my French professor had after I attempted to speak his beloved François.

"I'm sure it is very funny," he said curtly. "But we like to keep this on a professional level."

Professional? Ha! The poor fellow clearly hadn't read my ace carpentry book. He didn't stick around long after that little tête-à-tête. He knew when he was bested. Once you start speaking the language, you feel like a real stud. And I'm not talking about an upright beam in the building framework here.

When I wasn't sweeping sawdust, pulling old nails or baffling county inspectors, I rambled around visiting other workers to check on their progress. One day Chris was walking on a six-inch wide plank on the rafters high above the very hard concrete floor. He was hammering knotty pine boards onto the vaulted ceiling.

"Geez, Chris, that makes me a little nervous," I told him.

"Makes you nervous?" he replied without glancing at me. "How do you think it makes me feel?"

His feet proved as sure footed as his wit. I sauntered on until I encountered Maureen. She was doing a bit of architectural work, drawing a few sketches of how the cabin would look when the renovation was completed. Naturally, I offered my assistance.

"Remember, form follows function," I told her.

"Shush," she replied without looking up. "Don't bug me."

So I strolled over to assist Richard and Paul. I noticed they had lately taken to firing up very loud power tools when I approached. Poor timing on my part, I suppose. But the time Richard grabbed an electric saw and revved it to a high whine, holding it aloft while staring at me was troubling. He then turned it off and went back to nailing when I retreated. He obviously had started to use the power saw, then forgot what he needed it for. Forgetfulness like that can be a dangerous thing.

But I wasn't able to meander for long. Chris quickly came up with another chore to keep me busy. This time it was working on the old pecky cedar boards that incased the outer wall of the cabin. These were the cheapest cedar boards you could buy, the kind with holes large enough for a mouse to enter with a U-Haul and set up shop. Some were knot holes; others were gnawed or created from wood rot.

"One thing you can do to really help us is plug those holes," Chris told me. "We use pieces of metal roofing that is left over. You cut them to fit with tin snips. It will take you a while. Just make sure you turn the painted side out."

Professional that he was, Chris masked his disappointment that much of my time would now be taken up cutting little pieces of tin and painstakingly placing them over the holes. But I assured him I would finish it post haste and would soon be back discussing carpentry matters with him. "No hurry," he quickly countered, adding, "No hurry at all."

Not to boast but I turned out to be a hole-plugging fool when it came to the outer walls, finishing the job in one weekend.

"The holes, they have all been plugged," I told Chris the following Monday afternoon.

"That's too bad," he said, obviously saddened by the fact he had no more tasks to challenge me with at the moment.

However, just as I started taking about head jambs, he remembered one chore left to do.

"You know, there are some bullet holes in the roof," he said. "Someone needs to plug them with sealant. You want a crack at them?"

"That is a little out of my league," I replied. "I'm not afraid of heights. It's just that I find smacking on the ground after falling from the roof a little unsettling."

With that, I was the one retreating in case he pursued the matter. The bullet holes were apparently made by local urchins armed with firearms when the place was vacant. For whatever reason, most of the holes were high on the roof near the ridgeline. Yet one enterprising youngster had targeted the old chimney over the master bedroom. Judging from the angle, he was firing from a tree house which used to be in a broadleaf maple tree on adjacent neighboring property. The tree house is now gone so he would have to find another rest for his rifle barrel. Still, it is not all that difficult to sneak up on a chimney. Judging from the shell casings of a civilian AK-47 we found and what appeared to be four associated holes in a wood closet door, it was apparent one lad had ventured into the main bedroom to let fly a few rounds during the period the cabin was not lived in.

That gave me pause. I grew up with firearms, and hunted throughout my adolescence well into adulthood. I even killed an eight-point buck—eight one side, nine on the other—with a .303 British rifle in October of 1968. But, as wild as we were, we always knew there was a solemn responsibility when carrying a firearm. Regrettably, that respect for lethal weapons appears to have fallen by the wayside. After seeing the bullet holes, a friend who is an avid hunter observed that, while we have a right to keep and bear arms, we don't have a right to be armed morons. He may be on to something.

But I didn't need to worry about the bullet holes in the roof. Richard, who apparently has no fear of heights, climbed up onto the roof and plugged them. He simply tied a stout rope to the deck railing, threw the other end over the ridge of the roof, and used it to walk about the roof, plugging away. I cringed at the sight.

It was on the ground that Richard encountered his biggest danger. It happened while he was working outside near the old pump house, sorting through a pile of boards for one that would fit his needs. Rajah, a crusty old largely blind chow we had inherited from a daughter, promptly trotted up behind Richard and bit him on the calf. Richard shook him off, then resumed looking for the board he needed until he found it.

"Your dog just nailed me," the carpenter calmly announced when he returned to the cabin. He pulled up his pant leg to reveal indentions from two rows of teeth. There were a few drops of blood. Fortunately for us, the nefarious creature had his rabies shot and the biped was not the litigious type. But Richard did keep an eye out for the chow from that day forth. He was willing to work hard but he figured giving up a pound of flesh was taking one for the carpentry team a little too far. In defense of Rajah, he never bit Richard again. The dog preferred chicken.

As mentioned earlier, I am very much a chicken when it came to leaving the bounds of earth. Unfortunately, my other major chore would take me skyward. Richard had ordered a can of barn red paint to touch up several of the metal sections of the roof whose original color had been tinged by the fire. The carpenters had already replaced the rafters and plywood underneath. The paint, very similar to that used on cars, would be used to touch up the metal roofing sheets that had been scorched but were still serviceable. It was taking recycling to a loftier level.

"All you need to do is sand down the burned area a little, then paint over it," Richard said. "Most of it is just a little touch up work. It's pretty straight forward. You won't need to get off the ladder because it is all on the edge of the roof."

Apart from the ladder work, it did seem simple enough. After having turned chicken over plugging the bullet holes, I was determined to take on this mission.

"When I'm done with this roof, you won't be able to see any burn spots," I vowed. "With a paint brush in my hand, I'm a regular Vincent van Gogh."

Maureen, who had overheard the conversation, couldn't help herself. She was a little concerned about the height of the canvas I would be working on.

"Don't cut off your ear just yet, Mr. Post Impressionist," she said. "Remember, this will mean you will have to climb ladders. And you and ladders aren't the best of friends."

She had a valid point. After losing the full dexterity on my right side, great heights to me meant anything higher than a foot stool. I'm not really afraid of climbing but I can get mighty squeamish when facing a ladder. My right leg isn't very flexible and my right hand lacks the dexterity to easily grasp things such as ladder rungs. Nor do I bounce well. Think the Tin Man in the *Wizard of Oz* before oil was applied to his joints. Add the lack of balance or ability to grasp much on his right side, and the tin man is going to crash even after he is well oiled. In Ladder Climbing 101, placing one foot solidly on a rung while grabbing a rung directly in front of your chest with one hand while the other appendages are stepping or reaching for the next rung is apparently elementary. I never took the class, preferring instead to keep my feet squarely on terra firma.

The long extension ladder we acquired a few years before had never gotten much use from me. Yet I was tired of being mocked by a ladder. I decided it was high time to overcome my lowly fear.

There were three places on the roof that needed a little paint. All of them were on the edge of the metal sheets where flames had flickered. Two spots were easily accessible on the bottom of the main roof; one was on the south side of the spare bedroom, the other on the north side of the kitchen. That meant I only had to climb up to a point where I could peek over the edge of the roof, sand a little and dab on the paint. My feet would barely be six feet off the ground. They wouldn't be too nervous.

The other area needing paint was the crest of the gable roof on the west end of the master bedroom. At about eighteen feet above the ground, it was the most challenging for someone concerned about heights. I would need our tallest extension ladder to reach it. That spot would be saved for last.

After making sure the ladder's metal feet were firmly planted, I took a deep breath and began my ascent outside the guest bedroom. I figured it was prudent to start with the least scary and try to build up my confidence. I moved slowly, deliberately. It wasn't exactly pleasant but it wasn't as hair raising as I anticipated. The old feeling of terror subsided to an acceptable high anxiety.

It is an exhilarating thing, conquering your fears, or at least refusing to back down in the face of them. I was getting the job done. Better yet, I had not crashed to the ground and snapped a femur.

After sanding and painting, I even took a moment to enjoy the view. It was a bright sunny day with a nice breeze. I descended the ladder, and moved it to the north side of the kitchen. When I climbed this time, it was with confidence. There was no hesitation, no need to take a deep breath. I resolutely scaled the ladder, a fearless man scoffing at mere death. In a few minutes, I had sanded and painted the area which had been scorched by the heat. It was all going without a hitch.

But the old trepidation returned when I moved the ladder to the gable and looked up. To reach the peak, I would have to extend the ladder and stand at the top with my chest level with the gable ridge. But my courage hadn't completely retreated. I took a deep breath and began climbing. I took another deep breath and poked my head above the ridge. Butterflies fluttered in my stomach. That's when I noticed another scorched spot about four feet down the steep roof to my right. I figured I had better start there and work my way—and my courage—back up to the peak.

But I didn't want to have to climb all the way back to the ground, shorten the ladder and move it over so it was nestled against the roof line. After studying it for a moment, I decided I could drop down a few rungs, then simply reach over and do the job. No fuss, no muss.

In my mind, the plan worked flawlessly. I would lean over a little, sand the area, then apply a few brush strokes. No worries.

But there was a little glitch when it came to putting the theory into practice. When a ladder is square up against a gable, it tends to stay in place. But when you start sliding the top of the ladder down a very steep roof, the law of gravity takes over. The ladder also seemed to have a mind of its own. It apparently figured if it could slide down a bit, I would have an easier time painting the spot. The problem was that it slid more than a bit. It shot past the burned spot and was heading pell-mell for the ground. I applied the brakes by grabbing the board on the edge of the roof. Yes, it very well may have been a fascia board but I really didn't give a damn what it was called at that point.

Normally, when you are high on a ladder, you prefer to have the thing perpendicular to the ground far below. The ladder and I had left the perpendicular. We were now at a very awkward angle to the ground. I was clinging to the roof with my left hand while the fingers in my right hand had a death grip on the rung. The paint can and brush were sprawled on the ground.

The last thing I wanted to do was call out to Chris or Richard for help. They already correctly suspected I was somewhat of a bumbler when it came to all things related to carpentry. Finding me whimpering at the top of the ladder would have finished me off for good. Besides, I didn't want to see them hurt. Laughing uncontrollably can be hazardous to your health. They could have broken a few ribs, gasping for breath like that.

The voice of a whining little boy in the far recesses of my brain started yelling "Mommy!" But I managed to shut him up, the horrible brat. What I needed right then was the other general contractor to walk around the corner of the house, stroll over to the ladder and hold it up while I scurried down. "I can't leave you alone for a moment," she would say with her angelic smile.

But Maureen wasn't there to bail me out. She was in town, working at her shop. I would have to figure out another way to avoid being hoisted on my own petard. Webster tells us that a petard is actually an explosive device but I side with those who would argue that suffering multiple broken bones from a fall is akin to being blown up.

Oddly enough, I became very calm. But I knew I couldn't hold on to the roof indefinitely with my left hand. I also knew without looking down that the left foot of the tilted ladder was now a few inches off the ground. I needed to inch my way back up the roof to the gable's peak.

I tried pulling the ladder up with my left arm. It didn't budge. The ladder was pressing against the edge of the roof, creating too much friction to be moved. I would have to push the ladder away from the roof while pulling up with my left arm. The problem with that little plan, of course, is that you don't want to go sailing over backwards.

I took a deep breath and pushed away from the roof a few inches with my right hand while pulling hard with my left. The ladder hopped a few inches toward the gable peak. Ever so slowly, I began inching my way upward, using the push-away, pull-upwards method of ladder hopping. I didn't rest until the ladder was once again plumb with the terra firma. On shaky legs, I returned to earth.

The very top of the gable on the west end of the master bedroom remains as it was on that day. Unpainted. It mocks me when I walk past it so I avoid the area. But there are days when I look up and think about painting it. But I suddenly remember something far more pressing to do. One day I will get the tall ladder out, take a deep breath and climb up there to finish the job. Scout's honor.

Despite my shortcomings as a carpenter, I preferred to think I was making a contribution. More importantly, the old cabin, like a chrysalis stirring, was coming out of a long dormancy.

EIGHT

Snakes, Spiders and Other Charmers

A PIERCING SCREAM OF SHEER HORROR SHATTERED THE stillness of the Gilson Gulch night. Bears glanced fearfully over their shoulders while running away over a distant ridge. Nervous cougars leapt for the nearest big tree, climbing until they felt safe from the hideous threat below. In Jacksonville, parents locked their doors and held their children tight. Closer to the little valley, several residents rifled a cartridge into the chamber. At least one uncorked a bottle of stout liquor for a swig of courage. Others grabbed the crucifix and held tight. Some wept.

It was the summer of 2002. Something dreadful menaced in the night that was dark as a tomb.

To put it all in perspective we need to go back to the previous morning when everything was calm and bright in the rising summer sun. Maureen and I were leisurely cleaning up debris around the cabin. It was a lazy Sunday and a carpentry free day. I was pottering about with a rake; she had a shovel. By late morning, we took a break in lawn chairs under a big fir tree. It was one of those rare moments of peaceful beauty which makes one wish you could stop time. Life was pure bliss.

One of our cats, Tommy, was sitting near the old tack shed, studying something in a periwinkle patch planted decades before we arrived. A mellow fellow, the elderly orange and white tabby was often sober and reflective for long periods. Or perhaps he was having one of his despondent moments. Whatever the case, he would sit for long periods until he hashed it out in his mind.

"Tommy's pondering," I told Maureen. "He's likely wondering why we moved to this wild place and disrupted his once peaceful life. It makes him melancholy."

"He probably just heard a mouse nibbling in the periwinkle," she replied. "Besides, he loves it here. He's a very contented cat."

Suddenly he started poking with his right paw like a boxer jabbing at an opponent, looking for an opening to land a solid punch with a left jab. He jerked back a little, apparently to avoid a blow that his unseen opponent had thrown at him. Just when I started to fear that he had inexplicably turned into a shadow-boxing feline mime, we heard a telltale buzz. The sound chilled my blood.

In my Walter Mitty moments, I like to think I'm the sort of man who laughs in the face of danger. My only reaction to peril would be slight muscle twitch in a granite jaw underneath an unflinching steely squint. But what I like to think sometimes doesn't square with reality. My imagined bravery flees when faced with ladders or adders.

"Mother of God!" I yelled. "It's a rattler and he is going to kill Tommy."

Sure enough, there was a rather large rattlesnake coiled up in the deep grass in front of the cat. The snake flicked his tongue; the cat hissed back. The two combatants were about three feet apart. But the snake was roughly three feet long, and serpents are capable of striking within the length of their bodies. You can do the math.

Incidentally, I referred to the scaly creature as a male because I have never sexed a rattlesnake nor do I ever intend to. That is taking the political correctness continuum to a place where I refuse to tread.

Maureen, who respects rattlesnakes but isn't bothered by them all that much, moved in quickly to use her shovel to gently coax Tommy away from his serpentine boxing buddy. She calmly picked up the still hissing cat and carried him to the trailer for a timeout. Fighting an urge to flee, I tried to use the long handle of the rake to keep the rattlesnake from disappearing into the periwinkle. From a distance, it would have appeared that I was fencing at the patch with a rake, one-handedly parrying and thrusting.

The plant may be an attractive ground cover with its lavender blossoms and green leaves but it also a wonderful place for a buzzworm to hide if it turns off its buzzer. I didn't want it to become a green snake pit.

The snake, whose girth was only slightly smaller than that of a fire hose, was not impressed with the rake. He slithered passed it into the section of the periwinkle where I was now standing. I was suddenly wailing a la the Soggy Bottom Boys and jigging backwards like a member of Riverdance. I figured the jig was up.

"It's only a rattlesnake, for crying out loud," Maureen said when she returned. "And quit flailing around with that rake before you hurt someone. You need to start looking at rattlesnakes as our friends who help keep the place clear of vermin."

I can never, ever look at a rattlesnake as a friend. They give me the heebie-jeebies. A psychiatrist specializing in phobias would say I have textbook ophidiophobia. But I prefer not to describe it as fear of snakes as much as merely a healthy regard for their toothy snouts. Besides I am not afraid of all snakes. It's just those who inject you with poison that make me cringe. I accept they are part of the natural cycle, and that they feed largely on mice. But even the knowledge the snake probably wouldn't lower itself to nail a journalistic rodent, recovering or otherwise, gives me no peace of mind.

We were able to pinpoint the rattler's location in the ground cover by its continued buzzing. Using a large garbage can which I laid down with its open top facing the snake, we used rake and shovel to guide it into what it must have thought was a dark cave. I carefully turned the can upright and sealed it with the lid.

Our plan was to take it into the mountains to release in a remote site on public land. I already had plenty of snake blood stains on my hands. As a youth roaming the Illinois River during those long summer days in Kerby,

I had routinely slain rattlesnakes. But as I have grown longer of tooth, I have come to appreciate life. I figure there is room for rattlesnakes, providing they don't rattle around near—or in—our cabin.

I gingerly picked up the buzzing garbage can, making sure I held it away from me. If the container's manufacturers were a little skimpy with the plastic, I figured two long fangs could easily puncture the can. I placed the can upright in the back of the pickup truck.

There were still a little nervous jitters but the worst was over. After all, it was still a beautiful summer day and I was determined to enjoy it, even if it meant taking a ride with a buzzing rattlesnake. I'm not sure what is the preferred attire for buzzworm wranglers but I was wearing a t-shirt, shorts and tennis shoes. As I was roping in the garbage can to keep it in place, something slithered over the bare calf of my right leg. The Foggy Bottom Boy shrieked and began high stepping again. I knew instantly that the rattler had slipped out of the can and was searching for a soft spot in my calf to sink in his fangs. I could almost see my life flashing before my eyes.

And what was my beloved spouse doing while I was about to be snake bit? She was laughing so hard she had to hold onto the pickup to keep from falling down.

"It's the rope," she gasped after her peals of laughter finally subsided. "The end of it grazed your bare leg when you were pulling the rope up to tie it. Oh, my gosh, that was funny."

I like to laugh as well as the next man but I find nothing humorous about death-dealing snakes. Nor was the rattlesnake laughing, judging from his continued angry buzzing.

After Maureen finally sobered from her laughing spell which continued with intermittent giggling fits for a half hour, we took the snake to a forested site several miles from our cabin. I admonished the serpent to stay away when I poured him, still buzzing, out of the can. He stuck his forked tongue out at me and slithered off.

"Well, I'm glad that's over," I told Maureen as we headed back home. "I'm sure we've seen our last Sterling Creek rattlesnake for a while. The word is out they don't want to mess with us."

"But you have to admit it was entertaining," she said, and then collapsed into another round of helpless laughter. I may have chuckled a little at that point but I want you to know it was only out of relief the snake episode had slithered away.

Or so I thought.

We both worked fairly late at our day jobs the next day. After a quick dinner that night, I grabbed our flashlight. For a second, I thought about changing its weak batteries. But I figured it would be fine for us to take the dogs for a short walk and then round up the cats. That's when Tommy began following something crossing the driveway. Maureen focused the dim flashlight on the cat who was swatting at something wriggling across the driveway towards the cabin.

You guessed it: another rattler. Admittedly, it was a barely half the size of the monster that had wormed its way into our lives the previous morning. Yet it still had fangs and venom. And it was also underfoot and cabin bound.

This occurred when our only electrical lighting was a couple of low watt bulbs inside the trailer. Outside it was inky dark. My hair stood like bristles on the back of my neck as I grabbed the rake and what was now known as our rattlesnake can. This guy was fast. He kept trying to snake around the can to get at me. Maureen's job was to keep him in the dim spotlight.

It was just at the point where he was about to slip past the rake that she turned the flashlight away for a moment. I was in utter darkness. Not only could I not see my hands in front of my face but I couldn't see the rattlesnake that was just beyond my naked fingers.

The fright one feels when a fast-moving buzzworm is heading straight toward you in the dark is very difficult to describe. It overwhelms all other senses. As far as I know, those who regularly catch rattlesnakes don't much like nabbing them in the dark. When their bosses insist them work at night, I am fairly confident they don't use the Braille system of snake catching.

Maureen later claimed with a fairly straight face that she heard a noise behind her, causing her to turn the flashlight away from the snake. I wouldn't know about that. I was too busy backpedaling.

I stepped back onto what felt like the cold rubbery back of a you-know-what about to whip around and sink its fangs into my leg. Remember the bone-chilling scream that opened this chapter? This is the precise moment it was heard, a cry of terror filling our little valley. It was an involuntary scream, one I don't remember emitting.

When Maureen switched the light back to the business at hand, she beheld her screaming husband beating a garden hose to death with a rake. Her maniacal laughter that followed the scream sent coyotes hightailing up nearby mountainsides. The chortles continued for several very long minutes. Frankly, I found her hysterical mirth every bit as frightening as the scream but I'm probably a little biased.

The snake? The nervous wreck darted into the garbage can, seeking shelter from the shrieking man with the rake and the howling mad woman.

Early the next morning before heading to our day jobs, we took the snake up into the mountains. He quickly slithered off, no doubt relieved to get away from the very strange bipeds. Poor fellow probably developed a nervous tick and suffered nightmares, waking up in a cold sweat. Unfortunately, there isn't much counseling available for reptilians suffering post traumatic stress disorder.

Maureen likes to tell people about the night her husband beat a garden hose to death with a rake. But she can never finish the story before being overcome by a bout of uncontrollable laughter that continues intermittently, nearly stopping, then resuming full throttle. It reminded me of a car I once had whose engine would continue running in fits and starts after you turned off the ignition. I think it was bad gas in both instances.

Rattlesnakes have toyed with us periodically since we moved into the cabin. Perhaps it annoyed them that someone was renovating it and they would no longer have the run of the place. Or maybe they came out of curiosity, having heard about the weird humanoids from a jumpy snake with a nervous tick.

Our buzzworms haven't been content to threaten us underfoot. Take the summer day we were out minding our own business, cutting brush to reduce the threat of wildfires. We took a water and snack break, and sat down on the side of the hill overlooking the valley. There is always wildlife to watch and the day was no exception.

"Look at that hawk," Maureen said as a large bird of prey flapped its way toward us. "It's carrying something. Is that a stick? Maybe they are building a nest."

"It's kind of a fat stick for a nest," I said as I took a swig of water. "Maybe they are building a tree fort."

The stick started wriggling. It was a serpent, and a very stout one at that. The only indigenous fat snake in the state of Jefferson has rattles at the rear end to warn of venom-dripping fangs at the business end.

"Holy moly, it's a rattlesnake," I said as I craned my neck to watch the flying reptile. "And he is flying directly over us. Good God! What if he drops him on us?"

I wasn't exactly foaming at the mouth but there may have been a little spittle. It was bad enough the fanged worms were underfoot. Now we had to keep an eye out for them falling from the sky to drape around our necks like biting scarves. It still gives me the shuddering willies just thinking about it. For a fleeting moment, I feared the birds of prey were in cahoots with the venomous vermin, giving them an airlift to our place.

But the hawk's flight path was away from the cabin. What's more, the big bird didn't seem happy about the state of affairs. From the way the feathered pilot appeared to be struggling with the controls, the fat viper was causing quite a disturbance. Flying with a wiggling, biting passenger must be very challenging. The fact the talons had clasp it closer to the middle than the head would no doubt be a concern for the pilot. If the snake whipped its head around, the fangs could reach a drumstick. It was likely going to end with what helicopter pilots euphemistically refer to as a hard landing.

We never saw what happened with the hawk and the snake. Presumably, the hawk had dealt with similar troublesome passengers in the past. It probably had the snake over for dinner. We haven't seen an airborne rattlesnake since then, although one sighting more than satisfied my curiosity. The day it starts raining rattlesnakes is the day I buy a double-barreled shotgun.

Understand that I'm totally comfortable with most wild things. I've encountered bear and cougar in their natural habitats without much concern. I find them fascinating creatures that are interesting to watch, albeit neither ever hung around for long. They may be dumb animals but they are smart enough to know running into a humanoid is invariably bad news for them.

It's expected that an old cabin and its environs provide an excellent habitat for creatures you don't want snuggling up against you on a cold winter night. That's particularly true when you are happily reading in bed or starting to nod off. There is just something hideous about an unidentifiable creature creeping across a fluttering eyelid or slithering over a bare foot that causes one to sit bolt upright. Good books and bad words tend to fly at that point.

That's not to say they aren't interesting, even beautiful in a beasty way. We did find a western skink in the cabin that we both saw as attractive with its sky blue tail and silken skin. The Oregon fence lizards, who run vertically on the outside cabin walls all summer long, are also handsome fellows with their telltale cerulean blue bellies. On the other hand, alligator lizards are definitely not huggable, even though they are largely harmless. It's just that we don't want to wake up to see a lizard on our pillows, giving us the evil eye. Interesting as they are, we want our bedroom to be a lizard free zone. We're persnickety that way. The cold-blooded fellows sliding up against you at night would feel too much like a viper.

On the other hand, furry creatures are generally warm and fuzzy, although I've never considered rats and mice huggable. Granted, the kangaroo mice found around the place are cute little fellows. But we don't want them hopping about the cabin or perching on the end of our noses when we are asleep. Pet rats, too, could be construed as endearing by some folks who revel in rodentia. But I draw the line at Norwegian rats known to inhabit our region. Nothing wrong with Norway, mind you, it's just that the rodents whose ancestors hung with Vikings are a bit too toothy for our tastes. Like the seafaring pirates of old, they are also probably a little hygiene challenged. Calling someone a dirty rat is redundant in my book.

But there are a score of other crawly creatures that skitter out of their hiding places under cover of darkness en route to our bed that are far worse in our minds. Chief among that creeping, crawling mass are salamanders, scorpions and ticks. They are all bad actors who are not fit company.

Now, you may want to include mosquitoes in the list of unacceptable guests but you can swat a mosquito. Ever try to swat a rattlesnake? A rabid bat? I've never tried it but it seems like it would be a risky endeavor. You can swat a tick but he won't notice. He is too busy burrowing into your skin to suck your blood.

About now, you are thinking that ticks, even with those carrying Lyme disease, are not much of a concern since they are rarely encountered. I used to be guided by the same fallacy.

While writing for the *Mail Tribune*, I met a fellow named Jim who was a retired tick expert from California. He had settled in the Applegate Valley where he began raising wine grapes and studying the lifestyles of ticks north of the California state line. When I asked if I and a photographer could tag along when he went on a tick safari, he readily agreed. While I find the little suckers creepy, I admit they are interesting in a loathsome kind of way.

As it happens, we had just purchased the Sterling Creek property but had yet to move onto it. The place seemed as good as any for hunting ticks. Jim agreed to meet us there.

"This will do very nicely," he said as he surveyed the place. "You've got oak trees with moss, you have brush and tall grass. This place will be thick with ticks."

It wasn't exactly what I wanted to hear about a piece of property we had just bought. Jim brought along a white cloth flag which you would assume he would use to surrender when we encountered an army of ticks. Instead, he employed it to gather ticks. He waved it through grass and brush, and passed it over the moss. Nearly each time he would find a tick clinging to it.

"This is a deer tick," he said of one tiny spot which was crawling up the flag. "It's also known as a black-legged tick. They can carry Lyme disease."

He said it as though he was a proud parent introducing a child who was a prize pupil. He gently shook the tick off into the grass where it would bide its time until I happened along one day.

"After a tick latches on, it takes a while for the disease to be transmitted," he said. "Symptoms of Lyme disease include swollen lymph nodes, joint pain and a flu-like malaise."

He introduced us to several other members of the tick family and taught us how to differentiate between a male and female. Size matters when it comes to gender in the family tick, by the by. Females are larger. Wife ticks probably don't take any guff from the hubby.

After a few hours of studying ticks, I could feel my nodes swelling, my joints inflamed and a general malaise settling in. But I didn't develop a facial tick, er, tic.

Then there are Sterling Creek's flying blood suckers. Bats flew into our lives the moment we bought the cabin. In fact, they happily inhabited the old place when we arrived. Generations of bat families had probably been born there. They probably get together for family reunions and watch vampire movies.

I don't know about you but I'm not too keen on having airborne rats in the form of bats fluttering about the house when I'm reading or trying to catch a few winks. They aren't as worrisome as flying rattlesnakes but they, like journalists, have been known to become rabid. Better to let them flit outside after bugs.

While cleaning up the cabin, a few bats did a fly by over our heads, apparently to let us know they were on duty. We usually shooed them out of the cabin with a broom or whatever else was handy.

When we are removing the burned debris in the loft above the kitchen, we encountered our first roosting bat. The little brown fellow was under a partially burned board hanging from the vaulted ceiling.

Maureen, who was wearing thick gloves, gently picked him up.

"Do you think he is OK?" she asked. "I bet he is hibernating. He just needs to sleep a little more."

"He's probably sleeping off a long night of imbibing too much blood," I said. "But we are not going to start making pets out of little vampires. That is not going to happen."

Maureen gave me that serious look, the one she gets when I verbally step over the line to make a declaration without going through our spousal democracy. When her eyes become steely like that, I usually retreat to the Good Book. I've read it, but didn't come away as enthralled as Maureen when she finished poring over chapter and verse.

"If memory serves, I believe the apostle Paul instructed us that women should not usurp power over men but to sit quietly in silence," I said. "I don't believe I need say more on the matter, woman."

"But there is more to be said on the matter, little mister," she retorted. "If you had continued reading, you would have discovered that his significant other, a very small woman by the way, soundly boxed his ears and made him sit in the corner until he could say something sensible. I find reading that passage very empowering."

She finished her little sermon with an angelic smile. It's a sad day when you can't take quotes out of context from the Bible without someone playing one upswomanship. Little wonder our world is constantly plagued by religious wars.

Maureen took the little bat with its tiny fox-like ears and tucked him into a corner where she had made a little bed out of some old insulation. "Leave him alone," she instructed me.

Later that afternoon the little vampire began to stir, first with a toothy little yawn. He watched us for a while, quite possibly wondering if he was having a bad dream. He then stretched his wings and took flight, disappearing out the window opening.

The next bat close encounter of the third kind occurred when daughter Sheena was home from college and giving us a hand. She was working in the cabin when she came running over the trailer.

"We're parents," she announced. "More like I'm the parent and you are the grandparents. You've got to see this."

Our first thought was a worst-case scenario involving some wild college party. After all, she was living in Eugene at the time. But the responsible young lady quickly disabused us of that silly notion by announcing that a bat couple with a youngster had taken up residence in the cabin's master bedroom.

"The little guy is so adorable," she said. "I bet we could make a pet out of him."

I didn't repeat my unbiblical quote, knowing it could very well lead to two women taking turns boxing my ears. However, before Maureen could warm up to the idea, I convinced them that keeping a bat pup was a bad idea. A wildlife biologist had once informed me that little bats are called pups. This was after I kept referring to them as infantile vampires.

"They are wild creatures who need to be out enjoying the great outdoors," I told Sheena. "They don't do well in captivity, makes them want to go around biting necks. Besides, they eat a lot of mosquitoes. We need every bat soldier we can get on the front line of the war against those tiny little bloodsuckers."

We went over to visit our future bedroom which had turned into a bat maternity ward. The three were all hanging in a row from a beam—papa Dracula, mama Dracula and baby Dracula. The little guy was likely born a week or two earlier in the bedroom since they are flying about on their own within a month. We left them alone and they were all gone via a window opening within a few days.

A couple of weeks later the builders installed all the windows, closing off the cabin from flying visitors. For a time after we moved in, Maureen, whose hearing is far better than mine, informed me that she could hear a slight ticking sound against the window panes at night. She insists it was bats trying to return home. But it may have just been bats in her belfry. Either that or she got a kick out of seeing me hiding under the covers at night.

Funny thing, Maureen is not overly concerned about a couple of rattlesnakes slithering about the old homestead or bats going bump in the night. But she is jumpy as a frog when it comes to the tiniest spider. The psychiatrist who would conclude I have a deep fear of rattlesnakes would also diagnose Maureen with acute arachnophobia.

To say she gets a little apprehensive around the eight-legged creatures is like saying someone with a fear of heights gets a little squeamish while looking over the edge of the Grand Canyon. At the sight of a spider no bigger than a flea, the petite biped with the biggest heart known to humankind will grab whatever weapon available—ax, baseball bat, husband—and start flailing away.

"They give me the creeps—I can't stand them," she said, shuddering as though she was suddenly chilled. "I just want to smash them. Horrible things."

"You need to look at them as our dear friends who help keep out the insect vermin," I said, unable to help myself. "Perhaps yoga would be of some benefit. Think of the sound of one spider leg clapping. If you gave them a little time, you would find they have a warm and fuzzy side."

"I don't tease you about your little issue with rattlesnakes," she sniffed.

Beyond the silly sarcasm, I was serious about a spider's work being important in the world of nature. It certainly results in fewer flies and mosquitoes. But I am not a spider hugger.

While I don't collapse into a fit of the screaming willies at the sight of a spider, I have a healthy respect for those who are aggressive. Arachnids with the baddest reputation in these parts are the black widows, a dark spider with a red hourglass on her abdomen. While she isn't deadly, she will give you a nasty sore. She also has a habit of killing her mate, something I find in very poor taste.

Maureen says the fact spiders are predatory creatures, lurking in dark places, waiting for an innocent meal to stumble into its silken web, is what bugs her most. The meal, of course, is usually a small insect which is rolled into a neat little sushi snack. The spider munches on the delicacy at its leisure, something it conceivably has in abundance. I assume the insect sushi is crunchy on the outside and moist in the center. But I'm only guessing. I've sampled sushi in the states as well as in Japan but I've never become much of a connoisseur, and certainly not of the variety found dangling in a spider web.

I have met some spiders who give me the willies. The biggest I've ever encountered was during a journalistic sojourn to Vietnam in 1999. I stayed a few nights in an old French hotel in DaNang, an interesting city roughly halfway between Ho Chi Minh City and Hanoi.

My room had one of those showers in which the shower head dropped out of the high ceiling. The drain was a tiled low spot on the floor. The system worked fine but it did have a few bugs in the form of spiders. These were large, clay-colored arachnids about two inches in diameter. They lurked on the lower portions of the wall, apparently waiting for whatever prey that the funny-looking gecko lizards lounging a little higher up may miss. Either that, or the spider gang was waiting to attack visiting journalists foolish enough to close their eyes while shampooing. Vietnamese shampoo really stings when you shower with your eyes open, al a Psycho.

One morning before taking a shower, I picked up a shoe to give one spider a little nudge. Just to see what he would do, you see. He also needed to move out of my comfort zone. But as soon as the shoe touched him, he shot up the wall, causing yours truly to yell a very bad word which has to do with biped reproduction.

She—he?—was four feet from the floor one second, then at the edge of the ten-foot-high ceiling the next. It scared the bejabbers out of me. The spider was lightning fast. If he or his several other relatives in waiting ever decided to jump on me, there would be no leaping aside. I would be spider sushi.

I never did find out whether he was poisonous. Judging from his evil looks, he certainly appeared malevolent. The little commie definitely did not appear to be of the vegan persuasion. But perhaps communist spiders aren't as independent as our domesticated arachnids who have known only free enterprise for generations. Maybe he wouldn't have attacked without a go-ahead from party leaders. I wasn't going to take any chances. I wore my hair a little greasy during my sojourn in Vietnam.

Maureen doesn't share my sense of limited curiosity toward the eight-legged creatures. To her, they are the evil incarnate.

"I'll never understand what E.B. White saw in them," she sniffed one day while holding a splintered two-by-four board she had just employed as a weapon after a suspected spider sighting on a cabin wall. "There must have been a loathsome witch in his ancestral web named Charlotte. Probably a great aunt who never married, a bloated old hag with a crooked snag of a tooth. It's a terrible, terrible thing, scaring little kids with a book like that."

"I happen to think E.B. was a fine fellow in life as well as a terrific writer," I protested as I gently removed the broken board from her gloved grip. The fact her fingers were unrelenting told me a little humor was needed.

"Don't tell me the spider you were trying to bash had written "SOME PIG STY" in silk on the cabin wall," I offered, slightly rewriting what Charlotte had purportedly scrawled in webbed script above the pig pen. "If you remember your White correctly, you'll recall Charlotte was a barn spider. I suspect your common cabin spider is an illiterate lout."

"All spiders are louts," she pouted.

I had just come from around the other side of the cabin where I had been sweeping up sawdust left by the carpenters from earlier that day. I dropped my broom after hearing the sounds of the two-by-four slamming against the log wall. A quick examination revealed there was no structural damage to the wall's integrity, albeit the board I had previously denailed was now splintered.

"You've got to quit attacking every spider you see," I said as I ran my hand over the targeted log. "But I don't see anything now. You not only scared your husband and the neighbors, but the spider must have gotten a little jumpy. He's long gone."

"He's still right there, by your hand," she replied, causing me to pull my hand from the log as though it had suddenly become electrified. I may not be quite as immune to a spider's fearsome appearance as I sometimes pretend in her presence.

Yet I still didn't see the culprit.

"Where?" I asked as I peered at the log, careful to keep my hands off in the event it was a leaper.

"Right there," she said again, pointing to her targeted area. "I think I got him. He's not moving."

"He's not moving because he is not a spider," I countered. "He is a spider knot."

It was her turn to look at me as though I had suddenly become fluent in Martian.

"I told you to start wearing a hat," she said. "You've been out in the sun too long again. You know how you get."

"No, really," I said. "You've been attacking a knot—as in the remains of a limb that formed a knot in tree trunk—that looks a little like a spider. There was no spider. There is no spider. The log is spiderless."

"Now it is spiderless," she insisted. "There was a big one on it until I smashed him."

When it came to her fear of arachnids and my trepidation when confronted with a rattlesnake, it is about a draw. Yet, as you have seen, she is not afraid of other creatures that would scare most people. In my defense, I am not afraid of other reptiles, and even find many of them interesting in a cold blooded sort of way. I sometimes pick up nonvenomous snakes to relocate them on our property when they are underfoot or in harm's way of the mower or on the driveway. These are snakes that I know to be harmless, of course. Still, I do hold them at arm's length.

The problem with snakes is that some of them are actors. Take Gus, the large gopher snake that hung around our place for years. The snake was more than three feet long with diamond-shaped marks along its back. It liked to coil its scaly self and hiss at me while vibrating its tail. Although gopher snakes don't have rattles, they can mimic somewhat the buzzing sound of a rattlesnake by vibrating the tip against the ground. When you are already jittery, you jump to the conclusion it is the real thing. Should there ever be a horror movie made called "Death by Rattlesnake," Gus would make a nice double for the main bad guy. He is the hissing image.

Of course, experts will tell you that it's easy to tell the difference between the two. Rattlers have a flat triangular head while the gopher variety's head is more rounded, they explain in their cold-blooded fashion. Very clinical, these people. They are also quick to observe the pit viper has a heavier body. The gopher snake is more slender, they note.

The folks in the white lab coats insist you can tell the difference by looking the snake in the face. Rattlesnakes have heat-sensing pits between their nostrils and their eyes, allowing them to hunt warm-blooded prey in the dark, they explain. Gophers don't have those telltale pits, they smugly add.

Finally, they tell you that looking the snake in the eye reveals the real killer from the poser. Gopher snakes have rounded pupils while rattlers have vertical pupils like a cat, they explain. So all you have to do is get down on your knees and look into their eyes to determine which is which.

Yeah, right. This all goes to explain why you seldom see an old rattlesnake scientist who relies on eye-to-eye research. But there are young ones whose hair has gone prematurely white, the result of failing of a near miss while trying to differentiate gopher snakes from their poisonous cousins through the pupil method.

Not long after the nocturnal rattlesnake encounter and with the image of a lurking reptile with vertical pupils still coiled in the back of my mind, I stepped out of the driver's side of the car upon arriving home one evening. My left foot landed on top of what I assumed was the damned garden hose.

Until the hose slithered, that is.

Words that would make a sailor blush shattered the evening quiet. Maureen leaped out the passenger side, fearing I was having another hissy fit over the vagaries of life.

"Agrhhhh! It's a rattler!" I shouted.

Once again, I could almost feel the venomous fangs sinking deep into my leg. Darkness seemed to be closing in as I breathed my last.

It was rattlesnake nightmare déjà vu. Here I was about to leave this world and the last thing I would hear were peals of Maureen's laughter. Surely my departure would warrant a few sniffles, perhaps even a tear or two rolling down her pretty cheeks.

"It's just Gus," she said as she wiped away tears of laughter. "Quit jumping around. You are going to hurt him."

The lowlife jokester had been sneaking about our place all summer. Apparently born with a sick sense of humor, he likes to pop up when he's least expected, scaring the bejabbers out of me.

"He's got to stop doing this—my heart can't take it," I gasped after I stopped doing a jig.

Gus snaked off, no doubt smirking as he went. Maureen gave him the moniker, knowing that naming the snake Gus would make it harder for her husband to become an ax murderer intent on hacking him into bits. She hopes we will bond.

"See, he's wagging his tail at you," she said observed once when he surprised me under the large fronds of a zucchini plant in the garden.

When I reached down to harvest a young squash, Gus did his Oscar-winning rendition of a coiled rattlesnake, complete with hissing and tail shaking. But I like to think my performance of a startled man whizzing his pants would have also impressed the Academy.

I quickly moved on to the tomato patch where the wildlife in the form of insects was friendlier. I suddenly decided I didn't much care for zucchini anyway.

The tomatoes were nice and plump. They were also turning red. The fruit was just about ready to be picked. When I peered down under the foliage of the cherry tomato plant, a giant garden spider peered back. I didn't notice whether its pupils were round or vertical. The fearsome sight startled me for a second. Although perfectly harmless, a garden spider looks downright evil. And this enormous fellow was nearly as large as a large cherry tomato. Its housekeeping in the plant would be a good thing, resulting in fewer insects nibbling on our tomato plants.

Its presence also started the prankster wheels turning in my head. By now, you have noticed my humor tends to run strongly juvenile. Sometimes I can't help myself. This was one of those adolescent times. Never mind I knew it was a terribly immature thing to do. It was game on.

"Hey, honey, we're finally getting some ripe tomatoes," I told Maureen who lives for ripe tomatoes. "You ought to grab a couple of these cherry tomatoes. They are ready for the plucking."

God help me, but I was giggling when she headed, nearly skipping, to the cherry tomato plant, basket swinging in her hand. Now, there are those who say the scream from the garden that day would have horrified Jack the Ripper. But I found it lacked the gravitas as the one piercing the night of the rattlesnake. It just didn't have the chilling conviction that death was at hand. But I shouldn't quibble. It more than made up for those shortcomings by its sheer volume.

NINE

Chased by Fire

T HE UNEXPECTED ROAR OF A FIREFIGHTING AIR TANKER thundering low over the Sterling Creek drainage jolted me awake late one afternoon in July of 2014. I was sitting in my old leather desk chair in the loft that serves as my writing nook, and had started nodding off in the warm air while trying to come up with something vaguely coherent to write.

Glancing out the window, I saw the tail end of a large aircraft streaking over, its fuselage at a slight angle to the narrow Sterling Creek drainage. After calling a friend at the Oregon Department of Forestry district office in Central Point, I learned the airplane, flying out of the Medford air tanker base, had dropped a load of retardant on a lightning-caused fire which had just sprung up in the Little Applegate River watershed. The fire was about half a dozen miles south of us as the crow flies.

The aircraft was an aerial antique, although it was two years younger than yours truly. But the DC-7 built in 1953 seemed to be bursting with youthful energy, something I hadn't felt in decades. Instead of being put out to pasture, the aerial workhorse had been rebuilt for dropping fire retardant onto wildfires. The strategy is to dampen down a blaze before sending fire crews in to snuff it out before the flames have a chance to sprint off through the forest. Although the firefighting approach isn't foolproof, it is often effective. If a large fire breaks out, the aerial bombardment can also be used to slow its advance at strategic points, enabling ground pounders to have a better shot at protecting rural homes, culturally important sites or valuable natural resources.

The crackling late July thunderstorm had been the first substantial tempest of the fire season. It made up for its tardiness by igniting dozens of wildfires in our two-county area. Most of them were burning in the remote forests growing hard against the state line. The largest in the greater region would burn more than 100,000 acres near the northern California community of Happy Camp, a place name that is definitely a misnomer when threatened by a wildfire.

A few of the bolder lightning cells ventured north into the relatively more civilized region across the state line, creating high anxiety for local residents. Anyone who had spent a summer in southern Oregon knows the potential for a large fire to bust loose. Having one knocking at your door causes much fretting and wringing of hands. You want the unwanted visitor to stay away.

Like sorties on military missions, retardant planes were routinely flying over Sterling Creek en route to fires in the upper Applegate watershed or into far northern California. You could almost set your watch by the flights. About every half hour, one would rumble low overhead, heading back to the Medford air tanker base to load up with retardant. In addition to the DC-7, several modern aircraft had been drafted for the fiery battle.

"This is not good," I observed when the thunderheads first began stacking up like giant anvils over the valley. "The last thing we need right now is lightning."

"Maybe it'll bring rain," suggested Maureen, ever the optimistic one seeking to find a reason for hope. "We usually get some rain when we have thunder."

But she knew full well there would have to be days of torrential downpours to make up for the abnormally long dry spell we were enduring. Nor did I have to tell her that a dry lightning storm would be very problematic for the area. For weeks, we had endured daytime high temperatures that had crested

100 degrees. Previous record highs were being knocked over like dominos. One well-placed fiery bolt from above could torch the bone dry forests.

Not only had the summer been blistery hot but there had scarcely been enough rainfall during the winter and spring to turn the vegetation green. Rain had become a distant memory. Leaves and twigs crackled underfoot when you walked in the forest. At each step, dust rose up like puffs of smoke from the forest duff. Even the trees seemed to be feeling the stress of a thirsty year. Leaves began dropping from madrones in June, something which usually doesn't begin until late summer. Evergreens were also shedding some of their needles in an effort to reduce the need for water. Needles were turning brown on the lower branches of the smaller fir and incense cedar. Victims succumbing to the 2014 drought will be popping up in our forest for years to come. Douglas firs will likely be the species hardest hit, followed by pine and cedar. Darwin was right. In the natural world, it is survival of the fittest.

One of the few positive things about the dry summer was the fact there were no nasty little mosquitoes buzzing around our cabin. There was no surface water for them to lay their eggs. The local tick population also seemed have taken a substantial hit. I certainly didn't miss them but I would gladly exchange the drought for moisture and the accompanying gangs of flying and crawling little bloodsuckers any day.

The hillside meadows were brown and brittle dry, leaving precious little browse for the deer. Even the yellow starthistle, an invasive thorny weed from the Mediterranean region, seemed to be struggling to survive. And this, a weed that thrives in an exceedingly dry climate. Let the starthistle struggle. Too bad wildfires wouldn't restrict their burning desire for fuel to the invasive species that are now a constant nuisance to many rural areas in the Pacific Northwest. Both could cancel out the other.

In the days leading up to launching the air tanker sorties, there had been very little wind. When a rare breeze came up, it merely smothered you with hot air. The stifling heat wasn't just bothering bipeds. Even normally energetic grasshoppers would fly only a few feet, heading for the nearest bit of shade they could find. Turkey vultures circled overhead, optimistic about the chances of finding a heat stroke victim. Deer kept to the shadowy woods once the sun began baking the countryside. Our dogs slept on the cool concrete floor of the cabin, too exhausted by the stifling heat to even utter a sleepy woof when someone drove up the driveway. Best they could do was periodically lap the ice water we kept in their water bowl, then plop back down. The heat had turned them into grumps.

They weren't alone.

"I really hope we don't relive what we went through in 2002—that evacuation was no fun," Maureen said. We had just stepped out onto the deck to watch another air tanker disappear into the cloud canyons created by the thunderheads building up overhead. She was referring to what we euphemistically referred to as 2002's four days in hell when a wildfire chased us off our lands.

"What are we going to do with all our pets if we have to leave this time?" she asked. "We have more of them now. We can't leave anybody behind."

By anybody, she meant our two dogs and the cat herd. They are people to us. You notice she wasn't worried about our material stuff. Like me, she was more concerned about our furry friends.

"We won't have to evacuate," I said, although secretly wishing I felt more confident about my remark.

Normally, she is the one who has to shore up my pessimistic attitude towards nouns in general. I'm always pleasantly surprised when people, places or things turn out to be honest, pleasant and reliable.

"We'll be fine," I said. "There are lots of firefighters in our region right now. Besides, it's not as bad as it looks. If any fires start near us, they'll have them out before we know they are there."

I was only partially blowing hot air. There were significant numbers of firefighters as well as firefighting equipment in the region at that time. By early July, an air tanker from Alaska was already perched at the Medford tanker base, the Last Frontier having been drenched by summer rains at that point.

But 2014's explosive wildfire potential in the local forests was as bad as it was in 2002. That had been the first summer we spent on the property and the only time we had retreated in advance of a threatening wild fire. Even if we could shake the uncomfortable memories, the continued sorties by the fire retardant planes and the rumbling thunderheads were a constant reminder of that mid-July 2002 firestorm which engulfed our region. Back then, we were still doing time in the cursed trailer. There was a device in the trailer which the manufacturer laughingly labeled as an air conditioner. What kidders. When you turned it on, it emitted a warm breeze which you could feel only if you put your face next to a vent. A drooling mastiff's fetid breath down the back of your neck would have felt more refreshing.

We opened every window in our metal oven at night in a futile effort to bring the inside temperature down to where you could bake bread. Fortunately, there were only a few holes in the screens for the mosquitoes to slip in for a little nocturnal snacking. But most of them couldn't take the heat. They stayed outside in the comparatively cool air. There was no relief from the heat in the metal box that was our temporary home. At least we were able to shed our sheets. Our side-by-side pets were little more than furry sardines, enduring the heat in their heavy coats.

As thunder storms go, the tempest on July 13, 2002 wasn't anything out of the ordinary. But there were zaps of lightning early that Saturday morning, followed by what sounded like giants hurling huge bowling balls down the valley, knocking over pins the size of redwood trees. The fiery storm was followed by a heavy but brief downpour, one which would either drown or slow fires sparked by the storm.

By mid-afternoon, the storm was over, leaving behind a largely blue sky and the wonderful fragrance that only a summer rain can bring. Satisfied that all was well, Maureen and I hit the road, bound for Eureka to visit my elderly mom, Gladys Clara Cooke Fattig. For several years, we had been making the nearly ten-hour round trip once a month to the town on the northern California coast. Other siblings also visited her regularly.

She lived in what is euphemistically called a retirement facility. Such places used to be referred to as nursing homes. The name change was no doubt conjured up in a public relations gimmick to help guilt-ridden offspring feel less lousy about dumping their parents into what is little more than human kennels. It didn't make me feel any better about the crowded facility where she would spend her final years. One of the biggest regrets in my life was not pushing to have her moved north to the Rogue Valley.

Maureen and her sister, Teresa, had found a very pleasant home in Medford for their elderly father, Andy, a likable fellow with the same financial limitations as my mom. The large house where the World War II veteran spent his final years had only five other elderly people, including a former editor of mine. The patients were treated like family, thanks to a big-hearted lady named Debra who managed the well-kept place. Florence Nightingale could have taken lessons on compassion from her.

While the folks staffing the large nursing home in Eureka no doubt worked hard, it was depressing to enter the facility. Time-worn people in wheelchairs looked up at you wistfully, hoping you were there to visit them. Regardless of the sitting, mom was invariably perky, always glad to see us. Her buoyant personality was infectious, cheering us up. The kind, gentle soul who adored Maureen passed away in 2008 at age ninety-four.

Normally, we made the long trip down and back to Eureka in one day. Since we had gotten a late start, we elected to stay the night in Eureka, spend Sunday morning with mom, and then hit the northbound road for home early that afternoon.

Numerous down strikes had slammed into the Applegate River drainage but daughter Derra and her significant other Matt were visiting from Portland. They would be watching over our place, including keeping an eye on the pets. Everything seemed hunky dory.

We drove south along Sterling Creek Road to the Little Applegate River before heading west to eventually link up with Highway 199 which would lead us south into the refreshingly cool California coastal redwoods. Just as we entered the main Applegate Valley, we saw a tendril of smoke rising from Squires Peak. The 3,340-foot spire is several miles west of our cabin. Often after a summer rain or in the mornings, a wisp of what could be mist or smoke can be seen rising in the nearby mountains. Folks who staff fire lookouts refer to them as water dogs. However, this was no puddle pup. It rose up like smoke from a large campfire on top of the peak.

Several wildland firefighting rigs were parked along the road when we drove past, a surefire indication firefighters were already massing to attack the little blaze. No doubt a helicopter carrying a large bucket would soon be dropping water on the fire. Certainly an air tanker was available if need be.

"They'll have it out before we get back Sunday afternoon," I assured Maureen . "In any case, that fire is a couple of miles from our place. That's a long ways for it to travel. They are catching it early. It'll be snuffed out in no time. So, as they say in the Land Down Under, 'No worries, mate.'"

"Yeah, well, they also have kangaroos down there," she replied. "With an animal like that around, it's easy to 'jump' to the wrong conclusion. But let's 'hop' we have no worries."

She giggled as she reached over to tickle my ribs, her subtle way of asking for forgiveness for uttering two terrible puns in one breath. As a firm believer that puns are the highest form of humor, I couldn't help but laugh. In spite of the long road trip ahead, we were both in fine spirits. We were tired of baking in the inland heat. Driving along the far northern California coast would be a cool respite. What's more, it was always good to see my mom, her dismal surroundings notwithstanding.

Yet deep in the recesses of my mind was a niggling little worry, one I couldn't shake. It was a vague uneasy feeling. There was always the potential for embers to be fanned by a westerly late afternoon wind. Hungry flames could eat their way through the dry grass on the peak to reach the dry timber below. A conflagration in the woods would then be driven by late afternoon winds from the west, sending the flames racing toward our cabin. Despite what I had told Maureen, I knew a windswept blaze sprints through a parched forest, covering a few miles within a matter of hours.

But I pushed the inconvenient concern aside and focused on the trip ahead. By the time we reached the coast, all worries had faded away. The salt air was refreshing; mom her usual cheerful self. We were still in fine form late Sunday afternoon when we turned east off Highway 199 and headed up the Applegate Valley towards home.

However, upon entering Jackson County line, we could see a towering plume looming overhead in the distance.

"What in the world is that?" Maureen asked.

"Smoke from a wildfire," I said grimly. "Not good. It's coming from the mountains between here and Sterling Creek."

Our good moods literally went up in the smoke we entered. Wildfire trucks rumbled past. A helicopter carrying a large bucket was landing on a field near the Applegate River where a landing pad had been established to refuel and maintain the aircraft. But it was impossible to see the wildfire because of the thick veil of smoke over the mountains. With concern mounting at every mile, we drove on.

Yet everything was copacetic back in Gilson Gulch. The smoke was blowing to the west, away from our cabin. While firefighting aircraft could be heard in the distance, calm had settled over the cabin. Derra and Matt had enjoyed their night in the country and were getting ready to drive back to the city. Our pets were happy to see us, once they stopped pouting over us having left them the previous night. While it turned out that the Squires Peak down strike had escaped before firefighters could corral it, we were still confident it would soon be out.

The fire had other ideas. The sun was out in full force by late that afternoon and the wind began blowing from the west. More disconcerting was the fact the wind was gathering steam, a bad omen when you have a hungry wildfire nosing around, searching for a place to feed. An army isn't the only thing that moves on its stomach.

"I don't like this," Maureen said. "Are we going to be OK?"

"I'm sure we'll be fine," I told her, then repeated the balderdash I had spewed earlier in the day.

That niggling little worry smoldering in the back of my mind? It now loomed large, filling my head with concern about what the wind-fanned fire could do if it crested the ridge and plunged into the forest below. I kept the growing concern to myself, figuring it wouldn't do any good to air what had not yet become fact.

Although I am no expert when it comes to wildfires, I've warmed my journalistic pen around dozens of them over the decades. I'd covered massive wildfires in the Alaskan bush in the mid-1980s. The fires in the Far North would retreat into the thick caribou moss when it rained only to pop up again when the sun returned weeks later. There was the 100,000-plus acre Silver Complex of 1987 in southern Oregon which featured furnace-like crown fires. Entire stands were simultaneously torched as the flames raced through the forest canopy. Nor can I ever forget the deadly Oakland Hills fire in California's East Bay area in the fall of 1991. Fanned by a strong easterly wind, it raced up those beautiful hills, a virtual blowtorch razing homes and trees alike, killing twenty-five people. I recall seeing one house which emerged virtually unscathed, reputedly thanks to its tiled shingles. A fire's aftermath is like a war zone with survivors walking around, disoriented and shell shocked.

Like any good journalistic vulture, I've interviewed freshly hurting families who had lost all their earthly possessions to a wildfire. While they were uniformly thankful for having survived, they felt a helpless sense of deep loss for the photographs, family heirlooms and other irreplaceable items consumed by the flames. The worst was hearing the stories of grief-stricken people whose loved ones died while fighting a wildfire, often while working to protect rural homes like ours.

Few natural disasters are as deadly efficient as wildfires. Robert Frost, one of my favorite poets since childhood, was only half right when he wrote that, given fire or ice, either would suffice when it came bringing an end to the world. Unlike most water in the form of ice or even a flood, a catastrophic fire invariably obliterates, although you have to allow for the rare exception for houses like the one with tile shingles in the Oakland Hills. Frost's poetic version of a fiery ending to our existence had my full attention during the 2002 Squires Peak fire. This was no fire in which I could drop safely into the outer fringes, talk to a few folks, and then retreat to an air-conditioned news room. You get a whole new perspective on wildfires when you feel the dragon's hot breath at your own door. No longer was I a detached journalist walking away from the story at the end of the day. The sinking feeling in my gut settled in for a long stay.

After a smokefilled night we awoke Monday morning to the eerie calm of what could have passed for a nuclear winter. I was working the Tuesday through Saturday shift that week so I was home on Monday while Maureen went to her shop. I spent the morning feverishly trying to build a defensible space around the cabin, using ax, pole saw and pruning shears. We had been focusing on restoring the historic cabin since buying the property, paying scant attention to removing flammable brush and other material should a wildfire come calling. With the help of two daughters home from college, we cut brush, lobbed off lowlying limbs and removed smaller trees.

I considered getting out the chainsaw but figured it would take hours to find it in our unpacked tools. Besides, chainsaw use by other than for firefighting had been outlawed because of the extreme fire danger, one of the surreal realities during that period. I suspect I could have revved it up without any repercussions since I was contributing to the firefighting, albeit very indirectly. But the other tools answered well.

By late morning, my lungs burned as though I had smoked two packs of Camels. Non filter. All those decades have having never smoked were nearly negated in the smoke-filled days. But a mild panic had set in. Despite the hacking and wheezing, I was energized.

After a restless Monday night, Maureen and I were a little anxious when we went to our respective jobs the next morning. Maureen could focus better than me since she didn't have a scanner squawking in her ear, keeping her aware of the fiery battle going on just over the ridge from our cabin. I dashed home during my lunch break to check on the fire's advancement. It was still a safe distance away at that point.

Everything calmed down a bit around mid-afternoon, at least enough to allow the gallows humor hanging around the newsroom to come to life. One coworker suggested that the old cabin, which you will remember had partially burned a decade earlier, wills itself to burn like something out of a Stephen King novel. You must be on pins and burning needles, another one quipped to me. It was funny, albeit in the way smacking your funny bone is funny.

Just as I was starting to settle down to the job at hand and make up for hours lost to the jitters and jokes, the scanner announced late in the afternoon that folks were being evacuated in our rural neighborhood. I was out the door, pad and pen left behind on my desk. There were no more jokes from co-workers. They knew this could be serious.

Fortunately, the scanner was premature. There were no evacuations that day, at least not in Gilson Gulch or in adjacent Hukill Hollow, the inhabited ravine to our immediate south. Earlyday arrivals apparently had a penchant for alliteration when it came to geographic names.

But there would be precious little sleep that night. You don't sleep much when you can see the orange glow of a forest fire on the southeast edge of your property. Nor is it comforting to hear wildland firefighters yelling to each other in the dark, trees crashing to the ground and the clank of a bulldozer building a fire line.

No complaints about the noise, mind you. It's just damned difficult to snooze when folks are fighting a dragon within earshot. I would lie on my side and look through the trailer window at the orange glow of the fire on top of the ridge on neighbor Pete Bedingfield's property. His house was closer to the fire but was built in a meadow away from the forest. Even if the fire made a run down the valley, his house would likely survive the flames.

But I figured our place would be toast, the kind that turns black when you leave it too long in the toaster.

The worst part was the waiting. While we were sleepless in Sterling Creek at night, we spent our days riding an emotional roller coaster. Our utter despair would give rise to temporary relief in the still of early morning, only to have Mr. Despair return triumphantly each afternoon. The fire dragon seemed coldly calculating, as though the reptilian beast was looking for ways to get past the firefighters.

Wednesday began much the same as the day before. The fire lizard laid down early before dawn for a short nap, then came roaring to life as the wind picked up in the afternoon. I had taken the remainder of the week off, laughingly calling it vacation. Maureen also stayed home that day.

But it was no period of rest and relaxation. The acrid smell of smoke was in everything you breathed, ate or drank. Although the sky was gray, the days remained hot. The smoky heat was suffocating. Each breath drew in air baked by the sun. It was like breathing into a hot hair dryer. Rearing its ugly head was a brownish gray plume which towered over everything else. Partially burned leaves periodically drifted down, having been carried aloft by the plume.

When Chris and Richard arrived, it wasn't to work on the cabin. They hastily grabbed their tools and stowed them in Richard's truck.

"I'm sure everything will be fine," Chris said. "We just want to err on the side of caution."

"The fire is still a long ways from here," added Richard, speaking as an experienced firefighter. "They should be able to stop it. But if everything goes south, we would rather be safe than sorry."

No doubt they were wise in gathering their equipment and hurrying back down the driveway. But it did not leave us feeling optimistic. That sinking feeling in our stomachs took another plunge.

Like the journalistic jokesters back in the newsroom, firefighters assigned to Sterling Creek used black humor to cope with the seriousness of their business. One beefy fellow standing watch in our driveway noted that if the fire did burn into the nearby rural community of Ruch— pronounced Roosh—they would have to change the name.

"They'll call it 'Woosh!'" he said, prompting chuckles among his comrades.

Thanks, guys. As did the news room banter, the humor in the field helped to reduce the stress.

Gawkers didn't. Cars drove slowly past, their drivers and occupants staring at the column looming overhead. I gawked at the gawkers. But I understood their curiosity, having gawked plenty over the years.

Yet I wasn't ready for a reporter from a Medford television station when he came down the driveway.

"I thought you'd be up close to the fire line," he told me. "Getting a little color, huh? This is a great spot for it. Right in harm's way. These people around here are getting real nervous."

"They certainly are—we bought this place earlier this year," I replied.

"You're kidding, right?" he asked. "You don't live here, do you? I mean, really? This place looks like it would go up in seconds."

While his observation was spot on, I really didn't need to be reminded of the place's volatility. A crown fire fanned by a strong afternoon wind would make short work of our cabin, consuming it like a hungry dog snapping up a crumb.

Wanting to do something useful, we grabbed our tools to resume removing flammable material near the cabin. With the brush cut and the thick stand of trees thinned immediately south of the cabin, we began dismantling an old garage which was little more than a partially collapsed pile of dry cedar boards. The garage, which listed heavily to one side, stood less than thirty feet from the cabin. The large pile of kindling needed to be removed. And quickly.

Just we began peeling off the boards, a fellow whipped up our driveway in a vehicle whose door insignia announced he was from a structure fire department in southern Oregon. As soon as he opened his mouth, it became painfully obvious why he was alone.

"What do they think they are doing up on that ridge?" the charm school dropout demanded to know. "Who's in charge? They need to get off their asses."

I started to reply that at least they didn't speak out of that particular part of their anatomy but thought better of it. He obviously thought of himself as Gen. Patton, albeit he had no division to lead. With me as his private, he apparently figured he had an army of one. But this private, who was hefting a large crowbar used to loosen the garage boards, wasn't about to be slapped.

I already had a long day, one which hadn't included a meal, let alone a consultation with the fire bosses on how the fire should be fought. The last thing I wanted to listen to was some blowhard spouting off, especially when he seemed thicker than my crowbar.

"Do I look like a firefighter?" I asked him. "We just bought this property. 'They' didn't consult me. But 'they' are working on a fire line on the ridge which you can't see from here. And 'they' have been working their tails off."

"Fine," he said, then studied the work we were doing for a few seconds. "You are wasting your time here," he concluded.

With that, the horse's end that produces road apples galloped off down the road in search of someone else to annoy. I recall hoping he didn't verbally attack a battle-weary wild lands firefighter carrying a sharp Pulaski, only because I wouldn't want the ground-pounder to get into trouble. Now, a quirt well applied to the horse's ass, I believe that would have been permissible.

Maureen and I looked at each other after he left and shook our heads. "There goes a real jerk," she said. She was right, although I would have used a strong adjective and added a recommendation that he do something that was anatomically impossible. We never did find out who he was. He was the only firefighter we encountered on the fire who reflected poorly on their honorable profession.

But our sole asinine visitor wasn't worth a second thought. The heat of summer rose to simmering by noon. Despite the smoky haze, the wind picked up that afternoon. Ash began drifting down like large, dry snowflakes. The ash was followed by blackened yet unburned madrone leaves drifting upon the wind. The leaves appeared to have been stripped from trees, testifying to the power of the fire's updraft. Clouds formed over the column as it literally created its own weather. It looked like something out of Dante's Inferno. At times you could hear a low rumbling sound like a jet engine in the distance. That was no aircraft. The fire dragon was rearing back its head and roaring.

Scattered tendrils of smoke were sucked back into the base of the column that grew to Biblical proportions. The apocalypse seemed at hand.

Yet the mortals hadn't given up the fight. Overhead galloped the cavalry in the form of air tankers with loads of fire retardant and helicopters carrying huge buckets of water the size of small swimming pools. On the ground were the professional wildland firefighters, the infantry who fought the fire facetoface. Structure firefighters with their fire engines stood guard near our rural homes, waiting to step in to battle the blaze with a fire hose should the flames get too close. Neighbors, many of whom had worked in the woods, were building firelines around their homes. Each had a vital role to play in the Wagnerian drama.

About mid-afternoon the structure firefighter who had been assigned to our cabin received a communications on his radio from the powers that be. He wasn't smiling when he approached us.

"I'm sorry to have to tell you this but they want you to evacuate," he said. "It's getting too dangerous. They don't know if they can hold the ridge."

He had already advised us on last minute things to do to help, including wetting down what we could with the garden hose, removing any loose woody building material from around the cabin and leaving our ladder against the roof so firefighters could use it if need be.

"We can only spend about fifteen minutes fighting the fire here," he had warned us. "After that, we're out of here."

I'm assuming his time limit was because of a finite water supply, not some hot date in Medford. I never had a chance to ask. We all had more pressing concerns. It was a helpless feeling, facing evacuation. What to take, what to leave. The first thing, of course, was the pets. At the time, we had three dogs and half a dozen cats, all of whom were growing more anxious by the hour amid the smoke and roar of aircraft. Next were the important papers, irreplaceable photographs and a few clothes. Finding it was easy since everything was still in their marked boxes from the move. But the rest of our accumulated material had suddenly become immaterial. We left its fate to the fire gods and firefighters to hash out.

Friends and relatives helped us pack, protesting pets and all. We evacuated to daughter Amy's place in Grants Pass where we sat around for several very anxious hours. Later that night, unable to stand the waiting any longer, Maureen and I headed back to the cabin.

"You evacuated this afternoon and now you want to go back in there?" asked a dubious volunteer manning a roadblock. "You should wait until morning when we have a better handle on things."

I told him we had left a couple of important things at our place we needed to grab. It was the truth, albeit twisted and stretched a bit. We had remembered a few things we wanted to pick up. We would use extreme caution, I promised. After checking with his higher ups, he reluctantly let us pass.

"Don't do anything that'll put you—or us—in harm's way," he admonished us.

Fearing we may have already passed that milestone by heading back to the cabin, I drove off into the night. About a mile south of our place we saw what in the headlights appeared to be a large splash of blood across the pavement. It wasn't precious bodily fluid. Fire retardant had been dropped there when the fire attempted to jump the road late that afternoon. It was stark evidence of the day's battle.

Nothing had changed at the cabin. The smoke still hung like a shroud. Fire crews were still on the front lines up, although waiting until dawn to resume their battle. We spent the rest of the restless night in the trailer, waking frequently to check on the progress of the orange glow flickering on the distant ridge.

Once again we awoke to a gray morning. Once again we employed ax, pruning shears and scythe to cut brush and dry grass while we waited for word. We knew it was too little, too late. Yet it made us feel like we were helping in the battle.

Those who were really making a real difference, in addition to the firefighters, were folks like neighbor Pete and his extended family. They fired up Pete's bulldozer to charge the dragon and carve a roughly mile-long fire trail.

"We had kids stomping the grass out with their feet," he told the *Mail Tribune* in a story which ran that Thursday morning.

The tail end of the dragon's tale began Thursday, thanks to weak winds and hard work by firefighters and neighbors alike.

When the smoke cleared, only 3,038 acres were burned and four outbuildings lost.

Truly amazing. Only hours earlier I figured our cabin was toast. But the closest the dragon got was burning some twenty acres of Pete's property.

It was fitting that a Sterling Creek resident brought her alpin- horn to the site of the first evacuation on Sterling Creek that Thursday evening. To a quiet group of weary firefighters and neighbors, the talented musician played Amazing Grace. It was an apt tribute to those who had worked hard to stop the fire.

Later, a young man who lived in the area at the time, informed me in no uncertain words that the firefighters were all a waste of time. It was the local residents who stopped the Squires Peak fire, he declared.

I looked at him for a moment, wondering if he was serious. I considered asking him whose air tankers and helicopters attacked the eastern flank of the fire above our cabin. Perhaps he was joking. I was dead tired of the constant worry, of breathing smoke, of living on the run. All I knew for sure was the fire had been stopped dead in its tracks. There was no sound of a roaring fire in the distance, no thunder of an aerial bombardment. The air was smoke free.

"I suspect everyone contributed," I replied blandly. "The bottom line is that no one lost their homes. I appreciate what everyone did to stop the damned thing."

Unfortunately, the thunder storm in July of 2014 was remarkably like the tempest which triggered the Squires Peak fire a dozen years to the month earlier. Like its 2002 counterpart, the 2014 version was most belligerent in the morning. We heard several loud bangs but it was a dazzling flash to our immediate south, followed nearly simultaneously by a window-rattling boom that caused a jump in our blood pressures.

"That was really close," Maureen said.

"That was next door," I agreed.

When we looked at the tree-lined ridge line to our south, we couldn't see any smoke rising out of the forest. But within a few minutes, a helicopter began circling above our home, its ODF crew obviously looking for smokes. The helicopter made several passes over the ridge, and disappeared, heading south. But we could still hear its whop-whop in the distance as they continued the search for the down strike.

A call from neighbor Pete confirmed it had struck close. He had seen the flash and estimated it was within a quarter of a mile south of us. That would be a forested quarter of mile with nothing but thick, dry fuel between the strike and our cabin.

"I was wondering if you could see any smoke from your place," Pete said. "We could hear it hit. It was real close."

He and his wife, Rosella, were rightfully worried about the potential for another Squires Peak fire. I told them I would find out what I could and call back in a few minutes. As Maureen and I headed south on Sterling Creek Road, we were both wondering if we would soon be reliving the smoky 2002 purgatory. The similarities were eerily similar: extremely dry forest, a lighting storm rumbling through with a dazzling display of fireworks display, nervous bipeds scurrying about. All it would take is one well aimed down strike in deadwood.

We encountered an ODF fire rig parked along the road about a quarter of a mile from our place. I rolled down my window and asked the two fellows in canary-yellow fire shirts where the fire was located.

"Right up there a couple of hundred feet," the driver responded. "It was an old snag hit by a down strike. But we've already got a crew and a rig up there. They are mopping up now. No chance of it going anywhere."

We thanked them and returned home. I called Pete to give him the good news.

"They knocked it down right away—that's good," he said. "We sure wouldn't want another one like 2002. That was too close to home."

Spoken like the former logger he was who believed in culling any deadwood before speaking his mind. Many journalists could take lessons from Pete.

To paraphrase the incomparable T.S. Eliot, the fire season ended that year, not with a bang but a whimper. There was no great calamity. It simply faded away when the rains began early in the fall. Maureen and I walked, hand in hand, among the trees as the first heavy rains began to wash the fire season into history. We stopped to listen to the pitter-patter of raindrops on the leaves. The forest smelled earthy, like freshly tilled soil. Another fire season had bit the dust. The feeling of dread was gone from our neck of the woods.

I would accept that a wild fire is Mother Nature's way of a cleansing a forest. Certainly a low-intensity ground fire can improve a forest's health by removing the small vegetation, allowing the larger trees to flourish. I would even acknowledge that allowing a wildfire to burn in a wilderness area is not a bad thing. But I would draw the fire line where rural homes are involved, of course.

We humans have thrown a monkey wrench into the natural order of things by carving out homes in the woods, then working hard to prevent forest fires. As a result, many forested areas are unnaturally dense, creating thickets that explode when torched during the high heat of summer. I was reminded of that in a poem written, not by Eliot or Frost, but by my father. I had never read it until my older brother Jim discovered a copy of it late in 2014. Dubbed "Ruination," it was one our dad had written nearly eighty years ago. The poem had been published in the *Illinois Valley News* on July 15, 1937, fourteen years earlier to the day that my twin and I were born in 1951.

This was back in the day when newspapers published submitted poetry. It was also a time when Robert Service, otherwise known as the Bard of the North, was immensely popular. Our dad, who was working for the U.S.

Forest Service at the time, was obviously a fan of the man who created "The Cremation of Sam McGee." I suspect that's why our paterfamilias was drawn to Alaska where he lived for a time, trying his hand at mining before joining the merchant marines.

Back in '37 he and Smoky the Bear were worried about unattended campfires, a concern our father put to rhyme. When he attended Union Town School that once stood on the north edge of Little Applegate River, he would have seen Squires Peak perhaps a mile distant by a crow's flight path. Given my father's penchant for hiking, he likely climbed the peak as a young lad. While in the one-room school, my father no doubt read poetry, perhaps even that of Mr. Service.

While I am not an unbiased judge, I appreciate the poem, especially considering his formal education was limited to Union Town School. For those who don't appreciate his rhyming words, consider yourselves fortunate my maternal grandmother did not have Applegate Valley roots. She was a prolific poet who could—and did—make an orange rhyme. If I was of a slightly more mischievously malevolent nature, I would have trotted out a couple of dozen of her poems whose creative wording would have made Ogden Nash wince.

Instead, we'll end this fiery chapter with a poem called "Ruination" penned by the original Paul R. Fattig in 1937:

Into nature's playground a stranger came one day
Looking there for recreation and a quiet place to stay.
A place where he could rest in peace away from any town
For the hustling city life had sorta got him down.
Thru the forest he did wander, over hills and wooded streams
Until he chanced upon the place, the answer to his dreams.
A place God had had made to order for an office weary mind,
Where one could fish and hike and leave troubles far behind.
There, beside a peaceful lake, 'neath the softly sighing pine,
The camper stretched his tent, saying, "Isn't nature fine?
Here I'll spend my vacation, breathe the fragrant mountain air,
Feast my eyes upon the beauty of this mountain scenery rare."

But this over-anxious camper, in his haste some fish to take,
Left his campfire unattended while out fishing in the lake.
Soon a smoke was roaring skyward from a spark that got away
From the unattended campfire that was to spoil the camper's day.
Over hill and vale it spread: screaming, harsh, uncanny thing.
Consuming all before it, an agonizing death did bring.
Now with sorrow he relates a story sad to tell
How he made God's country look like that of hell.

TEN

Presidential Visit

J UST AS FIREFIGHTERS WERE ABOUT TO START mopping up the last of
the hotspots on the 2002 Squires Peak fire, political gasoline was
thrown onto the dying embers. Fueling the flames was the announcement
that President George W. Bush would visit the burned area.

Granted, it wasn't the relatively small Squires Peak fire that prompted
the presidential visit. Rather, it was the half-million acre Biscuit fire
burning largely in Josephine and Curry counties to our west. The Biscuit
was the largest wildfire in the nation that year, one which rightfully drew
national attention. Consider this: it was the largest fire in Oregon since
1865 when the Silverton fire torched 988,000 acres in the state's
northwest corner. The Biscuit was still baking when the president arrived.
A ground visit to that fire was deemed too dangerous for the president,
although the presidential aerial entourage did a fly over of the massive
fire. The blaze may have burned hundreds of thousands of acres of brush
and trees, but it would have been decidedly bad form to singe one
presidential Bush. The alternative was to visit the relatively safe area
burned by the Squires Peak fire.

As it happens, the site selected for his visit would be a ridge off Sterling
Creek Road on the U.S. Bureau of Land Management's Medford District.

He would pass through the historic little town of Jacksonville. Not since September of 1880 had a sitting president visited that hamlet. That would have been Rutherford B. Hayes, 19th president of the United States. While there would be protestors as well as supporters awaiting Bush, none of the records indicate there were any Rutherford protestors. If there had been, doubtlessly one wisenheimer would have held up a placard reading "We'd 'ruther' you leave." Protestors are an imaginative bunch with a flair for humor.

As expected, Jacksonville teemed with law enforcement officers the day Bush came to town. There were officers in uniform as well as others in plain clothes, mainly Secret Service agents. The latter all stand out because the male of the species look like no-neck college football players. The one woman agent I saw looked normal, albeit she also had the telltale habit of speaking into her collar.

Although the politics of our region are perceived by many pundits as reddish conservative with a blue dot marking liberal Ashland, that simplistic view doesn't reflect reality. We are more of a political potpourri. While Ashland is mighty progressive, it also has its conservative residents. Medford is basically conservative but has a liberal sprinkling of folks who lean left. The outlying areas also have conservative and liberal cells. Speaking volumes is the fact Jackson County voters endorsed Barack Obama in his first presidential bid, rejecting him in his re-election, with each outcome decided by a slim margin. We are a mixed bunch, which makes for feisty politics. Indeed, the body politic in these parts often emerges battered and bruised from family gatherings.

As for my politics, I would remind you I am a registered independent, often holding my nose when I vote. Admittedly, it is often difficult to tell who will do the least damage. When in doubt, I generally follow my father's one footstep and vote Democratic. But I have also been known to cross the political aisle on occasion. Maureen? A devout Democrat, like her father before her.

Lest you start pointing the bony finger of political indignation at me for focusing on the GOP here, it should be noted that we have had Mort Mondale over for a barbecue. I've also had lunch with him numerous times and attended his eightieth birthday bash in mid-December, 2014. You recognize the surname because Mort is the younger brother of Fritz Mondale, vice president of the United States during the Carter administration. You will no doubt recall he is a staunch Democrat. Liberal are the genes that swim in the Mondale family pool, at least the ones I've met.

When Fritz dropped in to visit Mort and his wife in their Josephine County home, we had a chance to chat with the former Vice President and his wife, Joan, who happens to have been born in Eugene. Sadly, she passed away in 2014. I bring up the Mondales to offer a little political variety. For name dropping purposes, too, truth be told.

In my political book, having a Republican president within a mile of the cabin and the brother of a former Democratic vice president over for a visit balances things out. I'll leave it to you to conclude whether George or Fritz was the better leader, although honesty dictates that I admit to believing that the latter would have made a fine president had he been elected to the highest post in the land.

My strange involvement in the 2002 presidential visit began with a phone call at work where I was minding my own business which largely meant trying to avoid meaningful work. From the outset, I suspected it was a call from a ruthless practical joker I was working with at the time.

"This is the White House we need your Social Security number, date of birth, race and sex for the upcoming presidential visit to Oregon, " the woman on the phone curtly informed me.

Yeah, right. It sounded suspiciously like a sophomoric prank. I was still smarting from one pulled on me a few years earlier. A very crabby old woman called to complain long and loud about a story I had written. About ten minutes into the irritating call I discovered the old crone was actually a practical jokester—you know who you are, Kathy—calling from her desk on the other side of the newsroom. Some newsies laughed so hard they were blowing snot bubbles. Disgusting behavior. I'd rather not talk about it.

But just as I was about to comment snidely concerning the audacity of juvenile jokesters when it came to presidential visits, I glanced at the caller identification on my office phone. It indicated the call was from area code 202, proof the person on the land line was calling from the District of

Columbia. The local jokester was ruled out, although I remain on my guard after all these years. Such is my prankster paranoia that when jokester Kathy called in 2014 to ask me to write an obituary for her husband, I checked to make sure one was warranted. Sadly, it was all too true.

The very real White House spokeswoman informed me in a very officious manner that I had been selected as the regional print media pool representative to join the full-time presidential press corps during Bush's visit to the Squires Peak fire on August 22. My personal information was needed for a security background check, she stressed. Without it, I would not be able to dive into the presidential pool.

No one ever told me why I was chosen to cover Bush's visit into the southern Oregon bush. Perhaps it was because I had been covering forestry issues for more than two decades and the visitor from the Oval Office would be addressing the issue. Or maybe it was pure chance, a selection made by the someone who, like me when I vote, held his or her nose and tried to choose the least offensive. What I do know is that presidential administrations, be they donkeys or elephants, don't have high opinions of the media.

The rest of the regional pool included a photographer from *The Oregonian* newspaper out of Portland and a reporter from a local television station as well as one from a radio station. As a journalist, I had finally won the lottery, never mind I had never entered it. True, being tossed into a pool brimming with news sharks from the White House press corps isn't most folks' idea of a good time. But I figured it would be a hoot, both as a journalist and a political junky. I had covered President Clinton in 1994 and the first President Bush in 1992, as well as President Reagan in the 1980s while working for another paper, all when they made stops in the Northwest. Each visit was definitely interesting, although I had yet to be able to pose a direct question to the Oval Office occupant.

Such a visit matters not one whit whether you love or loathe the person from 1600 Pennsylvania Avenue. We're talking about the President of the United States right in River City. As a journalist, I was stoked.

My instructions were succinct: Meet the White House representative precisely at 08:45 Aug. 22 at Gate 32 at the Medford airport. When I arrived, dozens of people already were being patted down and electronically violated by intensely serious security guards. Snipers with baseball caps on backwards stood on rooftops at the airport. It was clear this was serious business.

I reflected, not for the first time, that ours was a very strange profession. For the most part, journalists are somewhat normal folk, at least they start out that way. OK, a bit nerdy and perhaps a little full of themselves. Yet we come from all walks of life and throughout the nation. During my career I worked with or met journalists from nearly every state. Some come from old money; others had a hard scrabble background. But in the process of becoming print journalists, we all evolve into really strange humanoids. I'm not talking about progressive evolution here, the kind that improves the species. We become fixated on minutiae, a focus that would drive most people nuts. Who else goes to a city council meeting and comes home to prattle endlessly about the nuances of the late night session? If that isn't bad enough, we insist our poor spouses read every profound word we write on wide ranging topics from boring board meetings to equally mind-numbing budget sessions. It's a wonder that most journalists don't die violently at the hands of their significant others. Of course, the poor widow would likely get no more than a slap on the hand, what with having suffered through years of having been fed such an abusively dull diet.

As I stood on the tarmac, I pondered the unfair fact that we were the judge and jury of events. We decide what goes in the story and what is left out. A better form of covering events has never come to mind, however. You certainly don't want a government committee informing the public. But having it based on money-grubbing enterprises may not be preferable, either. I'm just saying it is not a pretty process, that's all. Moreover, we are all prejudiced by our life's experiences. Best we can do is try to present a picture that reflects accurately what is happening and let the reader-viewer-listener decide its merits.

My musings about the world of journalism were cut short by a Secret Service agent approaching the tall lean fellow two people ahead of me in the line. The fellow was wearing a baseball cap pulled low over his face.

He looked a little shady. Perhaps the security folks were about to round up a suspect. I watched with growing anticipation. This could be an exclusive.

Then the agent said politely, "You don't have to go through this, senator."

Turns out baseball hat man was none other than Ron Wyden, Oregon's senior U.S. senator. But the lawmaker elected to wait in line and be screened with the little people. That couldn't help but impress.

So did the nononsense security. The fellow conducting the littletoopersonal security check didn't lighten up when I told him I was happily married. Asking him if he was studying to become a proctologist would have also met with a cold stare. Apparently it is mandatory when you join the Secret Service to have your ability to smile surgically removed.

Shortly after 10:00 a.m. that day Air Force One touched down on the Medford airport tarmac. When the most protected aircraft on earth came to a full stop, the president of the United States stepped to the aircraft doorway and waved to the crowd of supporters allowed into the secured area. The crowd, made up of folks who had been hand-selected to attend the event, erupted into cheers at the sight of the biped known as the POTUS by veteran White House hands.

The woman from the White House staff who had called me quickly rounded up the four regional pool journalists, separating us from the rest of the journalistic herd like unruly calves being cut from the drove. We were herded into a white van with tinted windows marked "The White House Press Bus #2."

Minutes later, the two dozen vehicle presidential motorcade sped off on the twelve-mile trip to the Squires Peak fire. Escorted by motorcycle police, the drivers raced en masse through stoplights and stop signs. No other traffic was allowed along the route while we were on it. The VIPs in the group included the governors of four western states, three members of the Oregon congressional delegation, secretaries of Agriculture and the Interior, agency bigwigs and GOP dignitaries.

Albeit short, it was the most remarkable road trip of my life. We sped along, sometimes hitting seventy miles per hour in areas posted for thirty-five mph. We raced though Jacksonville, barreling through the historic hamlet that was filled with both protestors and supporters of the incumbent.

On sidewalks, where you can still see metal rings our ancestors once tied their horses when they came to town, people waved at the racing entourage. All the vehicles in the motorcade had tinted windows. Since they could not see inside the vehicles, they didn't know which vehicle contained the president. Like the rest of the media folk in my vehicle, I waved at a few of the street people. They didn't know me from Adam, of course.

Most of the folks along the route were shouting their support and waving signs. "Bush Kicks Tush," read one banner. Others demonstrated their opposition. "George Warlord Bush," declared one sign. Still others were there just to see history being made.

The dissent may have upset some but I figured motorcade cheers as well as jeers demonstrate a healthy interest in our democracy. Of course, had the majority known they were cheering journalists as well as Bush, there would have been gagging and hurling of projectiles instead.

At the time, none of us knew precisely where we were going. The Secret Service plays its cards very close to its bullet-proof vests. Those protecting the First Lady's hubby did not want anyone disrupting the event. They rightfully suspected there were a few wing nuts in our area, just as there are in any region of the country. OK, maybe the percentage is a bit higher here. But I like to think they are all harmless enough. Of course, I'm not the one responsible for protecting the President of the United States. No matter your political persuasion, no civilized person wants to see anyone in the First Family hurt or worse.

But we did know by then we were bound for the Squires Peak fire which at that point was well on its way to being snuffed out. I had been told our destination would be a ninety-acre site of BLM forestland somewhere off Sterling Creek Road whose stands had been thinned before the fire. But I was amazed when we turned off a little over a mile north of our cabin and headed west on a dirt road that led to Woodrat Mountain, a place where paragliders take a flying leap off the steep mountainside in hopes of soaring over the Applegate Valley. From our cabin, we sometimes see paragliders floating like giant butterflies over the ridge when the weather is favorable.

Bush was taking no flying leap, at least not off the mountain. Shortly after pulling off Sterling Creek Road, we turned south on another dirt road which led us south along a ridge top, stopping just northwest of our cabin. Talk about surreal.

The presidential dog and pony show at the fire site included a hastily erected bleacher for the VIPs. A podium had also been built for the occasion. Apparently no one hears a speech in the woods if a podium isn't there to demonstrate the speech is truly official. The press pressed to get close to the president, while Secret Service agents pressed us back. I felt like I was being carried along, my feet scarcely touching the burned ground. I was truly a fish out of water in the press pool.

The president was wearing boots, cream-colored slacks and a slate-green long sleeve shirt. His shirt sleeves were rolled up, apparently meant to convey the message he was ready to go to work. In his left shirt pocket was a black pen. The executive pen, no doubt.

Yet when he was taken on a short tour of the site, he walked with the assurance of someone who knew his way in a forest. When I told someone later that Bush seemed to be in his element, he remarked that was because the trees couldn't ask questions. He may have been on to something.

While you could not see our cabin from where Bush stood, I could have pointed out its general location below to the commander-in-chief. He did gaze in that direction for a moment, and remarked it was a beautiful area. I felt myself feeling really smug, what with the POTUS's comment. But I was glad the commander-in-chief could not see the toilet in the yard, let alone the partially burned cabin and the banged-up trailer from hell. He probably would have ordered an air strike at what looked like a terrorist training camp.

On most days, you can hear someone firing away with various weapons in the mountains overlooking Sterling Creek, apparently firing at targets or whatever wildlife they flush out of the brush. But there were no gunshots on this day. The sight of so many law enforcement folks no doubt caused some to stay their trigger fingers for twenty-four hours. Good thing. Who knows what kind of havoc would have ensued if a rifle shot, even in the distance, would have shattered the still air.

But all was tranquil. Bush strode a few steps into the forest which appeared to have withstood the blaze, although the forest duff was turned to ash. Two Oregon Department of Forestry firefighters, both dressed in canary-yellow Nomex shirts and forest-green pants, walked up out of the stand. One of the firefighters was Cody Goodnough, the son of Richard, our subcontractor. The president reached out to firmly shake his hand and thank him and other firefighters for their efforts.

Goodnough, the initial attack incident commander on the Squires Peak fire, told the president that the thinned forest slowed the fire's advance.

"It made our job easier as well as safer," the firefighter said.

"We're trying to bring a little common sense," the president told him, introducing a theme that was to be the hall mark of his short visit.\

During the tour, a BLM official had explained to his ultimate boss that the parcel had been thinned by logging its smalldiameter trees in 1996 and 1997, followed by a prescribed burn in 1999. The latter refers to intentionally setting fire to a specific area during times of low fire danger in an effort to remove brush and other vegetation. Because of the thinning, the behavior of the Squire fire changed abruptly when it came to the thinned area, the BLMinator told the president. Instead of raging flames of seventy to one hundred feet, the flames dropped to just a few feet when it entered the thinned parcel, the official added.

During the tour, we visitors did notice the fire appeared to have been less intense in the thinned area. The unthinned region beyond, with skeletal trees and deep ash, appeared to have been heavily burned.

At one point, the president stopped his walking tour to take a few questions from the Fourth Estate. Suddenly, all of us in the press corps were waving an arm and yelling "Mr. President!" as we tried to get his attention. Naturally, he called first on those who were old hands at covering the White House.

One woman asked him about punishing corrupt CEOs; a man wanted to know about the administration's relationship with the president of Egypt. To each, he answered that he would deal with those issues when he returned to D.C.

An arm just off to his left side shot up. A voice that sounded mighty familiar to me addressed the POTUS.

"Mr. President, getting back to the issue of wildfires…," I yelled. It felt like I was having an out of body experience. Yet it also seemed as though

I had been tossing questions to the nation's top political dog all my life.

The man who succeeded George Washington, et al, turned, pointed to me and said, "Yes?"

For once in its decidedly non-baritone existence, my voice didn't flee, although it may have been quavering a little.

"Does the nation have enough money in its coffers to pay for the thinning many feel is necessary to reduce the threat of catastrophic fires in the northwest?" I asked.

I know. It wasn't anything terribly brilliant or even remotely profound. But it was the best I could come up with at the spur of the moment given the fact I never in my wildest journalistic dream s ever thought I would be able to ask the top person in the White House a question. I'm just glad I didn't squeak or become incontinent on the spot. Or both.

"We'll deal with it," he said, adding the funds would have to come from congress. "My job is to make sure it is spent on the right priorities.

"The other thing is there are partnerships we can put together for the benefit of those who care about conservation and those who are employed in the forests," he continued. "If we don't (have the funds), we'll deal with it."

His program would have broad-based support, he predicted.

"It is a balanced approach with recognizing more than one party involved," he said. "We will achieve goals and prevent fires and help the forests."

You will notice that he didn't actually answer my question. You will also correctly suspect that I had an inkling of just what subject would catch his interest. Years of investigative journalism, you see. OK, so any village idiot could have guessed he wasn't there to talk about corruption or the Middle East. He wanted to talk about forest fires. Duh. But there would be no time for a follow up question. He was already moving to the makeshift podium to address the VIPs and tell the press what was on his mind without being asked annoying little questions.

His main message, as it would be in a longer version of the speech given at the Jackson County Expo an hour later, was that common sense needed to be brought to the fore when it came to managing federal forestlands. The problem with that pronouncement, of course, is that one person's version of common sense is another person's nightmare. Everyone wants to reduce the likelihood of a catastrophic fire. But they all have different views on how to achieve that goal.

Most who have studied wildfires agree that today's public forestlands are generally unnaturally overstocked because of more than a century of fire suppression. But that's just the beginning of the debate. There are sticky wickets in the form of management practices, climate change, litigation and other issues that complicate what would otherwise be a simple solution. The timber industry and others blame the environmental community for holding up thinning projects. Many environmentalists say the fault lies largely with past timber cutting practices. They say they only object to harvesting the big trees that are the most fire resistant.

To his credit, Bush seemed to be trying to bring the different factions to the table.

"This isn't a Republican issue or a Democratic issue," he told the group. "Managing our forests is an American issue. It requires an approach that understands there is a difference of opinion, and that we ought to work together to achieve common ground."

He also announced that he was directing federal land-management agencies to begin thinning projects on an emergency basis in critical areas on public forests. Pilot thinning projects that include partnerships involving residents, conservation groups and timber industry representatives ought to be made permanent, he added.

"We haven't had a strategy to clear the forests of builtup brush and densely packed trees that we have seen firsthand here and places around the country," he said. "The catastrophic wildfires killed the oldest trees, those which we long to preserve. They kill just about everything in the soil. They prey upon weakened forests.

"Come out and speak to a firefighter about good commonsense policy and you'll hear what I just said," he added. "Actively managing forests is going to be the centerpiece of this administration."

Then it was back to the motorcade. The drivers were ordered to step on it to get the president to the Jackson County Expo as soon as possible to keep him on schedule. Waved on by motorcycle police, our driver, a local BLM employee, once again shot past stoplights and stop signs.

"That was the first time I've ever driven seventy miles an hour in a thirty-five miles per hour zone," he observed as he pulled into the Expo.

When I drove home late that night, I had a mischievous urge to floor it. Traffic signals and stop signs be damned. But there was that pesky insurance thing to be concerned about, not to mention the emergency room care and the following incarceration, providing I survived. So I drove slowly, reflecting on the surreal day.

ELEVEN

Return of
the Cavemen

WHEN IT COMES TO CRAWLING INTO CONFINED SPACES, I've always been reluctant to venture forth. Not that I am claustrophobic. I just prefer strolling in wide open places where I can breathe deeply. It's just that worming my way through dark, dank holes while struggling to breathe is not my idea of a good time. Anything tighter than Autzen Stadium where the University of Oregon Ducks football team pummels its foes makes me loosen my collar and gasp for air. If it weren't for those pesky tornadoes, Kansas would be the closest place to heaven on earth to me. Nice and open. I suspect the Serengeti in Africa along with the steppes in outer Mongolia also have enough elbow room for a man to breathe deeply.

But the mountain valleys of southern Oregon are my ancestral stomping grounds. I am part of the region, cavemen and all. It is where my mortal remains will fade away to dust. Besides, as you travel through time and keep your eyes and mind open, there are always new discoveries to be made here. It keeps life interesting.

Yet I instinctively procrastinated when it came to investigating an old mining adit on the north side of our property. Located on a south-facing slope amid an unrelenting tangle of trees and brush where rattlesnakes like to stretch out and sun themselves while waiting to sink their fangs into a passing ankle, the horizontal tunnel isn't tall enough for an adult to stand up in without inflicting serious damage.

Less than five feet high, the round adit looks like it was built by Hobbits. The front has also sloughed off a bit, leaving only a hole just large enough for a fairly trim adult to slither through to reach the confining tunnel. When you consider the fact the tunnel could cave in at any moment, coupled with the reptilian critters coiled inside that had snaked in after getting a nice greenish-brown tan on their scaly skin, it wasn't exactly a place that beckoned. Did I mention my deep respect for buzz worms?

To find out more about the old diggings, my plan was to mine the knowledge of Jad D'Allura, a friend who was a longtime science professor at Southern Oregon University in Ashland. The genial geologist and his wife, Pam, also happen to live in the Sterling Creek drainage. I had interviewed him numerous times over the years, and knew him to be exceedingly bright with a penchant for humor. Students spoke highly of his wit and wisdom.

Although he recently retired from full-time teaching at the school after thirty-three years of breaking rocks over the hard heads of college kids, he still teaches a few classes. Before we could take a look at the entrance to what I have taken to calling Dante's Inferno, he had to wrap up a chemistry course he was instructing.

"You picked the only day I'm not committed (though I should be)," he responded in an e-mail to my suggested day for an adit visit. "I will bring my geologic divining rod. If that doesn't work, I can easily make up a story. If all else fails I can do research.

"I assume there are tailings (refuse debris) from the mines?" he added. "I am, of course, dismissing the Anthropocene debris left from the recent work in progress."

Following a quick consultation with Mr. Webster, I discovered the A-word was referring to debris left during the current geological age, particularly the period when human activity has been the dominant influence on the land. He was, of course, further referring to debris left from what I had told him was our work in progress. Told you he was no cave-dwelling troglodyte.

Shortly after we bought the place, in a moment of insanity, I had also mentioned the adit to Damian Mann, a writing buddy doing hard time at an adjacent cubicle while I was at the paper. I told him about having peered inside the adit.

"Now I understand what Dante was all worked up about," I said. "I swear I could hear the snakes hissing at me. The rock walls of the old mine look like they could cave in at any moment. It gave me the willies just standing outside the entrance."

With his journalistically-honed selective hearing, he did not register my concerns about safety or the strong possibility of fanged inhabitants lurking within. All he heard was "old mine." He was already framing a story in his mind about lost treasure found in the historic prospecting digs.

"There could be gold in there," he said. "Remember, there was the big gold mine just across the stream from your place. Your cabin is probably sitting on a vast horde of precious metals. You need to get off your duff and check this old mine out."

"It's not safe to go in there," I reiterated. "The very thought of being inside that cavern scares the crap out of me."

"Grow a backbone, for crimony's sakes," he responded. "Buck up. I'll be right there beside you so you won't be scared and run home to mommy."

There are a few things you should know about our man Mann. Born in England of Irish parents, he is well traveled, speaks French like a native and appreciates fine food. He also happens to be an award-winning journalist, a brilliant chap adept at breaking down complex issues into digestible fodder.

But his main mission in life is to be a jokester who enjoys verbal sword play. As a result, we continually banter back and forth in what we like to think is scintillating repartee. Some with more discriminating minds may refer to it as drivel. Since his verbal pen is a little sharper than mine, I normally end up wanting to strangle the big kid in him. The remaining adult Mann would be unfortunate collateral damage.

"Like the bumper sticker says, 'Getter done,'" he announced upon arriving at our cabin one morning looking like a seasoned spelunker, complete with a miner's lamp slightly askew on his head. "Let's go do some serious caving. Times a'wasting.."

Standing 6′4″ feet tall, he could be a mite large to squeeze into a Hobbit hole, I suggested to him.

"If you get stuck in there, I'm leaving you behind," I added. "Your marker will read, 'Here lies a maroon.' I'll charge admission for people to see your bony feet sticking up out of the ground."

"It will have to be a big marker because it will say, 'Here lies two maroons too dumb to stay out of old mines,'" Maureen interjected. "I don't want to sound like a nag but I'm going to say it one last time: it is beyond stupid to go in there. So don't. Both of you know better. Good grief, it's like having two kids around when you two get together."

"He started it," I protested.

"Did not. He hit me first," came the response from the other large child.

But we assured Maureen we were merely going to reconnoiter the area. With perfectly solemn faces, we somberly pledged not to do anything really stupid, certainly nothing crazy like going into the adit. Perish the thought. We were lying through our teeth, of course.

"We'll use our heads," I added for good measure.

"That's what concerns me," she said, shaking hers.

We hiked the eighth of a mile from the cabin up to the adit. A small mound of tailings can be seen just below the opening. Right above it, there is a large pine tree, one which took root after the hardrock miners threw down their picks and left. I couldn't help wonder how much the pine weighed as it pushed down on the adit.

"That entrance is even smaller than I remembered," I said, noticing my collar suddenly seemed a little tight. "It's really clammy today. Or is it hot? God, I need some air."

"What a wuss," he countered. "It's just a little hole."

"That's precisely the problem," I observed. "And it seems to be shrinking."

We sat there on the tailings for a while, staring at the entrance. The rock over the mouth of the adit looked a little loose. I tossed a little rock at the wall, causing a little landslide.

"It looks like it could cave in at any moment," I said. "If it weren't for the worms holding hands, it would have collapsed by now. Why do I ever listen to you?"

"Because you look up to your wiser elder," said the would-be caver who just happens to be a couple of years younger than yours truly. "You realize you are in the presence of a superior mind so you naturally capitulate."

Normally, he would be grinning while ribbing me. Yet his comment was expressed with a serious look as he studied the entrance to the cavern. Sensing he wasn't real keen on entering the adit, I pounced.

"What happened to keeping that stiff upper lip you Brits are famous for?" I asked with a vicious smirk. "Or is life in the colonies a little too tough for some scheisskopfs?"

"For your edification, I'm of Irish descent and scheisskopf is German," he said. "I'm just trying to figure out the best way for you to get down in there. I don't want to have to drag you out after you break a leg. Have to shoot you like they did horses in the old West."

Our verbal fisticuffs died again as we sat there in the tomb-like air. An open grave would be more inviting than the entrance. A turkey vulture floated over, optimistically watching us. The air was stifling hot, even in the shade.

"Well, hell, it'll at least be cool in there," I said, standing up. "Let's get it over with."

"Now you're talking," he said. "We can take a little peek, although we had better not tell Mo. It would be a real shame if you did something idiotic to cause her not to invite me over for dinner any more. I did promise her I would try to keep you out of harm's way. As long as it didn't jeopardize my safety, of course."

"Yeah, right," I said. "When it comes to keeping information away from Maureen, we're dead meat. She is better at winkling information out of people than a veteran journalist. I'm just going to spill the beans and blame you."

He suggested I go first, alleging his height made it difficult for him to move swiftly in the cramped interior should the need arise.

"Besides, you can squeeze in there better than I can," he said. "If everything goes south, I'll write down your last words so choose them carefully. Wouldn't want anyone to remember you as a babbling idiot."

"Write this down: I'm going to strangle you with my bare hands if I get out of here," I said. "Slowly, very slowly. I'm not worried about a jury of my peers. They would unanimously agree it was justifiable homicide."

Yet I somehow summoned the courage—otherwise known as insanity, depending on your responsibility quotient—to enter the portal. You will remember that when Alice slid down the hole to Wonderland, she discovered a fantastical world that included a Mad Hatter and a rabidly late rabbit, not to mention a vicious playing card with a penchant for lopping off heads. But I would remind you she did not live along Sterling Creek, although there may have been some during the moonshine days of Prohibition who frequently spoke with animals when they guzzled a bad batch. Come to think of it, there could have even been encounters with the wicked queen of hearts or an occasional March Hare during the psychedelic '60s.

The hole into the adit did not led to a Wonderland, despite the fact Oregon once had license plates declaring it the Pacific Wonderland. The cavern was as cold and silent as a tomb. The floor was flat with broken pieces of rock, ideal for accommodating a coffin. The temperature was as cool as the room where they keep the bodies at your neighborhood morgue. I involuntarily shivered as I tried to get the thought out of my mind.

"Step back—you're blocking my escape route," I snarled at Tweedledum, alias Damian, who was peering down into the entrance. "I want all the light I can get. And quit breathing. You're using up all the air."

I peered down the tunnel with my flashlight. Contrary to my wild imagination, there were no skeletons of long-dead miners inside, at least none near the entrance. While that brought some relief, the fact there was no supporting timbers gave me pause. True, the timbers would likely have started rotting by now, but they would have least demonstrated a good faith effort by the men who toiled with pick and shovel more than a century ago.

"This is not safe at all," I whispered. "They didn't even try to reinforce the walls."

"Maybe some of them tried but they didn't make it out," Damian said in an equally hushed tone. "Perchance there are body parts back there still, the skin little more than dry parchment. At night, you can probably hear their tortured souls wailing in the cave."

"Your brain is dry parchment," I muttered as I continued checking out the tunnel with the light.

At that point, I was about ten feet from the entrance. The tunnel seemed to continue largely on a horizontal plane about 100 feet back to the northeast, only to slough off at the end. Before ending in a pile of rubble, it took a slight twist to the east.

By focusing on the rocks under my knees and not dwelling on collapsing caves, rattlesnakes or poisonous gases, I maintained a sort of controlled panic as I inched along on my knees. I even found some areas in the mine somewhat fascinating, albeit in the same sick way a shivering victim on the Titanic may have found the layout of the deck chairs oddly engaging that ghastly night. Mental digressions are our friends when facing life's little horrors.

"This is interesting in an eerie way," I told Damian. "Look. You can see where they were digging into likely spots here and there."

There was no answer. I glanced behind me. He had entered the tunnel but was no more four feet inside the entrance. There he sat, his back against the west wall, watching my progress.

"I didn't want to trouble you but I get a little touch of claustrophobia now and then," he said. "I've presently got a wee bit. So I'll just sit this one out. It's nothing for you to worry about. Just let me know what you find in the back."

"You gotta be kidding," I said through clinched teeth. "You are the one who wanted to explore this hole in the first place. You lowlife piece of…"

"Yeah, yeah. Just check it out," he responded with a raised voice. "Pick me up a couple of nice nuggets while you are there."

"Don't yell," I hissed. "You'll start an avalanche."

"That's only in snow country," he corrected me. "It is referred to as a cave in when rocks crush you to death in a collapsed tunnel. But the end results are precisely the same."

I had enough repartee. I decided to hurry along and ignore Damian's smart ass humor. I just wanted to check it out, and get back to the surface as quickly as possible.

Strangely, his courage seemed to grow the farther back I crawled.

"Get a move on," he said. "I'm curious about what is back there."

After hurling blasphemes over my shoulder, I crawled forward to a point as far as I dared go. I was now some twenty feet from where the ceiling had fallen in, although that was likely near the spot where the digging had stopped. It appeared the miners had started to dig another tunnel toward the northwest, perhaps lured by some come-hither rock. Those who dug the adit either worked on their knees or were gravity challenged. Even if you were a Hobbit, you wouldn't have room to swing a pick over your head. At best, the work would have been extremely difficult as well as dangerous.

But there were no telltale signs of rich rewards for their hard work. The only rock I could see was the brownish-gray material that encased the entire adit. There was no thick vein of quartz containing gleaming gold or silver metal. It was apparently a probing mine that produced no riches.

My curiosity satisfied for the moment, I turned around and looked back down the adit. The entrance was now just a pinpoint of light which I could easily block out with the end of my thumb. The full dawning of just how stupidly dangerous my predicament was hit me like the morning sun popping up over the mountains. These walls and ceiling may have been made of stone but it was broken, fractured stone. The adit could collapse any moment. Mission over, I started crawling double time toward the distant light.

Unfortunately, my spelunking buddy, apparently having gotten over his touch of claustrophobia, was getting bored. He decided to start inspecting the adit roof. Given his height and Abe Lincoln arms, he could easily reach the top of the tunnel while sitting down.

"Hey, check this out," he yelled. "This rock breaks away from the ceiling real easy. Real crumbly stuff."

Just what I said to dissuade him of his mischief making need not be repeated here. As I watched chunks of rock fall from the ceiling, I reached deep for the foulest words I could muster, summoning them from the ghosts of Marine Corps drill instructors, loggers and Kerby urchins from the 1960s. I like to think I would have made them all enormously proud.

With me yelling incoherently while scrambling along the cavern floor, Damian naturally assumed the ceiling was caving in. He bailed out of the hole and into the sunlight. Scuttling along like a crab, I popped out only seconds behind him.

"Don't ever, ever do that again," I gasped as I flopped out on the ground in the open air. "I thought I was a goner."

He didn't hear a word. He was nearly in convulsions. But it wasn't a grand mal.

"That was priceless," he said after he stopped chortling and caught his breath. "It was the first time I ever saw anyone run on all fours. You were actually sprinting on your hands and knees. Talk about a Kodak moment."

"I thought the ceiling was giving away," I said as I looked up at the wide-open blue sky. "God, what a hideous feeling."

The sun may have felt stifling hot before we entered the adit but now it seemed warm and welcoming. The turkey vulture was gone, apparently having concluded there was no meal about to start slow cooking on the hillside below where it could later be pecked apart like pulled pork at a Southern barbecue.

"You aren't right about much but maybe you are on to something about not letting Maureen know about this little episode," I said after resting for a while. "We don't have to lie but we certainly don't have to mention that I crawled back in there. It'll just make her worry about our sanity."

"You mean about your sanity," he said. "Actually, I'm thinking now that it would be a shame not to be able to share such a great story. Inquiring minds want to know about strange people doing goofy things. It was as though you had the hounds of the Baskervilles on your tail. Too bad they don't have a crawling event in the Olympics. You would be a gold medalist."

He started guffawing again, stopping only when he had a coughing fit. When he calmed down, he put our experience in perspective in his unique way.

"In Latin, you just had what is known as a '*memento mori*,' " he said. "That means to remember that you must die at some point. It's a reminder of our own mortality. Maybe next time you will know better than to do something that dumb."

If I had not been so happy to be on the earth and not in it, I would have reached for a large rock to brain him. But the profound relief of being once again in the open air stayed my hand. Perhaps I did have a memento mori, although the unpremeditated rock-on-head urge probably also died because I am quite aware that prison cells are rather confined spaces, a lenient judge and jury notwithstanding.

While I had no intention of ever venturing back inside the cavern, I still intended to discover what I could about the mine and the mineral within.

"I'm never going in there again, but I'm going to find out more about what drew miners up here," I said. "However, the next time I come up here it will be with someone who knows about rocks. And one who happens to be an adult."

He ignored the jibe.

"Yes, as your behavior today demonstrates, you do need a babysitter," he replied.

I figured that Professor D'Allura, having spent more than three decades teaching would-be rock scientists at the college level, may be able to pound a little information into my thick skull. There was no question the educator who lives within a rifle shot of our cabin knew a lot about the earth upon which we live. The Indiana native had earned his science degrees, including a doctorate, at the University of California Davis.

But I was curious how he came by his moniker.

"They were my dad's initials," he said in response to my inquiry as we hiked up to the adit. "His name was Joseph Anthony D'Allura. When he was a first lieutenant in the U.S. Army Air Corps stationed in Iceland during World War II, he became known as 'Jad.' So that's what my parents named me."

As we neared the mine, he addressed the nomenclature of the earth beneath our feet.

"This whole area is underlain by what is called the 'Applegate group,' " he said as we made our way through thick manzanita brush to the mound of tailings below the adit. "Jurassic in age, it represents primarily ocean deposits, things that are washed off the continent. That would be the sands and the silts and the muds, things like that. They were deposited, buried, then metamorphosed—changed by the heat and the pressure.

"By the way, the rocks in our area haven't been age dated but ones near Applegate reservoir have a 173 million year old age," he added, noting that date was also a reasonable assumption for the rocks upon which we stood.

I started to tell him I knew all about that period, having seen the Jurassic Park movie several times. But I didn't know how sensitive my field instructor was to sophomoric humor. I have this theory that science professors develop a mental shield to protect themselves from juvenile jokes. They actually become deaf to students cracking wise. My theory holds that the shield eventually wears thin after decades of being bombarded by stupid comments and jokes with pimples still on them. According to my theory, one goofy observation eventually breaks through the shield, allowing its silly cousins to rush through and overwhelm the poor pedagogue. That's when the now mad professor comes at you, swinging a rock hammer, one just like the one Jad was clinching. So I nodded as though I had at least a dim idea of what he was talking about.

Actually, I did have a slight clue, having recently read about ichthyosaurs and other curious-looking creatures that evolved during the Jurassic epoch which began some 200 million years ago, give or take. I started to wonder aloud if it made a dinosaur sore to be saddled with the first name of ichthyo. But my theory and the sight of the rock hammer reminded me the shield could be worn thin after having been battered for more than thirty years in the collegiate classroom.

The professor picked up a rock, broke it with his hammer and held the broken piece to his nose. The geology class had resumed without any bloody incident which a tall English bloke of Irish descent would have written up in stellar journalistic prose.

"Quite often, when there is a mine with iron pyrite and you whack the rock, you get a little bit of a sulphur smell," Jad said, referring to what is commonly known as fool's gold. "But there is none of that here."

Catching my quizzical look, he noted that geologists are curious creatures who like to use all their senses when trying to solve a rock puzzle.

"We do all kinds of weird things," he said. "Every once in a while, you'll even see a geologist put a rock in his mouth and start chewing it. It's not because of the nutrient value. We are trying to determine the grain size. So if you see someone doing weird things along the side of the road, it's either a geologist or an escapee from a mental institution."

"Or perhaps it is one and the same," I offered, trying to help.

"Could be both," he agreed. "Yeah, that is always a possibility."

That's when it dawned on me that some really smart professors back up their adolescent joke shield with an offense that goes straight for the juvenile jugular. The soundness of my revised dumb-joke shield theory gained gravitas when he asked me if I knew how the name "adit" came about. No idea, I replied.

"When you are going after gold, you have to dig a hole to get 'ad it,' "he said with a straight face. He had obviously dug deep into the joke store tailings for that little nugget, proving once again that a good defense is a good offense. Having been bested, my prepubescent jokes slunk away to pout in my mental adit, refusing to come out for the rest of the day.

"Now, if we take a look at this stuff, a lot of it will be slatey," Jad said as he continued the class. "You can see it has fracturing developing in it that is the result of all that pressure. That pressure also generates these rocks. Some people thought there was a lot of volcanism but there really isn't. We are dealing with something that is from offshore deposits, from ancient seas."

That makes it some of the older rocks found in the region, he noted.

"But this is definitely a prospect," he said of the old dig. "At this point, we don't know what kind of metal they were looking for. There is copper in this area. There isn't much silver but there is gold. There is certainly the bedrock stuff from which the Sterling Mine derived a lot of its gold."

Of course, that was down in the bottom of the Sterling Creek drainage, not on a baking side hill a quarter of a mile as the crow flies from the mother lode.

He moved a little closer to study the broken rock forming a dome over the entrance.

"These fractures here suggest this thing has been put under pressure," he reiterated. "Essentially, that pressure develops the fractures. That is very unstable rock. You don't want to go into something like this. You never know when it might collapse."

It was about that time I confessed my misguided adventure into the mine. He looked at me for a moment, perhaps wondering if I was any sharper than the dull rock he had picked up.

"Well, you don't want to go in there again," he said, apparently concluding I was at least capable of learning. "It is definitely not safe. It's deteriorating. Especially near the entrance where you are at the surface and there is more weathering going on."

He poked around the tailings for a while, searching for anything that would give him insight into what drew the miners to the mountainside. Pulling out a loupe to magnify a rock sample he had chipped, he found something that caught his attention.

"See this really faint banding in through here?" he asked, using a finger nail to trace it along. "That's the original bedding. I can tell because there is a little grain size difference.

"The reason it is greenish is in the metamorphic environment there is, quite often, very little oxygen in the water," he continued. "So you get reduced iron. That produces the greenish color. You don't get the red or orange color you would have with iron oxidized at the earth's surface."

Like a detective in search of clues, he kept poring over the debris dug out of the earth back when you couldn't throw a rock without hitting a miner. Considering the rock is 173 million years old, it occurred to me that the 19th Century dig was but a second in time ago when it came to the geological clock. I said as much.

The professor nodded, knowing that at least a portion of his lesson was sinking into my cranium.

"Now, if you look closely at this rock, the way it fractured, you will see it has a lot of really fine silica," he said. "It's like quartz, but it doesn't have the structure of quartz. A lot of older miners looked for quartz when they were trying to find gold."

Yet quartz is not always an indicator of gold, he cautioned.

"It's interesting that, when these rocks are buried at greater depths, quartz, which is so hard, is mobilized in water under higher pressure and increased temperatures," he explained. "When that happens, it moves into cracks. Unless the material being dissolved contains precious metals like gold, then all you get is barren quartz veins.

"A lot of the quartz veins have nothing in them because the other rock has been what we call 'sweated' out," he added. "Having said that, other quartz veins associated with volcanism will sometimes carry gold. But, as I mentioned earlier, there is not a lot of submarine volcanism in this area."

I felt like a long distance runner, trying to keep pace with someone who was miles ahead of me intellectually. But I gathered correctly that submarine volcanism referred to an underwater eruption. I was a little hazy on the rest.

He gave me a few minutes to catch up mentally, then returned to the subject of quartz and miners.

"A lot of the old miners in the 1800s would find quartz and go for it, hoping they would find something," he reiterated. "Some people still believe that if you find quartz, there has to be gold. But that is just not always the case."

In fact, the quartz we found around the adit contained no dull glint of gold. Not even a trace.

"The quartz here has been sweated out," he said as he continued to check out rock samples with his hand lens. "This quartz was in a crack. You can see the elongated quartz crystals there. Usually, doing metamorphism, the rocks are moving and groaning, kind of like an old person getting out of bed in the morning."

Now he was speaking my language, one I would be grunting upon awakening the following morning, thanks to the hike on the mountain.

"The cracks will sometimes open up," he said. "When you have this water under high pressure, it goes right into the crack. And whatever it is carrying is precipitated there."

While gold miners of old may had neither the latest gadgets nor scientific knowledge to help them in their quest, they were no dummies, he stressed. They were quick studies when it came to the land they were working, he said.

"Miners were very smart," he said of their ability to find precious metals. "Don't forget. They had to make a living out of what they did. They had to work to eat. They either had to do this or turn to highway robbery."

Indeed, there was no social safety net back when miners first came in search of riches in what is now Southwestern Oregon and Northwestern California. They were swinging picks to break rocks to pay for a roof over their heads and for regular meals. Their very survival depended on how well they could read rocks, he noted.

"Hard rock mining like this is much harder than placer mining," he said. "When you think about removing all the overburden with a pick and shovel, that was hard, hard work."

Down at the Sterling placer mine, water was used to power hydraulic giants which removed the overburden, he observed, referring to the tons of overlaying gravel.

"The Sterling Mine was a tremendous operation," he said. "But those old monitors they used were horribly destructive to the environment."

He noted the miners, largely with the help of Chinese immigrants, dug what was known as the roughly twenty-six-mile Sterling Ditch from high in the Little Applegate River drainage to produce a hydrologic head to run the monitors, also called "giants."

"They were like nozzles on a huge garden hose to wash the overburden away," he added. "Tons of that gravel was washed into sluices where the gold was highgraded. Incidentally, most of the bedrock mines cost more to operate than the gold they extracted."

We hiked up the hill to get above the adit, and found a trench about 75 feet long running roughly perpendicular to the tunnel.

"They saw something that excited them, prompting them to dig this trench," he said. "This was a lot of work with a pick. This looks to me that it was hand carved. There were guys here with picks and shovels, digging around. But what they found on the surface that caused them to get excited is a mystery to me. This rock looks pretty barren."

After puttering around the trench for a bit, we hiked down past the adit to a smaller trench, one which had an extremely small hole bored into the earth on the northwest end of the trench. It was too small to be described as an adit, at least without digging into the hillside to see if it led to another tunnel. Digging into that hole was not, nor will it ever be, on the agenda, however.

If one were to dig four feet or so beneath us, we would likely hit bedrock, Jad surmised. He stood in the trench, studying the rock.

"This rock here shows where the quartz, over time, has moved into the cracks in the rock itself," he said, using his rock pick to point out a faint light-colored line in the darker material. "See that irregular fracture that occurred here? That is typical of the silica-saturated rock throughout this area."

It was there he found something that gave him an insight into what may have brought miners to the site.

"That green is a secondary copper carbonate," he said of a rock he had broken with his hammer. "They may have been going for copper here. Of course, they may have accidentally run across it. This is leaking out of the rock. I'm not exactly sure what this copper mineral is. I bet it will effervesce with hydrochloric acid."

Later, he would conduct a little research on the hard rock mines in the area. In addition to the Sterling mine, there were several small gold prospects in the area, both placer and hard rock mining. He found no copper mines in the vicinity.

It could be the time when the adit on our property was dug that holds the biggest clue to what prompted miners to dig in the area, he said.

"Those guys were probably just trying to find the mother lode," he said of the period when the hills were teeming with hungry miners searching for gold. "Now this is just a wild ass guess but it may have been they had found gold somewhere else that was associated with this rock with a greenish color. Maybe that's what drove them."

Miners often followed their gut instinct once they found a mineral associated with gold, he added. For instance, miners in Gold Hill, a historic community bordering the Rogue River, often looked for oxidized or decomposed rock from an ore and mineral deposit, he observed.

"Up in Gold Hill, they find gossan—material weathered out of the rocks which leave behind the iron oxides which come from pyrite," he explained. "That comes from iron pyrite which is iron sulfide. Old miners called it 'iron cap.' When they saw that, they went after it because iron pyrite, even though it is known as 'fool's gold,' is sometimes associated with precious metals."

A seasoned prospector could read the gossan like a book and determine the type of mineralization likely waiting below, he noted.

In an email following our field trip, he expanded on some of the points he had made while we were at the adit. He didn't mind stepping into the schist I was curious about.

"There isn't much schist on your property but there is what geologists call semischist (sort of a poor stepchild of schist)," he reported. "Schist has parallel layers with notable mica flakes that can be seen with the naked eye. Semischist has much finer grains than schist but can be seen with a squinty Popeye eye; slate has no such visible grains. So there is a gradation from slate through semischist to schist."

Much of what we found was argillite, fine-grained rock with crude fracturing that forms diamond shapes, he explained.

"That's what we saw at the mine," he continued. "There the argillite was dark gray to black caused by lots of carbon (that was likely organic critters or seagrowing vegetation). The greenish colored rock with specks of crystals in it we call green schist even though it isn't really schist (go figure) and likely represents altered marine volcanic tuff (ash) or ironbearing sediment washed into the ocean to settle slowly like floating dandelion seeds to the bottom.

"That's more than you wanted to know but I just can't turn off the teacher in me," he concluded.

Actually, he had provided the mother lode of information I had hoped for. I came away with a deeper appreciation for the adit as well as for those who dug it. The knowledge the rocks under our feet were part of a sea bed back when time was an infant is also a sobering reminder of how fleeting our lives truly are. And knowing we have neighbors who are brilliant, considerate and humorous is a reminder of how fortunate we are to live in the Applegate Valley.

Of course, it was also nice to know we were not in deep schist. Not even deep semi-schist.

TWELVE

Misery Whips, Drawknives and Ditch Diggers

W HILE DISMANTLING THE OLD STAND-ALONE GARAGE we discovered several antique tools buried in the debris, including a battered miner's pick which conceivably could have been employed to dig the two adits overlooking our cabin. Just looking at it made me tired. The miner had bludgeoned it against rocks until the heavy steel points were battered down to within a few inches of where the handle once was. During the early days of mining along Sterling Creek, a pick was a blunt weapon wielded by men with rawhide arms made strong by digging among rocks for a living.

If the pick head could talk, it would have an interesting tale to tell of the life and times of the region. Judging from the irregularity of its shape, it was forged by a blacksmith. This was no wimpy factory product. It had been pounded into shape by fire and brute force. Folks with knowledge of mining who have seen the old pick surmise it was used for hard rock mining. Since we had no prison farms with convicts breaking rocks in the vicinity, mining was the likely culprit.

Hard rock mining with a pick and shovel would have been exhausting work. Power tools weren't around to make the job easier. The dream of bellying up to the bar in the Sterlingville saloon for a cool beer after a long day of hard labor probably kept many a young man moiling in the rocky earth.

The pick's story will never be told, of course. While we may have more conjectures than a miner's hound dog has fleas, its past remains as silent as the adits. We could only add it to the growing number of curious artifacts we've found around the old place.

The old eight-foot-long crosscut saw that daughter Derra, then a college student, discovered buried alongside the southern wall of the garage also had a story to tell. Referred to as a misery whip by early-day loggers, it still had all its long teeth, albeit the metal incisors were a bit rusty.

Studying it, I had an inspiration. If we could find a couple of old handles for the saw, we could try it out on a log we planned to buck up for firewood, I told Maureen.

"It'll be fun," I said. "We'll make it sing. We'll be like loggers of old."

"Every old logger I've ever seen was a little stove up," she said. "I don't think their life was all that much fun. A lot of them also had missing limbs. Besides, where are you going to find some old handles for it?"

She was spot on regarding veteran loggers as well as the old handles. My dad had lost his leg in a logging accident. So did the father of one of my best childhood chums. And I had set enough chokers in the logging woods to know logging was a tough occupation where catastrophic accidents were waiting to befall anyone who let his guard down. As for the handles, we could buy new wooden ones via the internet. But that seems like cheating. Only old handles that had been gripped by calloused hands would do. So I agreed to shelve the idea, although it kept sawing away in the back of my mind.

What led us to cracking the whip was an elderly gentleman in Medford named Richard Powers who shared my interest in antique tools. When I told him about the old saw, the retired building contractor got an excited gleam in his eye.

"I've got an old pair of handles for that saw," he said. "But it might take a while before I can locate them."

The following year, long after I had forgotten about his saw handles, he called.

"I finally found the old saw handles I told you about," he said. "I was almost standing on top of them when we were talking about them. I just didn't see 'em. They're yours if you still want them."

To some folks, the old wooden handles would have looked like so much junk. After all, they were simply ancient pieces of wood with some rusting hardware attached. Most people would have chucked them into the garbage without a second thought.

But I couldn't have been more tickled. Not only were the handles old but they had come from a ranch that Richard's father bought in the Applegate Valley in 1936, according to the octogenarian. In fact, they were able to cut enough firewood on the property to pay for the land, he added.

Turns out Richard was an aficionado of old handsaws. As one who appreciates hand tools that have weathered the ages, he had a collection of thirty-five handsaws. However, the stump of a ring finger on his left hand attested to the fact he used power tools while in the building trade. The stump was the result of his breaking in one of the first circular power saws on the market, observed the Navy veteran. Ouch. Yet he was one you knew wasn't going to let something like a little amputation slow him down.

The human stumps I've seen over the years have made me gravitate toward people-powered cutting tools whenever feasible, although I do use a chainsaw and a table saw frequently. We have a circular saw but I only deploy that feisty little number when no other tool will do the job. I'm fond of my digits.

I also like working with wood. When King Tut's treasures made their first visit to the New World in the mid-1970s, I stood for an hour in front of his 3,000yearold chair trying to figure out how the ancient Egyptian sawyers fashioned it out of hand tools. Those folks living along the Nile 1,000 years B.C. were skilled craftsmen. I'm guessing most of them had the appropriate number of digits.

Back when I watched TV, my idea of time well spent was watching PBS'

"The Woodwright's Shop," the one featuring the fellow who worked with nothing but peoplepowered tools. Yankee ingenuity seemed to flow more readily back in the day when we didn't have power tools to do the job. Perhaps slowing down a bit inspires creativity.

The vintage handles Richard gave us reflected that ingenuity. They are equipped with what are known as a pinstyle design with a finger guard and a groove to accept the end of the saw blade. Two steel flanges saddle each side of the wooden handle. A halfinch diameter bolt passing through a hole in the wooden handle is tightened by a wing nut.

It took only a few minutes to attach the handles to our old saw. They fit perfectly. I liked the fact the wing of one nut had broken off, evidence of years of use in the Applegate country. Like the old pick, it had survived its share of hard labor.

The literature I dug up on old misery whips indicates ours is a bucking saw with a straight back, not a felling saw with its telltale tapered ends. A bucking saw was often used by one person, resulting in a thicker blade that won't bend easily when pushed. It also weighs more than a felling saw. In this case, weight is an asset to the poor sap working by his or her lonesome.

Our saw has what is called a lance tooth pattern. Picture an army of small Klingon blades lined up in a row to do battle.

Although the saw is a bit rusty, it appears the teeth were sharpened before the tool was left to rust in the old garage decades ago. They needed to bite wood.

"We have to try it out before putting it back into retirement," I told Maureen. "This is a bucking saw. It needs to buck wood."

"I'm not sure how much wood a bucking saw can buck if its teeth are old and rusty, bucky," she replied.

"Aw, come on," I insisted. "It'll be fun. Let's make it sing."

She sighed and her eyebrows dipped a bit but she agreed to humor me. That's why the sound of steel teeth rasping across the grain filled our woods one Sunday afternoon. It sounded like a beaver grating his buck teeth against the grain of a tree. No doubt the sound had not been heard in those woods for decades.

A visitor that day would have found no toothy beaver, only Maureen and

I pushing and pulling the old crosscut saw across a 20inch diameter fir log we were bucking up for firewood. Admittedly, I had cheated a little by cutting down the old snag with a chainsaw before we brought out the crosscut. Even this old fool had his limits.

And those limits were quickly met as we pushed and pulled the old saw across the log. With each pull, a bit of the hubris I had that I could make the old saw sing fell away like the sawdust spit out by the old saw. Suffice it to say the saw did not exactly sing. It was more of a lament, a funeral dirge of wailing and moaning, most of which was emanating from me.

That afternoon, I gained an intimate knowledge of why they called them misery whips. Your back aches. Your arms feel like lead weights. Sweat flows from every pore.

A half hour of the sweaty work more than satisfied my masochistic curiosity. My respect for those who wielded the old saws climbed with each exhausting minute. The whip had whipped me but good. I sat down heavily on the hillside, and fell back against the cool soft earth.

"OK, it's a misery whip—I get it," I gasped after catching my breath. "Let's call it a day. I'm about to drop."

"Don't be such a baby," Maureen said. "This is fun. Get off your duff and let's make this misery whip sing."

I groaned and rolled over to look up at her, ready to beg for mercy. That's when I saw her big grin.

"Got ya," she said as she flopped down beside me. "This is beyond exhausting. I'm ready to go home and collapse."

The old misery whip is now a conversation piece hanging under the gable roof high over the cabin's deck. We deployed our tall extension ladder to place it out of our reach so we wouldn't ever be tempted to whip it out again. But I love the looks of the old saw with its handles, all of which had bucked wood in the Applegate country, including one small log on Gilson Gulch early in the 21st Century. It gives one a sense of satisfaction, knowing it had been on the front lines. But there was a deep contentment in knowing that we will never ever wrap our fingers around those damn saw handles again.

Yet we weren't through working on logs with old hand tools. Our next antique weapon was a drawknife, a tool also known to make brutes whimper. It is basically a knife with handles at each end. Back in the dark ages, when the headsman's ax was too dull for a beheading, a drawknife could conceivably have been employed to do the job, although the process would not have been very tidy. That was before they became refined and invented the guillotine, of course.

Chris and Richard hauled twenty-four dry fir logs to the job site in July of 2002 and promptly announced the trunks had to be peeled with drawknives. I should have known that something was amiss since both were grinning. Those big kidders.

These were logs which would replace those burned by the cabin fire. They weren't large trunks, the biggest being only about ten inches in diameter. The longest logs would be used for four beams measuring a little over twenty-four feet. Those beams would tie in the north and south walls in what we refer to as the living room, although some pretentious types would sniff and insist that it be called the great room. But that moniker seems a little ostentatious to us. There are also another six beams over the kitchen and six log uprights holding up the ridge of the roof. Add the five log beams in the guest bedroom, along with the log handrail and two uprights for the stairs, and every log we peeled was well used.

But making them buck naked was a chore. The bark from a green log apparently peels rather easily, although I've never had the pleasure of debarking a green one. However, cured logs were necessary because green wood often twists and wriggles out of shape as it dries out. Green logs installed in the cabin would have looked like they had been on a drunken binge. In hindsight, that may not have been as bad as the alternative.

The contractors, still grinning, handed us two old drawknives to use on the logs. One was fairly large; the other was relatively small. Presumably, this would allow the user to attack different size logs. For reasons I could never fully fathom, Maureen also bought a new drawknife.

"You never know when you might need one of these to commit a felonious but necessary act to silence someone's sophomoric comments," she said cheerfully. Even now, I can't look at a drawknife without getting nervous.

Chris added yet another ancient tool to our growing arsenal of log-assaulting weapons. It looked like an old baseball bat with a particularly wicked blade at the end. A childhood chum and self-described ruffian would have referred to it as an equalizer.

"That's called a slick—it's a chisel that boat builders use," Chris explained. "My dad worked as a boat builder for a while."

It resembled something a flenser would employed aboard the Pequod. A flenser? That was the fellow who sliced whale blubber for a living back when Herman Melville sent Captain Ahab chasing after Moby Dick. This was a time when Starbuck was the whaling ship's first mate, not a place where baristas served coffee. Flensing is one of those jobs that would have made strong-willed bipeds blubber, even those of us who have munched on muktuk. Fermented whale skin smells and tastes nastier than your worst fears, by the way.

While Maureen had been reluctant to try out the misery whip, she was gung ho when it came to the drawknives. I whined a little about the thought of laboring under the July sun.

"Come on, where's your pioneering spirit?" Maureen demanded to know.

"Spirited away by Grandpa Jonas," I replied of my Applegate Valley homesteading ancestor.

Yet I imagine that my paternal grandfather, who was known as a mad dog worker, drew more than a few knives over logs in his time. Perhaps using a drawknife would help bind a family fragmented by time and space. Moreover, despite the oppressive heat, I was also a little curious about the prospect of trying out the old implements, a la the pioneers.

But when I mentioned it to a friend at the Tribune, he said the only way he would try peeling a dry log in July is if a hulking figure wearing a black mask and holding a long whip stood over him. In Maureen's defense, I quickly countered that the petite lady wasn't into masks and whips. But it was disconcerting the way she had taken to hefting the slick.

"Just getting the feeling for it," she said sweetly.

Just the same, I decided to put my back into the drawknife. So did Derra, the college kid home for the summer. You may have noticed the finder of the misery whip made sure she wasn't around when we tried out that tool. She wasn't an honor student for nothing.

For those of you who haven't drawn a knife to do grievously bodily harm to a log, a drawknife has wooden handles at each end much the same as a misery whip. You lay the eighteen-inch long blade on the log and pull the handles toward you.

In theory, it is supposed to slide down into the bark to the cambium layer, neatly removing the bark. It does work surprisingly well, until it does knot, er, not. Every time you hit an area where a limb grew out of the trunk, it was like striking a steel rod. There were also sections where Mother Nature used some kind of super glue to apply the bark. Once again, I found a few carefully selected swear words helped, especially when your knuckles drag against the bark. That tends to take the bark off your skin and makes one bark cuss words.

When we hit a knot, Maureen would grab the slick and decapitate the knot with the skill of a veteran flenser. Like any chisel, the slick is supposed to be pushed. Employing your shoulder against the heavy handle, the slick worked well, particularly with small knots. If the slick chisel and its user failed to be up to the task, I would step in with the ax and dispatch the knot. But the slick was mainly used to lift the bark loose, sometimes removing large swaths where it was already slightly loose from the trunk. An experienced flenser would have declared we did a whale of a job.

While the drawknives were our chosen implements of torture, it took a little on-the-job training to get a handle on how to use them effectively. We would begin by putting each end of the log on a saw horse, then pull out the drawknives. We tried sitting astride the logs and working with the knives but that proved a little awkward. It was also a bit dangerous since your thighs could conceivably be flensed. Our preferred position was to stand beside the log and draw the knife.

A drawknife has a flat side as well as a beveled side. I soon learned that pulling it bevel-side up causes the blade to dive into the wood like a wild Moby Dick beneath the waves after being harpooned. A deep cut into a log that is going to serve as a beam for all to see is not good form. But working with the bevel-side down seemed to dull the blade faster, a fact whose cause I was never able to fathom. Since honing a drawknife was not my forte, I usually pulled with the bevel up, taking care not to cut deeply by gently pulling up on the handles as you drag the blade forward. Pushing down on the handles or pulling up also guides the blade deeper into the wood or out of it.

When I made a deep gash in the wood, I would frown at the college kid and point to the blemish. A loud "tsk, tsk" would complete the transfer of the blame to the wrongfully accused. It's easy to impugn the innocent in the drawknife game.

Some drawknife practitioners advise you should start in the middle, drawing toward the end, then return to the middle and pull the opposite direction. But I found it easier to begin at one end, particularly if the bark was thick. If you can get the blade under the bark, you can usually work the steel forward. I also discovered it was easier to have the blade at a slight angle instead of a full on perpendicular assault.

"You pull at an angle in what I like to call the drawknife slither," I instructed my two coworkers. "It catches the log unawares."

"Mom is going to catch you unawares with the slick if you don't behave," the smart college kid retorted. "And quit making those gashes in the big beams. You will be reminded of your flubs every time you walk into the living room and look up."

Sigh. You buy them books and send them to school yet they still have no appreciation for their elders. But she may have had a point about the beams which were going to be in the open air for the world to see.

The cabin builders had used an ancient architectural design known as a log kingpost truss. In our case, the log kingpost truss consists of the horizontal beam tied into the walls at each end, and an upright log post upright connecting the beam and the roof ridge. It's apparently one of the earliest truss forms, one the Vikings reputedly used in their longhouses while resting up after an exhausting summer of pillaging. They may have been uneducated barbarians, but they figured out that the problem of a sagging beam could be mitigated by a installing a kingpost—a vertical log—between the beam and the ridge line, thus using the tension to support the beam. I don't understand it all myself but I have an excuse: I have a college degree.

When all the logs were put into place, we felt a pioneer's sense of pride in having done t he work. It was one of those chores that I wouldn't have missed for a million bucks. But it would take nearly that sum for me to do it again. OK, I'd do it again for a $100,000 but I'd bitch and moan the whole time.

It's easy to imagine the Egyptians who fashioned King Tut's furniture using drawknives. Their knuckles were probably scraped and bruised. There may very well be some really old drawknives in the bottom of the Nile where the pharaoh's frustrated woodworkers flung them in disgust.

Like the misery whip, our drawknife has been stowed away. I hid it where Maureen can't find it.

Our one major project that did not require antique tools was the most labor intensive task of them all. We had to dig a 350-foot-long narrow ditch for the electrical and telephone lines. An underground utility line was preferable to having power poles marching along the driveway with wires dangling from them. Fortunately, neighbors John and Rhonda Edwards, whose house on the hill to our immediate south overlooks our cabin, also wanted their view free of dangling wires. They readily agreed to let us tie into the underground power terminal on the southeast corner of their property. Turns out we had good neighbors in every direction.

The power company required the trench be three feet deep and six inches wide. While it is conceivable it could be dug by hand with something like the entrenching tool issued back in the Corps, the task would have taken months of very strenuous work. A power tool was essential for the job. So I drove into Medford to a place that rents out trenching machines.

"Who are you going to have operate this for you?" asked the beefy young man who introduced me to the monstrous machine I would need for the job. "That would be me," I replied with a cold stare.

I assumed he had noticed my limp and leaped to the asinine assumption that anyone walking with a limp is largely useless. I had spotted the telltale round bulge of a chewing tobacco can in his hip pocket and deduced that he wasn't the brightest bulb on the premises. Turns out my flying leap to a conclusion missed the target.

"Hey, I didn't mean anything by it," he said, throwing up his hands in surrender. "It's just that these guys can be a little tricky. It's always good to have someone around with a little experience with heavy equipment.

Even Arnold Schwarzenegger could be thrown around by this machine if he hadn't used one before. This mighty fellow can get rowdy, especially if you have to work at an angle on the side of a hill."

"All of it will be at an angle on a hill side," I said with a sigh. "But I'll be just fine. This isn't my first rodeo."

Actually, that was a lot of bull. I had never wrestled with a mechanical monster tipping the scales at 1,000 pounds. It was a three-wheeled affair with a three-foot bar and chain that rips into Mother Earth like a chainsaw tears into wood. A few rounds with it and I would be begging for the likes of Arnold. But the Terminator was wrestling with politics at the time and would soon be elected governor of California, a position from which he would eventually be terminated.

To get the entrencher to Sterling Creek required loading it onto a utility trailer and pulling it behind our pickup. Since our truck is no hulking mechanical Schwarzenegger, the tail wanted to wag the dog, making driving home an interesting adventure. Countless mailboxes came within inches of being wiped out every time I swung wide on a corner.

Once home, there was the matter of figuring out how to back it down the trailer ramp. It thundered to life with the turn of a key but I had to get a handle on the half dozen levers used to control the mechanical menace. Yet it seemed docile enough when it came to exiting the trailer. It could have been a little puppy on a leash, sniffing a little here and there but eager to please. It even happily chugged up the hill in the direction I wanted it to go. I was surging with confidence as I walked alongside the machine which you operate like a mammoth garden tiller.

We had traced the trench path with a can of biodegradable orange spray paint. I positioned the machine over the dotted line and lowered the bar to the ground. It immediately began chowing down.

But it ignored my frantic attempts to guide it. The machine wanted to wander around, munching the ground here, attacking a bush there. Then, apparently having spotted the cabin, it roared toward what would be our eventual retirement home. Fortunately, I was able to rein it in by furiously pulling levers before it took a bite out of the deck. With its earth-eating arm disengaged, I managed to steer it back to the dotted orange line.

But when it was directed back to its earth-eating mission, it protested again. The machine seemed to have a mind of its own, fighting me every inch of the way. It was baffling. About that time, a friend happened to be driving past and pulled in to check on our progress. He is a retired U.S. Bureau of Land Management forester as well as the forester for the town of Jacksonville. While he and Chris were often on different sides of the environmental debate over how to manage our public lands, I figure both had something valuable to say. We had hired Paul to do a required forestry survey of our land for tax purposes, a job he did with aplomb. Yet we have worked on the land in a fashion that Chris championed. When it comes to humanoids, none of us have all the answers. We can learn from each other. A thoughtful fellow not given to outbursts, Paul watched me wrestle with the machine for a moment before hold up his arms like a referee stopping a game. I turned the surging beast off.

"You need to turn the machine around," he said. "You are trying to make it go the opposite way it wants to go."

With his help, I turned the metal monster around. Sure enough, it began digging in earnest with little protest. I had been trying to force it to go bass-ackward. The forester had the decency not to laugh outright, although you know he was chuckling when he drove away. In retrospect, I have to shake my head at my ineptitude when it came to what amounted to digging a ditch.

Yet even when I had it turned the right way, it was challenging because we were going across the side of a hill. The machine's weight kept pushing it slightly off the path we had chosen. But it munched the ground as intended, creating a trench that met the required depth and width. The only time it started bucking was when I hit a large rock. At that point, we would use long-handled entrenching tools. One was a combination rock chisel and pry bar, the other had a trowel at one end. The hand tools did the job, although it was tough slogging.

At one point, we hired the neighbor's teenage son to do some of the rock removal work but he also found it slow going. I thought about salting the area where he was digging with a few old coins we had found around the place as an enticement to dig faster but figured the coins would only be lost. It was a good lesson for him: he discovered that digging ditches was not his forte.

Meanwhile, Easter weekend in 2002 was special for us. We completed the trench that Sunday.

"How did it go?" the young man asked when we returned the machine. "Everything went according to plan I trust."

"Flawlessly," I replied. "It saved us weeks and weeks worth of labor." Hey, there was no need to clutter his mind with minutiae.

After the trench was inspected and approved by the power company, we hired neighbor John to install the plastic conduit required to house the underground utility lines. John is one of those rare individuals talented in everything from carpentry to electrical installation. One night when we came home from work, we were welcomed by an outdoor light he had thoughtfully placed in the back yard, letting us know we were plugged into the grid. Suddenly, our world was looking brighter. Literally.

After the hard labor we've done around the cabin, we both agreed digging that narrow ditch was the most trying. The memory sits perched in the back of my brain, chirping like Edgar Allen Poe's raven the same word over and over: "Nevermore." I'd rather wrestle buck naked on the courthouse steps than tangle with that diabolical machine from hell again.

THIRTEEN

Digging Wells, Screeding and Pumping

D ID YOU EVER HEAR THE ONE ABOUT FRED the well driller, Sean the concrete guy and Doug the pump man? No, this is not a set up for a risqué joke, although it certainly has ample potential for lowbrow humor. Rather, it's a tale about restoring my faith in fellow Americans. In part because of my chosen profession, that faith had eroded a bit over the years.

Granted, when it came to cabin restoration, we had scored a home run with Chris and Richard. They were straight shooters who were pleasant to work with, not to mention possessing top notch skills. I figured we had just gotten lucky and that our skein of luck was about to peter out. We were entering into what was to me unfathomable depths, particularly when it came to well drilling. We needed folks like Chris and Richard who were problem solvers capable of quickly assessing the situation, rolling up their sleeves and doing what was needed. We also wanted them to be honest, completing the work on schedule and within the agreed cost. At the time, our nation was shaken by one business scandal after another, economic woes, ongoing wars and endless political bickering. OK, none of that has changed much in the ensuing years. But it seemed like it was more acute shortly after the turn of the century.

With our cabin finally plugged in to the power grid, we were closing in on our dream of no longer having to import water to our home. It would be a huge watershed moment, pun intended. Carrying water to the trailer was a mundane chore that we found very tedious. We bought it in bulk, then hauled it home and lugged it into the trailer. We showered much like my grandparents had done a century earlier by heating water and pouring it on ourselves. Maureen insists her grandparents were more civilized than mine. Given her better sense of decorum, I suspect she is right.

But it wasn't merely transporting the water that we disliked. The jugs of water invariably had a slight plastic taste or some other foul chemical flavor we couldn't readily identify, possibly fluoride. Now, I know what you are thinking. But you would be wrong. I do not have any problem with fluoride, and certainly nothing that smacks of Gen. Jack D. Ripper, the wacko officer in the comic movie classic *Dr. Strangelove.* You may recall his famously screwball question posed to Captain Lionel Mandrake. "Do you realize that fluoridation is the most monstrously conceived and dangerous communist plot we have ever had to face?" asked the paranoid general with a straight face. Just thinking about that line from one of my favorite movies always cracks me up.

I know that fluoride is a natural substance. I also accept the conclusion from the folks in white coats and wearing thick glasses that fluoride is not harmful and is beneficial when added in prescribed amounts to public water supplies. These white-coated folks would be scientists, not psychiatrists working to cure the deeply disturbed Jack D. Rippers of this world. Of course, we all know that scientists are pinko commies.

Communist or other diabolical threats notwithstanding, we simply wanted to drink cold, clear water that didn't taste like it was dipped out of a swimming pool. It was time to try out the old pump and our relatively shallow well. However, before we could fire up the pump, we first had to dig another trench to deliver underground electricity to the pump house and connect a water line from it to the cabin. This one would be shorter than the one linking us to the grid. Still, it was nearly 100 feet from the pump house to the area of the cabin where we could hook up both water and electrical lines.

Unlike the previous trench, this one would be on level ground in relatively soft dirt. What's more, it only had to be 18 inches deep. That was child's play compared to the one which requiring being tossed around by the monster machine. We finished it in a few days, using hand tools, and soon had the power hooked to the old pump.

From the outside, our ancient pump house looked like an askew outhouse. Leaning slightly to the northwest, its frame was covered in faded boards. Like an old privy, it had a door that sagged when you opened it. Inside was an old pump, an array of leaking pipes and a cracked concrete floor. The concrete pad around the well was poured on Aug. 6, 1948, according to the date written in the concrete when it was still wet. A kitten had also walked across the foundation before it hardened, leaving tracks in time. You had to wonder where that kitten was headed. It appeared to be bound for the cabin where its mom was likely the head mouser. Or maybe it simply wanted to play in the wet concrete.

The old pump may have been a state-of-the-art machine in its youth, but it was now old and decrepit. To get it to work, I had to beg and cajole. During those rare times when it worked, the pump, infirm as it was, drained the well in a few minutes. Never mind I had been told the well produced 5 gallons a minute. The output was more like a quart a minute. When you took a shower, you had to decide whether you wanted to shampoo your hair or take a quick body shower. Taking both was out of the question, even with the holding tank which apparently never filled up.

Few things are more miserable than having to stumble to the pump house while trying to keep shampoo out of your eyes. It makes one cranky.

One day while Maureen was in town I called a local pump company and described the pump situation as best I could. Since I didn't have the foggiest when it came to pump nomenclature, the fellow who answered the phone probably thought I was speaking Swahili. I couldn't take the land line telephone out to the pump house where the guy on the other end of the line could guide me through the tangled web of the pump world. As I indicated early on, we have a cell phone but there is no reception in our little corner of Sterling Creek. We had the phone hooked up in the cabin before we moved in.

By the by, taking a break from being in contact with the world 24/7 is not a bad thing. When we first got our cell phone, we got numerous calls demanding a fellow named Angel come to the phone. Angel was apparently no angel when it came to paying his bills.

"There is no Angel here," I would tell the insistent caller. "This is not his number."

"We are going to turn you over to a collection agency," the caller threatened.

"Trust me on this, I am no angel," I would counter. "Just ask anyone who knows me."

No matter how long and loud we told them they had the wrong number, they just knew Angel was on the other end, sneering. But they eventually quit calling. Like the kitten that walked across the wet concrete, Angel disappeared into the time continuum. I'll always imagine him with a devilish smirk.

Unlike Angel's bill collectors, the pump guy listened patiently. Like I say, it must have been difficult, given my convoluted explanation about the goings on or lack thereof regarding the pump that refused to live up to its name. But he was a good sport.

"Sounds like your pressure switch could be haywire, Bud," he said. "You sometimes need to reset them when they get old. It's probably 40-60."

"I don't know how old it is," I replied. "But I'm guessing it's closer to sixty. It's a geezer."

"No, I'm talking about your pressure," he said. "You have to adjust your pressure switch."

"And what does that look like, pray tell?" I asked, now completely lost.

"You're really new to this game, aren't you, Bud," he said. "No problem.

I can walk you through it. Your pressure switch is in the rectangle box right on top of your pump."

He instructed me to remove the top that popped off and peer inside the box. "Be sure to turn off the electricity to the pump first, Bud," he said. "If you don't, you'll be zapped but good."

I didn't want to be zapped but good. Nor was I too crazy about being called "Bud" but I figured it was better than being mistaken for a serial debtor. I walked out and did as instructed. With the cover off, I could see the two springs the pump guy had told me to look for.

"Based on your pressure in the system, your pressure switch turns the pump on or off," the pump guy explained when I returned to the phone. "You have your main spring and your smaller spring. Your main spring adjust both your cut in and cut off pressure."

He further noted that 40-60 meant the pressure switch turned on the pump when the pressure dropped to 40 pounds per square inch and clicked it off when the pressure reached 60 PSI. Turning the main spring clockwise would increase both the highs and lows, he said. I absorbed some of the information.

"You never want to adjust the cut-in pressure below 20 or the cut-off pressure above 60," he warned. "Bad things happen at that point." Already in over my head when it came to water pumps, I didn't ask what bad things would happen. Some things you just don't want to know.

I thanked him and went out to make some technical adjustments to the pump. Standing inside the small pump house, I could see the sky through the cracks in the roof. A knot hole in the wall provided a peek at the cabin. The pump house would leak when it rained and the pipes would freeze during a heavy frost. It wasn't raining that day but the concrete was damp. I turned the main spring clockwise a bit and placed the cover back on the pressure switch. Taking a deep breath, I turned the power back on, hoping I wouldn't be electrocuted. Nothing.

After trying several more adjustments to no avail, I went back to the cabin and called the pump man back.

"Hmmm," he said. "Could be your points, Bud. You need to clean them. In an old system, they can get mucky. Messes up your connection."

"I used to have a '56 Chevy when I was in high school that had points," I told him. "Are these points anything like those?"

"Now we're talking," he said. "Once you take the water and gas out of the picture and just look at it from an electrical standpoint, they are very much the same."

Armed with his latest instructions, I strode back to the pump house, a man on a mission. Sure enough, the points did look a lot like the points on that old V-8 engine which gave me fits when I was a teenager. Points look a lot like watch batteries. But these were black from use. I cleaned them until they shined like new, although they had a few small pits. After replacing everything, I stepped back and turned the power back on. There was a click and the pump came to life. We were in the water business. I called the pump guy back to thank him again.

"Glad to help," he said. "But you need to give some serious consideration to getting yourself a new pump and getting that well dug deeper, Bud. It'll cost you, though."

When Maureen returned home late that afternoon, I met her with a garden hose, spraying water on her car. She turned on the windshield wipers but I could see her grinning out at me.

"Bud fixed the pump," I told her when she got out. "And he didn't charge a dime. He's a stalwart fellow with a giving heart and smart as a whip. I don't think there is anything he can't do. Amazing man, that Bud."

"OK, smarty pants, what did you do?" she asked. I told her about the helpful pump guy who called me Bud.

"This Bud is for me," she said, putting an arm around my waist and squeezing. "To misquote the tongue-twisting Mr. Rumsfeld, you know more than you know you know."

"I'm afraid it is just a temporary fix," I said in a rare moment of candor. "This Bud cannot make a pump pump water from a well that has precious little water to pump. We need a new pump and a deeper well."

While it was a relief to no longer haul water to the place, the on-again, off-again pump was a major headache, even with Bud's vast pump skill and knowledge. After a few weeks of having to nurse the pump back from the brink of death only to have it suck the well dry in a few minutes, we agreed that a reliable water supply had to be a priority if we were ever going to make the cabin a comfortable place to dwell. We also wanted enough water for a garden. With the water we had, a cactus would have withered away of dehydration.

We decided to start with the top concern which, in this case, was the bottom of the well. We needed to find a well driller who wouldn't tap too deeply in our bank account. Unfortunately, we were about to plunge into a profession which was completely unfathomable to us. So we started calling around to test the waters.

One of the first well drillers we called insisted we would have to drill down at least 1,000 feet. "I know that Applegate country," he said. "You gotta go deep. Won't do you no good to pussyfoot around near the surface." The cost? At least $10,000 but likely a lot more, he said, all but rubbing his hands in anticipation of a big score. "But I can guarantee you'll have plenty of good, sweet water," he added.

While we didn't know anything about wells, we suspected it was bogus to make promises when it came to digging in the ground under our feet. As Mr. Rumsfeld would observe, there are no known knowns down there. I added the oily well driller to my mental list of BSing scalawags to avoid.

A friend suggested we call a well driller based in Ashland. "Fred is a very honest fellow who will treat you right," he promised. "No song and dance with him."

When Fred came to check the place out, he fit the description of a fellow who knew his way around a drilling rig. Wearing broken in coveralls and boots, he was ready to slop about in mud and muck. His handshake was firm; his eyes met your straight on. He was also rather large, giving off the impression he wasn't one to be trifled with.

When he talked about how drilling worked, he spoke with an impressive precision. By the time he got to the geology found in the Applegate Valley, particularly the characteristics of the metamorphic rock deep underneath, he was way over my head.

Yet he was also quick to observe that there was no way to predict how far we would have to drill to reach an adequate water supply.

"But we can be assured of finding good, sweet water, right?" I asked.

"No one can give you assurance of that," he said. "There are pockets out here where you can find salt in the water. You can also run into hard water with a lot of minerals. But, while there are no assurances of success, there is a good chance you will find decent water in both quality and quantity."

Our friend was right: Fred was no song and dance man. I told him we wanted him to do the job but said $5,000 was our well-drilling limit. He agreed to keep the cost above water and we shook hands on the deal.

During the week he came out to drill our well, I took a vacation so I could work around the place, assisting him when needed. My first task was to dismantle the old pump house before he arrived, including breaking up the concrete floor with a sledge hammer. We saved the broken slabs of concrete for a pet cemetery we planned up the valley. The slabs containing kitten tracks would be used as memorials for our cats that had completed their nine lives.

When Fred showed up for work, he was driving a drilling rig which was pulling a small pickup truck. After parking the big truck, he unhooked the pickup and announced he had to go back for his other truck which carried drill bits and other gear. He drove off in the pickup. When he returned, he was driving a truck which carried the twenty-foot long pipes he would connect together to extend the depth of the drill bit as it sank deeper into the ground. His faithful pickup truck was again in tow. He drove the pickup home that evening, returning in the morning.

Although a one-man operation, Fred worked the complex drilling rig with the skill of a maestro. He didn't really need my help but I assisted him with small things like handing him tools and cleaning up the ground-up rock brought up by the drill. It was great for filling potholes in the driveway, incidentally. Overall, I found the whole drilling process interesting.

Hailing from New York state, the driller also proved to be an intriguing character who had traveled and read widely. His insightful views and comments on our world piqued my interest.

"I'm just curious," I said as the diamond-edged drill bit chewed into the ground deep below. "What did you do before you became a well driller? You are well spoken. You are obviously well educated. I'm guessing you did something else earlier in your life."

"Yes, I did," he replied. "I used to practice law."

My jaw actually dropped as the former attorney explained that he had grown weary of the legal profession in the Southwest. When he moved to Oregon some thirty years earlier, he got a part-time job with a well driller while studying for the Oregon bar exam. He discovered he enjoyed drilling wells much more than legal haggling. He decided to change careers. No more sitting at a desk in a suit and tie.

"I wanted to work outdoors with my hands," he said. "I was tired of working in a law office and all the paper work associated with it."

My jaw continued to hang open. I may have even been drooling a little. After all, we have certain expectations in life. You expect white collar workers to stay with their brethren. The offspring of doctors and lawyers are expected to follow in those white-collar footsteps. OK, a blue collar worker may occasionally find a niche in a white-collar occupation. But it almost seems downright un-American to go the other way. And a well driller? Some snobs would sniff that's just a ditch digger burrowing a vertical ditch. All I knew was that the revelation of an attorney turned well driller turned my world on its ear.

What's more, we're talking about a former lawyer here. I have friends who are practicing attorneys, even one who is a retired judge. Fact is, a son-in-law graduated from law school at the same college that gave an onion skin to Richard M. Nixon. And all of them, save Mr. Nixon, are fine folks who are straight shooters. My problem is that I tend to place a hand over my wallet and back away when I meet a lawyer I don't know.

My distrust is irrational, although it's probably rooted in the fact I know they are a lot smarter than I am. It's a bit like voters who damn all members of congress but are fine with their own congressional representative. Attorneys are like journalists in that they are poorly regarded as a herd but once you cut one from the bunch they become tolerable, even likable. Second thought, strike that from the record. Journalists are not tolerable once you meet one. You wouldn't want one hanging around in polite company.

As a result of discovering we had an attorney turned well driller, I had worked myself up into a barely contained state of high anxiety by the time Maureen came home from work that evening.

"I've got some very bad news," I told her. "We are doomed. We might as well pack it in. It's over."

"What on earth are you talking about?" she asked. "Did Rajah bite one of the carpenters again?"

"If only that was it," I lamented. "Our well driller is a former attorney. An attorney! And I didn't get his promise in writing that the bill would be no more than $5,000. We are dead meat."

"How do you know he is not a man of his word?" she asked. "Are you saying that all attorneys are dishonest? That's like saying all journalists make things up. That's just goofy."

"Oh yeah, well I've known a lot more attorneys and journalists than you have," I said. "They are a shifty lot. I've known attorneys who would shaft their mothers. And don't get me started on what journalists will do for a story but it is not pretty."

"Your imagination is running wild again, sweetie," she said. "I'm sure everything will be just fine. Besides, I like one journalist very much, despite his uncontrollable imagination. No more coffee for you."

Fred arrived pleasant as usual the next day, the day he would be wrapping up the drilling operation. Yet he must have been wondering why his formerly babbling assistant had all but clammed up and was looking at him like a nervous mouse watching a cat. He probably figured it was just one of those weird things journalists do from time to time. A squirrelly bunch, he likely concluded.

Besides, he was busy with his job. He had punched the well 140 feet deeper, tapping into plenty of water for our household and garden needs. The water also stood up well to a rigorous analysis by a water-testing firm. What's more, it was the best tasting water we've ever had, bottled or from the tap. We were thrilled about quality and quantity.

But there was still the little matter of the bill. I asked him about it at the end of his last day at our place. He gave a verbal estimate which was below our limit but he cautioned that was merely a rough guess.

"I haven't figured it out precisely just yet," he said. "I'll send it to you in the mail. I've got to go over a few items."

His words sent a chill down my spine. Obviously, it was one of those the-bill-is-in-the-mail ploys from someone who didn't want to be there when I gasped at the bill and clutched my chest. In my frenzied mind, we were about to send Fred and friends on a world cruise with a long stop in Monaco where they would spend wildly in the Monte Carlo Casino. And it would all be paid for by the gullible goof on Sterling Creek. When I wasn't moping, I was mentally kicking myself.

The bill arrived a few days later in the mail, looking innocently enough. I took a deep breath and tore open the envelope. I gasped.

"Wow," I murmured and handed it to Maureen. "Wow," she agreed.

The bill barely topped $3,600, well below his rough estimate and far below our ceiling price. An attached note said he deducted part of the bill because of my week-long assistance, adding he appreciated the help and friendly chit chat. Like I said, wow. There was nothing to stop him from pushing the bill beyond our agreed limit. Nothing save a strong sense of ethics, decency and honesty, that is.

"See, there was absolutely nothing to worry about at all," I cheerfully told the wife.

"Well, you were right about some journalists making things up out of thin air," Maureen said. "They can certainly get a little overwrought over nothing. Really strange people, journalists."

OK, I admit I may have overreacted a tad. In one fell swoop, Fred made me re-evaluate my attitude towards attorneys as well as developing deep appreciation for those who drill wells for a living. But I still draw the line at journalists. They remain a shifty bunch in my overwrought mind, albeit very interesting creatures in the way turkey vultures are interesting when they are happily munching on the guts of some poor road kill.

With the well punched out, we were still not yet done with hiring the rest of the folks who would make our water well a gushing success. We had to build a well house, complete with a concrete pad and insulated walls and a watertight roof that would not allow Jack Frost in to freeze the pipes. We also wanted to be able to use the pump house as a cellar to store some garden vegetables like onions and potatoes over the winter. My grandparents likely had a cellar a century earlier on their Applegate Valley farm. While I don't believe they were all good old days, I figure some accouterments of their lifestyle would be useful, including a cellar to store homegrown veggies. Maureen agreed, although she cautioned she did not want to go completely pioneer. "Unless you want to sleep in it, don't even think about building an outhouse, buster," she warned me. What a spoil sport. I was going to bring up, for discussion purposes only, mind you, the feasibility of the compost toilets I saw in the arctic village of Wainwright in the mid-1980s. I suppose I'll have to sit on that idea for the time being.

Maureen drew a blue print of the pump house she had in mind, making the new concrete pad a little larger than the old one. The dwelling for the pump would be heavily insulated with shelves for keeping vegetables cool and dry. Furthermore, the pump would be submersible so there would be no points to adjust or clean. Just between the two of us, I didn't have a lot of confidence in our man Bud when it came to water pumps. Bit of a bumbler, truth be told.

There would be no dithering when it came to building the pump house. It was certainly doable for us, beginning with a form for the concrete pad. We found some old 2x8 planks around the place that were well suited for the job. It took but a day to dig out the area for the pad and install the form, bracing it to hold the wet concrete in place.

"As those who inhabit the architectural world are wont to say, form follows function," I told Maureen we stood back and admired our work. "We done good."

"When it comes to playing in the dirt, we bow to no one," she replied with a grin. "We know how to get down and dirty."

As a veteran couple working on projects, we are members in long standing of the Mutual Admiration Society. Granted, I've never been long on Yankee ingenuity when it comes to building anything. For that, I invariably turn to Maureen. But I don't mind dirty jobs. In fact, for callus building experience, I probably have more than most journalists: bucking hay, setting chokers in the logging woods, felling snags and bucking the tree into firewood, digging ditches and building countless carpentry projects over the years. Nor does Maureen mind dirtying those adorable pinkies of hers.

Early the next morning, shortly after we had placed the concrete wire mesh and rebar in the form, Sean the concrete man pulled up in his truck. Inside the drum, our future pump house pad was being agitated, keeping it a semi liquid until it could be pumped into the form.

As with the well driller before him, Sean had to go through what Maureen calls my inquisition. I've always been curious about people and their chosen professions. A gregarious fellow who brought his young son along to the job site, Sean was obviously happy in his work.

"I was a carpet layer down in southern California," he said. "I enjoy pouring concrete, particularly sense it allows me to get out and see the country. You have a very pretty place here."

As he talked, he was busy getting his rig ready to pour the concrete. He gave me a run down on the way a concrete mixer works, including how the liquid concrete is constantly mixed with a giant Archimedes screw to keep from turning into a solid. In transit, the spiral blade is turned so the concrete is continually pushed deeper into the drum, he explained.

"When you want to start pouring, you just turn it the other way," he said of the screw. "That forces the viscous concrete into the chutes, delivering it to where it is needed."

Like Fred, he worked quickly and efficiently. In short order, the form we had built was full.

"You need to work with it fairly fast at this point," he said. "You can start screeding now."

Before I could inform him we weren't that kind of couple, Sean explained screeding was using a straight 2-by-4 board to smooth out the concrete.

"Just saw it back and forth—it'll smooth over," he said.

We sawed. Sure enough, the concrete became as smooth as a baby's bottom. We were natural born screeders and didn't know it. Unfortunately, before we could round up a cat to walk across the wet concrete, it hardened to a solid. You can never count on a cat when you need one. They are very unreliable creatures.

Batting cleanup was Doug the pump man who arrived after we framed the pump house. I had intended to call the pump man who had dubbed me Bud but Doug came highly recommended by several folks we knew in the building trade. Originally from Lakeview in south central Oregon, Doug was a former logger who turned to the pumping business when the logging industry hit hard times. Before talking pumps, we covered the important business of what it meant to be reared in rural Oregon a few decades earlier, of our youths spent fishing and hunting.

When he mentioned his success in deer hunting, I naturally had to bring up the eight-point buck I had shot as a teenager in the Illinois Valley in the fall of 1968. We're not counting buck points like they do back East. To be precise, he had eight on one side and nine on the other. Doug was impressed, although he correctly noted that the mule deer east of the Cascade Range have larger bodies and wider racks than the smaller black-tailed deer found in western Oregon.

"But that is a mighty big rack," he conceded. "We were fortunate to grow up in Oregon at a time when we did. I wouldn't have missed it for the world."

With the small talk completed, Doug rolled up his sleeves and went to work. He installed the new pump, pressure tank and related gadgetry as promised and under budget. In one day, no less.

Of course, that's not to say everything went smoothly with all the subcontractors we hired. There were a few glitches, albeit nothing that detracted from the quality of their work. But the weird happenings did increase my suspicion that the old cabin has an odd sense of humor and likes to play games with its biped inhabitants.

The electricians who rewired the cabin were a likable pair. The foreman was an older fellow who was helping the younger man learn the trade. The graying gent was a short fellow with a wry wit. The strapping young man, barely out of his teens, looked like he played fullback in high school. Like his mentor, he was also a cheerful chap.

One day during his lunch break the budding electrician took a soda can out of his lunch bucket. After a couple of long drinks, he sat it down and went back to work. A few minutes later he walked over to take another swig, and let out a shout.

"I just got stung by a bee," he announced. A yellowjacket had apparently been taking a drink the same time as the electrician in training and didn't appreciate the competition. Perhaps electricians are used to dealing with being stung in the mouth but I was concerned.

"Are you OK?" I asked. "Are you allergic to bees? Do you need to see a doctor?"

He shook his head as he brushed his tongue with his fingers. His tongue was already starting to swell up.

"Naw, juth got thung on the thongue," he replied. He was still smiling but he was certainly having trouble enunciating.

"You what?" I asked, concerned that he was about to go into convulsions.

"He just got stung on the tongue," his mentor interpreted. "He'll be fine. He's a tough lad."

The young fellow just grinned and cheerfully went on with his work. Never mind his tongue was beginning to look like a slab of raw steak and had started to loll to one side like a hound dog that is tuckered out.

"Thung on the thungue," he would happily explain the rest of the day whenever someone dropped by and asked him what happened. He never lost his smile and returned the next morning raring to go as usual, his tongue back to normal. When you are accustomed to getting zapped by a jolt of electricity on occasion, something like a stung tongue is apparently mere child's play. It certainly didn't affect the quality of his work. The county building inspectors happily approved the electrical work when they checked it out.

For several years afterwards, whenever we tripped or had a small accident which prompted the other to ask if everything was OK, Maureen and I would invoke the young electrician's cheerful response.

"Juth got thung on the thungue," we would reply. We have no doubt the pleasant young man did well in his chosen vocation. Like his mentor said, he was made of stout stuff.

As was the three-man plumbing crew we hired to replace all the water pipes and faucets in the cabin. They were tough, working hard to get the job done. Like the other subcontractors, they also came highly recommended.

"They'll do a good job, although they are kind of rough around the edges," we were told by the builder who recommended them. "But it'll be done right, that I guarantee."

True enough, they were a boisterous bunch who didn't mince words when it came to announcing their angry frustrations upon encountering a stubborn pipe or a tight squeeze. Suffice it to say they didn't attend church regularly or, if they did, they spent hours in penance for uttering words which would have put a Marine Corps drill instructor to shame.

The ultimate height in sweardom was reached the day a member of the plumbing crew began working in the nearly twenty-five-foot-long narrow crawl space between the master bedroom and the main cabin which snakes under both bathrooms. It would be a tight fit for most adults, and this fellow, although short, was burly. But, despite his size, he was apparently the one who specialized in the worming work.

We probably should have slathered him with butter before he began slithering. The crawl space apparently gets a little smaller the farther west you go, something our burly plumber didn't know before he entered the worm hole. He was about half way when the swearing began. At first, it was innocent enough, the kind of swearing that you might mutter when you hit your thumb with a hammer.

"Damn!" he began. "It's tighter than hell under here."

There were loud grunts and thumping kicks as he wiggled westward. Suddenly, there was a Mount Vesuvius eruption of profanities that threatened to blow the cabin off its foundation. The plumber called down curses to forever damn any obstacle blocking his way. With a roaring expletive, he let the world know what the crawl space and cabin could do if they were sentient beings capable of reproduction. But even if they were, what he called for would have been an anatomical impossibility. He routinely threw out the name of a female dog along with that of a person born of parents not married to each other.

This was coarse language which curdled mother's milk and caused the devout to sink to their knees in subjugation to a higher power. The Rev. James Hamilton would have been mortified; my drill instructors awestruck. But the rest of the crew took the epithet eruption in stride as if it were all part of the job.

At one point, the verbal villainy suddenly stopped. I peeked down into the crawl space and asked him if he was all right.

"Oh sure," he responded cheerfully. "Just taking a rest."

A few minutes later, seemingly recharged, he resumed hurling curses with a vim and vigor that would have inspired a logger. He eventually squeezed out the other end, his work under the house completed. "A little tight under there but I got 'er done," he offered.

We were never certain but we had an idea what fueled the outbursts. Each evening when we cleaned up, we would find half a dozen or so empty beer cans left by the plumbers. These were tall beer cans, not those wienie ones for light drinkers. When I mentioned it to one of the plumbers, he said they just drank one can each at the end of the day. "It's our way of celebrating when we finish that part of the job," he explained.

They weren't shy about celebrating. By the time they were done, we had collected more than a case of empty beer cans. But it didn't seem to impair their work. Like the electricians before them, the plumbers earned high marks from the county building inspectors. We could have probably paid them in beer.

Despite the trials and tribulations that is apparently a prerequisite when restoring an old home, we now had water and electricity at our beck and call. And it was all because of Fred the well driller, Sean the concrete guy, Doug the pump man, fearless electricians and those feisty plumbers who were past masters at swearing. Perhaps one day I'll think up a ribald joke involving all their professions but for now I'm content in knowing they have restored my faith in the American worker. Our subcontractors proved to be competent, hard working and seriously fascinating humanoids. They also bestowed on me some choice cuss words to toss into my verbal tool chest.

FOURTEEN

Don't Fence Me In

WITH OUR WELL PUNCHED DEEPER AND WATER no longer a sputtering proposition, we decided it was time to vegetate. In a garden, that is. In these parts where deer are constantly nosing around for a tasty morsel, a fence is needed to keep the hoofed gluttons from laying waste to your succulent tomatoes. Of course, there are those who maintain that tomato-fed venison has a flavorsome piquant.

However, Maureen was growing more than mere tomatoes in her fertile mind, although she agreed the fence's main mission would be to keep deer out.

"But we also need a fence to keep our dogs in," she stressed. "They need a dog park. And we need space for a rose garden and more fruit trees. The boys will be able to romp amongst the roses and apple trees."

Our mutts were referred to as "the boys," despite the fact the alpha pooch at the time was a grand dame named Alyeska. She dominated the three-member pack with a queenly air. She was also the one who led them astray whenever they went outside without leashes. The fact the whiskers on her muzzle were growing white with age never slowed her down. She was clearly in charge of her fellow canines. What's more, she regally ignored disciplinary intercessions by the bipeds nominally in charge of her.

I acknowledged a small dog park was necessary for peace and tranquility since finding a dog lost in the Applegate country can be a daunting task.

"But let's don't make it too large," I cautioned. "They just need it to trot around in a bit. It doesn't have to be huge."

"We're on the same page on this one, honey," she replied. "Just big enough for them to run around in. Nothing huge."

Adjectives can be troublesome rascals when otherwise like-minded people have differing definitions of their role in the English language. To me, a huge dog park means it would hide a buffalo herd. To Maureen, the fact the park would accommodate a thundering herd does not necessarily make it huge.

That seemingly subtle difference became, well, huge when we began stepping off the size of the dog park. I stopped after pacing off at about fifty feet but Maureen kept going. And going. She disappeared into the trees.

"It's going to be 200 feet long," I protested when I caught up with her. "And that doesn't include the garden fence which will be another fifty feet or so."

"This isn't going to be big," she insisted. "The one in Medford is at least ten acres. They are going to need this room to run and play."

"The Medford dogs aren't going to bring their owners out here to run around in our dog park," I countered. "Medford mutts subscribe to the same philosophy as their hairy counterparts in Las Vegas: what happens in Medford stays in Medford."

Since that last statement left Maureen baffled and me momentarily befuddled, I decided another approach was needed. Perhaps my old friend Robert Frost could shed some light on the fencing debate. But the bard of New England isn't much help when you start spouting his poetry weirdly out of context.

"Something there is that doesn't love a huge fence," I began. "The fruit trees aren't going to be running around. And I'm pretty sure the roses won't start wandering off and stopping to smell people. Huge fences don't make good neighbors."

"You confused me about the Las Vegas reference, and you completely lost both Mr. Frost and I on that last one, sweetie," she said. "Let's just make the fence as big as we need it. We'll get back to mending that other wall of yours later. I know a good counselor."

Gibbering aside, I had a valid point somewhere in there when it came to the fence. However, although she is one of the nicest humanoids you could ever meet, my wife doesn't budge once she plants her feet. Her feet were set like fence posts when it came to the size of the dog park. I could bay at the moon all night long and never change her mind when it came to parking the pampered pets.

It wasn't just the fence's proposed length that worried me. Maureen's design called for the northern border to head west along the seasonal spring by the cabin, then wander south up the hill by the old tack shed, meandering east up through the conifers and finally on a northerly direction to connect with the garden fence.

"See, it's not going to be huge," she said with a perfectly straight face.

"I think we ought to give some thought to stopping the fence at the state line," I told her. "Otherwise, we will probably have to get California dog licenses for the mutts. All that red tape can be a real bother. Besides, our hairy boys will demand surf boards if we go too far south. You know how those spoiled dogs in Southern California like their fashions."

Her frown told me that it was time to muzzle my muzzle. While I had been joking when it came to exaggerating the size of the dog park fence, I was seriously concerned about the time it would take to build it. Little did I know it would eat up a year, largely because of an accident which was literally waiting to happen. No matter what form the fence took, my days of relative languorous somnolence were going to end. Mr. Fate was patiently waiting; leaning against a post and chewing on a straw while watching our little lives unfold.

The fence building began easy enough. We started with the garden, agreeing to make the fence around it fifty foot square with garden wire six feet high. Separating the garden from the dog park would be a shorter picket fence with pickets we made out of the weathered cedar boards which once covered the old garage. The idea was that the picket fence would stop the dogs from venturing into the garden while the six-foot wire fence around the perimeter would keep the deer out of the tomatoes. With apologies to

Frost's dogged neighbor, good fences make good neighbors providing the neighbors are furbearing.

When writing about our garden fence in a column in the *Mail Tribune*, I received a huffy e-mail note from a fellow who let me know quite tersely that a six-foot fence won't deter deer. I politely let him know that every garden fence I've ever had was six feet high and was deer proof. But that was no proof to him. He pronounced me a dunderhead. Perhaps his characterization about me had merit but I was right about deer fences. Some would sniff that southern Oregon deer aren't as good at high jumping as deer in other parts of the country. When it comes to high-jumping local mammals, I would be remiss if I didn't mention that Medford is the birthplace of the Fosbury Flop. That's a bona fide local-boy-makes-good story. In the 1968 summer Olympics in Mexico City, Dick Fosbury, Oregon native and graduate of Medford Senior High School, won the gold medal in the high jump with his heretofore unorthodox jumping style which involves going over the bar headfirst and backwards. He cleared 7 feet 4 ¼ inches, a record at the time. The "flop" he perfected in the Rogue Valley is now the standard technique for high-jumping bipeds world round. Fortunately, our deer have yet to adapt the Fosbury modus operandi of jumping. If they do, this dunderhead will add another foot or two to the fence.

We bought 500 feet of six-foot tall garden mesh wire and sixty posts for the fencing. After all, Maureen promised not to make it huge. We wouldn't want the buffalo herd to become lost in the dog park.

However, as with all things we undertake to build, it wasn't as simple in reality as it was in theory. We ran into a little glitch. More to the point, I ran into a glitch. Tripped over it is more like it.

About the time we were finished building the garden fence and starting on the dog park fence, we bought some commercial property in Medford. The half-acre parcel came with a metal and decorative block building that had gone through several owners since it was built in the 1970s. But it was solid and well built. With a few modifications, it would be ideal for Maureen's hairy enterprise.

"We will need a more efficient floor plan," she observed as she was giving the building a once over. "That means building some partitions here and there along with a little remodeling in some of the rooms."

You must understand that the word "little," like the four-letter "h" word, is a relative thing when Maureen deploys it into battle. In addition to building the partitions, revamping two rooms as well as the bathroom, we removed and replaced the flooring. We also painted all the walls. Fortunately, several friends stepped in to give us a hand, making the job easier as well as more fun. This meant the dog park fence project was kenneled for a bit, of course.

The work on her shop resulted in me spending a lot of time climbing up and down ladders, something that always gives my good leg a workout. You may recall the car accident I mentioned early on, a 1971 crash which left me with limited dexterity on my right side. As a result, I'm walking challenged. My pedestrian locomotion has a Frankenstein lurch whose execution has sent more than one frightened little kid running shrieking to his or her parents over the years. Apart from the occasional bruised ego, I don't mind the hitch in my gait all that much. It gets me where I'm going, although slower than your average biped.

What's more, my imperfect gait has taught me my one true expertise: falling down. I have perfected the fine art of falling flat on your face without getting hurt. I've fallen on stairs, rocky mountainsides, over curbs. Sometimes, for no apparent reason, I trip on a perfectly smooth floor. But I can usually fall without a scratch. If falling down sans a major injury was an Olympic sport, I would outshine Mr. Fosbury in the gold medal category. But even would-be gold medalists have off days. Mine came on the Sunday before Labor Day of 2008.

We had just spent the day in Maureen's new shop, climbing up and down ladders. I had completed the day without a major tumble. But my right leg was dragging and my good leg wasn't holding up that well since I tend to stand on one leg like a stork, even while on a ladder. I was exhausted. We agreed it had been a good day's work and headed back to the cabin.

It was a nice evening so we figured a barbecue was in order. After cooking a couple of turkey burgers out on the deck, I loaded our dinner onto a plate and headed back into the cabin. Remember our concrete floor?

As you can well imagine, it is very unforgiving for those who drag one leg while walking without paying attention. My right foot touched down on something slick on the kitchen floor and shot out from under me. I tried to turn in mid-kitchen pirouette to save our dinner.

Bad move. My right foot was pointing forward while my left foot found traction and twisted around to point the opposite direction as my other foot. Feet are not meant to take opposing stands. Something had to give. My left fibula volunteered. Fortunately, the pain in the back of my head from striking the concrete lessened the agonizing pain flaming up from my lower extremity. A couple words of warning: don't try this at home, boys and girls. Not only is it a difficult maneuver to replicate, but it really smarts.

Our newly acquired young pooch Waldo, who had been resting with his golden muzzle on his white paws in the living room after a hard day of snoozing, was the sole witness. He likely found the dumb human trick very amusing.

Being a well mannered mutt, the pup managed to stifle a canine chortle and immediately trotted over to check if I was all right. His big brown eyes peered down into mine. But his frowning furry face was only there for a second. His next priority was to clean up the far flung barbecue before some bothersome biped snatched it off the floor.

I wasn't worried about our dinner. The powerful pain shooting up my left leg almost made me upchuck. Maureen and daughter Derra, who was visiting from Portland, came running when they heard the commotion and cry of anguish. I was writhing on the floor; Waldo was munching on burgers which, not to be boastful, were done to a very nice golden brown. He was happy although he probably would have preferred to have had them served in his dish. He can be finicky that way.

Derra, who was working at the Oregon Health & Science University at the time and knew about things medical, immediately assumed command of the field hospital. The two of them helped this moaning patriarch to the couch, wrapped my already swollen lower leg and ankle, applied ice and elevated my leg. They ordered me to stay put.

The next morning brought Labor Day. The fellow in emergency care who had drawn the short straw to work that holiday had two large eyebrows that looked like furry caterpillars. When he checked out my lower left leg, one caterpillar shot up upon seeing the enlarged purple ankle and lower leg which looked like the owner had a severe case of elephantitis.

"Ouch," the man said. He certainly had a way with words, I'll give him that. My hopes that the lower leg was only a real bad sprain were quickly dashed when the fellow peeked under my skin with an X-ray machine.

"Congratulations, you broke your fibula," said the man upon completing the examination. OK, he wasn't warm and fuzzy but at least he didn't make a crack about the bone snapping like a bread stick.

Even though it was a holiday, medical people can be fussy when a patient comes in with a foot out of proper alignment. He announced that he would have to realign the broken fibula before putting my lower leg into a temporary soft cast.

"This will hurt a little," he warned, then pulled my foot down and twisted it slightly to bring it into line with the rest of the leg. He had apparently attended the same grammar school as Maureen when it came to adjectives. It didn't hurt a little. It hurt like hell.

I never did discover the caterpillar man's medical credentials. Could be he was a maintenance man sweeping up when we arrived and decided to fill in until the doctor on duty returned from a break. But he seemed to know how everything worked in the emergency room. The pain wasn't quite as acute when we left. Of course, the pain pills he prescribed may have had something to do with it. Cold medication will make me loopy so a pain pill, even a mild one, sends me into drooling unconsciousness. As a result, I generally stick to aspirin. But I suppose one has to branch out when a fibula snaps.

Fortunately, my ankle, although badly sprained, sustained no permanent damage. But I literally didn't have a leg to stand on since my right leg is an out and out fraud when it comes to providing locomotion, let alone support. I had to go under the knife. Two days later found me in a Medford hospital undergoing surgery to have a steel plate installed with eight metal screws. An X-ray after the surgery revealed a Franken fibula with a metal plate screwed on to the bone by what appeared to be wood screws you could pick up at the corner hardware store. The gruesome sight would have made Mary Shelley shriek in terror.

The surgeon, a bright fellow with a good sense of humor, told me I couldn't walk for six weeks. If I had a cigar and a Groucho mustache, I would have quipped that I couldn't walk for six weeks before the accident. Out of curiosity, I did ask him whether a refrigerator magnet would stick to my metal plate. His response was to frown the same way Waldo did when I crashed in the kitchen. I have yet to give the plate the old magnet test out of fear it would latch onto the metal and I couldn't get it off. I already excite the Homeland Security folks at airports with the steel leg plate and the metal in my neck. They would go for the guns at the sight of a metal device attached to the outside of my leg.

Obviously, with both legs stove up, the fence building project was put on hold, although we were able to move forward on the shop renovation, thanks largely to friendly helping hands. For two very long months, my only mode of locomotion was a wheelchair, a contraption I swore I would never sit in again after spending the bulk of 1971 in one. It's a problem of navigation, you see. Thanks to the lack of full dexterity on my right side, my right hand doesn't keep up with my stronger left hand when providing forward motion in the chair. The result is that I constantly veer to the right since my left hand has more horsepower than my right hand. It is very vexing.

Besides, being confined to a wheelchair is no fun. Contrary to what some former bosses may think, sitting on my posterior isn't something I do well. It seems counterintuitive, but sitting is exhausting after a while. What's more, too much sitting causes me to gaze at my navel and question my self worth.

But I was able to wheel back to work in the newsroom where friends did their best to help keep things rolling along. One wag asked if I had a nice trip. Another took to calling me "Wheelie." One referred to me as "The Gimp." Several offered to grab a screwdriver to tighten my obviously loose screws.

Readers also joined in after I wrote a column relating the experience. A retired mill worker sent an ink well holder that came from a dilapidated antique desk he had acquired. A talented woodworker, he made a little stand for it, figuring the holder would inspire me to write books, an aspiration I had shared with him. It has served as an inspiration ever since. Of course, the gallows humor I had trotted out in my column inspired some readers. One called to say he was sorry to read about the temporary loss of my good leg. "Maybe it'll even out your lurch," he offered, hopefully tongue in cheek. But my favorite was an e-mail from Lloyd in Longview, Wash. He is the twin brother of a friend of mine in Jacksonville, both of whom are retired teachers. "Since you have been comforted by so much black humor I thought I would add one more," Lloyd wrote. "I felt for you. I broke my leg and several arms over the years. I also have plates and screws. I run a crematory now and I love to burn people like you because I find so many treasures in the cremains like screws, plates, etc. that I have to remove before I grind them up." I will chuckle over that last missive for the remainder of my years. But I told Lloyd the crematory man that he can't have my metal parts until I'm done with them. He indicated he would be happy to bide his time.

While the humor helped, after those horrid two months of listing to the right in the wheelchair I was eager to graduate to the walker which Maureen picked up at a medical supply store. A sticker on the side included the warning, "Walkers may not be suitable for mentally confused people." Someone needs to inform the manufacturers that the sticker isn't suitable for mentally confused people since they wouldn't comprehend the gist of it. My wife insisted that she didn't buy the thing specifically because of the warning label. But she was giggling when she denied the allegation. The whole experience was mentally confusing.

With the walker, I was ready to take tentative steps back into the walking world. Even then I would be wearing a protective boot allowing only limited movement, a la Frankenstein. All that was lacking was a bolt sticking out of my neck. But I was mighty glad to be given the opportunity to walk again, albeit baby steps.

Naturally, I had to crack wise on such a momentous occasion. On the day I took that first giant step for mekind, I stood up before the walker, grabbed the two handles that serve as supports, squinted at Maureen with my best steely look and growled, "Walker—Texas Ranger." To understand the attempted humor, you had to know there had once been a television show featuring a martial arts fellow named Walker who was a Texas Ranger. Obviously, I had far too much time on my hands in order to come up with that clunker. The joke, like the television show, needed polishing. Maureen laughed the first time I took the lame pun for a walk, second bad pun intended.

As for the walker, it was no Texas Ranger. I hobbled along at first, moving ever so cautiously. The memory of that painful day I snapped my fibula was still fresh, causing me to be filled with trepidation when I took hold of the walker. But I quickly got the hang of it and was soon clanking around the news room and our cabin. It felt good to be bugging people and pets again.

I was still using the walker when I picked up the post hole digger and went back to work on the fence during the weekends. One of my first thoughts were that Henry, the central character in Ernest Hemingway's "Farewell to Arms" was full of happy horse hockey when he mused that "The world breaks every one and afterward many are strong at the broken places." My broken leg was not strong then, and now, nearly a decade hence, it is still not strong at the place it broke. Furthermore, my neck is not strong more than forty years after it snapped, despite being reinforced by steel wire and grafted bone. While Hemingway was a fine writer, his male characters were sometimes pushed by athletic prose to act like cowboy philosophers with an overabundance of chest hair. Henry was nestled in bed with Catherine at the time he made the observation. I seriously doubt if he was thinking about manly philosopher things.

As for me, I just wanted to be able to man up for the next post hole, all of which would be dug the old-fashioned way with a manual post hole digger. There would be seventy-four holes all told. A gaspowered machine would have been faster but I had enough problems standing straight with a relative lightweight post hole digger. A heavier, powered one has enough torque to twist an unsteady man with a walker into a pretzel. It also seemed appropriate in the land of my grandparents to install posts the old-fashioned way. I figure Grandpa Jonas hand dug plenty of fence post holes in the Applegate Valley a century earlier. But we did cheat by encasing each post in concrete, ensuring the pressure treated posts would outlast the dogs and us.

Oddly enough, digging the post holes turned out to be great therapy, both physically and psychologically. I tackled the flat areas first, leaving the steep sections until my leg was stronger. The walker was useful on level ground but was of little help on the side of a hill. Taking a downhill header with a walker is not as much fun as it sounds.

To avoid walking more than was absolutely necessary since I tended to hobble along, using the post hole digger as a cumbersome crutch, I became very efficient in my fence work. I made sure I never forgot a tool. After all, it would take me fifteen minutes to painstakingly work my way to the tool shed when I forgot something. If there were a race between a banana slug and me with my walker, the slug would leave me behind in a trail of slime. On the days she wasn't working at her shop, Maureen could serve as my legs. But that would be unfair to her since she was already doing her share of fence building. Better to remember everything before arriving at the job site.

Even with the careful planning my leg muscles tired quickly. When the body no longer did my bidding, I would sit on the hillside and contemplate life. Moving slowly and stopping frequently gives you a different perspective. Since I'm a natural-born daydreamer, I was in my element. There are natural-born captains of industry who live to build a materialistic legacy. Others have an innate ability to act or sing well, rare gifts to be sure. Some folks even believe there are natural-born killers, although I like to think that is an acquired taste. But we daydreamers rarely commit mayhem, at least not in the physical world. I daydreamed my way through primary and secondary education, even made it my primary MOS (military occupational specialty) while wearing a uniform. Somber university professors did scare my old dreamy friend off for a time but it was always there, waiting in the shadows. I suppose if I had been born a generation later I would have been diagnosed with attention deficit disorder and plied with pills. But I like to think my reveries are constructive daydreams that help me figure out how to smooth out life's wrinkles before getting to them.

Sitting on the hillside one sunny spring morning while waiting for the burning pain in my leg to cool off, I thought about our adit on the opposite hillside. The next thing you know I was in Greece, mulling over the famous piece known as the *Allegory of the Cave* written by Plato nearly 2,400 years ago. The Greek philosopher apparently concluded that our grip on reality is tenuous at best. You may recall Plato relating how his mentor Socrates had described reality, using the example of chained people in a cave whose reality was the view they had of their flickering shadows on the cave wall created by a warming fire. I've always wondered why they were chained but their transgressions were apparently of no concern to Socrates. Perhaps the felons were natural-born daydreamers sentenced to hard labor. Whatever the case, Plato seemed to feel that our senses did a mighty poor job of portraying the real world as it is. He apparently believed the best way to comprehend reality is to take an intellectual approach. I think Plato concluded that all of us have times when we have been mentally confused, periods when we would be challenged by how to deploy the walker. A walker has handles you can grab; reality does not. Plato probably fell down a lot.

My Greek reveries were interrupted by two bicyclists pedaling slowly past on Sterling Creek Road, heading north. The two young men were deep in conversation not meant for public consumption. Now, I am not a snoopy sort. But they had pedaled into my listening space. I wasn't the one traveling down the road, carrying my post hole digger under one arm and invading the world of cyclists. So, like any good natural-born post hole digging eavesdropper, I listened.

"She doesn't need to know what happened that night," said the fellow in a luminescent lime green suit, the same color the Oregon Ducks sometimes wear while crushing an opponent on the grid iron. "I'm certainly not going to tell her."

"You may want to reconsider," said his buddy who had elected to wear a robin's egg blue outfit. "She will eventually find out. It's better if it comes from you. Tell her you had too much wine."

Still debating the issue, they moved beyond earshot, leaving me wondering to this day about that snippet of mobile conversation. What happened that night? Did she find out? Did he man up and tell her? Was she his wife? But the unchained shadows in my cave had pedaled off. The bothersome affair caused me to look at bicyclists a little differently. Don't get me wrong: I like bicyclists. Like butterflies, they do no harm as they flit past in their colorful garb. They don't pollute, providing you don't count the visual pollution created by some of their more garish colors. But the fact some pedal pushers keep secrets from their significant others is a troublesome trend. It's just not right. I'm sure butterflies don't have dark secrets about what happened one wild night after consuming too much fermented nectar.

Not long the two bicyclists pedaled past, a couple of tom turkeys looking for romance strutted into my work space. Turkeys, too, can be psychologically trying to a befuddled hillside occupant with a post hole digger and two bums legs. Like the wheeled visitors, the toms were decked out in their finest attire. A male turkey in spring-time courting plumage is a sight to behold. Take the snood. Please. The red fleshy mass hangs over the beak like a brightly colored athletic supporter. It's almost embarrassing to watch a tom strut his stuff when he has that testicular-like thing hanging down over his beak. You want to cover it with underwear. The weird thing about it is that it seems to have a life of its own. Sometimes it dangles as though asleep over the beak but other times it shortens itself, then stands up and sniffs the air like an earthworm after a rainstorm. As if the snood wasn't bad enough, toms have wads of red wattles hanging from their throats that do little to enhance their appearance, at least from a human viewpoint. Topping off their courting outfit is a beard. I'm not talking about facial hair here. A turkey beard is comprised of a bunch of feathers sticking out of his jutting breast like an untamed cow lick on a male model having a really bad day on the runway. But the toms aren't embarrassed in the least by their gaudy garb. They strut about, puffing up their feathers to make them appear twice their size. They then fan out their tails and drag the tips of their wings, each trying to outdo the other. With the sunlight shining on the hillside, a tom's feathers are iridescent. Their plumage shines gold and green, bronze and copper, purple and red. Finally, they create a booming reverberation that sounds like a teenager driving slowly past in a car equipped with amplifiers that pound out annoying bass beats that throb like heartbeats. Come to think of it, we human males do act a lot like tom turkeys when we are teenagers. While we are without snoods or wattles, although those of is sporting a bright orange Mohawk is arguably in the neighborhood, we certainly have the preening and strutting down pat.

Scientists who study turkeys say a tom does this to attract hens, all of whom are so drab looking they make an Amish grandmother look like a hooker on Anchorage's Fourth Avenue. Apparently a male turkey practices polygamy with gusto, happily mating with as many hens as he can entice with his courtship display. Whether the size of the snood matters in the courtship is something we'll leave for turkeys to decide. There are things that even turkey scientists would rather not know about when it comes to the activities of their Thanksgiving dinner.

While wild turkeys are interesting critters, they can be a bit dense. You have to wonder what Ben Franklin was thinking when he suggested during the birth of our nation that the wild turkey become the national symbol. Perhaps Franklin was taking a few nips of what today is hard liquor named after the untamed bird. Or it could have been that Ben's experiment with the kite and thunderstorm fried a few brain cells. On the other hand, bald eagles are scavengers at best. However, having watched wild turkeys for several years, I'm amazed any of them survive in the wild. They are puzzled by things as simple as a fence and can spend an eternity gazing at a post. No doubt the latter is mightily relieved to have found something dumber.

When a tom turkey stares at you in his comical way, moving his head from side to side in an effort to sort you out, one can't just sit there quietly. It would be rude. But I didn't know what would be proper etiquette when facing strutting tom turkeys on a spring day. So I winged it. "What's up with the snood, dude?" I asked.

For whatever reason, the question seemed to infuriate them both. Flighty critters, turkeys. They both let fly a slew of gobbles. I write gobbledygook fairly well and speak the dialect a bit but not enough to converse with a turkey. I felt like a first year French language student being dropped off in downtown Paris: the Parisians' rapid fire French would leave me baffled. But I caught the turkey's drift. I had just been cussed out by turkeys who could apparently swear like drunken sailors. Perhaps they had caught a whiff of their brethren being barbecued on the grill the day I broke my fibula and was letting me know they hadn't forgiven me for searing a family member. Or maybe they just disliked humanoids in general. They probably subscribed to the same school of thought as that great flyfisher and writer Norman

Maclean in his classic *A River Runs Through It* when he, echoing the sentiments of his preacher father, concluded that humans are a "damn mess." Both toms strutted slowly off, all the while swearing in turkey about the damn mess sitting on the hillside. But they quickly forgot me as they sought out companionship with the dowdy feathered maidens pecking around in our meadow in search of bugs. It occurred to me that turkeys probably have bug breath but we'll leave it to turkey scientists to sniff that one out.

Despite the leg problems and the on-going distractions of bicyclists, turkeys and other visitors, the fence building work progressed fairly smoothly. We completed the perimeter at last. At Maureen's firm insistence, the dog fence worms along the contour of the land, climbing the hill and meandering a bit in its long journey. But she acquiesced to my doggedness that it didn't dip into California. I had to admit it looked good and would give the boys plenty of rambling room.

When we were done with the wire garden and dog park fence, along with the picket fence separating the garden and dog park, we had dug seventy-four postholes. Giver our interest in recycling as much lumber as we could, we were happy our plans worked out to use the old cedar siding taken from the ancient garage to make pickets for the wood fence. Wouldn't want tomatoes sneaking into the dog park and harassing the pooches, don't you know. Those beefsteaks can be real bullies.

The three gates into the dog park were built of wire with a wood frame. But we wanted a traditional picket fence gate on the garden fence. As it happens, there was an old one hinged to an historic apple tree growing adjacent to the garage. When closed, the rickety relic had hooked to the side of the garage. It was a little too large for our garden gate but we loved the shabby chic style so we cut it down to fit the garden gateway. The best guess is the gate was built during the 1920s or in the Great Depression. Given the fact it provides a portal into our property's history, we couldn't toss it out. The gate had been crafted by someone of sound mind and steady hand who knew how to use a handsaw. Simplicity personified, the gate has a crossbuck pattern along with eight vertical pickets and two horizontal slats. It has a graceful arch, suggesting the builder had a flair for the whimsical.

Like the cedar siding on garage, the gate's cedar slats had weathered to a battleship gray. The pickets were also so brittle you could break one over a knee. Fortunately, our burly boys have yet to discover they can run through the fragile garden gate without breaking stride.

When we finally finished the fence work, it was a day that that changed our lifestyle. We now had a dog park our pooches coveted. With silly grins plastered on our faces, we took the pooches into the park and released them. Before trotting off to explore the park, their first reaction was to hoist their legs and let fly. We hoped that wasn't a gesture indicating their displeasure with their new outdoor digs.

As for the bipeds, the completed a fence, a year in the making, was a major milepost that made us proud. For me in particular, it was built during a low point, a period when I wondered if I was going to bounce back from breaking my good leg. I discovered that I had lost none of my lifelong bouncing ability. Or quirky sense of humor, for that matter.

"Yar!" I announced to Maureen as we watched the dogs explore their park.

"What?" she asked, looking at me as though I was uttering Martian. "Why are you suddenly talking like a pirate?"

"I'm not—I said 'yar,'" I replied. "Don't you remember *The Philadelphia Story*, that old classic with Katherine Hepburn and Cary Grant? When she was talking about the *True Love*, the sail boat he built for their honeymoon, she described it as being 'yar.' That meant it was good to go. You know, shipshape, like our fence. Yar."

"Well, I guess you could put it that way," she replied. "But don't start talking about stringing someone up on the yardarm."

"No problem—we don't have a yardarm," I said. "For your information, a yardarm is the part of the mast where sails are hung. Apparently, Blackbeard and his whiskered buddies liked to hang people from them, too. We could always put a yardarm up in one of the old pear trees in the dog park."

"We aren't going to hang anyone," she said. "However, that is subject to change if you don't stop talking like a pirate."

FIFTEEN

Cabin Decorating and a Wedding Arbor

D ECORATING A CABIN IS A SERIOUS BUSINESS, particularly if the decor is intended to faithfully reflect the rustic woodsy culture. Naturally, I had to toss out a few less than serious suggestions about what would be required for proper cabin accoutrements. Just to get the logs rolling, you see.

"We need to honor the conventions of cabin living," I told Maureen shortly after moving in. "It must be a harmonious relationship with nature. You know, living with logs and stone, becoming at one with nature and all. Above all, it's got to be manly."

One pretty eyebrow went up. Never a good sign.

"A true cabin dweller should display at least one animal skin which can be hung on the wall or spread out on the floor," I quickly added. "And we'll need a stout set of antlers which will be the envy of any visiting hunter. Of course, prominently flaunting an antique farm implement is a must, preferably one representing a rugged lifestyle from pioneer days of yore on Sterling Creek."

The other attractive eyebrow rose. My time was short.

"We already have the natural fur carpet, although we'll have to get the cats and dogs to hold still," I hastily concluded. "But you know them: slippery little devils. Maybe we could tether them strategically around the cabin so we won't have to walk barefoot on the cold concrete floor."

Cursed by an innate sense of decency, Maureen calmly waited until I was done with my tongue-in-cheek offering, her elevated eyebrows notwithstanding. But my more sensible half was clearly not amused by my flippant comments, although she knew full well I was just joshing.

"First, we are not going to walk on our pets," she said. "That's mean to even joke about. Secondly, we are not moving into a cave. We are not going to start gnawing on raw bear bones and grunting at each other, for crimony sakes. As for manly, I'm not even going there."

Yet, aside from not having a living fur carpet, although the occasional dust bunnies come close, my fanciful suggestions did largely come to pass. True, she did select the furniture, including a beautiful wooden dining table with matching wooden chairs which tied in nicely with the log rafters we had peeled. She also found an easy chair and a futon, both with log frames. She chose some electrical lamps that are reminiscent of the old gas lanterns once found in a miner's cabin.

While we are still in the vicinity of the subject, it needs to be established that she was the one who began calling my writing loft the "man cave." It makes me proud to know I planted the idea.

The thing about cabin decorations, they should all contain memories. Cabin inhabitants are moody folk who need to look at a piece of rustic art and reminisce. On those walls should be the stories of our lives and tales of the wonderful people we met along the way. I want to be ready when our grandchildren point at an object and say, "What's that, grandpa?" Our grown children may suddenly remember a prior appointment, having heard the tale ad nauseam.

As for an animal skin, there is one hanging on the east wall of the living room above the French doors in the form of a very large beaver pelt. James Bridger would have been impressed although Francophiles would probably shudder at the sight of a beast's fur so close to their beloved entryway. The pelt is called a super blanket, meaning it was once worn by a big beaver. In accordance to traditional cabin décor, the fine fur has been mounted on a willow hoop. The fur hails from Alaska where it was given to me by my old friend Gary Soderstrom who lives in the hamlet of Trapper Creek. The name is appropriate since he had trapped the critter in the area located roughly halfway between Anchorage and Fairbanks.

My friendship with Gary goes back to the Illinois Valley and our high school days together. After he graduated in 1969, he joined the Marine Corps, retreating to the Last Frontier upon completing his hitch. He has lived there for some four decades where he runs sled dogs, hunts, fishes and traps when he isn't working in construction. When I lived in the 49th state, he and I ventured forth on some memorable winter camping trips with his sled-pulling pooches in temperatures that seldom warmed up to a balmy zero.

His lead dog was a champion named Dozer who never met a mountain of snow he couldn't plow through. Gary would stand on the back of the sled's runners and yell encouragement to the dogs while I sat in the sled, comfortably wrapped in blankets while munching smoked salmon Gary had made. When we sailed over a large bump in the deep snow, I sometimes wondered if it was a hibernating grizzly. I never poked a snowy lump with a sharp stick during those icy excursions. Some things are better left unpoked.

You get a new perspective on life when you are ice bound. In those conditions, you slept inside a sleeping bag stuffed inside another sleeping bag. You kept your snow boots inside your bag to avoid suffering frostbit toes after jamming icy feet inside frozen footwear. It sounds challenging but it was fun, despite the occasional frosty nip. Alaskan snow is high class stuff, a powdery icy topping fit for the Last Frontier. Western Oregon offers only its distant Cousin Sloppy, an embarrassment to any decent mountain's proper winter attire.

Out on the trail when the mercury had to rise fifty degrees Fahrenheit to reach the freezing point, Gary often carried those little packets of butter, the kind they serve in restaurants. He would periodically pop one in his mouth. "Taste like cheese," he said when I asked about the butter. He tossed me one. Sure enough, it did taste like cheese in the subzero weather. But I preferred the smoke salmon.

When I left Alaska in 1986, Gary and his wife, Annette, were busy building a log cabin on their remote property, using their dogs to pull logs they had cut. The work was done in the winter when he had time off and there was plenty of snow to make pulling logs easier for the powerful dogs. There was no road to the cabin they were building for their family which included three children. They were living their dream. Over the years I would send them post cards with what I hoped were humorous comments from Ireland, Vietnam, Egypt, Germany and other places I had visited while both working and playing. I don't know if they received them since I never left a return address. The pelt serves as a reminder of good times in Alaska.

But you can't help but feel a twinge of sadness when you run a hand across the beaver's soft fur. If you look closely at the nearly perfectly round pelt, you'll notice two little eye holes, two tiny brown ears and some bristly whiskers. Seems to me it's a sad little face. All things considered, I would have preferred the pelt remained on the beaver instead of hanging on our cabin wall. Yet I have grown fond of the fur.

On the same wall hangs a pair of snowshoes my father wore during Alaskan winters in the late 1930s and early 1940s. The three-feet long wooden shoes were essential footwear he needed for surviving the long winters in the Far North. This was before snowmobiles marred the white landscape. The snow shoes have wooden frames with rawhide bindings. After all these years, they still look like you could strap them on and go for a hike in deep snow.

The center piece on the west wall in the living room is a former Chugwater, Wyoming area resident, a fellow we refer to as Yorick. With apologies to the Bard's Prince Hamlet, of course. We don't know if he was a fellow of infinite jest like his namesake but he does wear a toothy smile, sans the lower jaw.

Our Yorick is a Rocky Mountain elk skull crowned with a six-point set of antlers. He was found by Matt, daughter Derra's significant other. But the likable lad didn't shoot the elk, although he was armed with a hunting rifle. At the time, he was on a deer-hunting trip with his father, Doug, some forty miles north of Cheyenne in that state's southeast corner.

"Dad had a friend who knew the area so we decided to go hunting there," Matt recalled. "It's an interesting place. I love the name 'Chugwater.'"

Indeed, it has a folksy ring to it, one that is hard to say without a smile. The last census indicated there were 212 souls in Chugwater. Those of a superstitious bent will note that, if you included Yorick, the count would have been an unlucky 213. Poor Yorick didn't have a lot of luck in his life.

Father and son were hunting in an area where there is a small mountain range, small in comparison to the majestic Rockies on the west side of the state. After a morning hunt, Matt decided to take a hike up a mountain canyon.

"It was a fairly deep canyon," he said. "When I got up there a ways, I could see this elk skull and antlers up on a barren hillside above me. It was all bleached out. You could see it for quite a distance. Really stood out."

After hiking up the hill to the antlers, he was impressed by the elk rack's nice balance. What's more, it was a 6 by 6, a six-point, also known as a royal bull in elk hunter's parlance. The young hunter became a gatherer.

"It was just the head and the horns—everything else was gone," he said, adding that it had probably been pulled from the main skeleton by a carrion eater. How poor Yorick came to meet his end is unknown. There are no bullet holes in the skull. Perhaps he succumbed to a cold Wyoming winter.

Upon deciding he was going to bring the skull and antlers back to camp, Matt faced a dangerous dilemma. Carrying a large set of horns through an area where there are armed people eagerly hunting for any animal sporting antlers could be a little dicey at best. Granted, most hunters are sensible people who think before they pull the trigger. But there is a brain impediment a few hunters suffer from that is known as buck fever come deer season, presumably bull fever in elk season. Its symptoms include a high state of excitement and shooting wildly at anything that moves. The mere snap of a twig can trigger an onset.

Unfortunately, there are also some hunters whose intelligent quotient falls short of the triple digits necessary for proper humanoid cognition. They are always itching to pull the trigger. An elk rack moving along through even sparse vegetation could cause that trigger finger to twitch. Never mind it wasn't elk season when Matt found the horns or that the rack had been bleached white from exposure to the elements. Nor would it matter one whit that it would be carried by a human encased in hunter orange. Elk are foxy creatures, don't you know.

"I was a little nervous about packing it out," Matt acknowledged. "There were quite a few people out hunting and I had about a mile to go to get back to camp."

Concerned he could become the target of a barrage by a hunter suffering from a feverish attack or what a Marine sergeant from Texas I knew with a rare but rough wit would have crudely described as "eaten up with the dumb ass," Matt wisely carried the horns facing downward when he strapped them on his back. He had also tied strips of brightly colored cloth on the horns. It would be a long walk, knowing full well he was carrying what amounted to a target on his back for those hunters whose thought processes were limited.

But he made it safely back to camp. The only casualty was the skull's nose tip which was broken off during transit.

"When I got there, dad thought it was cool," Matt observed. "But he wanted to know what my plan was to get it back to Portland."

His father, an experienced trial attorney whose job it is to ponder strategy, was wondering specifically just how his son proposed getting the antlers to his and Derra's Portland home on a commercial jet. Good question. After all, Chugwater is a long way from Stump Town. Then there is the little matter of presenting a large exoskeleton as baggage to airline folks known for throwing a hissy fit over something no larger than an extra tooth brush holder.

But Matt, an engineer who is also skilled at figuring out solutions, was not to be deterred. He worked it out with the airlines which sensibly required each of the points on the antlers be wrapped to avoid spearing anything or anyone. He does allow he was the target of staring fellow travelers when he trudged through airports with Yorick. Fortunately, none had a feverish desire to fire away at the man elk.

Yorick proved too big for their Portland house with its low ceiling so Matt asked if we might want to add him to our eclectic cabin decor. You betcha. The old bull now looks down on the living room where he is easily seen from the dining table. It's interesting to watch the reactions of diners during our annual Thanksgiving feast. Some see Yorick as an attraction worthy of note while others find it repugnant, bordering on the barbaric. In our defense, elk is never on the menu. Eating wapiti could be construed as cannibalistic by one cabin resident who may or may not be a fellow of infinite jest. I'd rather not be gored by an angry bull elk, thank you.

Yet Yorick has been a peaceful addition, one that adds a primitive, earthy ambience to the cabin. We prefer to think he likes the place. After all, he occupies a place fit for royalty high above the woodstove.

Both Maureen and I agreed that a woodstove was a must, although a fireplace is preferred by many cabin inhabitants. The problem with fireplaces, while giving the appearance of being warm and cozy, they provide precious little heat. We elected to replace the old woodstove that had been in the living room with a smaller but more efficient stove with a glass front. It has a catalytic converter which greatly reduces pollutants.

The stove would have probably impressed early-day Gilson Gulch occupants, although their eyebrows would have shot up upon learning it has a catalytic converter. But I'm sure the salesman was joshing when he glibly explained that it simply encourages folks with big families to change religious beliefs. Upon seeing my puzzled face, he quickly added that the main mission of the catalyst, which resembles a honeycomb, is to increase the stove's efficiency by literally burning the smoke once the temperature climbs to a certain point. His explanation perplexed me nearly as much as his lame joke but the device seems to work well. When it comes to religion, I'm sure it answers all persuasions.

As for the antique farm implement I had suggested we needed as cabin dwellers, we have a rather striking one. Overlooking the patio is a traditional wood-handled scythe, one the Grim Reaper would kill for. Here is a substantial scythe that would make Mother Reaper proud of her notorious son. But it was made for reaping crops, not bipeds. Unless they were vegans, of course.

When I laid eyes on it at a yard sale in Jacksonville for $18, I snapped it up. The business end on the six-foot-long curved wood handle is armed with a two-foot-long steel blade that looks mighty menacing.

"Why are you buying that?" Maureen whispered at the time. "It's kind of scary looking."

"Yes, and it'll make killer cabin décor," I happily responded.

Of course, we don't know its provenance. The folks we bought it from said they found it in their old Jacksonville home when they purchased it. There is no company name imprinted on the blade, although it doesn't appear to have been fashioned by hand. It very well may have been employed to harvest crops in the Applegate Valley back in pioneer days. Perhaps my grandfather once wielded it. Or it could have come from a farm in Nebraska where it was later presented as evidence in a grisly murder trial involving a cornhusker gone mad.

Maureen refused to allow it to be hung inside the cabin but agreed it could dangle over the patio. But I was happy with its placement. Protected by the patio roof, it startles first-time visitors to the cabin. Apparently, they are concerned it might fall on them. I just smile and advise them not to stand under it too long.

Overlooking the deck on the opposite side of the house is our old misery whip, the old saw we found on our property and tried out by using it to buck a log. While we appreciated the misery it provided, once was enough. We agreed to retire it permanently by hanging it high on the outside wall over the deck.

While Maureen acquiesced when it came to the scythe and didn't put up much of a fuss over the misery whip ornamentat, she was more than a little dubious when I suggested using a cow bell for a door bell to let us know when we have visitors on the deck.

"You want to what?" she responded. "A cow bell? Please tell me you are joking again."

"Far from it," I said. "I'm not talking about attaching it to the French doors. This would be to the gate leading to the deck. It fits nicely with the rustic look. Besides, Mary Paetzel would have loved it."

At the mention of Mary's name, Maureen's frown turned into a beaming smile. "That's truly a wonderful idea, honey," she said. "I had forgotten about Mary's bell."

She readily agreed we needed something to allow visitors to announce their presence in a suitable country fashion. The ugly, unnatural sound of an electric door bell would rip through the rustic ambience like a buzz saw through balsam wood.

Although it was meant for a bovine, the bell was actually worn by Mary's dog Sally and given to me after Mary passed away just shy of her eighty-eighth birthday in 2007. What kind of person would strap a cow bell on a dog? In this case, a wonderfully eccentric woman with a crusty exterior but a huge heart for all of nature's creatures. She also put up with some homo sapiens, providing they weren't braying idiots. Nonetheless, she and I got on well.

The self-taught naturalist attached the bell to the pooch out of concern she would run off while the two were on their nature walks in the Siskiyou Mountains where they loved to roam. It seemed appropriate since the black and white mongrel was largely a breed commonly known as a cattle dog. The canine didn't seem worried she had been mistaken for a cow. She happily ran about, exploring a willow thicket here or a rock ledge there. When you ran into Mary out in the woods, you always knew her dog Sally was nearby by the sound of clanging down in a ravine or up on ridge. The pooch always seemed to be running, always full of joyful energy. Sally knew how lucky she was to have been adopted by Mary.

If you are fortunate in your life, you will meet someone like Mary along the way, a rare individual who didn't give a tinker's damn about what folks thought. Of the countless colorful characters I've met over the decades, she stood out. That she was a feisty curmudgeon at times there is no doubt. She told you like it was, with the bark on. Yet she could be as sensitive as a butterfly landing on the tip of your nose. She was also brilliant, funny and insightful with a keen eye for detail. And she was a wonderful writer, one whose prose is pure poetry.

Born in Peru, Ind., on Sept. 21, 1919, Mary, always one to find her own way, quit school after the ninth grade when school administrators insisted she focus on cooking and sewing classes instead of hard sciences. She tried to enlist into the Army during World War II but was rejected because she had sight in only one eye. No problem, she simply got a job working as an aircraft mechanic to help the war effort.

It was after moving to Southern Oregon in the 1940s that she began exploring the Siskiyou and Klamath mountains. For thirty years she collected pollen for a pharmaceutical company which used it for allergy tests.

But her job merely paved the way for her to study nature in the wild. She stopped and smelled the roses along life's long and winding trail. For her, these were wild roses which included everything nature had to offer, from bees to trees, from crickets to caterpillars.

In 1986, she discovered a rare population of Mariposa copper butterflies in the Siskiyou Mountains. Her interest in butterflies led to a U.S. Forest Service contract job to survey butterflies on Dutchman Peak, the 7,420-foot high pinnacle that overlooks the Little Applegate River drainage, including Sterling Creek.

Back in 1963, she had written a "Writer's Prayer" asking that her written words be remembered.

"Dear God, if you heed my humble prayer, I only ask that you help me share this work of mine, this talent of Yours, with others—that I may brighten a little the dark places, that I may gladden a little the heavy heart, that I may make less dreary the sad day," it reads in part. "With your help I beg to bring the sun and blue skies and clean woods, the peaceful river, the tranquility of the hills, to all who need and want them."

Her prayers were answered by Oregon State University Press, in part thanks to the persistent urging of Lee Webb, a longtime friend of Mary's. Now a retired wildlife biologist for the Rogue River-Siskiyou National Forest, he also helped edit her work. Her three books on natural science, including *Solitary Wasps and Bees: Their Hidden World in the Siskiyou Mountains*, were all published by OSU. Each one contains her brilliant essays and wonderful sketches of nature.

Not long before passing, Mary penned her final essay, titled "No grieving my friends."

"The bird in the gilded cage has flown," it began. "The golden path of the moon over the marsh is irresistible and the swans are calling. I won't be too far away.

"When the leaves turn golden in autumn, when the snow begins to fall, when the birds return in spring, I will be there," she added. "When the geese are on the wing, I'll be there.

"For the sounds of the wild things of the earth will be heard in eternity, and I'll be there."

There was no doubt in any of our minds that her spirit was there when some two dozen of her longtime friends and admirers gathered atop Dutchman Peak to honor her shortly after her death. She had been brought home for the last time, to have her ashes gently placed under a mountain mahogany bush on the peak she loved.

"Mary wanted her ashes scattered on Dutchman—she left expressed wishes for that," event organizer Webb reminded us that day. "But she didn't say 'have a party.' I can see her now, saying, 'None of that crap. Just put it out there.' But, secretly, she would be enjoying herself today."

We all laughed, knowing Mary would have definitely harrumphed at the whole spectacle. However, we also knew that, as he had indicated, Mary would have been tickled to see us all there, enjoying the mountaintop she loved. It was probably just a coincidence that a solitary white butterfly could be seen flitting among the mountaintop congregation that sunny afternoon.

Later, her friends were invited to take as a memento one of Mary's personal items displayed in the back of a pickup truck. The young woman who was staffing the fire lookout atop Dutchman at the time picked up the cow bell and gave it to me, knowing I had known Mary in earlier days. "Mary would have wanted you to have this," she said. It was a touching gesture that gave me a lump in my throat.

Now, every time I drive home and glance up at Mary's final resting place atop far off Dutchman Peak, I can't help but think of that remarkable individual who stopped to smell the wild roses along the way. And when that cow bell clangs on the gate, I think of her and smile. Hey, I warned you there were memories with every item decorating our cabin.

You get the picture: the cabin is rustically furnished and decorated inside and out, just as it should be. To provide a hint of sophistication, Maureen insisted on placing her piano in the living room. When she tickles the ivories, pleasant and recognizable tunes fill the cabin. The piano has been placed off limits to me. Something about the dogs howling. Man's best friend? Hah.

I did manage to offset the shock of seeing a piano in an otherwise ruffian-looking cabin by hanging a large print of a grizzly over it. The bruin was sketched by Bob Dale, a western artist from Texas with whom I worked at the *Anchorage Times*. The grizzly gazes lazily over a log as though he is considering an easy meal of the piano player. The placement of the print would have pleased Bob, a fellow with a Texas-size sense of humor. He would have noted they don't shoot even poor piano players in Texas but a bad pianist is fair game to an Alaskan grizzly. Bob, who passed away in his native Texas in July of 2015 at age eighty-eight, was fun to go fishing with. Like Mary, he was a hoot.

We can't leave cabin art without visiting the strangest creation that Gilson Gulch has likely ever witnessed. It wasn't for the cabin, of course, but it was definitely of the cabin. Indeed, it reeked of all things cabin. After all, it is made of logs, albeit Manzanita, the gnarliest, densest wood in these parts.

The log thing—that's the technical term—grew out of the announcement that daughter Sheena and boyfriend Justin were getting married on the beach at Lincoln City in northwest Oregon. Justin is a lawschool graduate but is otherwise a mighty fine humanoid. Sheena is a vivacious director of food and beverages at a major resort hotel in Southern California. They are a matched pair: gregarious, intelligent and humorous. Their dream is to own and operate a bed and dinner in the Pacific Northwest. Knowing them, the goal is easily attainable. They are doers. But first we had to get them through their August 3, 2013 wedding.

Our main role in the nuptials, in addition to giving the bride a hand in trudging down the sandy aisle, was to build a wedding arbor.

"Keep it simple," the bride admonished us. "Remember, this is going to be on the beach. It needs to be rustic. Nothing elaborate."

Promptly ignoring the instructions with a loving smile, Maureen announced we would build it out of manzanita growing on our Sterling Creek property.

"It is beautiful wood that lasts forever and it's durable, just like a marriage should be," she said. "This arbor will be unforgettable."

"Oh, we'll never forget this little project," I assured her.

While I am also a fan of manzanita with its deepred grain and resilience to everything nature can throw at it, I know the wood to be hard, very hard. Making what amounts to log furniture out of it would be challenging.

"The stubborn stuff has no sense of direction, twisting and turning every which way, like it's fighting with itself," I warned her. "It could run for congress."

On the sunny south slope of our West 40 grows the biggest manzanita I've ever seen. The one I would cut down was a good eighteen inches at the base with limbs twisting twenty feet high. We're talking more of an old-growth tree than a bush.

Adding to the challenge was the fact it was already July when we were assigned our arduous arbor task. Gilson Gulch tends to bake in July. Never mind the difficulty of working with twisted wood. We also had to ignore the heat, yellow jackets, poison oak and the occasional cranky rattlesnake. Rudyard Kipling was wrong: it isn't only mad dogs and Englishmen who go out in the midday sun. We quickly morphed into frothing mad dogs.

But we didn't bite each other. After all, our marriage turned twenty-one in our cabin on Sterling Creek, making the union old enough to drink. God knows it needed a stout shot from time to time. Like all partnerships, even those with a close bond like ours, there are always a few bumps and bruises encountered along the way. In truth, Maureen is very easy to get along with while her husband, well, I can be a real pill at times. I'm given to mood swings that would make an acrobat dizzy. You've already witnessed some of my puzzling tangents. Actually, I have a theory on the cause of digressions. But perhaps you are right. We need to get back to arbor building.

After I cut down the huge manzanita and bucked it up into logs, we lugged and dragged them down the hill under the blazing sun to Maureen's designated openair arbor lab near the cabin. As her assistant, I was equally culpable in the felonious crime against wedding decorum. I assaulted the wood with saw, axe and rasps.

A few imprecations were deployed in the hand-to-hand combat with the stubborn wood, verbiage that would have mortified a veteran logger with a graduate degree in the fine art of cursing. But don't be too harsh on Maureen. Manzanita is vexing wood.

Like Dr. Frankenstein, she began assembling her wooden monster while carefully instructing me what to cut and trim. She grabbed a bony thigh bone here, a skeletonized arm there, weaving it all together.

I observed the thing was beginning to look like the tragic result of a pterodactyl crash landing into a monkeypuzzle tree at the dawn of time. The petrified wood and bones intertwined over the ages, I suggested as we both stood back and stared at what we had wrought.

"It you look at it from my angle, you can even see the open beak of the pterodactyl caught forever in a dying shriek," I offered.

Not only did Maureen accept my wacky comments with the levity intended, she countered with her own nonsensical assessment.

"What this really looks like is something I saw in a Viking movie a long time ago," she said while stroking her chin. "But it seems to me there was a body on it, and they torched the thing."

With that, we both burst into spasms of uncontrollable laughter. Full blown hysteria complete with snot bubbles was only a snort away. I like to think it was the heat. Understand this conversation occurred while the temperature flamed into the triple digits. Any rational thoughts we may have had had long evaporated from our baked brains.

Yet out of the wooden pile of manzanita logs emerged an arch that actually bore some semblance to the beachwood wedding arbor pictures Sheena had sent us, thanks to Maureen's artistic skill.

"If the light is poor on the beach, and the guests guzzle the wine, it won't look too shabby," Maureen concluded of her masterpiece. She agreed when I suggested we needed one more manzanita stick about three feet long to complete the job.

"Yes, and it will need a little heft to it," she said.

"Indeed, you don't want the wedding arbor club to break, what with all the wedding guests you'll be whacking for making snarky remarks about this thing of grace and beauty," I said.

Peels of deeply disturbed laughter once more filled Gilson Gulch. Vultures circling overhead wisely drifted away.

But the large piece of cabinesque wedding décor actually looked good. For all its elbows and serpentine twists, it was perceived as a thing of beauty at the wedding.

As the nine groomsmen lined up for the ceremony, I couldn't help noticing they were a beefy bunch. So it came as no surprise to learn that at least one played football at the University of Oregon, while half of them, including our man Justin, were Duck cheerleaders. These are the stout fellows who throw the female cheerleaders high into the air as if they were rag dolls. By the way, Justin agrees his cheerleader tossing days are behind him.

Yet when it came to lugging the heavy, three-piece arbor from the parking lot onto the beach, it had been the eight bridesmaids who stepped forward to do the heavy lifting. Marines couldn't have taken the beach any faster.

Unfortunately, I couldn't figure out how the arbor puzzle, having been dismantled for transport, fit back together. Nothing seemed to match up. And the clock was ticking with the ceremony minutes away. But Derra and Matt, both Duck science alums, stepped forward to offer the needed brainpower to quickly piece the arbor back together.

Maureen had chosen the wood well. Manzanita represents the strength of character needed for a successful marriage. The deep red grain is strong and durable, while interwoven gray wood reflects the wisdom gained over the years. God knows that life has as many fascinating twists and turns as a manzanita limb.

I came away from the wedding with a renewed optimism about our world. Our new in laws and their friends are bright and friendly, the kind of people with whom you look forward to sharing a lifetime.

As for the Gilson Gulch wedding arbor, it was dusted off and used for its second wedding less than a year later when friends Jim and Sara McNeil borrowed it for their son's wedding in June of 2014 to a young lady from Texas. The wedding, held on Jim and Sara's property near Grants Pass, drew some thirty Texans, all of whom were apparently impressed by the wedding arbor. It seems our cabin décor isn't too shabby.

Meanwhile, the arbor patiently awaits its next wedding date. There will be a slight rental fee for non-University of Oregon alumni.

Our beloved Alyeska crosses a footbridge over the ditch to check out the snow. Part Akita and German Shepherd, the canine Queen of Gilson Gulch died at 15 ½ years old.

Mother Nature lightly decorates an old scatter rake just in time for the 2015 holidays. Like the ancient sickle mower in the background, the scatter rake was found on the property.

A light snow powders Gilson Gulch while a wisp of smoke from the chimney offers promises of a cheerful fire inside.

Top: The author tries his hand at demolition, removing the vertical logs that were charred when the cabin partially burned in the early 1990s.

Left: Maureen, left, and daughter Derra, taking a break from college, prepare to use drawknives to peel log rafters.

Top: The author tries to pull a drawknife through a knot. He found that using strong language often helped the process.

Right: Some drawknife wielders would rather not have their picture taken, particularly when they are making little headway.

Top: The 1920s garage was beyond salvage but the old cedar siding made a great picket fence to keep the pooches out of the vegetable garden.

Left: The old wood stove is believed to have been the one which heated what the author referred to as the "mystery cabin." That structure burned to the ground during a fire.

A man without fear as well as unlimited talents, local carpenter Paul Tipton checks out the roof ridge during the early stage of restoration.

During the years when no one inhabited the cabin, local vandals left their calling card.

While it is still too early to move in, the cabin interior starts to take shape. Maureen chose a hanging lamp in the living room that reflects the days of yore.

Maureen peeks over the edge of the burned loft which had been gutted by the fire.

The author takes a break after removing burned logs which once formed the west wall of the loft. The small room upstairs was turned into a writing den.

Top: The west side of the cabin was little more than blackened walls after the early 1990s fire.

Below: The fire all but destroyed the interior of the cabin.

Maureen and hairy pal Rajah check out the antique McCormick Deering bar sickle mower with its 34-inch metal wheels that could have been drawn by either horse or early-day tractor.

Top: An old apple tree planted perhaps a century ago still provides fruit in Gilson Gulch.

Below: Rajah takes a springtime stroll down the driveway as the old apple trees blossom

Top: A venomous visitor to Gilson Gulch in the form of a large rattlesnake slithers away, leaving the humanoid inhabitants a bit jumpy.

Left: The old garage provided cedar siding for the picket fence on the west side of the vegetable garden.

During the 2002 Squires Peak wildfire, an air tanker skirts a
huge plume of smoke billowing up just west of Gilson Gulch.

Weeds, boarded windows and burned logs didn't deter Maureen from wanting to restore the old cabin.

After a snowstorm knocked out the electrical power, Maureen cooked a hot breakfast on the grill.

SIXTEEN

We Really
Dig a Garden

A N EPICURE MY TWIN BROTHER IS NOT. As long as the dish doesn't contain what he refers to as that "damned celery," George is not particular about what he eats. He loves food, perhaps a little too much, judging by his expanding girth. He likes to wade into his meal with a knife and fork at the ready, stabbing and slashing at anything that puts up a fight. When at the table, the army combat veteran takes no prisoners. He is on a mission to consume whatever is before him. No wasting time talking about the food's origins, freshness or presentation.

"It's all just grub, fuel for the belly," he will growl while digging in. "No need to make it fancy."

There is no sane reason he can think of why anyone would want to go to all the trouble of raising garden vegetables. It's difficult to convince him there are wonderful rewards in gardening: the joys of crunching into a cucumber planted from seed, of chomping down on a juicy homegrown tomato, of picking your own bugs from your teeth.

Too much hard labor, George insists. My mere mention of looking forward to spring planting in our newly minted Sterling Creek garden nearly caused him to go into an apoplectic fit.

"Didn't you get enough of weeding and hoeing when you were a kid?" he growled. "God, you really irk me. You couldn't pay me enough to weed a garden. Just go to the store and buy a can of beans or whatever you are hankering for. Heat it and eat it. When it comes to victuals, I want no fuss, no muss."

This coming from a lifelong bachelor who thinks a healthy breakfast consists of a soda and doughnuts with ghastly blue or pink frosting slathered on thick. Any insistence that fresh vegetables are tastier and healthier is met with a look of annoyance. He has this way of tilting his head forward and peering over his glasses at you that reminds me of a contemptuous professor I had in college. The professor had a reputation for making students feel like bothersome flies; George's exasperating behavior makes you want to smack him with a fly swatter.

For some odd reason, he sometimes talks like he stepped out of a western flick, despite the fact he doesn't know road apples about horses. Truth is, he is well read, despite continually changing his major in college and not bothering to earn an onion skin. He has also gone global numerous times. Yet he does his best to conceal any hint of a formal education or worldly travels. At the time of this writing, he makes his home in Vinalhaven, a hamlet on an island of the same name off the coast of Maine. "I like being 3,000 miles away from you," he grumped to me during one visit. "You get on my nerves."

My twin likes to tell folks that he got the looks and the intelligence. My feeble rejoinder is that all he got out of the gene pool was a sense of humor. But I have to admit he is on to something, although I am correct that he inherited a larger funny bone than his twin. He was also born with a gregarious personality. He has yet to meet a stranger while I've always been a bit reticent. It's probably the result of being continuously outsmarted by an outgoing twin while we were still waddling around in diapers.

As you have no doubt gathered, he delights in provoking people, particularly if the victim shared the womb with him. A walking contradiction, he sports long, stringy white hair down to his shoulders and a snowy beard nearly to his navel. Never mind that he is a fairly conservative fellow who doesn't appreciate counter culture folks, despite looking like a poster child for what he refers to as "hippies." Both his sense of humor and tolerance has shriveled as they have grown older. It must be all that white hair cascading down from his head and face, blocking his view of the rich wonders found in our amazing world. Sadly, we have grown apart.

As for his attack on gardening, brother George does raise a valid point when it came to our childhood of fighting garden weeds. We spent long hours in the garden under a broiling summer sun. It is also largely true that George's taste buds never had much of a chance to become discriminating sensors of culinary delicacies. They were stunted largely because our mom, dear lady that she was, couldn't cook for beans. In point of fact, beans she could cook quite well but things got a little dicey once she ventured into cuisine that required following complex recipes. A stickler for details she was not. "You'd be surprised what you'll find in there," she would say of one of her creations that invariably left the child taste tester gasping for water while trying not to upchuck. But it was the closest thing she ever came to child abuse. She was a kind and decent person, despite being cooking challenged.

Incongruously, she could make an excellent pie crust from scratch. It was what was sometimes tossed into the pie that would curl your toes and make you want to hurl. We will come to that ghastly concoction anon. That repugnant odor you just got a whiff of? It's a green tomato pie's repugnant flatulence wafting out of the oven a few pages ahead.

"We are going to grow lots of different kinds of tomatoes but there will be no green ones served in a pie in this Sterling Creek home," I assured George. "I like tomatoes only when they are ripe and when they behave themselves by staying out of pies before they ripen. And once ripened the only pie they are allowed in is pizza."

George, whose taste buds are not so far gone that he isn't also repulsed by a greenish pie, found comfort in that announcement.

"Then maybe I'll stay here for a while," he replied. "Just don't try to force any fresh vegetables on me. I'll throw them at you. The ones I don't throw up, that is."

Like I said, he likes to antagonize the one he has known since before we were born. His gardening comments were planted as he was about to spend six months with us on Sterling Creek, a period during which he was recovering from a stroke. We took advantage of his captive status by trying to improve his dietary habits with a nutritional regimen that prevented him from breakfasting on sodas and doughnuts. We cleared all the offending fare out of the cabin, caused no small amount of brotherly loathing.

"Another week here and I'll be skin and bones," he grumbled. "Christ, the Nazis could have taken lessons from you. What's next, tree bark? When did you become such a health nut?"

"We are just trying to eat healthier foods," I explained. "We all need to eat things that are good for us. Besides, your doctors told me it is imperative you lose weight. We do like fresh vegetables. But we generally stop short of tree bark."

"The thought of fresh vegetables makes me sick," he retorted. "They don't have those preservatives that give grub that lasting aftertaste."

But I knew a dirty little secret about the great provoker: he doesn't actually mind vegetables from the garden, providing he didn't have to do any of the work and no damned celery is served. Not even one slender little stalk. To him, the wonderful crunchy vegetable with a slight nutty taste is disgusting. "It ain't a food fit for man or beast," he would say, intentionally butchering one of W.C. Field's best lines. Naturally, the kid in me made sure to slip damned celery into every meal. Being the only adult on the playground, Maureen told him when she added a little of the vegetable to her homemade potato soup. The recipe called for a smidgen, she politely explained.

"I'm not going to eat that crap," he grumbled. "It'll taste like sewage."

"I've never sampled sewage myself but I'm guessing this soup has a slightly different piquant," I said. "More of a nutty flavor without the septic tank ambrosia."

"God, you make my ass ache," he groused before digging in. He continued grumbling about the damned celery he could neither see nor taste, stopping only to ask for seconds.

"I don't like it but I don't want to hurt your feelings," he growled.

Despite his over-the-top attack on our desire to eat fresh produce, neither Maureen nor I are fanatical when it comes to consuming only healthy foods. We also love doughnuts, although those caked with sugar. But we eat them rarely and Maureen doesn't let me over indulge. However, I have yet to meet an ice cream I don't like. Upon reading about a restaurant in *Sunset* magazine that offers jalapeño ice cream, I told Maureen we needed to try it. She wrinkled her face. "I think that would make it hot ice cream" she said. "I prefer mine cold, thank you." One day I'll surprise her with a dish of vanilla ice cream in which tiny slices of our jalapeño peppers are strategically hidden. Her taste buds are more refined than mine so she should try it first. It's only right.

All our garden plants, including the damned celery, receive minimum care. We don't slave in the garden on a hot summer afternoon, crawling around tugging on weeds that refuse to budge while trying to keep sweat from dripping into our eyes. But we enjoy spending time working among the veggies on a summer morning, watering or pulling a weed here and there. We mulch to keep weeds at bay and to reduce watering. However, until we are forced to don pith helmets and grab machetes to fight through a jungle of weeds, we don't mind a few uninvited plants popping up.

That said, we do try to keep weeds from becoming bullies, choking the life out of our tender young vegetables before they can fend for themselves. It's on par with making sure the bullies on the elementary school playground don't make life miserable for little tykes.

Like school, a garden is a great place to learn, no matter how long your green thumb. Consider the lowly bean which takes nitrogen out of the air and puts it in the soil through a bacterial process in the roots. Anything that can make its own energy out of thin air without depending on fossil fuel is not to be scoffed at.

And there are garden mysteries like the thornless blackberry starts friends Jim and Sara gave us a few years ago. We planted the starts about three feet inside the garden fence. Once they got tall enough, I planned to build a wire trellis for them to climb on and do blackberry gymnastics. But the plants didn't wait for me to get off my posterior. When they reached about three feet high, the green feelers began reaching out toward the garden fence. How did they know the fence was there? They can't see. The fence, running east and west at that point, doesn't cast a shadow over the plants, alerting them to its presence. Perhaps thornless blackberries employ the Braile system.

Incidentally, like me, the plants hail from the Illinois Valley. They were ones which Sara got from her parents. Her father was Dr. Charles N. Versteeg, the only legitimate medical doctor available in the valley during my childhood. As for the skilled doctor, he was well prepared for the IV ruffians by having served as an Army physician during World War II. In addition to seeing him for the usual childhood illnesses and battle wounds, all local boys had to get a physical before being allowed to play sports in high school. For this shy teenager, the scariest sound was his gruff voice uttering five words: "Turn your head and cough." It was mortifying. Even now, when walking by the thornless blackberries, I feel an urge to turn my head and cough.

Being able to plant plants whose roots tap into our past is gratifying. Knowing we are part of a continuum that began shortly after humanoids left their caves and began raising plants for food is what draws many gardeners to moil in the soil.

I particularly enjoy stepping into the garden before the sun is up. The dew is on the leaves and the morning air is fresh and crisp. The morning is rife with potential. When the sun rises, the rays are warm on your back. You may spot a praying mantis, as gray as a devout Amish farmer, taking a moment out for pious devotion on a broccoli leaf before heading to church. Or a swallowtail butterfly will flutter past, bound for Jacksonville to flit among tourists in flowery shirts. Overhead, a turkey vulture will eventually drift over, floating in lazy circles. A family of squabbling ravens always flies over the little valley each morning. Ravens are interesting birds who bicker in flight. There is nothing they wouldn't argue about, including arguing about whether they should argue. Maureen has named the two loudest squawkers, calling them George and Paul. I like to think the latter always gets the last word.

No bickering is allowed inside the garden, however. When that gate closes behind you, you are in a sanctuary where time seems to stop, allowing satisfying reveries filled with contemplation and reflection. The longer of tooth I get, the more I'm convinced that the farther you travel outside your garden, the crazier the world becomes. Surely that nuttiness increases exponentially the closer you get to Washington, D.C.

Let the world throw all the tantrums it wants beyond the garden gate. I simply smile and pluck a few weeds or help a little old lady bug across a muddy row. I can be in that happy garden trance for hours. To get my attention, Maureen once turned on the sprinkler, although she insisted she didn't see me standing there that morning.

But I didn't mind. I was deep in thought about an article I had just read.

"Our plants are communicating as we speak," I announced.

She studied me for a moment until her curiosity could no longer stand quietly by.

"I know I'm going to regret this but I can't help myself: what on earth you are talking about?" she asked after turning the sprinkler off. "Are you talking to the potatoes again?"

"Seriously, plant scientists have determined that plants talk to each other," I said. "But not the way we do. They communicate with each other chemically through the air and in the soil. Our old trees warn each other when there is an insect infestation, that sort of thing.

"They don't tell each other risqué jokes or make deprecating comments about the latest bunch of buffoons living in the cabin," I continued. "But they exchange information.."

I pointed to the three apple trees and two pear trees growing just outside the garden in the dog park. They are all old growth trees about a century old.

"They give photosynthetic advice to the juvenile trees we planted," I told her. "Yep, the old codgers will be giving them pointers for years."

She continued staring at me, trying to decide whether I was being serious or pulling her leg. She opted for the latter.

"Since they don't have cell phones, which wouldn't work here anyway, do they have underground telephone lines?" she asked with a sweet smile. "Or do they do sign language with their branches when we aren't watching? Wow, and all this time I thought the wind was causing the branches to move."

While I may excel at wandering off topic, Maureen runs verbal circles around me when she impishly takes the baton. It's very vexing.

"Now, I can see a lot of potential here," she said. "Once I became fluent in tree talk, I could stand under the Ankerwycke Yew on the north bank of the River Thames in Merry Old England and ask it what it was like when King John signed the Magna Carta. That was back in 1216 in the nearby meadow of Runnymede. The old yew is 2,000 years old, so it was there. While I'm at it, I'd also like to ask if Henry VIII actually romanced Anne Boleyn under its firry limbs. I wonder if the tree told him to cut off her head."

"Fine, make fun," I said, trying not to let her know I was impressed with her infomercial on traveling to jolly old England. "But what I'm telling you is indisputable scientific fact. Plants communicate by releasing chemicals. It may sound rudimentary but they communicate better than some humanoids I happen to know quite well, by the way. At least they aren't snarky."

"God, I just hope they don't start gossiping about us," she continued. "You are going to have to watch your swearing. I heard our peach tree cussing the other morning. And that swear word was a real peach not fit for polite company."

Her soft laughter turned into a full throttle chortle. But I took the high road. I didn't let her know it's only funny when I poke fun. Judging from their silence, my woody friends obviously agreed, although there may have been some snickering from one of the old apple trees. I suspect the McIntosh.

But the garden shoes were on the other feet when Maureen, who didn't just fall off the potato truck when it comes to gardening, first introduced me to companion planting.

"Some plants play nicer with one type of vegetable," she explained. "It's like you and your twin. You get along fine with other people but not with each other."

Since George wasn't there to defend our rocky relationship, which was fine until we reached middle age, by the way, I had to step forward.

"We get along well as long as he behaves," I said. "Besides, how do you know when plants are in a spat? Does a Hatfield and McCoy blood feud that breaks out in the garden when we are asleep? Perhaps we had better keep the sharp implements out of the garden so the veggies don't slay each other."

Maureen wisely reined me in from wandering too far down the garden path.

"Don't push your luck, bucko," she said. "You will be having a soda and sugary doughnuts for breakfast if you keep that up. I can almost guarantee your grandparents Jonas and Harriett did companion planting. It's a tradition that was used before our ancestors left the old country. Centuries ago, gardens noticed that some vegetables grew better near some plants while they seemed to stall around other ones. So they planted accordingly."

"But is it based on science? Is there empirical evidence to support it?" I asked. In this rare instance I wasn't being a smart ass. Honest.

"They have determined walnut tree roots produce a chemical that inhibits the growth of tomatoes," she said. "On the other hand, cucumbers and cabbage are chummy. In your grandparents' garden, they would have definitely planted you and George in different sections to keep you from growing up to become the Bickersons you are today."

"Then we had better not plant a row of walnut trees next to a row of tomatoes," I said. "And don't even think about putting the rutabagas next to the turnips. I bet they would get into a fist fight before noon. We'd have to set the sprinkler on them to break it up."

I knew I was in for it when her laughter was followed by a smile that morphed into a smirk.

"When I was a little kid, I used to think a rutabaga was a car," she said. "You know, like a 1956 Studabaga."

"That was just awful," I said, although I was unable to stifle a guffaw. "You need to compost that one. Bury it deep. And you poke fun at my juvenile jokes."

But I still chuckle about that one when anyone mentions a rutabaga. However, we don't plant rutabagas. Maureen doesn't care for the taste. And I always shy away from any vegetable that has a funny name out of concern it may taste funny. In the interest of fairness, I should give them a try one day. Perhaps I'll take the classic '56 model for a test drive.

Before planting any spring vegetables, we always sit at the dining room table to plan our annual garden and pore over seed catalogues. It's our annual rite of spring. The planning session fills us with eager anticipation. Leafing through the catalogues, I can almost smell the aroma rising from the freshly turned soil of spring that reminds you the earth is a mighty fine planet. This is clean dirt out of which life will soon emerge, filling the garden with beauty and bounty. I am invariably reminded of Lord Alfred Tennyson, one of my favorite poets from across the pond.

"In the spring a young man's fancy lightly turns to thoughts of love," he wrote in an 1835 poem called "Locksley Hall." He was only in his mid-twenties at the time and would likely have had a difficult time telling the difference between a radish and a rutabaga. I can imagine him, just before dying at age eighty-one in 1892, rewriting that famous line: "In the spring an old geezer's fancy stumbles out into the garden to play in the dirt." But the line doesn't quite roll off the tongue the same way as the original.

While peace reigns in the garden, war can break out in the planning process during our kitchen table negotiations. While I am always eager to try new varieties, Maureen tends to keeping us grounded, insisting we stick with the tried and true.

"Fine, but I would suggest we plant only one zucchini," I told her in the opening session over our first Sterling Creek garden. "We should try to find a seedling that looks stunted. That way we won't be overrun with zucchinis until late in the summer. You may not be aware of the little known fact that Henry Ford had zucchini in mind when he first envisioned a car factory spewing out one vehicle after another."

"Yeah, right, but perhaps we'd better get a couple in case one doesn't do well," she countered. "And let's make sure they are hearty."

For once, I had a rebuttal that was not to be dismissed lightly.

"Let's not forget what happened to the Zucchini Man," I said. "You will remember that zucchinis nearly ruined his life. Very sad."

We both started sniggering as we recalled the zucchini tale of woe. We met the fellow we dubbed the Zucchini Man when our daughters were in junior high. With several of their friends, they joined pig 4-H. Pigs, by the way, are very smart animals that aren't filthy unless they are forced to live in a pigsty. When it came time to take the porkers to the county fair, a lot of parents stepped forward to assist. The Zucchini Man was a friendly fellow who, like countless Oregonians before him, had moved north from an urban center in California. A muscular chap who looked like he lifted weights when he wasn't volunteering to help 4-H kids, he told us about his eagerness to try his own hand at growing vegetables when he first arrived in rural Southern Oregon.

"I was really looking forward to raising zucchini," he said, talking somberly like a serial sinner confessing his transgressions to a priest. "I had always bought them before in a supermarket. I loved zucchini then. This was my first time at gardening, you understand."

He stopped talking and looked away, the pain of the memory apparently too great to go on for the moment. But he took a deep breath, sighed and pushed ahead.

"I wanted plenty so I bought twenty young plants," he said, biting his trembling lower lip. "I honestly thought I would need that many to keep us supplied with enough zucchinis."

Maureen and I were also biting our lips, fighting desperately to keep from chortling. I may have snorted a couple of times but I was able to stifle the outbursts.

"Well, everything seemed fine at first," continued the Zucchini Man. "My wife and I would go out to the garden and marvel at how well the zucchini plants were doing. All of them were thriving. We thought they were so beautiful. Real lush with those big leaves. It seemed to me I had discovered some wonderful way to garden. I thought I was a natural."

He stopped talking again. You could see the bitterness creeping in as he gritted his teeth before plowing on.

"Then the fruit of the zucchini or whatever it was called started forming," he said.

"I believe it's called a squash," I interjected. He ignored me and continued his sad story.

"We were overjoyed at first," he said. "We baked them, stir fried them, stewed them, chopped them up into casseroles. We even diced them and put them into spaghetti sauce. But we couldn't keep up. They were multiplying overnight. To think I used to love that slightly sour taste of biting into a chunk of zucchini floating in sweet spaghetti sauce. Now I hate it. Detest it. Nasty, wretched stuff."

For a moment he looked like my twin George contemplating biting down on a damned celery stick. But the Zucchini Man courageously continued.

"Do you have any idea how much twenty zucchini plants will produce?" he asked us. "The cruel answer is that nobody does. Brilliant mathematicians have tried to work it out but it's impossible. The zucchini just keeps coming and coming. And they all grow big, like green torpedoes. Oh, we gave away a lot but after awhile our friends quit coming over. Then they stopped answering the phone. The neighbors refused to come to the door when we knocked. We started dropping some off at relatives. I don't need to tell you that we weren't invited to the annual family reunion that summer.

"I tried stacking zucchini by the mail box with a sign, 'Free Zucchini,'" he added. "When I looked the next morning, there was more zucchini. Some gardener with a mean streak had piled on his excess zucchini overnight. I nearly cried."

By this time, tears of laughter were trickling down my cheeks. I started to sink to my knees. Maureen grabbed me but she was also having a hard time maintaining any semblance of decorum. We hung onto each other, shaking uncontrollably. Our storyteller didn't notice. He was lost in his own world now, wandering about in a nightmarish memory in which he was being stalked by zucchini zombies.

"I naively thought maybe I could sell some at the local farmer's market," he said. "What a bonehead. Have you ever asked folks at a farmer's market about setting up a zucchini stand? I had to walk two blocks back to my car and I could hear their laughter all the way, stabbing me in the back like a knife."

Maureen and I could no longer hold it in. Our peals of laughter started all the 4-H pigs squealing and snorting. Not once in the telling did the Zucchini Man ever waver from his somber presentation or acknowledge our amusement. He had the thousand -yard stare reminiscent of combat weary guys I had met in the Corps.

"Our marriage barely survived," he said. "We had always gotten along fine. But the zucchini really went hog wild in August and September. The stress was unbearable. We started arguing a lot. The counseling helped. But it was really the frost that saved our marriage. It killed all the zucchini plants, you see. My wife went out to the garden one morning and started screaming for me. I ran out there and we both started jumping up and down. The zucchini plants were withering away. We knew it was finally over."

The Zucchini Man took a deep breath and let it out slowly.

"We still garden a little," he concluded. "Tomatoes mainly, sometimes a few watermelons. But that's as close to the end of the alphabet as we go in the garden. The memories are still too raw."

After reliving the Zucchini Man tale and wiping away the tears of laughter, Maureen agreed that perhaps we limit our zucchini to one plant the first year in the Sterling Creek garden. "Just to be on the safe side," she said. "But we really should make sure it is a healthy one."

"I suppose we could always stack the excess by the Zucchini Man's mail box late some night," I agreed. "It has been two decades but he may still be a little jumpy. There could be trouble. I'd hate to be shot for unloading zucchini."

While we have never been overrun by zucchinis, although the squash had threatened several times, we do usually produce more veggies than we can consume. So far we've been able to pawn the excess away on to neighbors and other friends. When they stop answering the door, we'll seek counseling until the first frost.

During garden negotiations, it is the tomatoes that spark the most debate. They may look meek and innocent but they are thin skinned and vindictive.

"Let's don't try any weird ones at first," she said. "We need to have one season of gardening under our belts here before we get a wild hair to try things just because they sound interesting. Let's don't forget the Robesons."

Touché. She was referring to six Paul Robeson heirloom tomato plants I bought one year after they were recommended by a friend and fellow

Applegate Valley gardener named Lou. We had also planted a few other tomato varieties but the Robesons represented the lion's share of our tomato crop that year.

"These are the best tomatoes you will ever grow," Lou assured me. "The tomatoes are kind of purple with a tangy yet sweet flavor. Very large and juicy. And I like growing something that pays tribute to a great American."

It was the retired teacher's last comment that sealed the deal for me. Like my green-thumbed friend, I also had a lot of respect for Robeson, a black man born in the late 19th Century who refused to let others judge him by the color of his skin. He was an athlete, attorney, actor/singer and advocate for civil rights the world round, excelling in every activity. Valedictorian in his class at Rutgers University, the son of a runaway slave would graduate from Columbia Law School at a time when black people were still being lynched by racist mobs in the deep South. He not only fought for his race but reached out to other minorities who were being persecuted. When Jewish refugees were fleeing Germany's Nazi regime in the early 1930s, Robeson donated his income as the star in All God's Chillun Got Wings musical to help them. Among his friends were writers Ernest Hemingway and James Joyce. Like my friend said, he was a great American.

In part, I also planted the Robeson tomatoes to pay tribute to a small mountain peak on the southern flank of the Applegate River. On today's maps it is identified as Negro Ben Mountain, a landmark christened after a black settler who was a blacksmith in the valley during the mid-1800s. When identifying the mountain, early-day maps used a pejorative term that is patently racist in today's world, rap music notwithstanding. I figured the blacksmith would likely have gotten a kick out of a tomato named after a black American.

So on Memorial Day weekend that year we planted the Robesons. The holiday weekend has always been the weekend we traditionally plant tomatoes in southwestern Oregon. We firmly believe planting them earlier in the spring invites a killing frost, much like washing a fishing vest puts a curse on a fishing trip.

But the tomatoes didn't do as well in our garden as their namesake with the deep baritone voice did when he sang Old Man River on the world stage. Lord knows I provided care and comfort for the tomato plants, including planting their tomato toes deep in chicken poop fertilizer. I've faithfully watered and weeded all season. I spread a blanket of straw around them to serve as mulch. I coddled and cajoled them.

The plants grew well at first, becoming heavy with fruit. Then everything went south. The leaves began to droop. Something dastardly had invaded our tomato town.

"Maybe we ought to talk to them, let them know we feel their pain," I told Maureen. "If they can communicate with each other, then it stands to reason they can understand us."

"Better yet, let's just talk to people who know what they are talking about, sweetie," she said.

After consulting the always helpful garden wizards at the local OSU Extension Service, she identified the problem.

"We've got thrips," she informed me.

"I always make sure I turn the garden hose off," I sniffed. "Besides, I've never known a little overwatering to do this to tomatoes."

"No, silly, our tomatoes have been invaded by little insects called thrips," she said. "They feed on leaves and buds, sucking the life from the plant."

Thrips? I looked but couldn't see any creatures that would appear to answer to the strange name. She insisted they were there.

"They are very small insects that are hard to see but they come in hordes and cause a lot of damage," she explained. "In addition to eventually killing the plants, they can also transmit viruses. They are not nice."

"If you can't see them, how do you know they are there?" I asked. "Maybe we just got a bad batch of plants."

"You can tell they are thrips by their droppings," she said. "They are black and shiny. You can also see the damage they are causing. Look how distorted the leaves are." I looked at the wilted plants but couldn't see any insect poop. Then again, I am no bug expert when it comes to the bodily discharges of nasty little bugs. Nor is it an expertise I hope to acquire. But I was curious about garden nomenclature.

"Why on earth would they be called thrips?" I asked. "You would think they would be called tomato assassins or some such thing to reflect what they do. Entomologists may be brainiacs but they really dumb down when it comes to naming bugs. God knows what they must name their kids. 'Meet the twins, Thrip and Thrap.'

"For that matter, I also have a problem with lady bugs," I continued. "How do they know they are ladies? Dressed like that, you would think they would be called harlot bugs. And take your praying mantis. I bet they aren't all that devout. They may pray by day but you know they go out to the nearest watering hole every night to get slobbery drunk on fermented nectar or whatever it is they drink to forget what is bugging them."

OK, I know a praying mantis gets its name from the way it folds its front legs but its moniker always pops up when I think of amusing names.

In any case, we were flummoxed. The bugs and the viruses the thrips spread caused the plants to wither away. We salvaged only a few edible tomatoes that season.

"Our garden wasn't ready for Old Man River," I lamented to Maureen. We later gave Robesons another try and now sing praises of the tomato named after the remarkable individual.

However, despite the pampering and pleading, some tomato years are not bountiful. One year we had plenty of fruit but all the varieties refused to take the next step to become ripe for salads, tacos and BLTs. The fruit hung there like so many Bartlebys the Scriveners, preferring not to ripen.

"You'd think they would turn red from the sheer embarrassment," I said. "We had lots of red tomatoes by the end of July last year."

"Perhaps they are green with envy," Maureen tossed out before popping one of the few edible tomatoes into her mouth.

"It wasn't that good—a little green," she added before I could sputter a protest reminding her that our wedding vows included halfsies.

But I didn't mind all that much. While I like tomatoes, my wife absolutely loves them, particularly when they are fresh off the vine.

"We need to figure out what we can do with all these green tomatoes," she said after finishing her tomato. "I have a recipe I'd like to try."

"NO!" I protested, knowing precisely where she was going. The garden that had seemed so peaceful seconds before was now a minefield. In this case, the land mines were green tomato pies.

"This green tomato pie recipe looks very good," she insisted. "It wouldn't hurt you to try just a little slice. Pretend it is an apple pie. Do it for your mom."

My late mom was as angelic as a human can get but her green tomato pies were the spawn of the devil.

"I'm sorry but I can't get past the boiled sweat sock odor, the slimy texture and the gag reflex I get when I take even a tiny bite," I said. "It is truly horrible. Did you know the Geneva Convention strictly forbids threatening a POW with even a small wedge of green tomato pie? It's considered a war crime."

Although never having supped on a hearty bowl of boiled sweat socks, I have no doubt the hideous concoction would taste very much like a green tomato pie.

"You commit a war crime every time you exaggerate like that," she said. "Be a big boy and let's give it a try."

OK, I may have gone over the top a bit there but you have to consider that green tomato pies haunted my childhood. When the goofy horror movie *The Blob* came out in 1958, starring Steve McQueen, I figured it was a gob of green tomato pie that had come to life after being exposed to radiation. If you saw the terrible flick, you may recall the blob was alien slime from outer space that arrived via a meteorite and promptly began eating the fine folks of a rural Pennsylvania hamlet. For an adult, it would have been more slap stick than horror. For an eight-year-old, it was frightening, particularly if you were already fearful of a green tomato pie attack.

On the surface, the dreaded pie could have passed for one of mom's truly delicious apple pies. There was the golden crust, the amber liquid bubbling up out of the holes lovingly punched out by a fork. There was even that wonderful aroma of freshly baked pie filling our small house.

As a child whose imagination was already working overtime, I just knew that under that crust awaited freshly baked fruit. Apple, cherry or peach, I loved them all. Besides, I was always hungry. I couldn't wait to dig in.

Of course, being a kid, I wouldn't take into consideration that it was early summer and none of that tasty produce was available in Kerby back in the late 1950s. But reality slapped me in the face when I sliced into that beautiful crust which would have received a knowing nod of approval from Julia Child.

When the crust broke open, out spilled ingredients that brought to mind that old folk tune for children, "Great green globs of greasy, grimy gopher guts." A revolting odor invaded my nostrils. You could not have pried my mouth open to accept a forkload of pied green tomatoes. It was deeply unsettling, especially when your taste buds are anticipating apple.

Were it not for the green tomato pies of my childhood, I would have become an upstanding citizen and not a journalist.

Several weeks after out green tomato pie discussion I innocently went to town on a Saturday morning for an errand, followed by coffee with a friend. Maureen elected to stay home and relax. When I returned early that afternoon, a fresh pie sat cooling in the kitchen. It had a golden crust with amber liquid bubbling out of the top where a fork had left a pretty design. Naturally, I figured Maureen must have picked some of our apples. What a sweetheart. I grabbed a knife and cut a small slice to stave off hunger pains until lunch. She was out puttering in the garden and wouldn't mind. I happily bit into the pie.

The sound of a man retching up what tasted like sweat socks worn by a hygiene-challenged logger for a week brought Maureen hurrying into the cabin.

"Urghhhh gack," I moaned while gagging into a napkin.

"Oh, come on," Maureen said. "Your mom would have loved it."

"As a green tomato pie, it is perfect," I said after washing away the foul taste with a glass of ice tea. "There is the robust aroma of crusty old sweat socks with just a hint of road kill. And lets not forget that wonderful mystery flavor, one reminiscent of an outhouse on a hot August afternoon."

"You are incorrigible," she said. "Let me try it."

She took a fork and cut a petite bite from my plate, chewing thoughtfully for a moment.

"Honey, you are so wrong," she said. "Boiled sweat socks would taste heavenly compared to this slop."

With that, she spat the contents into a paper towel and threw the contents into the trash.

"OK, that was truly ghastly," she said, laughing. "But we tried it. I'm sure your mom's green tomato pie was much better."

"Trust me on this," I said. "You make a green tomato pie just like the kind my dear old mom made. And, like hers, it is really, really bad."

I like to think that green tomato pies are forever in our past. But I recall that in *The Blob*, the viewer never quite knew whether the monster was killed off. I remain vigilant.

UP STERLING CREEK WITHOUT A PADDLE

SEVENTEEN

Digging History

T HE MOST EXTRAORDINARY ITEM WE HARVESTED from the garden that first year was not a vegetable, although it looked like a small white onion bulb when poking out of the newly tilled ground. I picked up it up and knocked off the glob of dirt stuck to one side, intending to chuck it over the fence for the deer so they could get onion breath. But the orb was hard, not soft like an onion.

We had unearthed a very old marble. Upon closer inspection, it turned out it wasn't really white. More like the color of dirty snow you would find along an Anchorage street come April. Unlike the marbles I played with as a kid, this one was not perfectly symmetrical. There are bumps and blemishes, making it wander a bit when rolled across a flat surface. Life has been hard on the tough marble that had been scratched and gouged over time. Getting roughed up by a garden tiller certainly didn't do it any favors.

"Cool," I told Maureen, slipping into the vernacular we used while first going together as teenagers in the late 1960s. "Just think: some kid used this in a local game of marbles 150 years ago or thereabouts. I can picture young barefoot kids from Sterlingville playing marbles around here. This one likely belonged to one of the little scallywags."

"They were probably like the Kerby scallywags, getting into fights over marbles," she mused as she rolled it between her fingers. "Yes, this is very cool. I've never seen one like this before."

Jeff LaLande, retired Rogue River-Siskiyou National Forest archaeologist and an historian with a deep interest in the region's past, was also impressed when I showed it to him. His expert estimate is that the ceramic marble's birth is circa 1870, placing it in the period when young Tom Sawyer was emerging from Mark Twain's creative genius.

I couldn't help but wonder what it had witnessed. It may not be up there with an honesttogoodness Barlow knife that Tom raved about, but it was the kind of treasure he would have gladly accepted from fellow urchins in exchange for an opportunity to slap whitewash on Aunt Polly's fence.

It would follow that the other items we tilled up—square nails, old pottery and bits of glass colored by time—also hailed from that period, give or take a few decades. Understandably, any dirt-sifting archaeologist would shudder at the thought of someone using a tiller to harvest artifacts.

While the other items are interesting, the marble was personal, a toy from the distant past. A local boy carried it in his pocket. Perhaps his parents bought him some marbles during a shopping spree in Jacksonville. Maybe it came from a Sterlingville store. Or he could have won it in a game of marbles.

Historians tell us we humans have been playing with small round balls of clay and stone for more than 3,000 years. Romans enjoyed marblelike games, as did the ancient Egyptians. Perhaps Mark Antony played marbles with Cleopatra, although he no doubt found it difficult to concentrate on the game, what with having to keep an alert eye on her asp.

As Maureen rightfully noted, we played marbles when I was a kid in Kerby. The Sterlingville kids likely followed the same rules as did Kerby urchins, despite the fact nearly a century had elapsed between the games. Of course, our marbles employed in the late 1950s were a bit different than those used by the Sterling Creek kid in the 1870s. Our marbles were beautiful glass marbles of every imaginable color.

The old marble represented the eclectic treasures we could always expect to unearth when we dug into the earth around the cabin. As our likable rascal Tom would have no doubt observed, you couldn't swing a cat without hitting a remnant of early-day life along Sterling Creek.

Consider the time Maureen began digging a hole out front of the cabin for a four-foot high ornamental tree we were planting. I was working on the other side of the cabin, trying to figure out why the old pump wasn't pumping. It was a slow process, one that took more than two hours, despite the liberal application of powerful cuss words.

Taking a break from my lack of progress, I walked around the house to check on how Maureen was faring. I couldn't see her at first, although there was now a mound of earth adjacent to her job site. I walked a little closer. The top of her head could be seen poking out of the hole where she was crouched.

"I started finding square nails, then some purple glass," she explained while wiping her forehead, leaving a dirt smudge above her left eyebrow. "So I kept digging. Dug up some curious-looking pottery. All broken, though. I think they are called shards."

She stood up. Her shoulders were barely above the top of the hole.

"This may be a little deep for the tree," she acknowledged as I reached down to help pull her out.

"If you had been on the beaches of Normandy in June of 1945, you would have been very safe in that foxhole, Sergeant Kilroy," I said. "But we are going to have to back fill so the top of the tree will at least clear the hole. It's probably not a good idea to bury the entire tree."

"Funny boy," she said, lobbing a small gob of damp dirt at me.

We sorted through her morning haul, lingering a bit over the pottery. The designs seemed to be handmade but there wasn't enough there to determine exactly what it was.

"Tantalizing," I said. "Maybe it was a pitcher."

"No, it is too fragile to have been a pitcher," she said. "I think it was part of a tea cup."

Monetarily, nothing she or I ever dug up may have been worth much but we found them all fascinating, nonetheless. Like the marble, the square nails—they are actually rectangle—and the pieces of pottery and glass were once handled by someone when Sterlingville was young. A settler had picked up that square nail, holding it between finger and thumb before hammering it home.

History, of course, is all relative. What is considered old on the West Coast is relatively new in places like New England, a region whose history with European arrivals goes back some 500 years. Yet the tomb of Newgrange in Ireland, which I and my twin and daughter Amy visited in the mid-1990s, dates back to 3,200 B.C. However, a sagebrush bark fiber sandal found in a cave in Oregon's Fort Rock is estimated to be some 10,500 years old. The sandal had already been in that New World cave for 5,000 years when the Newgrange builders first began showing up at the Old World job site, probably complaining about the working conditions and lousy pay. Scientists didn't say what size foot the native North American had who wore the sandal. It looks like about my size. That would be size nine.

If I had not crossed over to the dark side to become a journalist writing the first rough drafts of history and had my mental acuity been a tad sharper, I likely would have become an archaeologist or historian. There is just something about digging in the dirt for artifacts or poring over old documents that I find appealing. Archaeologists flit like time-traveling butterflies back through the continuum to land on a particular era. They are detectives who piece together the puzzles of our past. I've yet to meet one who wasn't interesting, filled with fascinating tales of yore. Then again, I do tend to be a mite nerdish.

For the history aficionado, especially one interested in the story of the West, our cabin and it's environ is an ideal setting. Sterlingville once bustled with life, and that activity spilled over onto what is now our property. Visitors to newly-minted Sterlingville noted that the Sterling Creek drainage was dotted with cabins and teeming with miners. It stands to reason that several would have staked out what came to be known as Gilson Gulch. After all, it was just a five-minute walk to one of the two Sterlingville saloons for a shot of rotgut.

We now have enough square nails from our property to nail a small shed together, although they are probably too elderly to stand up to a young hammer's blow. Other larger iron artifacts include horseshoes, broken pick and ax heads that had been battered down to the nubbins. Our friend Stuart, a surveyor we hired to formally mark the property lines since the back fence largely wandered from tree to tree, found a heavy hand-forged gate hinge. In fact, the wire on the southwest portion of the property appeared to be antique. The only time we had seen barbed wire that old was a museum in Wyoming, one which had a display of historic wire. Joseph Glidden, who received an 1874 patent for inventing that particular strand, would have recognized his handiwork, although our wire's vintage isn't quite that old. However, as the devil's rope goes, it is brawny wire. None of that namby-pampy little stuff such as that produced in the last half century.

With no county dump and no garbage service, rural residents commonly disposed of old stuff back on the North 40. Several small ancient garbage dumps, what archaeologists would refer to as middens, dot our property. We discovered one when we spotted what appears to be a radiator frame for a Model A or Model T sticking up out of the brush. When we walked over to investigate, we could feel and hear the crunch of buried debris underfoot. Perhaps the oddest item we found is what appear to have been ancient shoe chains. Think tire chains that fit around the bottom of a boot. They look like something a medieval torturer would have killed for. One of the niftiest items unearthed was an antique silver serving spoon. With a little polish, it could be passed off as a family heirloom during barbecues we regularly have. If you happen to be at one and are a little squeamish, you may want to avoid the dessert dish festooned with the nifty antique serving spoon.

We did not use the antique spoon when we invited history detectives over for a barbecue. That would be Mark Tveskov, professor of anthropology at Southern Oregon University; Chelsea Rose, historical archaeologist and SOU faculty member; and Ben Truwe of Medford, a retired printer turned history sleuth of the first order. I had pestered them all as a journalist and had found them highly intelligent, knowledgeable and just plain interesting to be around. They found me somewhat tolerable as journalists go.

As luck would have it, I ran into Mark when we were both giving presentations for the video archives at SOU in nearby Ashland in early August of 2015.

"We've been finding a lot of old items around our cabin near the old boom town of Sterlingville," I told him. "We like to have you come out and give us your assessment."

"Sounds interesting," he said. "We're going to have to pay you a visit." At my request, he contacted Chelsea and Ben, both of whom proved to be equally curious about our cabin and the old stuff we had accumulated.

The lure of barbecued salmon sealed the deal, along with my pledge not to annoy them with too many questions that smacked of a journalistic Spanish inquisition. We placed the artifacts on folding tables set up on the covered patio out back. Since we didn't want to overwhelm them with too much old stuff, aware that much of it was pedestrian, Maureen suggested we gather only a few representatives of our growing pile of pioneer flotsam.

"Hmmm, now this is an interesting piece of obsidian," said Mark upon his arrival, having made his way straight to the display tables and picked up a flat slice of the black rock. I submitted it may have been employed as a scraper by native people.

"Yes, there is a lot of rind on it," Chelsea observed as she checked it out.

"That's the patina, meaning it has been exposed to the elements for a long time," Mark explained.

"It definitely has been worked," Ben offered. "It is not indigenous. A human carried it here."

The piece, which is about six inches long and slightly curved, was dug up inside the dog park near the west gate by one of the pooches in a futile attempt to get at a burrowing ground squirrel. As Mark noted, the patina indicates it was not a fresh chip off a block of obsidian. We have several large chunks of obsidian at the cabin, apparently gathered by a previous resident who was an avid rock hound. Those chunks likely hail from central Oregon where they are found naturally. But that obsidian is glossy. The scraper, as Mark had observed, has a distinct patina.

"There is a somewhat controversial dating technique in which you measure how thick that rind is to tell how long it has been exposed,"

Chelsea said. "These were modified by humans therefore the thickness will tell you when the human made the tool. But there is a lot of variability in what environmental factors create the rind."

"Yes, an event like a forest fire could reset the hydration level," Mark said before moving on to other items.

Ben and Chelsea checked out the eighteen horse shoes we have nailed to the old tack shed while Mark continued to pore over the items laid out on the tables. Inside the historic structure is a small round log across one side where saddles would have been hung. As a nod to its original function, I've nailed the eighteen horse shoes we've dug up around the place on the front of the shed. All of them have been hung with the "U" facing up to catch any good luck that may come our way, of course. No, I'm not superstitious. I just have an irrational fear of bad luck.

"You have quite the gamut of horseshoes over there," Chelsea said when they returned from the shed. "There are machine-made shoes but you also have hand-forged shoes. That's a wide range."

"But you have no big draft horse shoes," Ben added, referring to the large equines who would have pulled the heavier farming equipment.

Certainly a Clydesdale or Percheron would have come in handy to drag the ten-foot wide scatter rake or heavy sickle mower we found on the property. One would have also pulled the hay fork Maureen uncovered in one of the man-made mounds up the valley. The hay fork, also known as a bale lifter, hooked the bales with its harpoons armed with contractible spurs, and was then pulled up to the barn loft via a horse-powered rope and pulley system. It's an odd-looking device; one I thought would surely stump our visitors. But I hadn't allowed for Ben's eclectic knowledge of off-the-wall stuff. He identified it at first glance.

"They used those bale lifters to lift bales of hay up into a barn," he said. "These ends (harpoons) reached in and grabbed the bales to hold them when they were lifted."

Like I said, these folks were sharp. Having sorted plenty of detritus laden with broken glass over the years, they were also on familiar ground when poring over the glass fragments we had found.

"This is the bottom of a wine bottle," Chelsea said, lifting up a broken piece of old glass. "It could be fairly old but it is kind of hard to tell because wine bottles haven't changed that much. They figured out a good way to make them and stayed with it."

She turned it over a few times, studying the indention on the bottom.

"This one is handmade," she said. "It is consistent with the 19th century."

For a few minutes, they discussed the origins of wine bottle bottoms, a discussion which had to be a first heard at the cabin. It turns out the notch at the bottom of a wine bottle, a feature I would have referred to as a dent, is known as a "punt." They were apparently first made when glass blowers began making bottles and wanted to make sure their creation curved inward to be able to stand on a table.

"In the 16th Century, they had these big pick ups," Mark said, referring to the fact the punts were also used to pick up the bottles. "But they were also made much later on."

And they were familiar with the maker of a broken piece of an old medicine bottle which reads, "The Great Dr. Kilmer's Swamp Root Liver, Kidney & Bladder Cure." Turns out some of our pioneering forefathers and foremothers, while swearing to be bible-thumping teetotalers, weren't above taking a couple of swigs of "medicine" that would have made a hardened drunk shudder with delight when it went down. Medicinal purposes, you understand. The piece we found near the cabin has an embossed kidney on it, indicating it was from the large bottle of the stuff. The fact it is described as a "Cure" indicates it was made before congress passed the federal Food and Drug Act of 1906. The law required the word "Remedy" be used with such dubious offerings since the word doesn't carry quite the sure-fire promise of "Cure."

One glass piece on the table was the top of a sunpurpled bottle that was identical to an unbroken bottle found during a 2010 archaeological dig led by Chelsea in Jacksonville. That bottle, also the color of amethyst, was a 1870s prescription bottle, she noted at the time.

I was particularly proud of the bottom of a pickle jar I found which is embossed with the date of June 9, 1903. The lavender-colored glass was stamped Kerr Glass Co. of Portland, Or. Were the pickles dill or sweet?

Like my late great aunt Gladys Ingersoll Carter, did the pickle maker toss in hot peppers to allow the pickles to bite back?

"That's a patent date," Chelsea observed, shattering my belief the jar was born on that precise date. "But this was probably made in the teens before World War I. The glass solarizes with the manganese which was used as a decolorant. After World War I, they no longer used manganese for a decolorant." Without the clearing agent, the glass would have apparently had a greenish hue.

But the 1901 date etched into the brass base of a .12 gauge shotgun shells we collected apparently did reflect its birth year. Whether the shot slew a fat grouse for dinner or sent a bear fleeing out of the fall orchard ripe with fruit we will never know.

Nor do we know what the musket ball, discovered with a metal detector near an ancient apple tree in front of the cabin, was fired at. But Mark, whose research has included recovering musket balls from battles during what was called the Rogue River Indian War, confirmed it was definitely a musket ball.

"This is a .36 caliber," he said as he rolled it between thumb and forefinger. However, he was quick to observe it is difficult to determine when it was fired.

"Effectively, most muskets were out of use by the 1870s," Mark said, noting they were replaced by rifles which could be swiftly reloaded with cartridges. "But that doesn't mean someone on the farm didn't keep one into the early 20th Century to use."

They are also musket aficionados who continue to use them today, mostly as collector pieces, although some still hunt with them, he said.

"The musket ball looks like it was nearly spent before it hit its target," Ben observed, pointing to the slight mushroom shape on one side. If it had struck an object while speeding along at full flight, it would have been more misshapen, he added.

All three were curious about the old religious cards in both English and Swedish that Maureen and I had found while cleaning out the packrat nest in the attic area. They were also interested in Rev. Hamilton's book, the one we found in the warming oven of the old woodstove. But no one could come up with a rational explanation how it survived the ages. It obviously hadn't been there since the cabin was built but had been placed in the woodstove's warming oven years ago, certainly before the cabin partially burned. Whether its jacket was singed by the cabin fire or by a long stay in the warming oven is also has to be left to speculation. Perhaps a previous cabin occupant or a descendant can shed some light on the antiquarian mystery.

They studied the old photograph of the Gilson ranch, 1900 era, which shows the western section of our property, including the old cabin which now serves as our master bedroom. Nearly a dozen buildings can be seen in the picture.

"That is a lot of out buildings for a hardscrabble farm," Ben commented. "It seems a little excessive." But he allowed the obvious activity on the land resulted in ample items left behind for posterity.

When we sat down for lunch, the archaeological discussion was the main fare, a dish I had been looking forward to for weeks. To start the verbal feast they were about to serve up, I asked them about the prevalence of locally unearthed artifacts. Turns out they are not that uncommon.

"In my backyard in Medford, I've dug up horseshoes, chunks of 100-year-old bottles and newer plastic toys," Ben said. "I've even found a couple of hammer stones and some trade beads."

Chelsea, who lives in the Applegate Valley, has also found some interesting latter-day relics on and around her property.

"One of the projects I'm working on now is recording the archaeology of the late 20th Century marijuana grows," she said. "There are 1980s platforms dug up in the hills. When I first saw them, I thought, 'Wow! Pit houses.' Then I saw there was irrigation going to them. So I'm working on that, doing a lot of ethnography and oral history."

"When you think about it, that was part of the off-the-grid cottage economy that has been going on around here forever," Mark said.

"Like what happened during Prohibition," Ben agreed. "Now is the time to study it, of course."

As gatherers of history, they know those then illegal grows will soon fade into the history of the region much like the evidence of moonshine activity during Prohibition has slipped away over time.

As we ate, the talk turned to how the world has changed since folks first settled in Sterlingville and its environs in the mid-1850s.

"Back in the day when it was less of a disposable culture, people were not generating trash like they do today," Chelsea observed. "And, of course, the kind of trash has also changed."

"I think it is also an issue of population," Ben said. "The early automobile tour books wouldn't tell them to clean up their campsites but to just be sure to picnic far away from a farm house so the trash they leave won't bother the farmers."

A close inspection of photographs from the early 20th Century shows plenty of trash along roads, he added.

"I remember as a kid seeing that," said Mark whose age is approaching the half-century mark. "Then along came the crying Indian in the 'Keep America beautiful' campaign. I remember that shift when it became socially unacceptable to toss stuff out of your car."

He was referring to Iron Eyes Cody, an actor who, as Ben observed, was actually a first–generation immigrant from Italy. But Iron Eyes embraced the Native American culture, marrying an Indian lady and adopting two Indian boys. His acting career was largely spent acting in Indian roles and promoting Native American causes. In the early 1980s, he was the grand marshal for the annual Boatnik parade held every Memorial Day weekend in Grants Pass. As a reporter for the *Grants Pass Daily Courier* at the time, I had interviewed him. He was a pleasant fellow who was serious about speaking out for indigenous people.

Given the geneses of Sterlingville, the conversation eventually turned to the interesting subject of gold mining.

"The mining stories out here are really an untapped vein from an historical point of view," Mark said. "We've touched a little on it with the Chinese miners. Jeff LaLande has as well."

Chelsea coughed to get his attention, noting her master's thesis was focused on the Chinese miners who once labored in these parts.

"Yes, that is true," he acknowledged. "But the non-Chinese, the

Europeans and the Depression era and through World War II, that has not been a major focus. That's what I'm talking about."

Because of the problems created by people squatting in many of the historic mining cabins perched in the local mountains, both the U.S. Forest Service and the Bureau of Land Management began removing the old structures in the 1970s and '80s, they noted. As a result of the cabin-removal program, much of the history has been lost, they added.

"For instance, you go down the Rogue River today and it looks like a pristine landscape," Mark said. "But it was very different during the '40s and '50s when there were all those mining cabins out there."

"Those cabins told an interesting part of the larger story," Chelsea said.

Until recently, the Depression era mining activity was not considered worthy of study, she said.

"People didn't consider that period archaeological," she said. "But it was a fascinating time. The automobile gold rush in Jackson County, in and of itself, was very interesting. They had mining classes. People would drive out to mine right here on Sterling Creek."

The Sterling Creek discussion naturally flowed into the challenge of keeping local history alive in an age when many newcomers lack any interest in what occurred before they arrived.

"A lot of people are totally oblivious to their environment and the nuances of what altered the landscape," Chelsea said. "Places that people think of as pristine were totally modified by the mining activity. What some see as old-growth forests have often been totally changed by human activity."

Like the cabins that have been removed, many historic communities are no more, leaving little trace of their once thriving existence, she said.

"There was Uniontown and Logtown," she said. "There were people all over the place, mining and farming. Now those towns are gone."

"That's the general theme for rural southern Oregon," Mark added.

The point, Chelsea concluded, is that homeowners should make an attempt to document history on their property when they can.

"On our place, we moved there fifteen years ago and have cleaned it up so much," she said. "Now, when I think about it, I wish I had taken more photographs of how it was when we moved there. There was this old dump truck down in the field. We thought, 'Get rid of that!' Now I wonder what the story was with that. Yesterday's trash is today's treasure. Literally.

"The person who lived here before and used a bulldozer to cover up old buildings or whatever, in his mind they were not historical resources," she added. "They were a hazard with sharp nails. Maybe they looked bad. The thing is, not everything you find that is old is pretty or charming. But it is all part of the story."

Like Chelsea, Ben agreed there should be more documentation.

"But, at the same time, if everything were saved, no one would give a crap about anything," he said. "It is only the things that packrats save that make it into the museums. If everything were saved, we wouldn't need museums."

"It's an interesting question of what homeowners should do about the history they find on their places," interjected Mark, having finished with a salmon steak. "I think they should do what they want to do. We are professionals in this field. It is our job to record and explain history. But history is in the eye of the beholder. Some people don't find it significant."

"It is a non-renewable resource," Chelsea said. "It may not be important at the time but it may be later."

"I agree with that but what if you don't believe it is important?" Mark asked.

"There are laws in Oregon which protect some historic resources," she said.

"But we only have laws when people don't agree on something, when they don't agree in behaving in the same way," he countered before turning to me. "Now, you are a guy who is interested in culture and history. You find meaning in all this stuff. But someone else may move in here and not care about it at all. Who is right and who is wrong?

"I am definitely in favor of historic preservation," he added. "But you can't make people care through laws."

In the 1930s, a rancher in Gold Hill on the Rogue River asked an archaeologist to check out obsidian artifacts at his place, resulting in finds that shed new light on the local prehistoric culture, he said.

"Today, we are lucky if we don't get shot when we go onto a ranch," he said. "Laws are great but you can't cudgel someone with a law to make them care about something they don't care about."

Not being able to help myself, I pressed Ben to explain what prompted the former printer to become a researcher and gatherer of local history. Too few other people out there care about local history. Why should he?

"I will not be put on the defensive for doing what every human should be doing," he replied, looking stern but fighting a grin. "Every human should be curious about the history of where they live. Every human should be researching the world around them. You got a lot of damn gall trying to put me on the spot. I am the normal person here. Everybody else is wrong."

With that, all of us, including Ben, burst into laughter. Maureen and I were sorry to see them leave at the end of the barbecue. The table may have been cleared and the dishes done but much food for thought remained.

EIGHTEEN

Firing up the Metal Detectors

W HEN MATT SWEPT THE METAL DETECTOR OVER the ground near the old apple tree, the device went off like a slot machine hitting the zillion dollar jack pot in Las Vegas.

"Now that looks very promising," offered the soft-spoken young man who is no fan of hyperbole.

He is daughter Derra's significant other, the kind of person you hope your offspring would link up with when it comes time to choosing a partner in life. He is a thoughtful listener with a dry sense of humor. When he speaks, the words are fired with laser beam accuracy.

I've grown very fond of him, despite the fact he has the same impediment that inflicts Derra. Sadly, they were both born with brilliant minds. They are the type of folks who made my college years much more stressful than need be. You know the kind: they ace all the tests without seeming to study while you are sweating bullets just trying to comprehend the introduction to the text. They met at the University of Oregon where they breezed through, earning biology degrees, minoring in chemistry. Upon graduating from Duck U, Matt, an honor's college graduate, naturally, decided to become an engineer. He promptly applied to the engineering school at University of Colorado-Boulder. Never mind he had no engineering background. He strolled through the program, quickly receiving a master's degree in engineering. Life is not fair.

The couple—he now works as an engineer for a Portland firm while she is employed at Intel—had come down for a weekend visit to our Sterling Creek abode. As usual, they brought their two rambunctious city dogs for a romp with furry country pals Harpo and Waldo.

While their uncouth cousins are pure mongrels, pooches Remy and Atti are pedigreed canines hailing from a long line of blue bloods. Remy, a German short hair pointer, answers to the formal name of Royal Remington Coco Baby. A yellow Labrador, Atti carries the equally officious moniker of Attis Sister Golden Hairs. We don't call them by their formal names because it would shame them in front of our country mutts who are always ready with a howling guffaw. Very uncouth, our boys.

However, the unadulterated urban dogs with aristocratic ancestry and the country canines of questionable parentage are the best of buddies. They run together until their tongues are lolling. With Harpo, thanks to his mastiff genes, you will notice a little drooling when he gets overexcited. But he does it very tastefully, unlike the slobbering purebred father who sired him. Fortunately, his mom was mongrel, through and through. She was a fine lady.

During their visit, our plan was to take in the "The Sound of Music" at the Camelot Theatre in Talent, one of several top notch theaters in the Rogue Valley. The Portland pooches would stay back at the cabin in their crates while ours would spend a few hours of quiet time in their kennel. For their anticipated good behavior, they would be munching on doggy treats while we were enjoying the musical. Our dogs aren't much for music, even when the hills are alive with it. As urbanites, Atti and Remy probably prefer a little Johann Sebastian Bach, perhaps a fugue in D minor. Me, I wouldn't know a fugue from a fuchsia.

Maureen has a fine singing voice but the only way I could carry a tune is to strap the poor thing down with duct tape and push it around in a wheelbarrow. Like many who can't sing, I've always loved music and refuse to give up my search for a key. Any key. My wife, ever the kind soul, quickly intercedes on behalf of all quivering victims within earshot the moment I let fly. When I ignore pleas to stifle myself, she employs the tough love technique, one that is usually effective.

"I don't want to hurt your feelings but, speaking for everyone in the vicinity, including neighbors John and Rhonda, don't try to sing," she said a few days before we attended the musical. "Your attempt at 'The Sound of Music' soils the wonderful work of Rodgers and Hammerstein. So just stop it."

Soils? Ouch. I had started to hum, a precursor to my bursting out with something about the hills being alive with the sound of music. But my wife was standing with that listen-up-little-mister stance, her arms akimbo.

"Honestly, you scare the dogs when you sing, sweetie," she said in an effort to soften her rare harsh words. "They think you are in pain and they want to join in your lament. So please give them a break."

Now it is true that both Harpo and Waldo have been known to accompany me in song, although I prefer to think they are the ones off key. But, unlike some biped meanies, I don't make fun of their misguided musical efforts.

On the day of the musical, Maureen and daughters Derra and Sheena decided to drive into Jacksonville that morning for a leisurely stroll among its well-preserved historic buildings. Matt and I volunteered to stay home and look after our furry brethren.

But we had an ulterior motive. Matt had brought along a metal detector his sister had just bought him for his birthday. Earlier on the phone he had suggested we might want to try it out on our old homestead.

"With all the square nails you keep digging up, it's likely there are more interesting items out there," he said.

He didn't have to convince me. Although there was no gold to be found in our adit on the hillside, I knew there had to be a pot of gold buried somewhere on our historic property. Moreover, I've always been intrigued by the thought of messing around with a metal detector.

"I suspect you're are right," I said, nearly rubbing my hands in anticipation. "Let's see if we can find a few gold pieces before the women folk return."

No, I don't use that term when they are present. And you don't need to mention it to them, either.

Anyway, I have this theory, an admittedly hyperbolic one at that, about our place being the depository for hidden precious metals.

"The way I figure it, some whiskered prospector, not trusting Jacksonville banks, let alone Uncle Sam's monetary system, buried nuggets mined from Sterling Creek," I told Matt. "Maybe he dug them up; maybe he purloined them from the Sterling Mine. Who knows? But, with the bunkhouse on our property, those nuggets could be on our land. We just have to think like a miner and find the cache."

The question, of course, was where to start to look for treasure. I suggested we scan the area just beyond our garden.

"I find square nails every time I till the garden," I said. "There must have been a building here back in the late 1800s."

"Let's go for it," said my prospecting partner.

You will recall that it was in the garden where I unearthed the 1870 era marble. Unless it was a steelie, Matt's device wouldn't detect marbles but there had to be more metal items in the area. Maybe there were even some gleaming yellow nuggets that weigh heavy in your hands.

I randomly chose a spot near an aging apple tree largely because I like the old wooden sentinel. If you stand on one side of the tree, it appears to be a foot and a half thick at chest height, the distance forestry folks use to measure tree diameter. But when you walk around it, you discover the trunk is no more than two inches thick. For a trunk, there is only a thin band of wood, a mere half shell of the original trunk. What happened to the tree? Perhaps it was partially girdled by hungry stock once kept on the ranch, killing part of the tree. Or maybe it nearly succumbed to disease. Each year we think it will finally be felled by the Grim Reaper. But it keeps coming back, first with bright green leaves of spring, followed by red little apples each fall. Like the square nails we unearth, it is as tough as, well, nails.

"I've always had a good feeling about this old fellow," I said of the tree. "Maybe it'll bring us a little good luck. Let's try here."

Sure enough, about six feet from the base of the tree, the very first place we scanned, the metal detector went ballistic. Using the pick, I carefully dug about six inches down, peeling back a section of grass to expose the roots and bare earth below. Matt stepped in to begin nosing around with a trowel.

"Here it is—a coin," he said as he reached down into the dirt to pick up the item. He quickly wiped off the dirt to expose a small copper disc.

"An Indian head penny—not too shabby for the very first place we detected," I added.

Grabbing a water bottle, we poured the liquid on the coin to further clean it, although it was in relatively good shape. "It's a 1907," Matt said as he wiped it off with his fingers. "Wow. More than a century old, even before World War I."

In fact, it was minted the same year my grandparents homesteaded in the Applegate Valley. Maybe it was among the coins that passed through the calloused hands of my farming ancestors who would have counted their pennies. Whatever the case, chalk the date up to another odd coincidence in a series of seemingly unrelated events that would raise the eyebrows of those who find meaning in such things.

Unlike coins that have been handled by countless hands over the decades, the penny was not noticeably worn. Judging from its depth, we surmised it had also likely been in the earth for many years, undisturbed by the comings and goings of various property owners going about their business.

A quick internet check indicated the penny had been minted in Philadelphia, and that it was not a particularly rare coin. In 1907, the Philly mint clinked out 108,137,143 Indian head pennies, the most for any year since it started minting them in 1859. Its value? You may be able to sell it for twenty bucks today, providing the buyer is not well versed in numismatics. It certainly wasn't a gold coin like the two the Mayles found in Provence. Apparently the 1909 version of the Indian Head penny, minted in San Francisco, is worth nearly $1,000, providing it is in excellent shape. That was also the last year the U.S. minted the picturesque coin.

"Well, even though it's of little monetary value, it does increase our riches in making a connection with that past," I said as I held the 1907 coin in the palm of my hand. "We can hold a piece of history which meant something to those who had come before us.

"Perhaps it was handed out as change at a Jacksonville store after a hungry miner came in for supplies, slapping down a few nuggets to pay for his grub and a new pair of hob-nailed boots," I added. "Its provenance will always remain a mystery. But it's certainly tantalizing to think about."

"Yeah, it is an interesting little find," he agreed. "It's not something you see nowadays. It feels like you're holding a little bit of history."

I was impressed. Not only could he shovel happy horse hockey with his elders, but he could do it in fewer syllables.

"But we are looking for gold coins, damn it," I said. "Let's go find it."

"Damn straight," he said with a big grin. "Let's go for the gold."

Told you he was a keeper.

Both of us had the same thought: since we found the penny in the very first spot we dug, coins would be popping up left and right.

"We probably should keep all the coins we find, including this one," I said, tongue held firmly in cheek. "We can toss the smaller gold pieces into an old coffee can or something but we lets set aside all those in denominations of, say, $10 or more."

"It might be quicker to just toss the little ones into one pile and the larger ones into another," he suggested, tossing another shovel full of road apples on the growing verbal pile.

But the results did not sustain our dreams of untold wealth. Square nails kept popping up, as did pieces of iron whose original purpose was lost on us. The best we came up with was what looked like half a pair of ancient scissors, the kind used for sewing back when folks still mended their torn clothes.

We were still looking for pay dirt when the Jacksonville tourists returned. While they were impressed by the penny, they insisted we get ready for the musical. Like elementary kids told that recess was over, we moped off our playground. It wasn't that we didn't want to go to the musical. We just knew that the next coin was waiting.

As anticipated, the musical was fun. The singing was superb. I hummed along, albeit silently since Maureen was only a sharp elbow away. But I was slightly disappointed the family von Trapp wasn't there. Don't laugh. They very well could have been. Four descendants of the original family troupe now live in Portland where they have teamed up with the Pink

Martini band to continue the von Trapp musical tradition. With a twist, of course.

When the music died away in the hills during intermission, I couldn't help but think about that penny. I suspect that Matt was also mentally back on Sterling Creek during the lulls. Me, I kept walking across our front meadow with his metal detector, thinking that if we had just gone a little farther south—or north, or east, or west—we would have hit pay dirt. I knew the treasure is out there. Waiting.

Finding the penny prompted Maureen and I to add a metal detector to our bucket list. But we never seriously gave it much thought until after I retired and started writing at home. Out of the blue early in 2014, I received a call from the National Park Service which was seeking a content editor for an anthology written by various experts on the ecology of our fascinating region. The agency has jurisdiction over the Oregon Caves National Monument in the Illinois Valley and the Crater Lake National Park in the Cascade Mountains some seventy miles north of Medford. The spectacular lake, created by the eruption of Mount Mazama some 7,000 years ago, is the deepest in the Lower Forty-eight states. And the caves contains fascinating fossils going back well before humanoids ever trod the land. The region is a veritable treasure trove for those with an interest in natural science. As a lifelong avid reader not accustomed to being paid to pore over a book, I was stoked. As expected, it was an interesting read. The book was written mainly by scientists, most of who could wax quite eloquently. Later, I would edit the 450-page manuscript. Talk about manna from heaven.

"You know what," I suggested to Maureen, "I think we should use this to buy that metal detector we've been talking about. We'll never get one if we keep putting it off. This money came from a fun project. Let's spend it on something that is going to bring us years of fun."

"Sounds good to me," answered my best friend.

After doing a little homework and talking to folks who own metal detectors, we discovered that Oregon has a renowned maker of the unique devices. That would be White's Electronics, Inc. in Sweet Home, a town located in the northwest quadrant of the state.

Although we are well traveled when it comes to traversing the Northwest, we had somehow missed Sweet Home over the years. We drove north to check out the community and the facility. Turns out the town is a cool hamlet on the banks of the beautiful Santiam River in the western shadows of the Cascade Mountain range. It is also has its share of early Oregon history. Nice place. But isn't as historically quaint as Jacksonville. And keep in mind that Sterlingville was already dying away when Sweet Home was incorporating. The Cascades are beautiful but the beauty of the Applegate Valley is exceedingly hard to beat. I'm just saying.

Although I am no fan of touring facilities, the electronics plant, complete with its own little museum, proved fascinating. The family-owned business began in 1950 and now makes the machines for everyone from backyard recreationists to the military. In fact, it now has a second facility in Inverness, Scotland to serve the Asian and European markets. We came away with a newly-found appreciation for Oregon entrepreneurship, a rudimentary understanding of metal detectors and a spiffy machine of our own. We were ready to roll up our sleeves and find treasures on our historic property back in the picturesque Sterling Creek drainage.

But the fellow who demonstrated the model we bought offered a few cautionary words.

"It's encouraging you have found a lot of square nails and other relics on your property," he said. "Just be aware that means you will be finding a lot more of the same with this detector. Not everything you find will be coins. And no metal detector is fool proof. When you pick up a metal detector, be ready for both excitement and disappointment. It can be frustrating at times. Remember, the hunt is half the fun."

He was right about both the quantities of square nails found and the entertainment value. Spending a couple of hours nosing around with a metal detector is fun, even when finding only detritus left by earlier dwellers on our land. Unfortunately, the summer quickly turned into a blast furnace, cooling our enthusiasm for outside activity. Mother Nature punished me for some forgotten past transgression by broiling us in triple-digit temperatures nearly daily in July of 2014. We put away our metal sniffer, waiting for cooler weather. Besides, the user's manual noted the device sniffs better when the soil is damp.

"The way this gadget works is by transmitting an electromagnetic signal from the search coil into the soil," I explained to Maureen. "What happens is the metal target within range becomes excited, then retransmits an electromagnetic signal back. It's like they have a romantic interest in each other. But their electromagnetic romance is stifled when the ground turns as hard as a brick like it is now."

Like you, Maureen snorted at that fanciful explanation. However, she allowed the electromagnetic romance was a nice touch of balderdash.

But one morning in early August the god of metal detecting was magnanimous, offering clouds which actually dropped a little rain. After writing for about four hours, I fired up the metal detector late in the morning. For the most part, writing is a relaxing endeavor but I do need to step outside periodically. Otherwise I start typing, "All work and no play makes Jack a dull boy." Makes our pets nervous, particularly if I happen to be lugging a double-bitted ax.

I decided to go up the valley a bit and into our forest. As expected, I found a few square nails as well as round ones which are known as wire nails. The square nails were enough to keep me interested.

I began sweeping an area about ten feet from the base of a large tree when the detector lost all sense of decorum. All the bells and whistles were going off, causing startled birds to fly from nearby trees and the neighbor's donkey to start braying. If it were an opera singer, the squealing metal detector would have shattered our cabin windows with its elongated high C screech.

The electrical screen indicated the machine was fairly certain—ninety percent—that a coin was embedded in the dirt below. Judging from the mechanical fuss, I figured it was at least a $20 gold piece.

"Man, oh, man," I muttered. "Matt is going to miss out on the big find."

Incidentally, in addition to the 1907 Indian head penny, Matt has also used his metal detector to find the .36 caliber musket ball and a 1917 Lincoln head penny on our property. When it comes working a metal detector, he is a past master.

Using a small pick, I gently dug about half a foot down. The signal became stronger. The screen informed me the buried treasure was about six inches deeper.

"Holy moly," I told myself. "Wow, this could be it."

But I wanted Maureen, who had the next day off, to be there when we uncovered the lost Sterling Creek treasure. With great reluctance I turned off the metal detector, gathered my pick and trowel and trudged back to my writing loft.

"This is it—the big one!" I told Maureen when she got home late that evening. "There is no doubt in my mind that I've found it. We're talking mother lode. Go ahead and schedule that trip to Ireland and Scotland. We are in the money."

"Geez, honey, calm down," she said, laughing. "Let's not spend the money just yet. We don't know what it is. Maybe it's just some junk or something."

"I know this is a big mother," I insisted. "We should go out there tonight with flashlights and dig it up."

"We are going to do no such thing," she said. "I'm tired. It will be there in the morning."

Yet she was the one who brought it up during our taco dinner. If you ever stop by for dinner, you have a fifty-percent chance of eating tacos. It isn't just that we love tacos as much as the fact it is one dish I do well.

"Do you really think there is something valuable buried there?" she asked as she munched on one of my culinary master pieces.

"Of that I have no doubt," I said. "I'm still getting used to our metal detector but I've never seen it act like this. It actually seems like it is excited."

"Well, I hope you haven't started talking to the machine," she said. "It's not a person. And don't you dare bring up electromagnetic romance again. This fork is very sharp."

I went to sleep that night trying to imagine what awaited us. The potential for a big pay off was there. I reminded myself that our little valley once housed the bunk house to the Sterling Mine which produced more than $20 million in gold over the decades it was in operation. Like most groups, miners are a mixed bag with some being a little more honest than others. Perhaps one miner had a couple of gold nuggets or bright yellow coins he wanted to keep safe from his coworkers. Maybe the paymaster filched a few gold coins from the payroll and hid them away, intending to retrieve them in later years. The possibilities were endless.

I awoke at 5:00 a.m., got up and made us something hot to drink before returning to the bedroom to wake Maureen. But she was already dressed, having succumbed to the metal detecting fever. We were like two kids on Christmas morning, waiting for daylight. Of course, I was the most eager to open the big present under the cedar tree.

The dogs had also perked up. They sensed our excitement and suspected that a dumb human trick was about to be performed. Their tails wagged in anticipation.

"This must be what gold fever feels like," Maureen said as she sipped her hot chocolate. "You know there is something out there just under the ground. Then your imagination goes wild, and you start planning on what you are going to do with all the money."

"This has nothing to do with an imagination," I insisted. "The machine has no imagination. It is like a scientist. It weighs the facts. The facts told it there is something incredible in the ground.

"But, since you brought it up, I was thinking we might want to upgrade our canoe," I added. "It's more of a lake canoe than a river canoe. It doesn't have enough of a banana turn. Makes us look less than adventurous."

"Let's wait a little on the canoe, mister," she said, laughing. "There may be nothing there. Or maybe it is just an old horse bridle attached to a standing horse skeleton."

She spread some blackberry jam on her toast before taking a delicate bite while keeping her mischievous grin intact.

"Besides, I love our canoe," she continued. "That curve you are talking about on the canoe, well, a real canoeist would know it is called the rocker. Your banana turn is what canoe makers refer to as the amount of curve in the hull. Obviously, the more pronounced the rocker, the easier the canoe is to turn."

"Wow—those are mighty impressive facts," I said. "Since when did you become a canoe expert? You're the one who would insist on wearing a life preserver if we launched in a kiddie's pool."

"I read an article about canoes the other day," she confessed. "You should read it. It had some good tips on how not to flip a canoe, not that I have ever done that. Taking a plunge in a cold river is just a little too adventurous for me, thank you."

She was, of course, referring to the Eskimo roll—half, that is—that friend John Decker and I did in the chilly Wood River.

"Fine," I replied. "I flip a canoe once and it will now be written on my tombstone: 'Here lies a canoe flipper. What a doofus.' Better be nice or I won't take you to the treasure trove."

"Oh shush," she said. "Harpo and Waldo know where it is. They would show me, then help me dig it up."

By now the sun was beginning to peek over the mountain towering over Sterling Creek. It was time. Not wanting to jinx us, I purposefully didn't shave that morning. Although I'm new to the sport of metal detecting, I do know from sad experience that it is bad luck to shave before you head out at sunrise on a fishing expedition. After all, I had shaved the chilly canoe-flipping morning. In any case, I figured the two activities were close enough to be influenced by the same gods of good luck. Unfortunately, we departed from good fishing/canoeing protocol by brushing our teeth on the day we sought the treasure. I did it without thinking about the repercussions. It was only when I was putting the toothpaste away that I realized it could cast an evil eye on our fortunes.

I grabbed the metal detector and headed toward the spot which I had marked with two crossed sticks, forming an "X." Maureen was right behind me, carrying the tools of the trade. I also brought along a little rock hammer in case the gold coins were stuck together. Hey, you never know.

As we were walking to the site, a doe and spotted fawn walked past the big cedar tree. I figure a spotted fawn has to be a good omen. Perhaps the fawn would also help counter the teeth brushing faux pas.

Turning on the metal detector, I swept it over the spot. Sure enough, the machine came to life, emitting telltale electronic screeches alerting us there was treasure below. Farther up the creek, the donkey began braying again.

"Wow, maybe you have found something," Maureen said, then looked at me with stern eyes. "Hey, you had better not have salted the ground with a few coins, buster. That would not be funny."

"I swear on all the graves in our pet cemetery that I did not," I replied. "Look, you can see the ground hasn't been disturbed."

She scrapped the ground a little more. It was undisturbed.

"OK, it seems like it hasn't been dug into," she said. "But I haven't forgotten the fake pirate coin you buried for me down by the driveway. I really thought I had found an old Spanish doubloon. It was not nice. One day you will pay for that."

In my defense, that prank was unavoidable, given my weakness for practical jokes. We had been removing dirt from where the old structure had sat behind the cabin, using it as fill to cover a culvert we put in the ditch alongside the driveway. We had found several square nails in the dirt. When I found one of those fake pirate coins given out by a fast food chain, I couldn't stop myself from burying it in the newly placed dirt over the culvert, making sure Maureen would see the tip of it sticking out. Sure enough, she began shrieking when she saw it. That was before a closer inspection determined it looked like it came from a *Pirates of the Caribbean* movie set. Suffice it to say she called me a name which questioned my parentage.

"Again, I profoundly regret that little prank," I said. "It will never, ever happen again."

"OK, I'm trying to forget the juvenile doubloon hoax," Maureen said. "Lets focus on this. We need to dig a little deeper. Maybe we ought to use the trowel instead of the pick. We don't want to damage anything."

Taking up the trowel, she began scraping the dirt in the bottom of the little pit I had already dug. An archaeologist would have been impressed by her technique of patiently uncovering the dirt covering whatever hidden treasure awaited us. However, I am neither patient nor an archaeologist. Up in southeast Alaska, the Mendenhall glacier retreated another inch. The wind along the Oregon coast built a dune out of beach sand, then slowly eroded it back to nothing. A mushroom emerged from the ground, completed its life cycle, and gradually disintegrated back into the soil. An inch worm advanced a mile.

"Honey, this is not King Tut's tomb," I hissed. "Please dig faster, already."

"Oh phooey," she said. "We're going to do this right."

She continued scraping at a pace that would have made a snail yawn. Suddenly, there was the unmistakable sound of metal scrapping against metal. She passed a gloved hand over the dirt, exposing about three inches of a metal edge which looked like what could be the top of a treasure chest. I was sure it was about to serve up a treasure.

"What could this be?" she asked as she resumed scraping. No response was expected. The answer was in the ground. I was on my knees beside her, using my own trowel to speed up the process.

We exposed more metal. It was flat for about five inches, then made a ninety-degree turn.

"Hmmm," I mumbled. "Do we have a silver container of some sort here?"

We continued digging, coming to another corner, until we exposed the top of a rectangle about ten inches wide and some fifteen inches long. We started digging down along the sides of what, from our perspective, had to be a container. For some odd reason, one of my favorite articles written by James Thurber for the New Yorker magazine back in the early 1940s popped into my head.

"Let's hope it isn't a metonymy," I whispered.

"Say what?" she asked as she continued scraping.

"That's the container for the thing contained, a figure of speech that Thurber wrote about," I whispered back. "If you said you were going to hit me with the water, the metonymy would be the water bottle. Or something like that. Metonymies are confusing creatures at best."

"So are you," she fired back. "So stop it or I'll hit you with the water bottle."

Since we had brought a metonymy in the form of a large bottle to hold our cold drinking water, I wisely shut up. Obviously, she was no fan of metonymies.

We continued scraping, exposing nearly an inch all around the silvery sides. The sad state of metonymies was given the bum's rush from my brain. We focused on the treasure hunt.

"It probably holds something of great value," I whispered. "Let's do this correctly. Gold is a very soft metal. We don't want to damage anything inside."

Slowly, carefully, we began scraping off layers of dirt around the sides. About two inches down on one end, I reached the bottom of the side. Something seemed amiss. I gently scraped the end of the trowel along the top of the container to remove the loose dirt. It felt like I was hitting little speed bumps.

"What the hell?" I asked as I pried one edge of the thing out of the dirt. It was no container but an upsidedown paint tray and an aluminum one at that. "You gotta be kidding. An old paint tray! This doesn't make any sense. Why would anyone bury an old paint tray out here?"

"Maybe there is something underneath it," Maureen said. "Maybe they used it to cover something."

No longer content with using the cautious archaeologist's approach, I grabbed the pick and dug deeper. Dirt flew. Maureen wisely retreated a few steps.

"There is not a damn thing here," I said, stopping to catch my breath. "What kind of a rotten, lousy bastard would bury this out here where someone would find it years later? What a crappy trick. Those dirty SOBs..."

"No need to be a potty mouth," Maureen interjected. "Look at it this way: now we know where there are no gold coins."

She pursed her lips while looking down at the paint tray, then burst out laughing. "You know what this is? This is bad karma coming back on you for the fake doubloon trick. I told you it would happen."

Her chuckles quickly turned into a helpless chortle, causing her to sit down on the ground to regain her composure. I plopped down next to her. We were both laughing at this point, albeit there may have been a few whimpers from the male of the species.

"I'm beginning to wonder if our early-day predecessors on this land had a cent to their name," I groused as I laid back and gazed up at the cedar boughs overhead. Maureen joined me in checking out the forest canopy.

"Actually, they did—and Matt found both of them," she said, sparking another round of giggling and snorting before we both stopped to catch our breath.

"So we just need to keep looking," she said. "Maybe we'll find the roller. Then we'll have the complete ensemble."

More peels of laughter floated up through our forest, causing a gray squirrel to bark at us from the top of a nearby pine.

"He thinks we are nuts," I said, reaching over to hold her hand. "We are," she happily replied, giving my hand a squeeze.

"Well, you can't quibble with what the guy told us back at the metal detector place," I said. "This has been both exciting and disappointing. The hunt is certainly interesting."

"Quibble? Isn't that one of those flying games that Harry Potter does on his broom stick?" she said, giggling again as she tickled my ribs. I couldn't help but laugh some more.

When she starts her infectious laughing, it sometimes takes a while for the chuckles to run their course. Think of a car whose engine continues to turn over after it's turned off. In her case, it would be a very cute car whose purring engine is easy on the ears.

As it always does, her humor perked me up. I filled in the hole we had dug as she picked up the paint tray and cleaned it off.

"This looks fairly old," she said, turning it over in her hands. "It's heavier than the paint trays you buy today. I bet it is at least fifty years old."

"Be careful you don't scratch the patina," I said, tongue held firmly in cheek. "We don't want to lose the value."

"I'm serious," she said. "This is still interesting, finding out a little more how they lived. Somewhere out here is a dump from the 1800s. That will tell us a lot."

"Yeah, finding a really old midden would be interesting," I agreed. "But I'm not too keen on finding the refuse left by people who lived here just a few decades ago, particularly if they buried it."

I picked up the metal detector and resumed sweeping along the forest floor. The machine immediately squawked. We began digging up parts of an old iron stove, one which had unaccountably been broken up into small pieces. We found the ubiquitous square nails and an old horse shoe. The horse was not attached. The most interesting find of the day was an odd knife.

"I think this is one of those old throwing knives I saw in the county fair when I was a kid back in the 1950s," I told Maureen. "It's evenly balanced.

What you would have thrown it at, I have no idea. But it's kind of cool in a carney sort of way."

"What, pray tell, is a carney?" she asked as she examined the knife.

"One of the guys who works at the carnival in the county fair," I said. "Seriously, I recall seeing something like this at the county fair when I was a kid. It was in one of those booths where the challenge was to land all the loops over this square block. If you did, the top prize was either a stuffed Teddy bear or a throwing knife. I really wanted the knife but I never got anything. I think it was rigged. The loops were probably too small for the target."

"No offense but I'm glad you didn't win the throwing knife, sweetie," she said. "Kerby residents didn't need a knife-throwing urchin in their midst. This seems like a real bad thing to offer kids, particularly those from Kerby. You guys were a little rough around the edges."

I would have argued with her but she had a point. Besides, we already had plenty of guns and knives. What I could have used as a kid was a metal detector.

NINETEEN

Sterlingville's Paper Trail

W HILE WE HAD FOUND PLENTY OF ARTIFACTS, we weren't able to put faces on the people who once handled them. Those faces began to come into focus when Medford historian Truwe, a fellow you would recall from an earlier chapter had you been paying attention, made one of his forays to the National Archives and the Library of Congress in Washington, D.C. He dug up a large Sterlingville nugget in print: James Mason Hutchings' early 1855 journal of his journey through the state of Jefferson, one which included a visit to the tiny boomtown. His diary was insightful, particularly his notes about surviving a memorable stay in the defunct little town.

Consider the night of Feb. 8, 1855, when the man who would become famous as the "Father of the Yosemite" tried sleeping in what was obviously a very rustic Sterlingville hotel. The presidential suite was apparently taken.

"Last night it rained for about threequarters of an hour, and as I felt it pattering on my head I didn't approve of such an unfeeling course," he noted in his diary. "I however moved further down in bed and covering my head with the blankets told it to rain on but it didn't for long."

Yes, he wrote "further" instead of the correct "farther." Perhaps getting a wet head dampened his grammatical ability.

"Still, it is an unpleasant situation, sleeping in the best hotel of the place to find that when the rain can get at your head you feel its cold fingers down your back," he continued. "Such is hotel accommodations here."

The largely sleepless night in Sterlingville followed what was an offering of mystery cuisine which he found well short of appetizing.

"There is moreover two women to cook, yet nothing fit to eat," Hutchings noted. "Went without dinner rather than go to eat it."

His sleeping quarters that night was perhaps a quarter mile of where our cabin now stands. In fact, the well-known traveler's trek more than 160 years ago crossed on or near the edge of what is now our property. His observations of Sterlingville and its environs provided a rare hands-on glimpse of what life was like in our rather bustling little neighborhood back in the day.

Hutchings could occasionally be a little snide when it came to judging folks he met along the way. I find this curious, given the fact he hailed from a blue collar background. Moreover, everyone he met, aside from indigenous Native Americans, came from somewhere else just as he did. It wasn't like they were rustics who had been holing up in the hills after generations of inbreeding. If they had settled into a routine in which family members routinely married relatives and committed unbiblical sex, then pointing the bony finger of indignation would be justified. But the Oregon Territory was peopled by folks searching for a place to call home. They were adventurers, eager to take on challenges. It seemed a little unfair to judge them before they had established themselves.

His condescending attitude reminded me of a journalistic coworker who, when talking about folks living in the Applegate Valley, always mimicked Billy Bob Thornton's character in the 1996 movie *Sling Blade*. Never mind that many Applegate folks are better educated, farther traveled and brighter than the journalist. And, as far as I've been able to ascertain with a relative high degree of certainty, no one I know living out here ever murdered their mother as did Karl, the character played by Billy Bob. At least not when they were twelve years old and armed with a swing blade which, as our troubled boy observes in the movie, is also called a Kaiser blade. Regardless of the name, it is apparently a farm implement meant for harvesting agricultural crops, not for slicing people. Admittedly, after listening to the journalist's Billy Bob routine for the umpteenth time, I did entertain thoughts of acquiring a swing blade but then recalled Karl's contemplations about committing more murderous mayhem. "I don't reckon I got no reason to kill nobody. Mmm," he concluded. Billy Bob was right, of course.

As Hutchings noted, Sterlingville was less than a year old when he arrived. Carpenters were throwing up store fronts, merchants setting up shop, miners wielding pick and shovel. Like all boomtowns and its new inhabitants, Sterlingville had no gloss, no glitter. It was crude and uncouth, much like Hutchings in his youth.

Born in the tiny English town of Towcester in 1820, Hutchings was the son of a carpenter. He had only eight years of formal education before being apprenticed at age 16 to his father to learn the carpentry trade. At the time, Towcester had about 2,500 people, making it comparable to Jacksonville when Hutchings arrived in the Oregon Territory. Chances are, he may have stayed in Towcester as a carpenter if an American named George Catlin hadn't visited nearby Birmingham in 1843. Catlin was an artist whose colorful paintings depicted Indians and the Wild West. There is no doubt the young carpenter was influenced by Catlin's lively art, the likes of which he had never before seen. In 1848, Hutchings left England for New York. He was in New Orleans in 1849 when he learned that gold had been discovered in California. By mid-October of that year, he was among countless gold seekers mining for the precious metal in Northern California. He found some gold, lost it when a bank failed, then wrote a pamphlet in 1853 titled, "The Miner's Ten Commandments," which sold a respectable 100,000 copies. Somewhere along the line, the miner morphed into writer as well as an illustrator and photographer. He would spend two years exploring California and venturing north into the Applegate and Rogue River valleys.

"He was a significant guy in the history of the West," Truwe said of Hutchings. "He was doing surveys and censuses as he traveled. He was really fixated on the number of eligible marriageable women in each community. He had it broken down into the number of marriageable women, children and prostitutes."

Hutchings was just two days shy of his thirty-fifth birthday when he began checking out the southern tip of the Oregon Territory. In addition to Sterlingville, he also spent time in Jacksonville, then a major hub in the vast territory. The traveler, who would later publish the *California Magazine*, was intent on capturing the life and times in the upper Rogue and Applegate river drainages.

Hutchings had traveled north to Sterlingville from Cole's Station in what is now Hilt just south of the California line. On Feb. 5, he wrote about the rough route between Cole's Station and the Rogue River Valley.

"The road is very heavy and clayey mud," he wrote. "The horse's feet when drawn out go off like corks from large bottles, such is the suction of the mud. At other times the water from an old hoof hole would squirt six or eight feet above one's head when on horseback. Plug! Plug! Plug! would be the music."

Upon reaching the summit, he was impressed by the valley opening up before him.

"When you get a distant view of the Rogue River Valley, you are struck with the beautiful green slopes and clumps of oaks and pines on a rounding knoll here or there with the smoke curling up from one of those woody dwelling places," he wrote.

In addition to the occasional woody dwelling places, otherwise known as a log cabin, he also ran across pack trains bound for Yreka by way of Jacksonville and Crescent City. As was his wont, he kept an eye out for women, marriageable or otherwise.

"Met a lady sitting astride her mule the same as the two men with her," he jotted down. "She didn't exhibit much of the beauty or ugliness of her understandings. I must say I like to see a neat ankle on a woman! She had one, and I of course had to admire, consequently, looked!"

He would spend the night in what was then known as the Eden District— now called Talent—at a place dubbed Rockafellow's Tavern. He and his horse were charged $3 for the night, a fee he described as good.

From the tavern he took a twelve-mile trail through the mountains that took him to Sterlingville. Reaching the mining boomtown at 2:00 p.m. on Feb. 6, 1855, he described it as a "busy little spot."

"This is a small town that has newly sprung up, the diggings not having been found more than seven or eight months," he wrote. "There are now in the vicinity about 550 miners—about 20 families—no marriageable women—about 35 children."

We don't know for certain how he determined whether a woman was marriageable. She obviously couldn't be sporting a wedding ring. She also had to be old enough to give consent. Perhaps he had qualms about whether they were too ugly or too old. Having all their limbs would have also likely been a plus, particularly lower limbs with neat ankles attached. It could be the two cooks in the Sterlingville hotel were available but he may have considered them unfit for marriage on the grounds they were cooking challenged.

"The hillsides and gulches are alive with men at work either stripping or drifting or sluicing or tomming or draining their claims by a tail race," he noted, referring to a method of mining that employed water to separate the gold from other material.

"Yet the water is thick with use, being very scarce, as a large number of men are using it," he added of placer mining. "Here you see a prospector with his pick on his shoulder and a pan under his arm, and his partner coming along with the shovel upon his shoulder."

Hutchings traveled down Sterling Creek to a hamlet he called "Bunkumville," where the stream met what he referred to as Applegate Creek. The stream is now called the Little Applegate River.

"On the hillsides men are very busy the same as in town," he observed. "Many are doing remarkably well with the little water they now have."

Farther downstream he reported more miners in the hills as well as working the stream.

"Then cabins are seen and in the distance a flag—perhaps a piece of old canvas tied to a pole (although sometimes the stars and stripes are floating proudly as if to say 'walk in—there's liberty here to get drunk if you have money or credit)," he wrote.

"At all events it indicates a trading post," he said of the place now known as the tiny ghost town of Buncom. "Opposite to that the rocks and the water and the pick or the shovel or the fork are rattling in or about the sluice boxes. People are all hard at work. What a contrast to some places."

It was that night he spent under a dripping hotel roof in Sterlingville. The next morning found him heading back north in the rain to Jacksonville, where he spent a few days observing life.

"The population is about 700—22 families—and over 200 families in the Rogue River Valley," he wrote. "There are 53 marriageable (women) within a circuit of 12 miles of Jacksonville—nine within Jacksonville."

He was certainly one for taking census. He listed ten stores, three boarding houses, one bowling alley, one saloon, four physicians, one tin shop, one meat market, one livery stable, one church and one schoolhouse. Apples grown in the Willamette Valley were being sold in Jacksonville for ninety cents a pound, he noted.

When it came to religion, our man Hutchings obviously had little patience for judgmental zealots. His following unChristian zinger was obviously aimed at men, not marriageable women.

"There seems a number of longfaced religionists—how blue and mean they look," he wrote on Feb. 10. "They want credit, hum and hah and rub their hands and hang their head on one side as if deprecating their unworthiness to be a man."

Feb. 12 found him slogging south back up over the Siskiyous in the rain and ensuing muck.

"Oh, horrible—horrible has been the road today," he wrote. "The road over the Siskiyou Mountains had enough before, is now from the recent rains much worse. Mud Mud Mud.

"Horse drawing long corks for ten miles," he added. "Now he would only be up to his knees, now again he would be up to his belly...This may have been a good stage road, but I wouldn't think so now. It is the worst road I ever traveled."

But we can't leave his diary without highlighting another illuminating point. Remember that ongoing but tiring tiff I mentioned early on between some Oregonians and folks who hail from the Golden State? It seems that our man Hutchings very well may have fired the first volley in that goofy war of words.

Hutchings brought the issue up in his diary right after mentioning the two women whose meals he could not eat in the leaking Sterlingville hotel.

"But then they are from Oregon!!" he chortled, adding, "The majority of men here are those who crossed the plains last summer to Oregon and utterly disappointed...Oregon people do not seem to be in good favor anywhere north. They are generally called 'Wallah Wallahs,' as a large portion talk the jargon of the Hudson Bay Co."

The latter referred to the Chinook jargon which originated in the 19th Century as a form of rudimentary communication between trappers and indigenous people in the Pacific Northwest. Perhaps some had taken to talking like mountain men to put the scare into those civilized California wussies. After all, California became a state in 1850, something the rowdy rustics in Oregon wouldn't achieve until 1859. I have to snidely add some Oregonians swore there was a sign at the point where the Oregon Trail split, a marker indicating that one path lead to California while the other to Oregon country. Those who could read took the path to Oregon, they insist.

After surviving Sterlingville and Jacksonville, Hutchings in July of 1855 led either the first or second—depending on whose version of history you read—tourist trip into the now famous Yosemite Valley. Hutchings featured Yosemite Valley in the first edition of his *Hutchings California Magazine* in July 1856. He also produced a lithograph of Yosemite Falls that was widely distributed. And he wrote a book on Yosemite called "In the Heart of the Sierras."

Following the magazine's merger with another publication, *California Mountaineer*, Hutchings stepped down as publisher and editor and moved to Yosemite where he opened a hotel, presumably one which did not offer mystery dishes. It was for his promotion of that region that he became known as the "Father of the Yosemite." In 1869, he hired a sheepherder from Scotland named John Muir to build a sawmill in Yosemite Valley. Muir, who later became perhaps the nation's most famous naturalist, led the fight to create Yosemite National Park. During a return trip to the park on Oct. 31, 1902, Hutchings, eighty-two, was thrown from his buggy after his horse spooked. He was buried near the base of his beloved Yosemite Falls, safe from any Oregon bumpkins. He is surely the only one buried in Yosemite National Park who spent a wet night in a Sterlingville hotel.

While Hutchings' lively journal is likely one of the earliest first-hand accounts of Sterlingville we can hope to find, other articles have popped up which captured the history of the little town along Sterling Creek. One which caught my eye was a 1947 clipping from the *Mail Tribune* under the headline, "Gold in Buckets, Rugged Men and Women, Recalled by Native of Sterlingville." The article was a feature on Alice Gilson Ulrich who was interviewed just shy of her ninety-first birthday. It was sent to me while I was writing for the paper from one of her descendants now living in California. It arrived less than a month after Truwe had unveiled the Hutchings diary he found in D.C.

A cyberspace check on her history indicates she was born in Sterlingville on Oct. 26, 1856, a little over a year and a half after Hutchings was rained on in the hotel. She was the eldest of Thomas H. and Mary A. Gilson's eleven children, seven of whom were daughters. Prolific breeders, Thomas and Mary.

"She remembers well the clink and the gleam of gold when she was the only little girl in a thriving mining town about nine miles from Jacksonville," the article observed of Sterlingville. "Now only rocks and cavities in the earth reveal that man was once there. The old Delmonica house in which she was born was the last to go down."

Chances are there were other young girls in the vicinity since Hutchings had counted thirty-five children in Sterlingville during his visit but perhaps Alice never got to know them. As you shall soon see, her childhood was briefer than most.

"It is hard to believe that dance halls, saloons, livery stables and stores once stood in the now forsaken area," she told the paper. "Sterlingville had its housing shortage, too."

When her father, a native of New York and the son of an Irish emigrant, couldn't find a suitable house, he built one in Gilson Gulch, the little valley which now bears his name. The property we own was once the Gilson ranch. We like to think that young Alice, when she wasn't being farmed off to neighbors, would have romped where our cabin now stands.

But we don't know if she chatted with the reporter about where she played as a child. She did talk about gold from the Sterlingville area being minted into $1, $2.50, $5, $10 and $20 gold coins.

"They used to carry the gold out in buckets, then bring it back from San Francisco in the form of gold coins," she explained. "Many men traded with the raw gold. They carried it in buckskin purses sewed with a welt so the gold would not leak out. For the fellow who found it, kept it."

Despite what we like to believe about the "good old days," all the folks back then were apparently not as honest as the day is long. Trustworthiness was not always a staple in the days of yore, according to the clipping.

"Stealing went on then, too," the article observed. "There was much talk of gold being stolen from the gold blower."

Then there was the day a farmer rolled into Sterlingville with a wagon full of produce to sell.

"An Applegate farmer came into town and boasted that no one could get away with stealing from him," according to the article. "He had a load of watermelons in his wagon. When he came out from the store, the melons were gone. He searched but couldn't find one melon. When he had gone home some of the boys lifted up the floor of a building and brought out the melons."

Another constant over the ages was the impact booze had on people, Alice told the paper.

"Hard liquor, for instance, made people do strange things just as it does now," she observed before launching into a tale about a fight she saw at a Sterlingville dance hall.

"I was the only little girl there," she began. "I always wore dresses of tarleton...long full skirts. The men used to pick me up and dance me around the floor.

"This night two men just started talking about the oyster supper which was always served at the dances," she said. "They began arguing. Too much hard liquor, you see. One pointed his finger at the other and he bit it straight off."

Yow. Those Sterlingville folks were made of tough stuff. Fortunately for the finger pointer, the biter apparently didn't have a swing blade handy or the incident could have been much messier. Perhaps Hutchings was on to something, after all.

Interestingly, neighbor Pete, who bought his property half a century before we moved onto Gilson Gulch, says an old dance hall once stood near the northeast corner of our property. The building was on a little flat area near where we have found a lot of old colored glass and square nails. But we have found no human finger bone, although I suspect they are difficult to recognize once they have been chomped off. Besides, we don't know if the biter spit it out. Moreover, a Sterlingville mutt would have probably snatched it up since unattached human fingers were rare treats then. Still are, unless some Billy Bob character goes wild with a sling blade. Mmm.

But the biggest fright of Alice's childhood was not in Sterlingville. Thomas Gilson decided to try his hand in the Smith River drainage of far northern California hard against the Oregon border. Unfortunately, they arrived when that river, tumultuous even during summer, was flooding.

"Mrs. Ulrich remembers well the fear which 'chilled her heart' as she saw horses and wagon, containing all her family's belongings, food, clothing and gold, claimed by the river and swept out to sea," the article observed. "Fortunately, her parents and the children were in the other wagon, which was rescued."

The Gilsons turned the wagon around and began the long trek back to Sterling Creek. It had to be a low point in their lives. But, like most people of that era, they didn't give up easily.

"Stopping for the night in an old shanty along the road, the family found some potatoes," the story continued. "These they roasted in the ashes, adding the remaining ones to their wagon to have something to eat until they reached Sterlingville and friends again."

Much of Alice's childhood was spent living with friends. When she was nine, Alice began attending what was called the Sisters School in Jacksonville. She boarded with a German family, becoming fluent in the language of Deutschland. At age thirteen, she began earning her own board and room while still attending school. Three years later she met Christian Ulrich, the man who would become her husband. Sadly, on April 4, 1879, the *Jacksonville Democratic Times* reported the death of John, infant son of Christian and Alice Ulrich. He was just ten days old. Yet they would have four children who lived to adulthood.

"People were different then," lamented the Sterlingville native who had lived in Jacksonville more than seventy years when she was interviewed. "They never have time to visit anymore." She died on Feb. 29, 1948.

The Gilson family apparently recovered from their ill-fated Smith River trip. According to the 1880 census, Thomas and Mary had ten children living at home, although Alice had already fledged. He was respected in the area. On April 19, 1884, the Table Rock Sentinel listed him as one of three appointed judges for the Sterlingville Precinct in the June election that year. And he bought a house in Jacksonville before the century was out. "T.H. Gilson of Sterlingville, one of the pioneers of Jackson County, has purchased D. S. Youngs' residence and will soon take possession," the *Democratic Times* of Jacksonville reported on March 29, 1899. "The consideration was $650." After nearly half a century of roughing it along Sterling Creek, the Gilson paterfamilias was moving into town. He waseighty-one when he died on Oct. 23, 1911.

Obviously, none of the Gilsons lived in the cabin we now call home since they were gone before it was built. The main ranch house and several outbuildings was on the south-facing slope of Gilson Gulch, judging by an old photograph given to us by Vernon Arnold, a former president of the Southern Oregon Historical Society. The black and white photograph from the SOHS archives was identified as the Gilson ranch. Vernon correctly noted the photograph, which we have enlarged, is of the eastern front of our parcel. Although the photograph is undated, several large fir trees perhaps more than a 100 years old now growing where none existed in the photograph indicates it was taken around the end of the 19th Century.

By the by, Vernon's family history can be seen in the peaks overlooking the Applegate Valley watershed. Collings Mountain, standing a respectable 3,625 feet above sea level in southern Jackson County, was named after Freeman Oscar Collings, Vernon's great-grandfather, who was known by his initials, F.O. Collings Mountain is immediately west of the Applegate Dam reservoir created around 1980. Over in southeastern Josephine County, Arnold Mountain, rising to an impressive snowcapped 6,642 feet, is named for Ezra Albert Arnold, Vernon's grandfather. Both mountains stand in the Rogue River-Siskiyou National Forest.

"Not many people have mountains named after them," acknowledged Vernon, seventy-five, when I interviewed him in 2013. "I'm very proud of my ancestors and their legacy. I'm glad they came here in the early days."

A history buff and former high school teacher with a master's degree from Oregon State University, he noted his grandfather was a miner; his great-grandfather a farmer. Both settlers arrived in the Applegate Valley when the state of Oregon was still in diapers. They would have traveled periodically to Sterlingville when it was flourishing.

According to an article Truwe unearthed on page 5 in the April 27, 1900, *Medford Enquirer* newspaper, the Sterling mine across the creek from the Gilson ranch was still going gangbusters at that point. Under the headline, "Gold Bricks," it noted that the Medford Bank president had contacted the paper, suggesting a reporter might want to check out some gold bricks from the Sterling mine on display at the bank.

"On a table in the center of the office was piled up seven large gold bricks, representing a cash value of $17,000," the article stated. "On the same table was a pile of twenties to the value of some $13,000, making a total valuation of a little over $30,000. The gold from the Sterling mine was only that which had accumulated in the sluice boxes and which are cleaned up about once each month, the general cleanup taking place later on when the season's run is over.

"As this has been a good year for placer mining, it is expected the Sterling's cleanup will amount to some $150,000, while the other placer mines will show a large increase here this year," it added. Remember, this was when $150,000 was a substantial sum. Still is, for some of us.

An article in the paper a little more than two decades earlier also shed a little more light on life at the mine and its surroundings. Written by Abigail Scott Duniway, described as an editorial correspondence for the *New Northwest*, a Portland-based weekly newspaper, the July 17, 1879 article begins with describing her party leaving Jacksonville.

"The morning is glorious and the scenery grandly magnificent," she wrote. "A ride of ten miles, up and down the billowy, zigzag vales and hills, and the little village of Sterling comes to sight, and we are soon met by Mr. Ennis, the gentlemanly superintendent of the mine, who, after a bountiful lunch beneath the trees, conducts the party to the hydraulic works, where a head of water, brought in a ditch from Applegate Creek, eighteen miles distant, and conveyed into the mine through a twenty-four inch pipe, which at the base of the gulch is divided into two branch pipes of fifteen inches in diameter, and from thence into five inch nozzles, pours a thundering, incessant stream of angry water as a vigorous broadside into the resisting heart of the rockbound mountain, disemboweling the complaining earth and sending it crashing to the gulch below."

Whew. She could certainly pack a lot of information into a sentence, nearly bowling over the reader with a torrent of words. Incidentally, most historical documents give the length of the mining ditch as twenty-three miles but we won't quibble over her entertaining description. Let's read a little more.

"Rocks, some of them weighing half a ton, are torn by this doubleheaded hydraulic monster from this ledge's side, and placed by miners upon dumps, from which they are lifted by a mighty derrick, also worked by hydraulic power, and cast in piles..." she wrote. "After the hydraulic ram has spent its heaviest power against the mountainside, it gathers its remaining forces at the head of the gulch, whose depth it constantly increases, and forming a roaring, muddy cataract, is collected in sluice boxes, and goes tearing onward toward the lowlands, leaving behind in the boxes an auriferous deposit sufficiently captivating to tempt the cupidity of even a political missionary."

Interesting that she should describe herself as a political missionary, albeit an honest one who wouldn't give in to the temptation of taking a few nuggets. But she had a reason: at the time, D.P. Thompson, the mayor of Portland, was president and principal shareholder of the Sterling mine. President U.S. Grant had earlier appointed him governor of the Idaho Territory, a position he held until 1876, when he moved to Portland where he was twice elected mayor. In addition to guiding the Sterling mine operation, he was a banker and state legislature. Even Hutchings would have been impressed by his accomplishments and, as Duniway did, have likely written favorably about the mining operation.

"We learn that the company...has spent a hundred thousand dollars in developing his mine, and when we look at the character of the country over which the ditch has been carried, and note the stability and power of the machinery employed, we consider the estimate reasonable," she wrote.

"There are but few men engaged now in the mine, the hydraulic power easily accomplishing the work of many hundred pairs of human hands."

If you are a fan of Oregon history, you will recognize Duniway's name. Traveling west on the Oregon Trail at age seventeen in 1852, she would see her mother and a younger brother die en route. Yet she soldiered on with her father and remaining siblings, becoming a school teacher. When her husband was crippled by an accident in 1862, she became the sole supporter for her young family, an experience which opened her eyes to how women were not treated as equals on par with the male of the species. While the article may have listed her as the editorial correspondent for the New Northwest, she was also its publisher. As such, she led the regional fight for equal rights for women, helping create the Oregon State Women Suffrage Association in 1873. Indeed, before visiting Sterlingville and the mine, she had already been speaking out. She is credited as the tireless leader of the effort which helped women in Idaho receive the right to vote in Idaho in 1896, followed by their counterparts in Washington in 1910, and Oregon in 1912. Never mind the powerful publisher of the *Portland Oregonian* was a staunch opponent of giving equal rights to women. That would have been Harvey W. Scott, her brother. Family gatherings were no doubt rather feisty.

We will never know whether Duniway was trying to butter up Thompson for political purposes. It is obvious she appreciated the beauty of Sterling Creek and its environs. Like Hutchings, Duniway traveled on down the stream to its confluence with the Little Applegate River.

"Here our party spent a half hour in sightseeing, and then we retrace our steps, viewing as we come down the mountain gorges a magnificent thunderstorm on the adjacent heights, its fresh breezes filling the air with the balmy odors of Araby the blest," she wrote.

I couldn't help but chuckle over her poetic description of the Sterling Creek drainage. None of the hundreds of old newspaper articles about our region that I have pored over have ever come close to her prose of equating July in the upper Applegate Valley to Saudia Arabia and its fragrant breezes.

Back in 2010, a kindly soul dropped off a pile of historical clippings about our region for me to peruse. One *Oregonian* article written in 1959 by a fellow named Lancaster Pollard cited Jacksonville as the state's top historical hamlet.

"Even the record of early Jacksonville is entrancing," Pollard observed. "Alice Applegate Sargent of the famous pioneer family wrote in 1920 that the thenmetropolis of the Rogue River valley 'had been settled by people of education and culture.' "

Sounds good, particularly for those of us with historical roots.

But Pollard goes on to note that S.H. Taylor, writing home to Wisconsin in 1853, had a different take on our esteemed Jackson County ancestors.

"The first time I was here I saw but one woman and she kept a bowling saloon and a drunkery," S.H. wrote to folks back home about Jacksonville. It seems that some may have been driving under the influence back in the horse-and-buggy days.

One article that caught my eye was a piece in the *Jacksonville Democratic Times* newspaper on May 23, 1901. It was what amounted to an infomercial back in the day.

Under the headline, "A Most Remarkable Case," the article began with a letter to the editor by a Mrs. Jonas Fattig of Ashland, my grandmother. Her full name was Harriett Viola Lounsbury Fattig. She died in 1940 before I was born, but family lore indicates she was a pleasant lady who doted on her children.

Her letter, under the subhead, "Another Ashland Cure," was about her daughter, Bessie Belle, age three.

"For some time my girl has been suffering with partial paralysis, extending to her hands, feet and bladder, so she could not pass urine," the letter began. "Through Dr. Darrin's electrical and medical treatment she has recovered. I cannot say enough in praise of Dr. Darrin's new mode of curing the sick.

"My husband is employed by John Cherry, who is getting out wood for the Ashland mine," she concluded. "I will gladly talk to anyone in regard to the cure."

The article, which includes two other testimonial letters to the editor along with information about the good doctor, was uncovered by historian

Truwe. While he rightfully noted there was sound, science-based medicine being practiced around the turn of the 20th Century, Dr. Darrin's electric shock treatment was iffy at best, although the article tried to convince the reader the good doctor was breaking new ground.

"Dr. Darrin makes a specialty of all diseases of the ear, eye, nose and throat, catarrh and bronchitis, la grippe, consumption, dyspepsia, constipation, heart, liver and kidney diseases, varicocele and hydrocele," it read. "He permanently cures diseases of the geniourinary organs in either sex, such as blood taints, scrofula, stricture, seminal weakness, spermatorrhoea, loss of manhood."

Reading that list makes me cross my legs and wince. The article observed that he will take on all peculiar female troubles as well as "nervous diseases of whatever nature." What's more, he promised to provide the "worthy poor" with free treatment.

"He will furnish batteries and electric belts for any patient requiring them, and will give full directions for their use," the article assured the reader. "The afflicted should not lose the opportunity to consult this eminent physician while here," it added.

He held court each day at the Hotel Oregon in Ashland until May 26 of that year, and then moved his mobile medical business to Medford's Hotel Nash, staying until July 1. No doubt he felt it best to keep on the move.

It turns out Dr. Darrin popped up throughout Oregon and Washington, traveling to small towns to hook folks up to his electrical device or administer medicine.

Consider the article in the *Eugene Register* newspaper on Sept. 8, 1905, the one with the headline, "A Most Remarkable Cure of Heart Disease."

"Perhaps one of the most wonderful results on record is the wonderful cure of Mrs. S.E. Clark by Dr. Darrin," it began. "Mrs. Clark was carried to Dr. Darrin's office in an almost dying condition afflicted with a complication of diseases."

Turns out she had been treated by the doctor on Dec. 24, 1897—more than eight years earlier—in Pendleton. But she had sent a letter to the Register in 1905 stating he had completely cured her of heart, lung and stomach troubles.

As it did in Jacksonville, the article indicated Dr. Darrin would provide the cure at no charge to the worthy poor. But it also noted he would charge others $5 a week. Curiously, Dr. Darrin's first name never surfaces in any of the articles.

We will never know whether his treatment helped little Bessie Belle. I try not to think how the three-year-old, whose angelic photograph hangs in my writing nook, must have been terrified when hooked up to an electrical gadget with its assorted wires for a shock. What I do know is that Bessie Belle died at age six on June 10, 1904, in the Fattig home at 1 Wimer Street in Ashland. Cause of death was high fever brought on by pneumonia following a bout with measles, according to her death certificate.

I can't help but wonder if my grandmother ever tried "The Great Dr. Kilmer's Swamp Root Liver, Kidney & Bladder Cure" on Bessie Belle. It couldn't have been any worse than torturing her with an electrical shock.

TWENTY

Sterlingville Area Dwellers

A LL DENIZENS OF STERLINGVILLE ARE LONG GONE, their souls resting for eternity after what was for many a hardscrabble life. When you walk through the Sterlingville Cemetery, many of the surnames greeting you on the tombstones are those of families who put Sterlingville on the map, be it only for a few brief decades. Names like Saltmarsh and Yaudes, folks who gave their all to help settle the area.

These were times when merely surviving day to day could sometimes be difficult. Poignant evidence of that can be seen in the markers for the graves of three Yaudes siblings, Aaron, 5; Lettie, 8; and Albert, 10. All three died on May 23, 1884 during a diphtheria outbreak. It is hard to imagine the profound grief their parents must have felt that terrible day in May. It should have been a time when the family was out in the nearby woods and meadows, admiring the spring flowers, not sadly picking flowers to gently lay them on fresh graves.

Yet, even then, the shining potential of the boomtown was beginning to lose its luster. The Sterlingville post office, which opened in 1879, closed a year before the Yaudes children died. But the Sterlingville School District, founded in 1869, managed to draw in enough local urchins to continue until it finally closed in 1937. The Saltmarshes had donated the land for the Sterling Creek School as well as the cemetery, in essence providing for both life and death. The Sterling Mine, founded in 1877 by Tod Cameron and others, continued to operate until the early 20th Century. But as gold became more difficult to find for those who did not have access to water for hydraulic mining, many miners moved on to fresher digs in northeastern Oregon and elsewhere.

While newspaper articles provide a rough estimate of a town's population, a more exacting count can be found in the U.S. census records. The 1860 census reveals that Sterlingville had 123 souls, including men, women and children. Just what constituted the "city" limits is not spelled out. In greater Jackson County, the 1860 census listed the population as 3,736. Over in Josephine County, there were 1,623 residents. A decade later, Jackson County's count had risen to 4,759 while Josephine County's 1870 population had dropped to 1,204, the latter likely because of miners leaving for better opportunities.

Many Sterlingville buildings were cannibalized to be used in other structures by local residents. A portion of the old hamlet was also undermined by gold seekers. And the descendants of the founding families would scatter like autumn leaves before the winds of time.

But there is still some Sterlingville gold to be found. Not precious yellow metal, although there are likely nuggets yet in the ground, but in the stories of those who knew the Applegate country when it was younger. Tales told by those who came before us are the real riches to be mined today.

Although this tome has already been salted with nuggets from old newspapers, we'll toss one more out there, sluiced up by our friend Truwe, to shed a little more light on early-day inhabitants. This one was printed in the *Crescent City (California) Herald's* Jan. 9, 1856 edition, page two.

"Sterling is a pretty little mining town, situated about eight miles from Jacksonville, on one of the tributaries of Applegate River," began the article, reprinted from *Jacksonville's Table Rock Sentinel*. "Sterling gold diggings were discovered about the 1st of June 1854," it continued. "This village has grown beyond all precedent—containing a population of five or six hundred—amongst whom are some of the most energetic and enterprising spirits in the country, well calculated to build up a town and keep matters and things ahead."

While the article's date citing the discovery of gold in our little watershed allows for a modicum of wiggle room, it matches the time frame Hutchings alluded to in his diary during his Sterlingville visit in the first week of February, 1855. It also provides a window in time, giving us a glimpse of what James Sterling and fellow miner Aaron Davis would have encountered. If today's climate is any indicator, which it may not be, the stream would still have been flowing around June 1 before largely drying out by mid-summer. Its flow depends on how much rain soaks the ground the previous winter. Unlike the higher mountains whose winter snow packs directly impact the rivers Applegate and Rogue, the immediate mountains from which the little stream pours are not high enough to provide a winter snow bank.

Unlike Hutchings, the journalist back in 1856 obviously felt Sterlingville inhabitants had something on the ball. Lets split the difference and agree some folks merited commendation while others deserved condemnation. Perhaps a few warranted both. As for those I've met whose ancestors had roots in Sterlingville and its environs, I have to side with the 1856 observation. Despite growing long of tooth, their spirits remain energetic and enterprising.

When I told former Southern Oregon Historical Society director Vernon Arnold about finding the 1907 Indian head penny, he put me in contact with a lady who had stayed briefly on our property more than eighty years earlier. Medford resident Myrna Turnbough Bradley was still in diapers when she lived on the land with her parents during the spring and summer of 1934. At the time, the world was deep in the Great Depression. Life was hard.

Her parents—Vernon "Bill" and Thelma Emmons Turnbough—lived in Phoenix, a small town between Ashland and Medford. Her father was a carpenter by training but owned the Bedrock Mine on the west side of Sterling Creek. The mine was just across the road and roughly 200 feet upstream from the northeast corner of our property.

"I was only eleven months old when we started living there." she said when I interviewed her for a newspaper column in the spring of 2013, not long after we found the penny. "But I remember the stories my mother told me, that we lived in a tent with a wooden floor. My playpen was a piece of plywood with a chicken wire fence around it so the rattlesnakes couldn't get me."

If the octogenarian's feistiness is any indicator, a visiting buzzworm would have likely been used as a whip by the youngster.

After getting permission from the owner, her parents chose a spot near the southeast corner of what is now our property to set up their tent. You could have smacked it with a tomato from where our vegetable garden.

"They walked back and forth over the hill from Phoenix to the mine on Sterling Creek," Myrna said. "There were a lot of miners camping along Sterling during the Depression. We were in the corner just past your gate."

Joining her in the interview was her sister Georgia Turnbough Blankenship, then seventy-eight, also of Medford. Although the younger sibling never lived on the property, she also remembered the stories their parents told of those distant days.

"Daddy said those were the best years of his life," Georgia said. "His ashes are scattered out there."

Rightly so since the Sterling Creek drainage—the sisters fondly refer to it simply as "Sterling"—was once rich with their ancestors.

Their paternal uncle Harden Turnbough was born in Sterlingville and lived up Gilson Gulch. Unfortunately, their father and uncle had a disagreement as young adults and never spoke to each other again.

The property to the immediate west of ours was once owned by their father's uncle, a fellow name Zeke Calhoun, who crafted jewelry when he wasn't working in the mines or making wooden boxes for Rogue Valley orchards.

Their grandmother Jessie Emmons lived in a small house that still stands half a mile from the mine. She owned the mining claim before the Turnboughs began working it around 1930. The sisters' father would build a small cabin on the claim.

"They found nuggets like this above your place," Myrna said, indicating some were the size of quarters. "They were huge."

We have not found—nor have looked for—any nuggets, but we did encounter the aforementioned rattlesnakes. It's likely they are scaly descendants of the rattlers who slithered around looking for a way into her chicken wire playpen during the Great Depression.

Although the 1907 penny was discovered not far from where the Turnbough tent would have been pitched in 1934, the sisters did not lay claim to it. Never mind there is the oft chance a family member may have dropped it.

"Yes, you can keep it," said the smiling former baby girl whose makeshift crib was protected from rattlesnakes by chicken wire when Yankee ingenuity thrived along Sterling Creek.

While there are other local folks with family roots tapping into Sterlingville's gold-bearing ground, few compare with Stan Smith, 91. Here was a remarkable individual who survived a plane crash at sea while in the Navy at the tail end of World War II, worked as a timber faller to pay his way through college where he was a star footballer on an undefeated team, coached and taught in high school, owned upper class restaurants and worked as a chef. He packed a lot of living into those nine decades.

I first met Stan and his wife, Thomasine "Tommie" Swoape Smith, a quarter of a century ago. A wonderfully matched couple, they were bright, gregarious and not ones to suffer fools gladly, although they graciously agreed to my interviews for history features. Sadly, Tommie, hailing from a pioneer family in Josephine County, passed away in 2009. They had been married for sixty-five years.

When I interviewed Stan in their comfortable Medford home in the summer of 2015, he was using a walker but still offered a vigorous handshake that would crush a clam. I engaged in a little small talk before the interview, waiting to regain the feeling in my right hand so I could take notes. I use a digital recorder as well but can't seem to shake the old habit of jotting down notes with pen and paper.

"I remember when there were still some old buildings in Sterlingville," recalled Stan who was born on March 24, 1924. "But even when I was a kid they were mostly gone. Wasn't much left by the '30s. Most old towns are like old people, they eventually fade away."

Be warned: to really appreciate Stan's pioneer bona fides will require a genealogical background to understand the bigger picture. Now, now. Compose yourself and stop whimpering. We're not going back to Japheth and Shem, some of the original begetters you may have read about in the Old Testament. But there will be enough of a genealogy lesson here to punish those of you who committed some misdeed in your past and thought you got away with it.

Stan's great grandmother was a lady with the weighty moniker of Ellen "Ella" Clarinda Pool Saltmarsh, born in 1854. As a young lady, she married a fellow named Samuel Cameron in Chico, California. They had a baby girl who they christened Mamie, but the marriage did not take and mother and child returned to Oregon. Incidentally, Samuel Cameron was not related to Theodoric "Tod" Cameron, the man who headed the Sterling Mine Company and helped establish Uniontown on the Little Applegate River.

On Nov. 24, 1881, shortly upon arriving back in Oregon, Ella married Joseph Saltmarsh, twenty-nine years her senior and one of the founders of Sterlingville. Her husband was a mining partner with his brothers Reuben and Sylvester Saltmarsh along with George Yaudes and C.K. Klum, all Argonauts on the ground floor of mining ventures on Sterling Creek. They sold out to the Sterling Mining Co. in 1886. You recognize the Yaudes surname because George Yaudes was the father of the three Sterlingville children who died of diphtheria on the same day in May of 1884.

In Sterlingville where Joseph and Ella moved in 1882, Joseph had years earlier donated land to house the school and cemetery. It was in the latter where the grieving couple buried their son Madison Saltmarsh on Oct. 14, 1884. The little fellow was barely two years old. Joseph followed suit in 1906 at age eighty, and rests for eternity near their young son in the Sterlingville Cemetery. Ella lived on until 1915.

While her husband was a founding father of Sterlingville, Ella's ancestry matched his pioneer history in Jackson County, albeit on the other end of the county in Eagle Point. That was where her father Arthur Pool had settled after coming west on the Oregon Trail. Stan's great, great grandfather, who begat ten children, built what was then a swanky place called the Eagle

Hotel in Eagle Point in 1872. Stan noted it was known largely for its fancy dining room. You will notice that nearly everyone perched in his family tree knew their way about a kitchen. In fact, the chefs spicing up the family cookbooks—we'll explore them a bit as dessert to close out this chapter— go back five generations to early statehood. The resulting scrumptious food meant they had to work their buns off to avoid becoming tubbies who have to be hoisted out of the house with a construction crane.

"He also had a blacksmith shop across the Little Butte Creek," Stan recalled of family folklore about Arthur Pool. "The Indians would bring their horses over from Klamath Falls and trade him huckleberries to shoe their horses."

In fact, Pool Hill, a prominent geological feature overlooking Little Butte Creek, was named for Arthur Pool. You have to admit it's impressive to have a chunk of real estate named after one of your ancestors.

But enough with the main genealogical lesson, though we'll periodically throw in a pinch more here and there for flavor. Lets get back to Sterlingville and Ella's daughter Mamie.

"My grandmother Mamie was a little girl when Sterlingville was still around," Stan said. "The family lived on a ranch right there on the left just before you get to the cemetery. It was practically in Sterlingville."

Unfortunately, some of the family tales were lost to the years but a few Sterlingville historic nuggets survived.

"One story my grandmother used to tell was about this freight wagon she would hear coming because the horses had bells on them," he said. "And she knew Charley Offenbacher was driving this team. As a young girl, she always ran out to the gate and waved. He brought her candy."

As they would have said with a wink and a nudge back in the day, the young man was sparking the young lady.

"The years went on and they got married," her grandson noted of their 1891 nuptials which united two pioneer families since the Offenbachers are also deeply rooted in Applegate history. The couple had a baby boy but husband Charley died in 1893 after being kicked by a horse. As we have repeatedly seen, what many tout as the good old days could be unforgivably harsh.

But the young woman who lost her first love would eventually marry again, this time to Horace Venable in 1894. Her second husband, who arrived in Jacksonville in 1884, operated a saloon in that town for a short time on the corner of California and South Oregon streets.

"My granddad didn't like running a saloon," Stan said. "He wasn't suited for the saloon business. He didn't care for it."

Horace traded the Jacksonville saloon for a 160-acre ranch on the south side of the Applegate River near Ruch where he could raise his own food and not have to babysit drunks.

"My grandfather had the Applegate ranch," Stan said. "We were across the river there by the hill. We always had the river to fight during high water. You couldn't get across. Yeah, that river used to get awfully low in the summer and awfully high in the winter. We were at its mercy. During high water, we didn't cross it. Our connection to the rest of the world was a swinging bridge. My sister and I crossed it to get to school."

He spent his childhood years of the Great Depression at the ranch.

"We barely even knew there was a depression," he said. "We always had a lot to eat. Of course, it didn't hurt to have those chefs in the family while you are living on a ranch. My mother was a fabulous, fabulous cook. So was my father. They were too good. We were all overweight."

His mother was Bessie "Nonnie" Venable Smith, born in 1900 in what is now known as the Grapevine Gallery building in Jacksonville. His father, Ralph Smith, was a chef who had worked in restaurants in Chicago and San Francisco. Ralph and Bessie met in 1921 at the Crater Lake Lodge where he was the hotel chef steward and she the hostess.

"After they got married, they moved down to California where I was born," Stan offered. But after seeing the error of their ways, his parents eventually moved back to the Beaver state.

As a youngster, Stan attended elementary school in Ruch, a tiny community just over the hill from Jacksonville in the Applegate Valley. "We played Uniontown School once a year in baseball," Stan recalled. "First base was a stump."

A dozen years earlier one of the Uniontown players racing for that stump after hitting the ball would have been my father. We have a 1922 photograph of the Uniontown School, one with my father standing in the back of the student body which consists of two dozen students. By far the biggest kid in the school, the eighth grader appears to be fighting the urge to ape at the camera. In the background stands Squires Peak, the mountaintop struck by lightning in 2002, sparking the wildfire that threatened homes in the Sterling Creek drainage and prompted the visit by President Bush. Back when the Uniontown School photo was taken, the man in the White House would have been Warren G. Harding, the first president to have his voice transmitted on the radio. That historic transmission was on Flag Day, June 14, 1922, three days before my dad's sixteenth birthday. When I was a kid, I recall seeing dad's eighth grade report card from Uniontown and being mighty impressed. Nothing but A's. That wonderment faded when, as an adult, I realized how old he was at the time. No doubt he was a bright fellow but it helps when you are allowed to age a bit in school.

That one baseball game a year with Uniontown apparently whetted Stan's appetite for sports. After completing a hitch in the Navy, surviving a crash at sea while serving as a crew member of a Navy patrol plane, he would play football at what is now Southern Oregon University. In 1946, with Stan starting as right tackle, the Raiders were undefeated. But it wasn't until 2015 that his alma mater won the national title among small colleges, an honor whose mention caused him to grin from ear to ear. During his senior year, Stan was named an All American for small colleges.

Like his father, son Dane was a standout footballer, playing for the University of Oregon where Stan had earned his master's degree. Dane owns and operates Mr. Smith's Sports & Grill in Medford, carrying on the family tradition of serving up tasty food to those with hearty appetites.

Back in 2009, when Oregon celebrated its sesquicentennial—its 150th birthday—the family dusted off and revised its *Smith Family Heritage Cookbook* whose first edition was served up three decades earlier. Stuffed with handed-down recipes and bite-size anecdotes of local history, the book has culinary and cultural roots reaching all the way back to Sterlingville. Consider great grandma Ella Saltmarsh's pioneer sour cream pear pie, Grandpa Ralph Smith's special Applegate breakfast or Uncle Ray Offenbacher's cowboy potatoes. The book reflects Southern Oregon pioneer custom of cooking locally grown food to make hearty meals, albeit some would make a cholesterol-fighting dietician cringe.

In an interview at the time, the book's revision, in addition to commemorating the state's birthday, was a labor of love for her mother who was gravely ill, explained Dana Tuley of Medford, eldest of Stan and Tommie's three children.

"Mom compiled the first cookbooks with my grandmother," Dana said. "The earlier cookbooks included recipes from family and friends. With this new cookbook, we're sticking to family from the Applegate Valley and Jacksonville."

In addition to capturing local history, the cookbook is liberally spiced with family poetry and notes reflective of earlier times, including the Sterlingville days.

Stan's mother wrote about making a foray into an early-day supermarket after being accustomed to the general store. Remember, this was a time when bringing a box of instant anything would have likely gotten you the bum's rush out of the kitchen.

"Foods with additives, preserved to delay the rot," she wrote. "The more I looked, the less hungry I got."

Dana is the proud owner of one of her grandmother's iron skillets. We're talking about cast iron here, the kind of frying pan you could use to knock out a bull. The heavy-metal cooking, including Dutch ovens, made memorable meals, Dana observed.

"In 1900, they had the first fair in Jacksonville and my great, great grandmother won for her pear cream pie my family still makes today," she said, referring to Ella Saltmarsh.

Because wood stoves were used back in the day, old recipes included directions such as "cook on a hot stove," Dana said, noting the updated recipes were adjusted for modern-day culinary tools.

"They all cooked on wood stoves back then," Stan recalled. "With an old wood stove, you had to have the right temperature for making bread and cakes. But they knew how to adjust the heat just right. I know out in the Applegate my mother put eggs in the warming oven of the wood stove and kept them there until they hatched."

For a moment, he reflected on his formative years spent on his grandparents' ranch in the Applegate.

"We all had our lard pails," Smith said of attending the Ruch school. "At home, we had biscuits and pancakes all the time for breakfast. So lunch was maybe a pancake rolled up with jelly in it. That was a treat. A biscuit with a fried egg in it left over from breakfast was also our lunch sometimes."

These were fresh eggs full of flavor from the farm, the kind with yolks that look like a bright orange sun floating in cream if you like them sunny side up. Naturally, the biscuits were made from scratch.

"Everybody in those days had a grease pot," Stan recalled. "When you fried bacon, you poured it into a little container. It would keep forever. When you wanted to make gravy or something, you used your grease pot. It made the best gravy."

Back in those distant days, hogs were commonly raised by local families to be butchered for home use, he said.

Those meals provided fuel for the long hours of farm work. As a young teenager bucking hay in the Applegate Valley, he received $1.25 a day. His pay was cut by twenty-five cents if he ate the big lunch provided at the farm.

"We worked from what they called 'can't see to can't see,'" he said, referring to the dawn-to-dusk work day.

The farm workers earned every morsel they consumed, he said, noting he always went for the bountiful lunch.

"My God! Lunches were great," he said. "Those gals could really cook. Homemade bread, everything you could want."

But you would need to buck hay the rest of the day to work off the food that was packed full of cholesterol and fats avoided by today's health-minded society. Yet for folks like Stan, it simply fueled a full life.

As I rose to leave, the man with Sterlingville roots stood up, leaning on his walker for support. He looked out the window of the home where the woman he loved spent her final days. Outside the window lay a vast green lawn as flat as the billiard table his grandfather likely had in his Jacksonville saloon. In the distance rose the mountains his ancestors threaded through to reach Sterlingville a century and a half earlier.

"This has been a good place to live," he said. "I have so many good memories here."

He studied the mountains for a moment before looking down at his strong hands firmly grasping the walker.

"Now I live in fear of falling," he said. He wasn't complaining but merely commenting on the inevitable changes coming at the end of a long life well lived.

After we said our goodbyes, I drove slowly back to Sterling Creek on the road which largely follows the same route his great grandmother would have taken from Sterlingville in the late 1800s en route to Jacksonville. I thought about all the lives linked to Sterlingville that are now all but forgotten. Stan passed away at the tail end of 2015, leaving this world a little less interesting.

TWENTY-ONE

Gods, Ghosts and Old Bones

R IGHT UP FRONT, REST ASSURED I'M NOT GOING TO TRY to convert you
to my way of thinking when it comes to the question of religion or
spirituality. Truth be told, I don't have any answers, just a lot of
questions. Hey, I'm still not fully convinced there is intelligent life on
this planet. So we'll leave the subject of whether there is a superior being
watching over us from the great beyond to another day. Perhaps I'll have
another epiphany by then.

Unfortunately, old religious items found in the cabin require that we
tiptoe into that hallowed minefield. Yep, give me that old-time religion.
But we'll try to stay on the path of history and not wonder about like
Diogenes in search of an honest man. Parenthetically, I've always thought
it would have been easier for him to find an honest woman.

As for the ghostly apparition and old bones in this chapter, you will have
to decide their merit. But I suspect you won't have a bone to pick with the
latter, even though it did involve a visit to our cabin by my grandfather
Jonas Fattig who was born before the Civil War. Actually, he had been
dead for more than half a century. We'll get to him in a bit, by way of the

Oregon State Hospital and Ken Kesey, Oregon's late great writer. You can't deny I warned you early on about meeting some strange bedfellows in this Sterling Creek tale.

First, we need to talk woodstoves. There were three woodstoves in the old place, including a humongous one in the living room, indicating the previous owners spent a lot of time chopping wood to keep the place warm come winter. In addition to the small one in the master bedroom, we found an identical little stove in the back yard, apparently to warm the adjacent cabin which once sat there.

The large woodstove was large enough to burn wood logs as long as your arm and as thick as a sumo wrestler's leg. The sumo stove weighed in at a little more than 300 pounds, according to the metal recycling place where we dropped it off in 2002. Moving the heavy metal heater proved to be a challenge but I enlisted the aid of my twin brother George who had stopped by for a short visit from Alaska where he was living at the time. We needed to move the stove across the concrete floor to the deck where we could load it onto the back of the pickup truck.

"Now isn't that a fine howdy do," George said. "I come to visit and you make me work for my victuals."

He got on one side of the stove while I stood on the other side. We both grabbed the edge of the heavy stove top and looked at each other.

"One, two, three—lift," I said.

We barely budged it. It was as though it was welded to the floor.

"OK, since you can't pick up your end, we'll have to try to walk it," my other half observed, adding, "You really need more sodas and doughnuts to get fired up for the day."

"And you need to quit exercising your mouth if you expect to get any victuals tonight," I grumbled.

When we began walking it toward the double door, we tilted it forward. What appeared to be a burned piece of wood slid out of the warming oven at the bottom. I kicked it aside. The "wood" opened up, revealing itself to be a hardback book whose covers had been singed. I carefully picked it up. The book is *The Mount of Olives and other Lectures on Prayer*, a 212-page hardback containing the sermons of the Rev. James Hamilton of the

National Scotch Church. It is more than a century and a half old, having been published in 1846 by James Nisbet and Co. in London.

How the small Presbyterian book, which is three inches wide and six inches long, came to reside in the cabin, let alone the warming oven, will forever be a whodunit in our minds. Like the 1907 Indian head penny, its provenance is a mystery. But it is at least half a century older than the cabin, obviously deposited there in the years after the cabin was built. To put it in perspective, it was published two years before the Oregon Territory was created. Good Presbyterians in Scotland were poring over it before cheap booze was being poured in Sterlingville watering holes.

The handwritten signature in pencil on the upper right corner of the first page reads "J.E. Bliss." Perhaps Bliss was an ancestor to one of the former owners of the property. He may have even been a resident of Sterlingville, although the lion's share of 19th Century miners did not have a sterling reputation for strong adherence to religious practices.

While I'll stick to my promise of skirting the religious debate, I am fascinated by the topic of where we came from and where we are going. The sermons in the book addressed those very questions in a philosophical manner that impressed. It struck me that the volume was appropriate for the cabin nestled in the picturesque mountain setting. Consider the opening words of the first lecture.

"The mountains are nature's monuments," it begins. "Like the islands they dwell apart, and like them they give asylum from a noisy and irreverent world. In their silence many a meditative spirit has found leisure for the longest thought…"

Obviously, Rev. Hamilton was not a blustery fellow given to raging rants about hellfire and damnation. He wasn't spouting off about saving souls while trying to reach behind you to grab your wallet. Here was a meditative spirit with something worthwhile to share. With a little morning mist and men wearing kilts, the mountains to which he referred could have been those rising above the Sterling Creek drainage.

Although I haven't read the entire book, the first thoughtful sermon doesn't appear to be an aberration. Check out Lecture IX which begins on page 171.

"Some have no turn for poetry, and others have no taste for science," reads the opening paragraph. "Many have no aptitude for argument and dissertation, and no comprehension for abstract statement. But almost all men have an avidity for history. And what is history? It is truth alive and actual—truth embodied—truth clothed in our kindred clay. It is knowledge, not afloat on the mist-bounded sea—the shoreless abyss of speculation—but knowledge coasting it in sight of the familiar landmarks of time and place; knowledge anchored to this human heart , and coming ashore on this our every-day existence."

You get the gist. Mr. Hamilton was a minister the kirk would have looked forward to listening to come sabbath morning. Brother George, who has tried on several religions for size over the years, was impressed.

"That's mighty interesting," he said after I read the above passages out loud. "They knew how to write back in those days. They surely did."

We both wondered aloud if our maternal great, great, great Scottish grandfather James Gordon, who left a village near Inverness in 1804 for the still fledging United States, knew of the Rev. Hamilton. Our Scottish ancestor was a learned man, if the fact his first job in his new country was writing for a Boston newspaper is any indicator. There is the school of thought that journalists don't need to be all that learned, of course.

It was only a few weeks later that Maureen and I encountered more religious material, this time from bible-thumping rats. Communicating in Swedish, no less.

This strange turn of events occurred was triggered when Chris and Richard began working on the ceiling where the pantry is now. Chris was removing the scorched ceiling, using a pry bar. He would loosen a section with the bar before pulling it down. The work was going slow but steady. But one piece directly above his head proved particularly stubborn. He gave the piece a few stiff jabs with the bar, followed by a powerful yank. The piece broke, showering Chris with mucho guano. Down came a veritable Niagara Falls of rat poop and other savory items generations of rats had packed in to make their home nice and comfy.

"Now that was a little disgusting," announced the king of understatement before heading home to take a hot shower. He wasn't completely covered with the foul stuff. There was one spot under his left ear that wasn't coated with rodent detritus. His right shoe was also partially spared.

Sterling Creek rats apparently have a penchant for the eclectic. There was all matter of household debris, including shreds of old newspapers that looked like parchment, pieces of cloth, twigs from the nearby forest, parts of toys, short lengths of twine, even antique zippers. Unable to find suitable plaster at the local rat hardware store, the hairy vermin used rat pellets and urine to bind the nest together. The latter seemed to do the job quite nicely, although we stuck to spackle when we needed filler material for our dry wall. Guano may have a pleasant bouquet to the family rat, but we find it a little musty, not to be unkind.

Maureen and I took over the job of removing all rat remnants in the attic space above the pantry and main bathroom. Chris was wrong about it being a little disgusting. It was major disgusting, even with our face masks.

"One more scoop of poop and I'm going to hurl," I told Maureen.

"Hurl away," replied the lady with a stomach of steel as she continued shoveling debris left by the rat congregation. "Just make sure it is away from me," she hastily added.

Despite my complaining, we worked the weekend so the ceiling material could be taken down without causing a cascade of rat dung to descend upon an understated carpenter. That included removing the stuff pack rats had put in the space between the old cabin shingles and the framing boards. Since the area had not burned and it was part of the original cabin, it was likely there for many decades.

The work prompted me to wonder if rats are like humanoids when it comes to packing things away and promptly forgetting them. Perhaps grandma rat stacked things neatly in the rat hole, later dismissing it from her mind. When she died of old age or got caught in one of the antique rat traps we found around the place, her grand rat kids would have had no idea what goodies she had carefully laid away for them.

In this case, the rat clan matriarch was very devout, although likely not as well read as the good Rev. Hamilton. Among the odd items we pulled out of what passed for the rats' attic were five religious cards which were very similar to baseball cards. All of them were printed from 1905 to 1910 in Kane, Pennsylvania. There was a color painting of Jesus or one of his disciples speaking to members of the flock. Under the art work was a short text in English while the reverse side has no painting but the same text in Swedish.

"Wow," Maureen said as she carefully examined the religious cards. "Who in the world had these? How did they get in the cabin?"

Good questions. Totally stumped, I couldn't even come up with a decent weisenheimer remark. I was particularly gobsmacked by the subject matter on the card dated Aug. 6, 1906. It was the most stained card with only God knows what on it, pun intended. But you can make out the pastel painting of three men dressed appropriately for an outing some 2,000 years ago in the Middle East. The print, which had a 1906 copyright by the Providence Lithograph Co., was titled "False Excuses."

I turned it over and let out a gasp. "I'll be damned—it mentions us in Swedish," I said.

If you've read the Bible, you will know that false excuses refers to the parable in Luke 14:1524. To refresh your memory, Jesus tells about the master of a house getting really ticked off after several folks came up with excuses why they couldn't attend a dinner he offered. One said he needed to go look at some land he just bought. Another had just acquired five oxen and wanted to take them for a test drive. Yet another used the excuse he was recently married. So the master tells his servant, "Go out quickly into the streets and lanes of the city, and bring in here the poor and the maimed and the lame and the blind." The Swedish version on the card reads, "*Tjanaren gick darefter ut och bjod fattiga och krymplingar, halta and blinda.*" In Swedish, "fattig" means poor.

"That's kind of freaky," Maureen said. "What are the chances we would find a card with 'fattiga' written on it? Maybe somebody up above is trying to tell you something."

I wouldn't go that far but it did strike me as mighty odd that our surname would pop up in the cabin in the form of a century-old card written in Swedish. Coincidence? Perhaps. It's one of those mysterious things that will leave me scratching my head until it no longer holds thoughts.

"Yeah, that's just plain weird," I quietly agreed.

Perhaps those cards were on my mind when we hit the sack one night shortly after we moved into the house near the end of 2002. Our bedroom is basically the old cabin that was built before the larger adjacent cabin to which it is now adjoined. Although it is most rustic part of our home, it is a pleasant place to snooze. Unlike the rest of the dwelling, it has a wood floor which feels warm to your bare feet. An open bedroom window on a summer night invites a soft cool breeze, drawn by an open loft window which expels the warmer air.

Yet I tossed and turned that night, unable to get comfortable. Maybe I was thinking about some frustrating writing project I was involved in at work. Or it could have been heartburn from pouring too much hot sauce on tacos we had for dinner. Whatever the reason, sleep came fitfully that night.

It was shortly after midnight that she appeared. A stout elderly lady with her gray hair in a bun walked into our bedroom, around the foot of the bed and over to the far corner. She didn't seem unfriendly, this doppelganger of Aunt Bea, the character from "The Andy Griffith Show" of the 1960s. It was as though she was looking for something. Maybe she was searching for little Opie.

She was wearing a house dress that was lightly colored with a flower design. Over that she wore what appeared to be a darker Mackinaw jacket over her dress, the kind of coat available at Cabela's if you are the outdoor type. The jacket, which may have belonged to her husband, suggested she was used to wearing a coat indoors. Perhaps she lived in the cabin when the winter wind blew in between the logs.

After walking to the corner of the bedroom, she simply disappeared. She didn't say anything, never made a fuss over the stack of books I always have on my dresser. One thing was certain: she acted like she was home. Of that, I am dead sure.

What is in doubt is whether I was awake. Or was I dreaming? I honestly don't know. None of our hairy creatures made a stir, if that means anything.

Naturally, I woke Maureen up.

"Honey, I just saw a ghost," I told her as I shook her shoulder. "She looked just like Aunt Bea."

"That's nice," she mumbled. "Tell Aunt Bea and Opie to go away and quit waking me up."

She rolled back over on her side, pulling a pillow over her ears. As a childhood fan of the show, she knew who Aunt Bea was, even upon being awakened in the middle of the night. She also knew that I have a sophomoric sense of humor, one which she humors during the day. But juvenile nocturnal jokes are not tolerated, particularly in the wee hours.

Only I wasn't joking. To this day I don't know the truth of what I did or didn't see. I don't believe in ghosts or other things that go bump in the night. Perhaps it was just some bad guacamole.

After sunrise, Maureen, fortified with a cup of hot chocolate, was more amenable to listening to the ghostly tale, although still wary of a prank.

"How can you be sure you weren't dreaming?" she asked as she bit into some toast. "Maybe you were dreaming that you were awake."

"It was so real," I replied. "I've never had a dream like that. She just walked into our bedroom, then over to the corner and disappeared."

Maureen picked up another piece of toast and began slathering blackberry jam on it. The mischievous glint in her eye warned me she wasn't too serious about ghostly guests.

"Well, we can be glad you didn't dream you woke up as a giant cockroach," she said with a big grin.

"That was really mean," I said. She knows full well the Franz Kafka story is one of my favorite short pieces of literature. I've always felt bad for traveling salesman Gregor Samsa who, at the cruel hands of Kafka in *Metamorphosis*, awoke to find himself turned into what appears to have been a giant cockroach or a close cousin. Just what Gregor did to deserve such a fate is never explained by Kafka, although I suspect underhanded sales practices in his biped life.

"Not as mean as waking me up in the middle of the night to announce you just saw Aunt Bea in our bedroom, bucko," she said. "Besides, it must have been a dream if you could see her. The bedroom was dark."

"She was kind of illuminated," I said. "You know, glowing a little."

I knew full well the conversation was headed south at that point. Ghost stories told in the light of day lack gravitas.

"Ghosts usually have a fairly low wattage," continued my toast-nibbling tormentor. "Would you say she was forty watts or so? Maybe she and Barney Fife were meeting for a saucy interlude. You know those Mayberrians get real wild at night."

"Fine, make fun," I said, chuckling despite my best attempts to pout. "See if I ever tell you about any more of my dreams."

As she headed for the kitchen to heat up her chocolate, she kissed me on the forehead, letting me know it was all in fun.

In retrospect, I suspect it was likely one of those dreams which seems real. No doubt deep in my subconscious I've always thought the woman who lived in the cabin when it was young must have looked like Aunt Bea and had her strength of character to survive. Perhaps I just conjured her up during a deep sleep.

In any case, she never returned. I'd like to have chatted with Aunt Bea as well as her paramour, if the bumbling deputy was indeed in the picture. As for that little thing they had going, we'll let them sort it out back in Mayberry.

While Aunt Bea was the closest we have ever come to an apparition, we have found plenty of old bones. That includes a skull found near the tack shed. But it wasn't human. When it was covered with fur, it appears to have been that of a large domestic cat. We're hoping that it died naturally of old age but we are harassed by doubts. Its teeth are not worn down, indicating it probably didn't die from old age. Likely it met its fate in the larger jaws of one of the fierce creatures that lurks in the Sterling Creek drainage, including bobcats and cougars. That's the reason we make sure all our pets are safely inside come nightfall.

It seemed cold to throw the skull in the trash or bury it in some soon forgotten hole. So I hung the skeletal remains on the outside of the old shed, under the eve where it would be sheltered from storms. I like to think it is a place of honor. A strong and silent type, he's one of the best cats we've ever had. He never coughs up a hairball. But, alas, he is not much of a mouser these days.

Perhaps the oddest bone we have yet to unearth is a two-inch long ancient tooth I dug up while cleaning debris out of the ditch that runs along the driveway. The tooth is about two inches long and a little over an inch wide with deep ridges running down the front. One friend suggested it could have been from one of the elephant-like creatures that roamed our region back in ancient times. Don't laugh. A mammoth tusk was found in the Sterling Creek mine in the late 1800s, Truwe reported. On page three of the Aug. 12, 1892 *Jacksonville Democratic Times* newspaper, he found an article about ancient pachyderms that had been lifted from the *Portland Oregonian.*

"Vin Cook, who has been at the Sterling hydraulic mines all summer, is in the city," the piece began, referring to Portland. "Every summer the fossil remains of mammoth or some other huge prehistoric animal are found in the mine; but this season they worked out a portion of a tusk, the largest yet found there."

The article doesn't mention it but Vincent Cook was the son-in-law of Henry "Cap" Ankeny, superintendent of the mine. After the senior Ankeny died in 1891, his son, Henry, and Cook took over the mine operation. They were in charge when the huge tusk was uncovered.

"The point was gone, so it was not possible to tell how long the tusk was originally, but the piece found was 11 feet long and 28 inches in circumference," the 1892 article reported. "The animal that sported a pair of tusks like that must have been a daisy."

No doubt it must have been quite a doozy, to put it into Baby Boomer vernacular. Makes one think President Jefferson wasn't far off the mark when he exhorted Lewis and Clark to keep their eyes out for mammoths during their exploratory 1804-06 cross continent trek. Of course, they would have found only fossilized remains since the big hairy fellows were inhabitants of the Pleistocene epoch, a period when glaciers abounded.

However, if bones could talk, those with the strangest story to tell would be the remains of my paternal grandfather, Jonas Fattig, a man who died before I was born. Obviously, I had never met him. But his earthly remains came for a week's visit to Sterling Creek in March of 2006.

This bizarre tale began after I read an article in January of that year in the *Portland Oregonian* newspaper about some 3,500 unclaimed cremated ashes, dubbed "cremains," stored in the Oregon State Hospital in Salem. The copper canisters had been discovered in a storage room during a 2004 tour by state legislators. Then Oregon Senate President Peter Courtney, D-Salem, had rightfully called it "the room of lost souls." The fact the canisters were left unclaimed in a storage room is a sad commentary on every next of kin who knew of their fate, including the family Fattig.

I knew my grandfather, who had been a late homesteader in the Applegate Valley, had been committed to the hospital when he was elderly. I thought he had been buried there, although I wasn't sure. After reading the article, Maureen suggested we contact hospital officials to see if his remains were among the canisters. Sure enough, after filling out the required forms and providing documentation proved I was related, we were informed that Jonas Fattig, rather his remains, resided in a copper urn marked 3414. He had been cremated and shelved nearly sixty years earlier. No family member had bothered to claim him. It seemed heartless.

My research on the paterfamilias revealed he was born on in Iowa on Jan. 22, 1858, three years before the first shot was fired in the Civil War. He farmed on the Greats Plains before arriving in Oregon shortly before 1900, first working as a laborer in Ashland before homesteading in the Applegate Valley in 1907. He moved the family to the Illinois Valley in neighboring Josephine County in 1921 where he bought a farm. Although family lore painted him as a stern authoritarian, he played the fiddle at barn dances in the Applegate. So he must have let his hair down and kicked up his heels once in a while.

According to the hospital records, the old farmer had been committed to the state asylum in the spring of 1947 by Charles Savannah Fattig, his eldest son and one of my uncles. Jonas was eighty-nine at the time. He died alone, far from family or friends. Harriett Viola Lounsbury Fattig, his wife of roughly half a century and my grandmother, had passed away in 1940.

Included in his medical records we received from the hospital were copies of two Western Union telegrams. One was from the hospital staff to Charles Fattig, then living in a hamlet called Wonder in Josephine County. It notified him that his father had died Sept. 17, 1947, and requested him to wire back with funeral instructions.

"In regards to remains of Jonas Fattig am leaving to your disposal," my now defunct uncle replied in the terse reply via telegram. Like I said, cold.

The medical records listed the cause of death as "bronchopneumonia." The folks in the white coats added his clinical diagnosis was "senile psychosis." They also noted that he was extremely sad, and that he did not know why he was locked up in what at that time was tantamount to a prison.

According to the family's considerably less than professional diagnosis, the elderly gent was as ringy as a church bell. One story is that he was sent to the asylum after strolling buck naked amongst a flock of church ladies on a Sunday picnic near his farm in Holland, startling them like a brace of quail surprised by an old hound dog. This particular Holland is an old community in the Illinois Valley, not the place with wooden shoes and windmills. Another tale told is that his eldest son was very keen on gaining control of the family farm, which he promptly acquired and sold after the patriarch was removed. We will never know the truth, naked or not. All who knew the gospel of it are long dead. Like those who have gone before, the answer belongs to the ages.

The hospital staff offered to mail gramps, but we figured his remains had been through enough without having to go postal. Maureen and I drove up to the state capital to pick up old No. 3414.

I couldn't help feeling depressed by the sight of the old section of the hospital where he was likely housed during his final months of life. It resembled a gloomy prison with its barred windows. Dark clouds threatening rain added to the dismal atmosphere. I kept thinking about a bewildered old man sitting alone on his bed in that gloomy brick building, wondering why he was there.

When most people think of the hospital, they reflect on the 1975 awardwinning flick *One Flew Over the Cuckoo's Nest*, based on the novel by Ken Kesey, who once worked there. It was a good read, although not Kesey's best work. In my Forrest Gump moments, I had covered high school wrestling in the Eugene area during the 1970s, and periodically ran into Kesey at the matches. His son had wrestled for Pleasant Hill High School whose team wrestled squads from several of the schools I covered. Since high school matches don't draw a lot of people, we kept bumping into each other. We ended up chatting about wrestling. I had wrestled in high school; he was a standout wrestler at the University of Oregon. I never asked him about his writing, figuring he would talk about it if he felt like it. He never brought it up. Now I wish I had broached the subject to that grand master of the pen.

Back at the gloomy old hospital, we found no rabblerousing Randle McMurphy, domineering Big Nurse or silent Chief Bromden, only a pleasant staff ready to hand over what was left of the family patriarch. But the visit left me with a distinct feeling of melancholy. Bothering me was the thought of so many lonely lives ending there in the dark and dreary, dilapidated old yellowbrick building with rusting bars on its narrow windows. The state has since razed the hospital's circa-1883 main building, replacing it with a new 620-bed facility. The cremains still at the hospital— less than 200 of the 3,500 have been claimed by family members—have also been removed from the copper containers and placed in ceramic urns to better protect them.

As we drove south, I thought about the changes in Oregon since he died. There were strip malls and mauled strips, folks chatting on cell phones and watching videos in SUVs speeding down the freeway that didn't exist in his time. We cruised along at sixty-five miles per hour, far faster than grandpa had ever traveled. The product of the horse and buggy era didn't seem to mind that the modern American society is a nimble bunch.

Our plan was to reunite him with his daughter, Bessie Belle, six, buried in 1904 in the Hargadine Cemetery in Ashland. Hargadine was where Jonas bought the north half of lot 40 in 1904 for $5 to bury his daughter. There could be nothing more anguishing for a parent to have to bury a young child. My father was born in Ashland on June 17, 1906, two years after she died. Perhaps his birth was intended to make up for the painful loss of Bessie Belle. In any case, we have the burial plot deed signed by Jonas.

Before making his final trip to the cemetery, Jonas spent a week in our cabin. I suspect he had been on Sterling Creek before since his homestead had been less than half a dozen miles from our cabin as the crow flies. He likely saw the cabin when it was still young.

We placed his copper urn, portions of which were covered with a green patina, on the small Baldwin piano in a nook under the stairs. When I sat gramps on the piano, I was reminded that he once played fiddle at barn dances in the Applegate Valley.

"You may have been the only one in the family with musical talent but there will be no tunes on the piano while you are here," I told him. "Nor will be there any naked sauntering. If there is any bad behavior, you will be kicked out on your ash."

Maureen groaned and looked skyward.

"Hey, he was an authoritative figure—he understands discipline," I said, adding, "Besides, a little humor is what we need right now."

He behaved splendidly while staying in the Sterling Creek cabin. Perhaps he was busy chasing Aunt Bea.

As it happens, Maureen has an old copper canister which she keeps for odds and ends. It looked remarkably like the urn on the piano. Across from the piano stands our woodstove. Inside were ashes. Sophomoric wheels started turning.

"Don't you dare," Maureen said when I suggested pulling a little practical joke at the cemetery. But it's hard to understand her when she's talking and giggling simultaneously. You will notice she didn't exactly forbid my adding a little mischievous levity to the otherwise somber event.

Cremains are more granulated than wood ash. In fact, it you were to shake the urn, you would notice it contained what sounded like several bone remnants that had not turned to ashes, not to put too fine a point on the ghastly subject. But to the uninitiated, ashes and cremains are alike. The wood stove ashes would serve nicely.

The informal ceremony to lay the remains of Jonas Fattig to rest was scheduled for the last day of winter in 2006. He had arrived in southern Oregon more than a century earlier. No one who knew him was there for the event. Most of his descendants have moved away but a handful showed up, including his greatgreatgrandchildren Erik and Meghan. The day was sunny and bright. There was also a nice little breeze.

I carried the urn as the solemn group walked from the parking area towards the grave site. It was all very prim and proper.

You may remember that early on I noted that I walk with a substantial hitch in my gait, one which often causes me to trip on the smallest things. Fiendish grasshoppers have been known to stick out their toes to trip me.

As a result, I've become an expert at falling down. Feigning having tripped, I threw the copper container into the air as I went down, making sure to give it an energetic spin as it flew through the air. The lid, which I had already loosened, fell away. A cloud of ashes erupted from the twirling canister.

Just that moment the breeze picked up, wafting what was purportedly our ancestor's mortal remains into the small group. There were startled gasps. His descendants, save his only grandson present, were utterly mortified.

"Don't breathe the ashes!" screamed my sister, Delores, as she grabbed her grandchildren and run with them away from the ghoulish cloud that seemed to be intent on enveloping them. She is by far the nicest of us siblings, by the way.

I was on my hands and knees, laughing. Maureen frantically tried to get everyone to calm down as she explained it was all a practical joke. Gramps' remains were still in the real urn back in our vehicle, she assured them.

The relatives were not amused. With the exception of Erik, that is. He broke into a peal of laughter that filled the entire cemetery. Erik graduated from high school in 2014 and has set off to make his way in the world. I hope the little joke didn't stunt his sense of humor during his formative years. We need all the laughter we can muster to flourish in this world.

We quickly retrieved the real urn and gently placed it adjacent to where the remains of Bessie Belle rests for eternity. A few words were said over the graves and we departed. Maureen and I make a point to place flowers on their graves each Memorial Day. We hope reuniting father and daughter will somehow make up for what happened in the distant past.

In retrospect, I freely admit the woodstove ashes incident was an adolescent act, one that any responsible adult would find disgustingly juvenile. Obviously, the one responsible must shoulder all the blame. That would be Maureen, of course. She was the one who should have been keeping an eye on me. What on earth was she thinking? Surely she must know such undignified behavior is intolerable in civilized society, even if you live in a cabin along Sterling Creek.

Cretin that I am, I still chuckle at the memory. And I like to think my fiddle-playing grandfather would have gotten a kick out of it. Rest in peace, grandpa.

TWENTY-TWO

The Gilson Gulch
Cat Herd

T HERE IS AMPLE EVIDENCE THAT THOMAS STEARNS ELIOT could be a little jumpy at times. His biographers—Eliot's poems spawned a litter of them—reported that he had a nervous condition for which he periodically sought medical attention. That he could sometimes be twitchy is perfectly understandable because the poet, known fondly as "T.S." by his fans the world over, was unabashedly a cat man.

An argument can be made that "The Waste Land," his most famous poem which was published in 1922, was largely about cats. But only one who has long suffered at the paws of feline fiends can truly understand the poem's painful mix of dread and desire. Just reading the poem makes me feel like a cat is sharpening its claws on a bare shin. Take the unforgettable line, "April is the cruelest month." Any cat person knows that mean month is often rife with new born kittens, the most demanding little monsters on the planet.

While Mr. Eliot did his best to cloak his cat obsession in that poem, he let it out of the bag a decade later in his *Old Possum's Book of Practical Cats*, a volume of poetry exploring the psychology and sociology of *Felis catus*. It was turned into the long-running Broadway musical "Cats" by Andrew Lloyd Webber. The poet knew full well that no cat is practical, of course. He was just taking his poetic license out for a walk. If you part the fur in his feline poetry, you sense he lived on the hairy edge of fear. As I said, jumpy. He knew that adding one cat could tip the balance, plunging his world into Dante's "infurno." When one starts giving cats monikers like Macavity, Mr. Mistoffelees, Skimbleshanks, Mungojerrie and Old Deuteronomy, you know the end is nigh.

I bring up the cat-suffering poet because the feline population in Gilson Gulch has reached that precarious point where our sanity could be tipped over. We stand on the edge of the precipice, looking down into a hellish maelstrom of mewling, demanding felines. The census-keeping Hutchings, a Brit like Eliot, never mentioned how many cats were living in Sterlingville where he spent that soggy February night in 1855. But I'm willing to bet a half dozen cats that we had all Sterlingvillians beat paws down when it comes to feline occupancy in our fur-lined cabin.

At last count, there were ten cats allowing us to share the cabin with them. Our cat colony no doubt skewed the survey released in 2013 by the American Veterinary Medical Association revealing that Oregon ranks third in the nation when it comes to cat ownership. A suffering cat person would laugh derisively at the term "ownership," given a feline's penchant for independence.

Of the cats we have nominally owned, at least five of them, possibly six, were indirectly bequeathed to us by my father-in-law, Andy Gaskin. The affable cat-loving World War II veteran died in Medford on Jan. 19, 2013 at age eighty-eight. I'm a little iffy about the last one because I do not know if Andy was—or is—associated with it. You be the judge. We'll get back to that cat in a bit.

When it comes to pets, Maureen obviously didn't fall far from the paternal cat tree. It wasn't just cats: her father never met a furry animal he didn't want to provide food and shelter. He was a kindred spirit to all creatures, domestic or wild. When the winters were particularly brutal when he lived on his remote ranch east of the Cascade Range, he would buy large bags of dog food to feed coyotes on a nearby lonely ridge. He would raise cattle but couldn't bear to have them butchered. For him, it was truly a case of the tail wagging the dog. Or cat. Or cow. The only animals he didn't cozy up to were rattlesnakes. He visited the cabin once when we caught a rather large buzzworm which had a rather feisty disposition. While we were nervously placing the angry viper into the rattlesnake can before transporting him into the mountains, Andy refused to come within twenty feet of our irate guest. Andy was no dummy.

But we can't blame all of Maureen's love for those hairy little spitballs solely on genetics. Nurture also played a role, in part thanks to her sister Teresa and cousin Sharon, both a few years older than Maureen. When my future wife was about five, their mom dashed to the nearby grocery store for a few minutes, leaving Teresa and Sharon to babysit. Being mischievous, big sister and their cousin couldn't help themselves. When their mother returned, Maureen was sitting at the kitchen table, her little legs swinging back and forth as she noshed on a tuna sandwich. Only it wasn't Chicken of the Sea. It seems the babysitters had decided to conduct a scientific experiment to determine whether baby sister could differentiate between human food and cat food. The empirical evidence indicated she was just as happy with the latter. Mom was not amused, albeit the anecdote still draws chortles at family gatherings some sixty years later. You also have to wonder if sampling cat food at a tender age created at cat fetish in the love of my life. I'm just saying.

In any case, the first I heard of Andy's cats heading our way was one morning when I was sitting innocently at the dining room table, sipping a cup of Earl Grey after carefully inspecting the surface to make sure there were no floating cat hairs. I had already flossed, you understand. That's when my other half lobbed a question that might as well have been a fragmentation grenade.

"Do you realize we have had seventeen cats over the years?" she asked out of the blue from the kitchen where she was making a cup of mocha. "I just counted them all."

"Like the married man said after his wife informed him they had been married for twenty-five years, 'It seems like a lot more than that,' " I replied, taking another sip.

"We have been married twenty-five years," she retorted, frowning as she peeked around the corner to make sure I was grinning. Like a Cheshire cat, I was.

But the cat question was worrisome. It had a distinctly rhetorical feel to this confirmed dog man. I felt like a mouse being toyed with by a very sly cat.

"Do you know how many cats Hemingway had?" she asked.

"Too many," I replied. "Some say there is probably a connection between his large cat herd and the fact he eventually took his life. Not many people know this but he only wrote on the side. He mainly raised cats for fur. That can be very stressful, even though there is more than one way to skin a cat."

Ignoring my weak attempt to change the subject, she pressed on.

"At one point, he had more than sixty cats," she said. "I was just reading about it. They were cool cats, too. They had six toes instead of the normal five. They are called polydactyl cats."

What prompted her interest in Ernest Hemingway's cats was the fact Derra and Matt had just returned from a trip to the Florida Keys. They made a point to stop in Key West and paid their respects to the house where the writer churned out his memorable works amid what must have been an endless cacophony of meowing. While they were already fans of his books, they became enamored with the polydactyls. So did Derra's mom.

"What started it all was a six-toed cat he was given by a ship's captain," Maureen said. "It was a white cat which Hemingway named Snow White. It just goes to show that you never know what will happen if you have the kindness to take in a cat that needs a good home."

Aha! The cat was finally poking its head out of the bag.

"No way!" I sputtered, nearly spilling my tea. "We already have too many cats. We don't need another one."

Don't get me wrong. I'm no ailurophobe, one of those wildhaired characters with an abnormal fear or hatred of cats. My concern was upsetting the cabin's very delicate cat equilibrium. There was no need to rile them up by tossing a hissing stranger into the mix.

"I agree with you—we don't need another one," she said. "But this would only be temporary. They are just tiny kittens that need to stay here a little while."

"They?" I asked in a near whisper. "Are you serious?"

"Yep, five little ones—just for a while," she said. "You won't even know they are here."

It seems that my fatherinlaw, who spent a small fortune on having feral cats fixed over the years, had discovered the kittens at his place. A feral mother cat that had eluded the spay dragnet dropped in one day to give birth to the five little tortoise shell felines. The furry floozie nursed the little guys for a while, then lost interest in the whole family values thing and wandered off with a tom to go permanently out on the town. Damned liberals.

"Again, it will be for a little while, unless we decide to keep one or two, of course," Maureen said, prompting another round of protest from yours truly. The dogs and I were cringing. It was pure pandemonium for a while, what with all the whining and whimpering.

"It's really embarrassing when you act like that," my wife said, adding, "At least Waldo and Harpo have the decency to be more mature about this."

"The poor pooches aren't being decent—they are catatonic," I protested. "They are terrified at the thought of being dogged by more cats. Telepathically, they are barking at me to stop this cat invasion."

But Maureen was not to be denied. "We'll just fatten 'em up a bit and find good homes for them," she said. "That means bottle feeding them, of course. They aren't weaned yet."

Despite my continued verbal handwringing, the furry little hairballs were moved into the cabin. One was so small it curled up in the palm of Maureen's hand.

"We're going to call this one Mouse," she said. "She's the smallest in the litter."

The dogs and I looked at each other, knowing we had lost the first battle.

"You can't name her if she is only going to be a temporary guest," I said. "Besides, naming a cat 'Mouse' is sure to cause some deepseated psychological problems. Who knows what mental depravity will be unleashed."

"You can always get therapy," Maureen replied. Mouse looked up at me, yawned and fell back to sleep. The hairy munchkin knew she was home free.

Maureen would rise early each morning to feed her furry friends. It was also the first thing she did each evening. She would heat their special cat milk—I don't want how nor do I want to know how one milks a cat—in a little pan, put it into a tiny baby bottle and gently feed each one until a tummy pooches out. She began referring to them as the "Little People." Never a good sign for a spouse worried about being overrun by felines.

"You little guys are soooo darn cute," she purred as they clambered onto her lap for each feeding. Mouse may have been the smallest but she was a bulldozer, pushing in to be the first fed. She then wandered off to explore the cabin and terrorize the rest of us. The pooches and I learned to tolerate the cat herd. After becoming used to serving as scratching posts and cat pillows, we found it best to suffer in silence.

But I did notice Waldo and Harpo had started taking turns sniffing Mouse's petite pink nose and furry little rump. The former man's best friends had apparently found a new best buddy. Curs can be so fickle.

At the outset, we received sound advice in the art of raising kittens from the great crew of volunteers at CATS—Committed Alliance to Strays—in Medford. It's a wonderful non-profit program to help strays and educate bipeds about becoming life-long servants to felines. Maureen's stated goal was to raise the kitties, then adopt them out through CATS. Bottle-fed kittens are apparently in high demand because the hands-on process creates extraordinarily lovable cats. In addition to adopting them out to good homes, the program also included spaying or neutering the kittens once they were of age.

The hitch for us, of course, was Maureen's bonding with the little fellows. They became her furry babies. For the dogs, fickle though they were, I had to make a stand against turning our domicile into the Sterling Creek cathouse. This was obviously a case where the best defense would be an aggressive offense.

"Don't even think about keeping any of..." I began.

"I think we'll put them in the living room until they are a little bigger," Maureen interjected. "That way they can get used to having us around."

"Yeah but..." I countered.

"Perhaps you are right," she responded. "We should let them out periodically to feel like they are part of the family."

"There is no way in..." I concluded.

"I'm glad that's settled," she said. "We can start taking proper care of the

Little People now. We'll need to bring the big cage into the living room so they'll feel safe and start socializing with the other animals."

Then she stepped up close and gave me a hug. "You love 'em, too—you just won't own up to it," she said.

Admittedly, I periodically had to stretch a muscle in my arm while reading, resulting in accidentally brushing my hand along the back of a nearby Little Person. Mine is simply a nervous disorder, an affliction perhaps similar to the one suffered by Eliot. But I had to move gently to avoid waking the one sleeping on my lap.

Living with a cat herd gives one an opportunity to study the curious creatures. Like bipeds, each has a different personality. Some are lazy louts, albeit they are difficult to spot, given the fact they all sleep about 18 hours a day. The one and only job of a cat is to bring peace and tranquility to a home. But our cats routinely ignore this simple rule, just as they typically refuse to acknowledge a simple summons. A subpoena from the highest court in the land would receive a cold furry shoulder from a cat.

Maureen added to the mouser mayhem by giving them little balls to play with. They fight over them constantly. Howling felines in a soccer scrum defeats the purpose of having cats in the house. The winner of the match invariably grabs the ball in its mouth, and dashes through the cabin yowling about the incredible victory. As is in American football, there really needs to be a rule against such unsportsmanslike behavior. Not that the hairy hellions would pay any heed to it, of course.

When it came time to present the five little bottle-fed felines to CATS for adoption, we took them in as agreed. "It feels like we are giving away our kids," Maureen sniffed when we drove away from the facility after dropping the Little People off. "It is a little sad," I admitted.

A few days later, at Maureen's insistence, we were back, ready to adopt. OK, so maybe I didn't protest that much. But when we got there, two of the five kittens had already been adopted out to good homes. Our little Mouse was still there. "We are adopting Mouse today," Maureen said. In a moment of weakness, I agreed, but only on the condition we could also adopt Evinrude, the kitten whose purr sounds like a little outboard motor. I nicknamed him the "Rudester" because when he wants attention it has to be now. Very spoiled, that one. But a reading cat par excellence.

Neither of us could bear to say farewell to Miss Chievious, the young cat who was forever attacking a bare ankle or swatting at a nervous tail attached to Waldo or Harpo. But we concurred at the time we could only take two cats.

Two more days passed. Maureen couldn't stand it any longer and called CATS to check on little Miss Chievious. The poor thing had all but stopped eating and had developed a life-threatening case of dysentery, according to the facility's veterinarian. Her chances of being adopted were not good, acknowledged the worried lady on the phone.

"We are going to adopt her and bring her home," Maureen announced. The statement left no room for debate. Since it was my day off, I went in to pick up our last bottle-fed kitten. She perked up when she saw me and made no fuss about being put in the cat carrier.

There is a permanent video in my mind of what took place when I opened the cat carrier in the cabin. Miss Chievious ran over to her two siblings who trotted over to meet her halfway. All three meowed greetings. They immediately started tumbling over each other, forming a miniature dog pile. Mouse and Evinrude began licking Miss Chievious' face. That they were happy to see each other there can be no doubt. From that day forth, Miss Chievious has been as healthy as a horse. She had only been homesick.

For reasons not clear in my cat-hair addled mind, Miss Chievious has decided that the two of us are an item. She pesters me constantly. When I am working at my desk, she often comes walking across the keyboard. I'll take any help I can get, although I don't appreciate her constantly pressing the delete key.

But I draw the line when she tries to follow me into the bathroom. The moment I close the door behind me, she starts caterwauling to be let inside. It's embarrassing. Once, when friends were visiting, I ducked into the guest bathroom for a second with Miss Chievious hot on my heels. The high-pitched wailing began the second I closed the door in her face. "What on earth is that?" asked one startled guests. "That's just Paul going to the bathroom," Maureen replied with a smile. Little wonder T. S. Eliot's nerves were jangled.

After all the cat hair had temporarily settled following the final Little

People acquisition, I expressed confusion to Maureen about how many cats we had.

"It's simple, sweetie—we had three, took in five, gave five back, brought three home and then added one more," she explained, then added with an impish grin, "It's 'purrcisely' the same number of cats we had at the beginning."

The explanation was well short of being "purrfectly" clear to me. Keeping tabs on our tabbies has always been a challenge but I believe I can lay out for you our cat numbers, although it may not match the magical seventeen Maureen tallied. Our numbers are blurred by the fact some cats are allowed to roam outside while others are inside cats. For instance, the Little People have never been allowed outside the cabin. Do cats become agoraphobic? I worry about that, albeit they seem totally content. When we open a door to let an outside cat out, the Little People show no desire to venture forth. But invariably opening the door to let one cat out means another outside cat will stroll in. Sometimes the cat coming in is even one of our cats.

I do know for sure that we originally brought three cats with us to the cabin. That would be Spud, Tommy and Ambrosia. Spud and Tommy both moved back north with us from California. Like all urbane Californians, they were at first a little overwhelmed by rural life. But they quickly fell in love with the Applegate country.

Spud, initially called "Angel" for reasons I could never ascertain, had been adopted from an animal shelter when he was a little white cotton ball. He was a lovable couch potato, hence the name I gave him. He was lazy, sleepy and would purr at the drop of his name. He never met a book he didn't want me to read, providing he was able to curl up on my lap. Here was a cat who took his responsibilities seriously. After twenty wonderful years, our old couch potato completed his ninth life. He died of cancer in August of 2009. Fittingly, he was purring when he was put to sleep.

Tommy, adopted from a neighbor in California, was a big orange and yellow fellow with a friendly disposition like his pal Spud. He was 21 when he died on Christmas eve in '07 with our family gathered around him. He spent his final hours curled up in the basket he loved. He died peacefully, never waking from his winter's nap.

Ambrosia arrived as a very small Himalayan kitten brought home from the grocery store by one of our daughters, a senior in high school, who had stopped to get a gallon of milk. Another time the honor student brought home a puppy from the same store while on a milk run. We quit sending her to the store for milk. We had Ambrosia for a little more than a dozen years before that wonderful little cat succumbed to feline diabetes.

For more than a year, we took care of an elderly, nearly toothless tabby named "Mama Cat," one which Andy had for more than two decades. After Andy broke his leg, he could no longer care for Mama Cat. We stepped forward to take her in until he mended. The cat stayed with us for the rest of her days, of course, moving slowly about the cabin until she died of extreme old age. She reminded us of Grizabella, the very elderly cat in the Cats musical. I wouldn't have been surprised if one day Mama Cat had started belting out "Memory."

Living inside the cabin when we bought it was a beautiful cat we named Sable because of her black coat with a reddish tinge. She lived happily with us for eight years before suffering a stroke. Thanks to Maureen's gentle care, Sable recovered and lived three more years before dying of old age.

There were also a few walkon ferals who made the team. They simply strolled up to our door and scratched. These felines knew a Sterling Creek gold mine when they saw it.

Our big boy Fitz showed up on our deck one day, two dozen pounds of muscle and meow. He is big on eating but not much on socializing. In the Cats musical, he would have been the fat cat Bustopher Jones, a "twenty-five pounder" according to Eliot. But our Fitz is sullen and withdrawn, reminding me of Mr. Darcy in the Jane Austin's *Pride and Prejudice*. Austen devotees know that Mr. Darcy's first name is Fitzwilliam. As his namesake would say, this cat is tolerable. While Fitz gained weight at the cabin, he lost nearly a pound when he was neutered. Understandably, the once well-endowed cat did not appreciate being gelded when Maureen had me take him in for the surgery. It has been six years and he still glares at me. Can't say I much blame him.

Odysseus is a long-haired tom who is always the last to come in every night. Nicknamed "Odie," the black and white cat was named after the Greek adventurer because of his penchant for roaming. Like all long-haired animals, he is a shedder.

"Promise me we will never, ever get another creature with long hair," I begged Maureen after Odie had joined the cat wrecking crew. "Not everyone enjoys a hair ball sandwich, let alone flossing with cat hair."

"That was completely unintentional, sweetie," she said.

A few weeks earlier she had packed us a lunch to take to work. We took turns making lunches but hers were invariably better than mine. I looked forward to lunch outside in the fine autumn air. It looked to be a pleasant day.

Unbeknownst to me, the newly arrived Odie had apparently ambled past while Maureen was preparing the sandwiches that morning. Naturally, she had to reach down and pet him.

Unfortunately, he was in his shedding stage, a period when he leaves large clumps of hair behind. Maureen, who is definitely not physically hygiene challenged, apparently forgot this once to wash her hands before returning to my sandwich.

Later that day I happily bit down on the sandwich, innocently enjoying the moment. The next thing I remember was the sound of someone—me—trying to hack up what must have looked like a wet kitten to shocked passersby.

"Oh, my God! You actually coughed up a fur ball!" Maureen recalled before lapsing into a series of gasping giggles.

Once she regained her composure and wiped her eyes, she insisted it was an unfortunate accident. But I am harried by doubts.

Naturally, the next cat to join the cat pack was longhaired, despite my begging to the contrary. The black cat has a white spot on his chest, making it impossible to label him anything but Spot. He showed up on the deck one night, sauntering into the cabin like he owned the place. He ate, curled up on a cat bed and slept until dawn. He has been us ever since. Perhaps in one of his other lives he did own it.

We try to keep Odie and Spot apart since they are always ready to scratch each other's eyes out. The reason for their on-going spat is unclear. Both of them have been fixed but it has done nothing to bring a lasting peace. Perhaps you are right: one must be a Republican, the other a Democrat.

But the instigator may be Freckles, our cute little calico cat. Despite being snipped, all the male cats are hopelessly and madly in love with her. They often get into a hissing match when she comes sashaying along. The first time we saw her, she was sitting at the edge of the forest, watching the cabin. Maureen began putting food out, hoping to tame her. She watched us from the safety of the woods for nearly a year. She would eat the food but refused to come close to us. One morning I was out on the deck, calling all cats when one came running up and jumped into my arms. It was Freckles. I initially thought I was being attacked by a wild cat but she was purring. The little tyke with the heart of a lion had finally decided that we were suitable to adopt as human pets.

When I took her to our veterinarian to have her spayed, they discovered she had already been fixed. Yet there was no microchip. She either had been fixed, then dropped off in the country or she had run away from a home where she had been spayed. She does have a worrisome habit of periodically slipping away for a week or so. Such is the ebb and flow in our catdom.

Spartan was a furry gift to us from daughter Sheena when she got married. Her fiancé sadly informed her that he was allergic to cats. But his love for Sheena must be powerful. After all, he had seen how his mother-in-law collects animals like the Borg gather civilizations. He correctly assumed that his bride was also an animal lover but knew they could work out furry details. They did adopt a hypoallergenic pup shortly after their honeymoon in Ireland. Alas, resistance is futile, Justin.

Yet Spartan is a pleasant fellow who never gets overly excited about anything. Maureen describes him as a working cat, a description that causes me to scratch behind my ear. We're talking about a cat that would have to diet to see 18 pounds again. Spartan is definitely not spartan. A curious fellow, the big orange and white tabby likes to survey the job site when we are working outside, monitoring our progress. But I would point out that his is a supervisorial role. He doesn't do a lick of work.

Despite not being on the payroll, Spartan gets all the accoutrements of a paid staffer, including medical should a veterinarian be needed. I discovered just how cushy he had it after I had worked a long morning cutting brush and thinning the overgrown forest near our cabin. I was looking forward to refreshments. Maureen was also ready for a break.

Pulling off my gloves, I eagerly lifted the lid of our little lunch cooler we packed for the day.

"What is this?" I asked as I fished out a plastic bag filled with what appeared to be dry pet food. "I'm not finicky, but there are things that even my Kerby stomach will not tolerate. This looks like cat food. Have you fallen off the catfood wagon again? "

"That is cat food and, no, it is not for me, goofus," Maureen replied. "Spartan gets hungry when he's out here. His little legs work hard climbing the hill. Our working cat needs an energy boost."

"Packing a lunch for a cat seems like a furry precedent that could come back to bite us," I groused as I continued pawing through our cooler to find a non-feline snack.

"And this?" I asked, pulling a small dish with cute little paw prints painted on it.

"Spartan's water saucer, of course," she replied. "You can hardly expect him to drink straight out of a water bottle. The poor little guy doesn't have opposing thumbs."

Yep, there was even a water bottle for Spartan in the cooler, apparently filled with special feline water.

After laying out Spartan's lunch under a tree, I started munching on a snack I found in the bottom of the cooler, one I hoped was intended for bipeds. Spartan ate and plopped on his back, holding a furry paw over his face to block out the sun while he took a cat nap. Working cats tire fast.

We obviously already had a plethora of pusses. But two more were about to be added, despite my protestations. This is where my father-in-law comes in again. A feral mom had been run over on the mean streets of Medford near where Maureen's dad was in an assisted-living facility. She had left behind two kittens huddled together near a fence, mewing forlornly at the sight of their mother's dead body out on the street. One kind neighbor took in one kitten. Maureen suggested we adopt the other which had been taken in temporarily by another caring neighbor.

Granted, it was a terribly sad story. The little cat deserved a good home. But the dogs were counting on me to at least put up token resistance.

"We are approaching a double-digit cat herd," I warned. "When you get into double digits, that's hoarding. Hemingway and Eliot may have been great writers but they were also cat hoarders. That will be their lasting legacy.

"We are going to be become known as the crazy cat people of Sterlingville," I added for good measure. "People will lock their car doors when they drive past. Little kids will cry at the sight of us."

I even trotted out a short article in the January 2013 of the *National Geographic* magazine, a story well told about the potential threat found in cat litter boxes. Incidentally, the magazine's editor at the time was Chris Johns, a Medford native who has since retired. Like all of the magazine's articles, it was a story well told, albeit was about cat urine. Call it engrossing gross reading.

Turns out there is a Czech evolutionary biologist named Jaroslav Flegr who has been infected with a brain parasite called Taxoplasma gondii. Apparently this bug is usually found in cats but can jump to bipeds who, among other catty things, mess around with litter boxes. His research found that rats whose brains are inhabited by the parasite are "less risk averse" toward cats and somehow become sexually attracted to the smell of cat urine. The obvious result is that such rodents are more likely to become rat sirloin for kitty.

Moreover, the scientist has determined that males of our species who get the bug can also become less risk averse and find the smell of cat urine pleasurable. There is no cure, per the article. Yikes.

You do the math. It doesn't take a scientist to figure out that my chances of catching the beastly little bug would give you good odds in Las Vegas.

"That's silly," my wife replied after I laid out my concerns about contracting the dastardly malady. "You never clean the litter boxes."

This coming from someone immune to any illness that would bring Superman to his knees. Indeed, she has missed only two days of work in the past twenty-five years. I can truthfully say I have never missed a day of work in my entire life. But it is also true I've called in sick numerous times.

"I would clean the litter boxes, but I have a hypersensitive gag reflex," I sniffed.

The upshot of it was that *National Geographic* did not come to my rescue. Besides, one would have a cold, cold heart to turn away a little furball who saw its mother killed. So another cat joined the herd.

Maureen promised I could name the furry little fellow with batlike ears who has what looks like a gray cape pulled over his white body. His gray mask stops just below his eyes, ala Batman.

"Meet Batman, the Caped Crusader," I announced as I held him aloft.

"Lord, give me strength," the wife said, sighing.

Yet she acquiesced, knowing that, as Robert Service wrote, a promise made is a debt unpaid. However, insisting the Batman moniker is unacceptable, she prefers the nom de guerre of "CC," short for the Caped Crusader.

The short-haired cat is unique among our feline team. He is long and lean, somewhat resembling a lemur. For a profession, he has chosen to be a cat burglar. But the hairy thief doesn't steal anything. Instead, he just pokes around our bedroom as though he is looking for something he misplaced. His target is always the same: the drawer where I keep my underwear. There are half a dozen drawers in the chest of drawers yet he always goes for the same one.

We've caught him in mid caper countless times. He climbs the chest until he gets to the top drawer, then pulls out on that particular drawer until it opens. He fishes in the drawer for the underwear, throwing them on the floor.

Take it from me, there is nothing special about my underwear. But I keep them in the drawer because these are fresh from the laundry. If they weren't, I could understand him throwing them on the floor, although I would prefer he toss them into the dirty clothes hamper at that point.

Short of putting a lock on the drawer, I'm unsure what to do about it. Having a cat with a fetish for your underwear is disturbing on so many levels. It's hard to concentrate on writing when you know that downstairs a mad-dog cat is furiously throwing your underwear on the floor. I'm sorry I brought it up.

Our last feline acquisition was Andy the cat, named after my father-in-law. It was on the night of his memorial service the cat appeared at the cabin. Coincidence? Again, you be the judge. We are not superstitious folks but we have lived long enough to know there are things about this world that defy rational explanation.

There are also religions in which some folks purportedly come back as animals. It's puzzling to me but it apparently has something to do with whether you were a good person or a lousy jerk during your life. I wouldn't mind coming back as a furry creature if I am fortunate enough to return as a mutt adopted by Maureen. That would be the life. I can almost taste those dog sandwiches now. Yet there are some people I know who would do a great disservice to the animal kingdom if they returned in a coat of fur. Indeed, I know several dogs on a first name basis that are far better creatures than some humanoids. That goes for cats, too.

Getting back to my father-in-law, he was buried on Jan. 29, 2014 at the beautiful Eagle Point National Cemetery two dozen miles from our Sterling Creek abode. He was buried holding a stuffed cat Maureen had given him. After the memorial, we went out to dinner with relatives to share a few stories about Andy.

When we pulled into our drive way that night, Fitzwilliam could be seen loping playfully after a small gray cat that ran under the deck.

"Did you see that?" Maureen asked. "That wasn't one of our cats. Are any of our cats other than Fitz outside?"

"They are all in except the big guy," I responded. "That definitely was not one of ours. Just remember the Sterling Creek cathouse is full. There is no more room in the manger."

Sure enough, all of the cats, save Fitz, were deep in various states of slumber inside the cabin. We called Fitz in but didn't see the other cat. Perhaps it had been a furry figment of our imagination. It had been a long day.

But the next morning Maureen discovered the gray cat sitting on a shelf in the laundry room which has a cat door. The skinny little animal looked more like a rat than a cat. Its fur was matted and dirty.

Maureen was a little hesitant when it came to offering the ratty-looking newcomer some food. It had every appearance of being a wildcat capable of lacerating the feeder. So she handed me the bowl which I sat on the floor. The cat jumped down, meowing softly as it walked over to the food. Its yellow eyes were calm and kind. There was no sign of aggression. Life may have been hard but there was no resentment, no hostility. The cat was sweetness personified. Even though it would put us into cat-hoarding double digits, I didn't even fake a protest.

"We'll name it 'Andy,'" I said.

"Dad would have loved that," Maureen said, tearing up. "The poor thing is so skinny. It couldn't have survived much longer."

Having eaten, the cat sat there, cleaning itself. It apparently wanted to be presentable before meeting the rest of our hairy household.

"Isn't that odd that a stray cat would show up on the night of Dad's memorial," Maureen observed. "There hasn't been a stray around here for a long time. Some people would think that is a sign from dad, letting us know that he is thinking of us."

"Then again, it could just be a present from a jerk wanting to get rid of a cat and dumped it off," I replied as I stroked the purring cat.

Yet it was hard to completely dismiss her suggestion, strange as it was. Andy the man certainly loved cats, as he did all animals.

Within a few days, feline Andy was completely at home. It purred constantly. No longer could you see its ribs. The once ratty gray coat developed a beautiful silvery sheen.

"Andy is what is known as a Russian blue," Maureen said as she picked the cat up and turned it over on her lap to tickle its tummy. "Oh, my gosh!" she declared. "Andy is a she!"

How that could be explained in terms of humans coming back as animals is lost on me. You would be talking about a tough World War II vet cross dressing after he crossed over. For propriety's sake, I'm not even going there.

What I do know for certain is that yet another surprise awaited us when I took her to the vet to be spayed. As directed, we didn't feed Andy that morning, even though it was difficult to ignore her plaintiff meows. She didn't put up a fight when we put her in a little cat carrier. As the retiree who works at home according to his own weird hours, I was the one who would be driving her to the vet. She let out a few soft meows to let me know she was hungry.

"You'll thank me for it later," I told her. "Actually, you won't. You will wonder what in the hell is up with those people. They take you to this place where there are a whole bunch of other animals, put you to sleep and you wake up with stitches in your tummy. It'll be one of life's little mysteries."

I know that felines don't understand much English beyond "Here, kitty kitty." If Andy was present, he would suspect I had been hitting the cat nip. But it never hurts to cover all the bases.

Since I had already brought in one feral cat to be spayed only to discover she had already been under the knife, the vet elected to shave Andy on her lower tummy area to check whether spaying had already been done.

"She has been spayed," concluded the vet as the gray cat with the shaved tummy sat purring in the examination room. "She has a nice disposition. And she is very healthy. You should get twenty years out of this one."

A few months after she arrived, I was sitting out on the patio, mulling over a challenging writing project. Andy the cat strolled up. Three deer were munching on grass about twenty feet from us. I was motionless, not wanting to startle the deer. Andy plopped down about five feet from me when a deer, a young buck with velvet-covered nubbins for horns, started walking toward us. He went over to Andy and touched noses. Both deer and cat seemed totally at ease with each other. Having greeted Andy, the deer then walked back to the rest of the herd.

Andy rolled over and looked up at me. Perhaps I was imagining things, but her yellow eyes seemed to have that same humorous glint that my father-in-law always had.

"I'm beginning to think she is a sign from Dad," Maureen said that evening after I told her about the incident. "It's all too weird."

"I'm starting to wonder myself," I said. "But I still prefer the theory the cat was dropped off by a jerk. Either that, or my wife is catnapping."

"Well, I am not bringing these cats home," she countered. "What's more, if someone is fixing feral cats, that's not necessarily a bad thing. It stops them from reproducing and still lets them live. It's thoughtful."

"It's thoughtful like dropping your kids off at a stranger's house then moving away is thoughtful," I groused, then added, "On second thought, that might not have been a bad thing when our kids were teenagers."

"You're funny," she said, patting my hand. "But I'm glad our kids have fledged."

For the sake of sanity, I'll stick to the assumption Andy the cat was dropped off by some thoughtless jerk. Yet a psychiatrist would find it troubling that I'm worried the feline giggling I faintly hear at night is CC the cat burglar and Miss Chievious the bathroom cat conspiring to slowly drive me over the edge.

TWENTY-THREE

Gone to the Dogs

ALYESKA WAS DYING. WE WERE GATHERED AROUND the front of the woodstove in our Sterling Creek cabin where the old dog lay on her side. Her front legs were stretched out in front of her. Her pillow was the edge of the stone hearth, a place she had sought warmth on countless cold nights. Her beautiful brown eyes that once glowed as bright as Venus in the winter sky were now fogged by age. Her breathing was slow and shallow.

The queen of our muttley crew, the regal Akita-German shepherd mix who had led us and our other pooches through fifteen and a half years wonderful years, was nearing the end of her joyous trail. She could no longer walk, let alone race the wind as she did for so many years. Old age had finally caught up with her.

We had called a gentle veterinarian who made house calls to administer a shot which would put her to sleep forever. It was Feb. 21, 2009.

Maureen was on her knees beside the dog we had raised from puppyhood. She buried her face in Ally's furry neck as she had done countless times in the past. But, unlike those happy hugs of old, my wife was crying.

"We love you so much, baby girl," she whispered. "We will never forget you."

I was kneeling beside Maureen, holding one of Ally's front paws in my hands. In better times, she would have placed one of those big paws on my knee to comfort me when she saw I was hurting. It was with these paws that she trotted up ahead to walk point when we hiked in the mountains, always on alert. She would trot back periodically from the front to check on me, the straggler who was usually bringing up the rear. It was a good feeling, knowing Ally was keeping watch. Few things she loved more than herding humans.

Now she was sprawled out in front of the stove, her grizzled muzzle resting on the stones for the last time. For the previous week, she had been curled up on a doggy bed in the living room, eating and drinking little. Her skin sagged where her powerful leg muscles used to propel her like a bounding deer. Her eyes were closed.

A tear rolled down my cheek. I quickly brushed it off, taking a deep breath and clinching my jaw to keep from sobbing. It's a silly thing that, having never seen my father cry, I invariably try to emulate that seemingly unfeeling behavior in times of great sadness. Only in my gray-haired years have I come to understand that striving to avoid any show of emotion at such times is not a sign of manliness but of weakness.

"We'll always miss you, Oopers," I said softly. Several more tears flowed down my cheek. Again, I hastily wiped them away.

Maureen got up, wiping her red eyes. We stood quietly together, our arms around each other as we looked down at our Ally. The vet knelt down and carefully inserted the needle into her neck. Just as she had when engaging life, Ally didn't flinch when facing death. She breathed in a few times, each exhale a little slower than the one before, then let out her last sighing breath. The dog we loved so deeply was gone.

In his introduction to *James Herriot's Dog Stories*, James Wight, undoubtedly the world's most read veterinarian, wrote from the heart when he addressed what every dog owner must accept. "Everyone who acquires a dog has to face the fact that they don't live long enough and that there is sadness ahead...," he observed. James Herriot was, of course, Wight's nom de plume. No matter what his moniker, he knew of what he wrote so well.

Unlike our cats, our canine count in Gilson Gulch is not an approximation.

Five dogs have lived with us in the Sterling Creek cabin, thankfully not all at once. Three of them are now buried in our pet cemetery under the spreading oak tree up the little valley. Each was a good dog, one of a kind.

Maureen discovered the dog we would name Alyeska, alias Ally, as a tail-wagging puppy in the Humane Society of Southern Oregon's Medford facility. When Maureen visited a room with several puppies, one of the little bundles of fur avoided the puppy scrum and trotted around the side to get Maureen's sole attention. That was Ally, a born strategist. She instantly and forever won my wife's heart.

Maureen began working on me that evening, beginning by mentioning her earlier visit to the animal shelter.

"She's just a little puppy with big ears and a tail like a whippet," she said. "Nobody is ever going to adopt her. It's really sad to see. She has these big brown eyes that just melt your heart."

"Funny, I know a person with eyes just like that," I replied. "And her very brown pretty eyes are pleading now for us to adopt a puppy."

In theory, our household is a democracy in which each biped's vote carries the same weight as the other. The reason there is never a stalemate is simple: Maureen's vote is the one with a little more weight. But I'm happy to live in the Republic of Gilson Gulch since I trust Maureen's vote more than mine.

At the time, we were still in the house at the lower end of the Applegate Valley but the voting procedure was the same. I protested a little to at least give the appearance of not being a pushover, then agreed we needed to go see the pup together. As Maureen knew full well, one look into the pup's brown eyes and I would be a goner. And so it went. We adopted her that day.

As a former Alaskan, I suggested we named her Alyeska, the native name for Alaska, meaning "great land." While we usually called her "Ally," I sometimes called her "Alley Oop" after the old comic strip character about a caveman by that name, shortening it to "Oopers." A friend who counsels bipeds suggested with tongue lodged in her cheek that our pets might develop multiple personalities since each one has a couple of aliases. She may be right about the rest of the hairy bunch but not Ally. She had but one mission in life: to take care of us.

As Maureen had observed, Ally had big ears for a pup, along with a tail that was as skinny as a garter snake. But she would grow into her ears and develop a full, bushy tail. She blossomed into a solid ninety pounder, becoming our hiking buddy, camping pal and overall protector. She strode through life with an air befitting a queen.

With her passing, we placed her body in a wheelbarrow and gently wheeled her to the little but growing pet cemetery up the little valley. It seemed more dignified and personal to place her gently in a wheel barrow rather than tossing her in the back of the pickup truck.

The deep topsoil made for easy going as we dug down. But it is hard to dig when your hearts hurt. To help us through, we started talking about the unforgettable times we had with our furry friend. A mélange of memories poured forth.

"Do you remember when she started barfing on the way home the very first day we got her as a pup?" I asked Maureen as we worked. "I had to stick my head out the window so I wouldn't upchuck. You wouldn't have thought a puppy could have held that much."

"Yeah, but she was so cute," my wife answered, smiling at the memory. "You were smitten the moment you saw her."

She laughed when she recalled how Ally had looked like the proverbial ugly duckling as a pup. "But she grew to be so beautiful, so regal," she marveled.

Like all royalty, she didn't appreciate buffoonery. We both recalled the day a braggart came over during a family barbecue. The BS artist brought his purebred dog, for which he was quick to observe he had paid big bucks. He repeatedly hounded us about how valuable the dog was, how it was bred to be smart and courageous.

I didn't blame the dog—who was about the size of Ally—for his master's bilge. But Ally, who was sitting quietly beside me, was not amused. When the canine wunderkind canine pranced past, Ally grabbed him by the throat, flipped him over on his back and stood over him, her teeth clamped firmly yet not puncturing his skin. She was deadly silent, her front feet placed on each side of his chest. The prize purebred whined ever so softly, afraid to move. His four feet froze in midair.

His blowhard master sputtered indignations for a few minutes, then left shortly afterward with his dog in tow.

"I've never thanked Ally for that," I said, chuckling at the incident. "I think she did it to shut him up."

Unhappily, her final year had its difficult moments. After a full life of running and romping, she had a major stroke on Dec. 14, 2007, the day of our 16th wedding anniversary. Her left side was paralyzed.

But the Grim Reaper of dogs nearly met his match when it came to Maureen. She massaged Ally, babied her, and cajoled her. Ally eventually regained her feet, albeit she would never run again. But she walked in a stately manner without a limp. Thanks to Maureen's effort coupled with Ally's strong disposition, she had another year of life. If it is true that dogs age seven years for every year, she was at least 105 years old in human years when we laid her to rest. While we were grieving, we also knew she had a very good life.

When we dug down about three feet, my pick struck metal. After working it loose, I pulled up an old horse shoe. Perhaps it was one once worn by a Gilson horse. After gently placing Ally in the grave beside her favorite bowl, we covered her with dirt, making a tidy mound that she would have appreciated. On her grave we placed the horseshoe, linking her with an animal from the distant past. She belonged to the ages.

At the head of her grave we placed a chunk of concrete that had once been the floor to our old pump house. Her grave was next to Rajah, the fur ball of a chow who, you may recall, had nailed Richard the subcontracting carpenter while he was working on the cabin. Rajah was just starting his second decade when he had to be put to sleep a few days before Thanksgiving of '04, the victim of cancer.

As is the case for nearly all our pets, we did not pick Rajah. Daughter Amy's boyfriend, long since gone, had given the pooch to her as a pup. When Amy went to college, we started dogsitting Rajah while he was still a pupr. Amy went on to earn her master's degree and become a teacher but the degreeless pooch stayed on. It would have been cruel to take him away from our home at that point. He had fallen in love with Ally who may not have reciprocated but she seemed to like having him around.

Our old dog Ona, short for Onomatopoeia because she sounded like what she was, joined Rajah and Ally in the cemetery early in October of 2009. Part golden lab and Irish setter, she came to us as a pup by the milk-fetching daughter, the same one who brought kittens home from the store when on a milk run. Trying not to look into the puppy's big golden eyes that could melt cold butter at fifty paces, I informed everyone that we already had two dogs. The puppy must be returned immediately, I insisted before stomping out to the garden and sitting down to pout. Being a keen strategist, the daughter simply put the puppy inside the garden gate, quietly closed it and walked away with a smile.

The puppy trotted over to where I was sitting, plopped down, let out a deep sigh and fell asleep with her head resting on my feet. A half hour later I sheepishly came out of the garden carrying the snoozing pup and gruffly allowed that perhaps we ought to keep the fur ball until a proper home was found.

Had Ona been human, she would have been one of those rare individuals who was a golden ray of sunlight breaking through the clouds. Never a harsh bark or a snarl. She was with us for fourteen and a half wonderful years. When her time came to exit this existence, we called the same kindly veterinarian who was there for Ally to make a home visit. The elderly golden lab mix with an easygoing disposition died the way she lived, peacefully and without stress. Like her buddy Ally, she died comfortably next to the woodstove.

It makes me smile to know that kitten tracks made in the pump house concrete floor in 1948 link all our pets together in the cemetery. After all, our dogs and cats belonged to the same mutual admiration society.

James Herriot had some wise advice for those who lose a dog: get another one immediately. Even before we lost Ally and Ona to old age, Maureen was keeping her eyes out for a young pooch that we could adopt.

"Ally and Ona could use a little puppish inspiration," she explained. "They'll live longer if there is a pup around."

"That is called dog rationalizing," I replied. "And let's not forget that the year they gain is one I lose because puppies like to harass me."

Ostensibly, we went to a large pet store in Medford in February of 2007 to pick up some cat food. In retrospect, I suspect a set up. Maureen knew it was the day the Jackson County Animal Care & Control Center volunteers were there, every one armed and dangerous with a cute little puppy. I was dead meat the moment we stepped inside the store.

The pups were all cute as a bug's ear, particularly the brown one who looked like a clown, thanks to a white face with a brown patch over one eye. One ear drooped forward; the other flopped over to the side. The furry Bozo made straight for Maureen. They immediately started conspiring in puppy talk, which my wife speaks fluently.

"Excuse me but we already have two perfectly good dogs—remember Ally and Ona?" I reminded her as she cuddled her new best friend.

"I know, but this one's not very big," she said as she stroked his ears. "He wouldn't take much room."

Not only was I concerned about becoming overrun with dogs but I was a little apprehensive because the pup was an American Staffordshire terrier, one of those breeds some folks refer to as pit bulls. Although the puppy was cute, I feared his adult face would cause a mafia hit man to wet his pants. Little did I know I had just met the most lovable dog we would ever have the good fortunate to share our lives with.

I wasn't able to pull my wife from the harlequin hound before she got his name—Smuckers—and a rundown on his history from the volunteers. The little fellow had been found abandoned in Medford late in 2006. I like to think Hades has a special place for people who abandon domestic animals.

No matter that the pup was immensely huggable. I had to put up some resistance, fruitless that it was.

"How would our old dogs feel if we brought this goofylooking guy home?" I asked. "And what about our cats? It took them years to train our dogs. It'll be a zoo."

"You know they'd all love him," she replied. "He's so cute."

But she agreed to leave the pet store with only the cat food. As we were leaving she looked back at Smuckers, who sat there grinning. It made me nervous.

Sure enough, Maureen dropped the other paw a few days later.

"I called about Smuckers—he still doesn't have a home," she said.

"I told them we would visit him."

Perhaps weakened by the flu bug that would floor me by the end of the week, I followed Maureen like a welltrained pooch into the shelter where she asked to see Smuckers. I was a little foggy in the head as Maureen filled out a long form. Among other things, it apparently asked if we were felons. She indicated we were not, ignoring the fact some folks consider journalism a felonious profession.

"What was that paper for?" I asked Maureen.

"It's just a formality," she replied.

"For what?" I pressed.

"For adopting Smuckers," she said, causing a groaning protest from her hubby. She patted me on the back.

"Everything will be fine," she said. "You'll love him."

After checking our credentials and ignoring my simpering protest, the pound people pronounced us dog worthy. We would be able to pick up the pup at the vet's after our newest pooch had been neutered. Maureen happily began making a long list of what we would need for the canine addition.

"We want him to feel welcome," she explained.

He must have felt like a canine king. A quick addition of the dog damage told the story: $75 to adopt, including neutering; $453 for expanding the kennel, $59 to buy a doghouse, which I didn't have time to build; $35 for doghouse insulation; $45 for a rabies shot and heart worm pills; $29 for puppy chow; $12 for a dog bed; $12 for dog toys, including a moose that squeaks; and $6 for a dog dish. That came to $726 for the princely pup.

"We still need to get a doggy coat for him," Maureen said.

"Why not," I said, adding snidely, "but make sure it matches the shirt I've already given him off my back."

"We also need to come up with another name—Smuckers sounds like a jar of jelly," she said, ignoring my amusing remark.

"We could just call him 'Expensive,'" I quipped.

She again ignored my witticism but agreed to my serious suggestion we name him Waldo. The name came from both a likable old fellow named Waldo Bodfish who I had met in the village of Wainwright in the Alaskan Arctic and for the old mining community in the Illinois Valley. Besides, I wanted to be able to come home and ask "Where's Waldo?"

When I picked him up the next afternoon, he seemed plenty spry for a fellow who had just been neutered. He hopped onto the passenger seat and grinned at me.

"Well, Waldo, you've just won Maureen's animal lottery," I told him.

He lay down on the seat, let out a long sigh and closed his eyes as I scratched his velvet ears. He was one happy hound, no doubt having heard through the dog grapevine about Maureen's wondrous dog sandwiches. He knew his life was going to be good.

How good it was to be for him was beyond his—and my—wildest imagination. While he had his new dog bed, Maureen decided that he would be sleeping on our bed.

Now, I love animals as much as the next biped. But I was determined to hold my ground when it comes to co-habitating with them at night.

"No way!" I informed her. "We are already overrun with cats. There is so much purring at night I can't sleep as it is. There are limits beyond which I refuse to go."

"But he is so little," she said. "Look at him. The cats are bigger than he is. He would be afraid to sleep on his dog bed all by himself. Poor little guy. He looks like he doesn't have a friend in the world."

Being the fine actor he is, Waldo stepped nicely into the role of poor-little-me, complete with a woebegone face resting on his little white paws. His pleading brown eyes looked like they were about to burst with tears. It was an Oscar-winning performance, although the long sigh seemed a bit over the top if you ask me.

"Fitz may be larger but the rest are definitely smaller," I said, knowing if I continued looking at him I would be a goner. "But that's beside the point. Very soon, he will be as big as a donkey. I already don't have enough room to turn over without disturbing a fierce creature."

"Just think about it, sweetie," Maureen said, patting my hand. "He could sleep down at the foot of the bed. It's a king size. We won't even know he is there."

"Hrrrumph," I snorted, knowing I was losing yet another pet battle.

And little Waldo? As God is my witness, I swear the mutt was smiling again as he trotted after Maureen. He had just confirmed his growing suspicion about who was the top dog in our cabin. No more dog beds for him. Life was doggone good.

A pooch who takes eating seriously, Waldo weighed in at 100 pounds upon reaching maturity. Because of his bulk, he and Maureen decided it was necessary for him to sleep in the middle of the bed. That can be a problem when he decides to sleep cross ways. King size or not, that means Maureen and I are then clinging to the edges, usually sans blankets. But I am just glad I'm not relegated to the dog bed. It's too short for my legs.

While he doesn't purr, he does have a very unusual habit of moaning contentedly throughout the night. It isn't as constant as a purr but it is decidedly louder. If you put a dog blanket on him, he moans. If you take it off because the night is too warm, he moans. He moans when you reach over to pet him. He moans when you turn over. If there are any ghosts in our old cabin, they are all nervous wrecks by now.

When Waldo first took over our Sterling Creek home, Queen Ally was still in charge. She adopted the pup as her own but was not amused by our perpetual fawning over him. In retrospect, I realize she must have noticed she was no longer receiving the lion's share of our attention. Early one morning I hooked a leash to Ally to take her out to the kennel. Once inside, I unleashed her and walked over to refresh their water before going back for Waldo and Ona. But when I turned around the gate was open. Ally was no longer fleet of foot but her highness had already disappeared down the driveway. She disappeared off Sterling Creek Road before I drove down in pursuit of the escapee.

At her age, both her eyesight and hearing was failing. I pictured her lost, hungry and thirsty. Maybe she had been hit by a car, knocked off the road into the brush, unable to answer my call with her customary "woof!" It dawned on me then I had been paying so much attention to Waldo that I had neglected my old buddy Ally. I felt like a twotiming cad, the pond scum of pet owners.

Maureen had gone to work earlier and didn't know about the missing pooch. I dreaded having to tell her. After calling a couple of folks who live around us, none of whom had seen a dog answering her description, I went to the office. But I skipped lunch and raced home to resume the search. I called a few more people to see if they had seen her. No one had. Intending to check the sides of the road for her, I headed back down the driveway, expecting the worst.

That's when I saw Ally trotting back up the driveway. The queen of canines was panting and thirsty but otherwise retained her majesty. Just where she had spent the morning was a mystery. But there was nothing mysterious about the lesson she taught me: pay equal attention to all pets, be they canine or cat.

Several months after Ally was put to sleep, Anna, a friend of ours, called to let us know she had discovered nine puppies and their mother living in a hollow log near Butte Falls, a hamlet nestled in the western foothills of the Cascade Range. Interestingly, Anna had rescued an earlier litter of eight puppies from the same feral mama dog on a snowbound January night in 2008 from another hollow log. Elk hunters had found the pups that time.

The pups' wild single mom is part black Labrador. This time she was also rescued, spayed and adopted out to a good home. The absentee father is believed to have been a randy mastiff farther down the mountain. Like all Americans, the pups hailed from a healthy ancestral stew.

After I wrote a column about the log dogs, the mom and six puppies were quickly adopted.

Since Anna had twice stepped in to save two different litters of the puppies, we figured the least we could do was take one off her kind hands. Waldo was then about three; Ona was going on fourteen. We figured a puppy would give Ona a rest from the energetic Waldo.

We wanted one of the pups that no one else wanted. But they are all equally adorable. Anna solved our dilemma by reaching in the squirming mass of fur and pulling out what looked like a tubby little black bear cub with a white mark on his chest.

That was on July 11, 2009, the day before the Oregon Caves National Monument's 100th birthday. Since cave discoverer Elijah Davidson back in 1874 had a bear dog he called Bruno, I originally dubbed our pup Bruno.

But his humorous personality dictated we change his name.

"He is definitely a Harpo," Maureen concluded.

Like the silent Marx brother, he has a deadpan expression yet is a constant clown. As a pup, Harpo perfected a wiggling assault onto your lap. It was unstoppable. He began by innocently placing his muzzle in your lap, followed by a front paw, then the other. Next came a back leg, followed by the other. He curled up, let out a soft sigh and fell asleep, exhausted from the ordeal.

He is also the most verbal of any of our pooches, past or present. He constantly gives me instruction on the finer points of life when he and his best pal Waldo aren't cooking up some mischievous scheme. He is always making comments about the world around him, be it the food he is fed or a smell he is catching a whiff of as it drifts down the valley.

"I've never heard such doggerel," I tell him, causing him to launch a vocal protest. The problem is that it's a real challenge to decipher his dog speak. Maureen thinks he may be fluent in Klingon but I disagree. What's more, Harpo perked up when I suggested it was pirate. "Arrr!" he said. He can't seem to get his hairy lips around "avast"and "ahoy" but he is working on his enunciation.

During our training period, he would bark out commands that left me baffled. It also became apparent that my trainer obviously felt I was a little slow on the uptake. He also insisted on running from one project to another without finishing the first one. And he didn't give a whit that I was dog tired.

"He just keeps hounding me," I complained to Maureen. "He's a canine provocateur."

But my wife was there for me. Sort of.

"He just wants to prove you can teach old dogs new tricks," she observed. "I'm sure you'll get the hang of it. Besides, you have to admit he is having fun trying to train you."

The pup had just untied my shoes with his needlesharp teeth, then started growling and pulling on a pant leg with all his might to get my attention. His stubby little legs kept pumping, but the fat feet got no traction on the floor.

"The only thing I will admit is that this rolypoly little log dog is a very rare breed, indeed," I said after the squirming fur ball crawled onto my lap, where he quickly fell asleep from exhaustion.

"He has you wrapped around his hairy little toe," Maureen observed.

"Pshaw, you're supposed to let sleeping dogs lie," I replied as I stroked the snoring pup's soft black ears.

Harpo and I became the best buds. He was happy to greet me when I come home from work. Nothing made him happier than to slaver me with a tongue that is nearly half as long as a fly swatter and stickier than flypaper. A fatherly influence, no doubt. As a pup, he would break into a wide, tonguelolling grin when his doggie bowl was filled. He still does, for that matter. We have never been able to persuade him that a loud burp after chowing down is not appropriate doggie decorum. Again, I would point to the father.

But I've also love the fact he never leaves my side. He particularly likes to lie down at my feet when I read. Since I am myopic, I read without my glasses.

Shortly after our puppy moved in, I was relaxing one evening with the legendary Lt. Joe Leaphorn created by the genius of writer Tony Hillerman. I tend to lose myself in a book but I did notice on the blurry edge of my vision our boy Harpo at my feet happily gnawing on what appeared to be one of his canine toys. As is his wont, he was chomping with gusto.

Adorable little tyke, I recall thinking. A few minutes later I got up to get my glasses so I could see my way into the kitchen for a glass of ice tea. I'm blind as the proverbial bat without my glasses when focusing on anything beyond arm's length.

But I couldn't find my glasses. Strange, I distinctly remember putting them down nearby.

They weren't on my desk. I couldn't find them on the table. Nor were they on the kitchen counter.

That's when Harpo's chewing sounds seemed to increase in volume. I recognized the sound of sharp puppy teeth scraping on hard plastic. Hard plastic as in an eyeglass lens.

Hurrying over to my chair, I leaned over to see what the furry fellow was munching on. He looked up with a poopeating grin.

Sure enough, his pudgy paws were holding down the wire frame while his teeth tended to the business at paw, as it were. His needlesharp puppy teeth were chewing away on my left lens, trying to grind it down to meet his demanding specifications.

When I retrieved my glasses, there were more than a dozen teeth marks on my left lens. Unfortunately, the glasses were fairly new and I had to wait another year before I could replace them under our health insurance policy. For nearly a year, I had to turn my head slightly to the left in order to focus on a subject with my right eye. It was a bit of a nuisance.

But my day would come. On that day, Harpo was laughing as we pulled out of the driveway. After all, the happy hound was riding in the car's back seat on the way to town on a sunny day. He squeezed his bearlike head out a side window, let his long, pink tongue flap in the wind and greeted the passing roadside with a goofy grin. A tailgater would have been sprayed with sticky drool.

At the time, he was nearly a year old. Life couldn't get much better.

"Hop in—you are going to the vet to be tutored," I had told him, paraphrasing that classic line from my favorite *Far Side* cartoon. The manly mutt, who would need a bra down there if his thingamajigs grew any bigger, was about to get neutered. Castrated. Gelded. Unsexed.

Sitting next to Harpo was Waldo upon whom the dastardly deed had already been done. Come to think of it, I also was the one who accompanied our cats when they were turned into eunuchs. Perhaps Maureen was trying to tell me something with these neutering expeditions.

But there was no delaying Harpo's date with the knife. We were concerned that he may soon begin looking for likely fourfooted lasses with a come-hither look in the Sterling Creek countryside. Harpo already was showing a growing curiosity in acquiring carnal knowledge. A coarse individual would describe his recent behavior as that of a Mississippi leg hound.

Stuart, a friend whose wife also collects furry creatures, had sent me an email upon learning of Harpo's appointment with the scalpel.

"If your dog needs consoling, you can tell him that virtually all of the male politicians in our congress have gone through the same operation and their approval ratings are still above fifteen percent," Stuart wrote. "He may not want to go with the full spine removal though."

Good point, although in our home, Harpo's approval rating is 100 percent.

Whatever Harpo's genetic makeup, the combination has resulted in a pup that is always happy to be here, no matter where here is. Harpo loves life. If he isn't going for a ride, his nextmost favorite thing, aside from eating, is to sit next to me, lean over and whisper "psst" in my ear. Like one of those slowthinking humanoids from *Far Side*, I invariably cock my head to hear what the pirate has to say. That's when the canine jokester unleashes his massive mastiff tongue to slather my ear, hair and neck. I swear he lets out a chortle afterwards. It's humiliating and not a little disgusting.

But there was no chortling when we arrived at the vet. The waiting room was filled with furry animals and bipeds, all of whom seemed a little stressed. Our pooch immediately peed on the floor, much to the disdain of a toy poodle with a pink bow on her pearly white coiffure.

I apologized as someone in a white coat began mopping up the piddle. With Harpo in tow, I gladly retreated into an adjacent room to have him weighed. The scales read eighty-five pounds, but that was after our boy flooded the machine with nearly another quart of pee. Fortunately, the vet's assistant giggled, as she did when she started to check to see whether his testicles had descended properly. A quick glance at the tennis balls covered with fur confirmed they most certainly had.

When I returned late that afternoon, they and Harpo's grin were gone. Unlike Waldo, Harpo was devastated by the experience. He walked gingerly out to the car, slowly stepped up onto the back seat, laid his big head on his paws and sighed. No doubt he felt he had just been betrayed by dog's best friend. It was a long, sad ride home.

But it wasn't as bad as some rides to and from a veterinarian appointment with the pets. We once took some 200 pounds of canine in Waldo and Harpo and more than sixty pounds of cat, all in our Subaru wagon. Maureen waggishly dubbed it the Fur Wagon Express. Anyone taking an innocent stroll along Sterling Creek Road would have been startled by a racing vehicle emitting what sounded eerily like wailing lamentations from the underworld.

The vehicle sped down the road, its five cats yowled and two burly dogs woofed at the world. The whining and whimpering quickly got to Maureen.

"Oh puhleeez!" she finally protested. "I don't know how much more of this I can take."

The poor woman had a point. The noise was unbearable.

"I don't want to offend you, but you are scaring the animals," she added. "Are you coughing up a hair ball or trying to imitate two cats fighting?"

"Fine, have your little fun at my expense," I replied. "But I thought a little singing would help calm them down."

But it apparently caused distress deep in the bowels of the Fur Wagon Express. Creeping up on cat's feet from behind the driver's seat came an eyewatering stench. One large scaredy cat had lost the battle to control his intestinal tract.

"Good God! That must be Fitzwilliam!" I yelled as I hung my head out the window to gulp untainted air. "I told you we couldn't take him."

"You said what?" Maureen yelled while sticking her head outside the passenger window. "You were the one who insisted we bring him."

It was pure pandemonium. Next to him was an equally upset Odysseus. He was loudly lamenting that his cage was next to Fitzwilliam's. Then there was the "Little People," gleefully caterwauling out of one big cage.

Taking it all in in the back seat were Waldo and Harpo, both adding a baritone bark now and then to keep the cats fired up.

The noise was bad enough, but having a rearview mirror filled with the image of Harpo's goofy grin was more than I could take. He had on his Elvis look. Raising one hairy lip slightly, he looked like he was about to start barking out, "A hunka, hunka burnin' love."

Such caring on is bad form for a log dog.

But we made it to the vet on time. Turns out not all of the fur bearers needed a shot. Waldo and the Little People were apparently along for the Fur Wagon joy ride.

"We'll have to take most of them back next month for booster shots," Maureen observed after all the creatures were back home. "But I think they will be OK with it now. But it will take me that long to recover."

I was also troubled by a recurring nightmare in which I'm was in a cage in the Fur Wagon flying down the road bound for the vet's. In the dream, Harpo is driving and grinning back at me in the rearview mirror. He is doing that Elvis lip thing of his. But the most worrisome part of the dream is that he keeps telling me I am going to be tutored.

At the outset, I figured Harpo would be a fine dog but not the brightest in the litter. After all, he was large with a big grin and a lolling tongue. Boy, was I wrong. He is the smartest pooch I've ever been around. I started suspecting he was smarter than he let on when I discovered he had figured out how to escape from the kennel. It has a metal gate that swings both inward and outward. You can step in and close the gate behind you. The click you hear is the metal bar dropping into place, locking the gate. To open, you simply lift the metal bar. The ingenious system works the same when you step outside. It is very handy.

But the simplicity engineered into the system for humans made it an easy matter for Harpo when it came to planning his great escape. He would push the bar up with his nose until it opens, and run off to explore the valley. I had to install a safety catch to keep the Houdini hound corralled.

It's risky business to anthropomorphize your pets' behavior, but empirical evidence cannot be ignored. It seemed that our dog Harpo has been hiding the fact his intellectual prowess is on par with most of us bipeds. But one day, perchance pondering the theory of relativity, the pooch let his hairy guard down.

It happened when I took both Harpo and his furry pal Waldo out for a walk on the back acreage. Like Ally, Waldo needs to be kept on a leash because of his wanderlust. The quickwitted pooch made good his escape when I relaxed my grip while opening a gate. He gleefully ran off, paying no heed to my calls.

Harpo sprinted after him, grabbed his leash with his pearly whites and loped back to me with a pouting Waldo in tow.

"Our dogs are pulling the fur over our eyes," I warned my wife later after relating the anecdote. "They pretend to be as dumb as turnips but in reality they are just scamming us.

"We trudge off to work, they sleep," I continued. "We toil away all day, then come home and feed them a sumptuous dinner and take them for a walk. And that's all before we grab a quick bite. Something is wrong with this picture."

Maureen rolled her eyes the way a babysitter does when a child declares that trees moving make the wind blow.

"Harpo and Waldo are smart dogs but they are not canine Einsteins, sweetie," she said. "They are not trying to deceive us. Really. Sometimes you scare me."

The poor lady had fallen for that old dog trick in which pooches act intellectually challenged in front of humanoids by sniffing each other's posteriors. Obviously a dog diversion cooked up to throw us off the scent, so to speak.

While my wife is more than a bit dubious about my doggone theories, she does acknowledge that Harpo and Waldo have a leisurely lifestyle.

Take the dog sandwiches she makes for them between meals. These are soft taco shells and cheese which look mighty appetizing. In fact, the first time she made them she failed to tell me they were for the dogs.

"Hey, you could start a franchise with these—mighty tasty," I told her as I happily munched away.

"You are eating dog food," she said, instantly wiping the road apple eating grin off my face. "Please don't start eating out of their bowls."

As if I would sink to that level. Sure, there are times when I look longingly at their dishes routinely filled with tasty tidbits meant for my bowl. But I would never get down on the floor like that. Bad knees.

As dogs go, both are nearly sane, although Harpo does have a wolfish leer that makes some visiting bipeds very nervous. He looks like he is about to take a pound of flesh when he merely wants nothing more than to slather a bare ankle. I like to tell nervous visitors that he is a just big baster. The bad pun doesn't allay their fears.

When I'm in the garden, he invariably sprawls just outside the weathered gate, happy in the belief he is protecting me from the big, bad world. Any student of the human animal has concluded we seem to be making a mess of things on this planet. In fact, when someone tells me our country is going to the dogs, I tell them they are being overly optimistic.

As I write this, Waldo is turning nine years old and already showing signs of slowing down. If we are fortunate, we should get another three years out of the terrier. I try not to think about having to go up the valley and dig another grave for a beloved pet. From the world's standpoint, Waldo will have made no more difference than a pebble being tossed into Crater Lake. But to us, he will be greatly missed.

Yet there is comfort in knowing those that have gone on before are all in peaceful repose in our pet cemetery up Gilson Gulch. The remains of nine of them reside for eternity in the pleasant spot. Collectively, the dogs and cats were with us for nearly 100 years, bringing a chorus of joyous barks and purrs to our lives. If they were human and there is an afterlife, they would all be heaven bound. With the possible exception of Rajah, although I know a lot of church-going bipeds that weren't as pleasant, kind or giving as that irascible pooch.

One day, Maureen and I will join our furry friends in the pet cemetery. When I spring from this mortal coil, Maureen has promised to spread my ashes on their graves. If she goes first, which I fervently hope is not the case, I have pledged to do the same for her. Our grown children will do the job for the last man or woman standing in Gilson Gulch.

Ideally, it would be nice for us to die in our sleep at the same time of extreme old age in our cabin, holding hands and dreaming of our wonderful times together. But life—and death—is seldom tidy. It will likely end with one going before the other, leaving a lonely soul slowly walking each morning up to the cemetery to visit loved ones.

"I miss you, sweetie," Maureen will say. "I look forward to seeing you in the hereafter. You are in my heart. Always."

I like to think she will be talking to me but once again I will be harassed by doubt. She does love those furry creatures of ours.

UP STERLING CREEK WITHOUT A PADDLE

TWENTY-FOUR

Creature Feature

B EFORE WE HAD OUR WELL DUG DEEPER AND REPLACED our old leaky pump house in Gilson Gulch, two little green guys were living in the old structure. They seemed quite happy in their digs. But Maureen alerted me one morning that their accommodations were not quite up to the hospitality expected by such discriminating guests.

"The frog water in the pump house is getting a little low," she noted. "We need to freshen it a bit."

On the surface, that would seem like a rather strange comment. But the really scary part was that changing the frog water seemed perfectly normal to me.

"I'll hop right on it," I replied. "And I'll try not to throw the baby frogs out with the frog water."

Rest assured that my wife and I don't drink frog water, at least not knowingly. As for tossing out tadpoles, I wouldn't do that. Honest.

But the anecdote illustrates how I had come to accept Maureen's menagerie much like a zookeeper accepts lions and bears as he goes about his day of scooping up do-do and attending to his charges. Going to the frogs? Just tell me how deep to dive.

Apparently having heard of Maureen's big heart through the amphibian rumor mill, the frogs jumped into the pump abode and set up house. Most people would merely observe there were frogs in the pump house and let it go at that. Not Maureen. She promptly installed a frog swimming pool in the form of a little stainless steel basin filled with water.

"Now they can take a cool dip when it gets hot during the summer," she explained. "It'll be nice for them."

"I think they are tree frogs," I volunteered. "They probably don't take dips all that much."

Nonetheless, the amphibians happily joined our expanding zoo. At least I think they were happy. It's hard to tell with a frog. They always seem to be grinning. Perhaps our frogs are merely simpletons who grin their way through life.

To help you fully understand the just plain weird pet-related challenges I face in our cabin, you need to meet the odd visitors I've come to know. We are not talking about the strange fur balls you've already met in the cabin, namely the dogs and cats. The subjects at hand are creatures not normally found in or near a normal home. But you already know that normalcy is a stranger to us.

There is something about the cabin and its environs that attract strange creatures like moths drawn to a light. Moths would be no problem, of course. They are interesting little winged gadabouts. Nor are the other usual wild suspects all rural residents encounter in southern Oregon and northern California a major problem. We have indigenous creatures in abundance, such as deer, coyotes, raccoons and skunks.

We also have plenty of non-native types such as wild turkeys, thanks to their introduction in the West a few decades ago. At last count, wildlife biologists estimated there were more than seven million turkeys in the Lower 48 states after being nearly extirpated in North America by the early 1900s. Despite their weird appearance and uncanny ability to poop where I'm about to step, turkeys are interesting to have around the place. Unfortunately, they are very low in the pecking order when it comes to survival of the fittest. This past spring, a hen with a brood of about eight chicks was hanging around our property. By fall, it was just her and a lone chick. When last seen, the chick was constantly in her shadow. I'm hoping it beats the odds.

Our animal problem is caused by the fact Maureen is an animal magnet. Every furry, feathered or scaly creature in the region seems to know she is an easy mark. To say she loves them would be like saying James Herriot didn't mind animals all that much. The lone exception, as you have already read, would be the eight-legged creatures and their web spinning ways.

Our unusual visitors have been beasts of all shapes and sizes whose presence and behavior make you want to scratch your head and wonder what is next. Some are fun to watch. Others not so much. Their common denominator is they were all uninvited. They apparently saw the cabin and, like us, decided it was going to be their home. All, save one, hailed from the wild. The one that wasn't was a bovine canine who came to stay for a rather long week. We'll save him for last.

Speaking of bovines, we did have one drop by for a brief visit. One day while I was working outside, minding my own business, a huge bull cow came trotting down the valley. Not being a cattle person, I'm assuming he was a bull. He certainly had all the necessary hardware swinging to and fro.

He stopped, looked at me and snorted in derision. The ill-mannered brute crashed his way up through the forest on the south side of the valley and disappeared. The stout bovine obviously wasn't impressed with me or our little spread.

I called neighbor Pete to shoot the bull about the unsolicited cloven hoofed visitor. I knew our westerns neighbors had a couple of head of horses but didn't know if they were still running a few head of cattle.

"Not one of ours—we don't have any cows now," Pete said. "Sounds like somebody is missing a fine animal, though. This isn't open range so he probably came from one of the local little ranches."

"He had Grade A beef written all over him," I said. "I was kind of hoping he would stay around for a barbecue."

Pete suggested I call a few Applegators who ran cattle but no one in the vicinity was missing a big bull, certainly not one with an attitude. Whatever happened to that particular cabin caller is anyone's guess. Perhaps he was headed to California where there are reputedly more vegans per capita than in Oregon.

With frogs popping up in the pump house and a snorting bull trotting past out of the blue, along with the preponderance of wildlife in our midst, both inside and outside of the cabin, it takes a little to startle me when it comes to odd creatures. But I knew we were in for it when Maureen posed the following question: "Do you happen to know where we can get some squirrel's milk?"

When such a question arises in our cabin, the safer course is not to act shocked. That's akin to blinking in a game of chicken.

"Are we out already? Geez, those containers are just so darn small," I said, all the while knowing that one of us in the room was the proud parent of a baby squirrel orphan.

"It's so hard to find a reliable squirrel milker who will put up with those mean little rodents kicking over those tiny buckets," I added for good measure.

But I was just putting off the inevitable news that yet another toothsome creature had joined the furry mob in our humble abode. In any other household, her squirrel-milk question would have been considered a little daft, prompting suggestions that medication levels were in dire need of adjustment.

Yet those who know us will tell you that Maureen is slightly saner than her hubby. They would also add, with a heavy sigh, that her deep love of all critters is slowly but surely nudging him closer to the funny farm.

It seems that earlier that morning shortly after I had left for work, she found a baby ground squirrel crawling down our driveway. She placed the squirrely toddler under a protective bush with a little picnic of seeds and headed off to her day job. She was hoping the squirrel mom would find her wandering babe. Upon returning home, Maureen discovered the little critter once again in the driveway, this time unconscious in the rain.

When I returned that evening, he was in a shoe box, sprawled out on a bed of paper towel strips. His wet fur clung to his pink skin, his breathing was shallow and his eyes were closed.

"It was so sad finding him cold and wet like that," Maureen said. "I'm afraid his mother has been eaten by a coyote or something. We have to help him."

I didn't ask her how she knew it was a "he," particularly since he was small enough to curl up in a tea cup. Squirrel sexing, like determining the sex of a rattlesnake, is one of the things I prefer to be blissfully ignorant of.

I tried the nature-can-be-cruel approach, although knowing it was futile.

"It is sad but we live in a coyote-munches-cute-little-critter world," I said. "The coyote probably needed a squirrel to feed her pups."

And I observed the little tyke appeared ready to meet the big squirrel in the sky.

"Maybe it's for the best," I said. "Most people consider ground squirrels nothing but pesky rodents, vermin that should be shot on sight."

"He doesn't look pesky," she replied, then observed, "See, he's already starting to perk up."

Sure enough, within an hour she had him wide awake and checking out his shoe box apartment. He looked bright eyed and bushy tailed like those of his ilk are supposed to look. He even seemed to be smiling, although his humongous bottom incisor appeared ready to chomp into my wife's husband's hand.

"He looks dangerous," I said. "Perhaps we ought to have that thing filed down."

Ignoring my snide suggestion, she carefully picked him up and placed him into a bigger box, one which included a king-sized bed of paper towels. Next to it was a little plate of lettuce, carrots, sunflower seeds and strawberries, her version of a healthy diet for a growing young squirrel. I couldn't help thinking those strawberries would have otherwise been wasted in a strawberry short cake.

"Look, he ate a strawberry and crawled back under his little blankets," she said when checking on his later. "I'm thinking we really should give him a name."

For the first time in my life, I was one step ahead of her. I had already called Wildlife Images in Grants Pass, known far and wide for its wonderful efforts to rehabilitate fierce creatures and release them to the wild. Over the years we have delivered two owls and a Stellers jay to the non-profit facility started by the late Dave Siddon. His son, Dave A. Siddon, continues the wonderful family legacy.

Orphaned baby squirrels were welcome, said the cheerful voice on the phone. "Just keep him in the dark and make sure he has water," the fellow said. I didn't mention the little guy's penchant for strawberries out of fear they would think I was unloading a spoiled squirrel.

Although saddened by her little friend's departure, Maureen agreed it was for the best. "Your weird sense of humor would have probably driven him nuts anyway," she said.

"Squirrels like nuts," I countered.

In any case, we had squirrels aplenty. Western gray squirrels periodically run along tree limbs near the cabin. They also bark at us from their arboreal homes. But the most entertaining guests by far have been the squadron of small squirrels who first began leaping through the trees in the dog park late in the spring of 2014. They are acrobats of the highest order whose arboreal skills are truly amazing. They run along branches as though they were sidewalks, making death defying jumps where the limbs are sparse.

"They are about the size of juvenile gray squirrels," I told Maureen the first morning we saw them. "But they seem awfully coordinated for being so young."

Moreover, they are too small and their dark brown coats the wrong color, I added.

"This group is from the Sterling Creek Gymnastic School," she said, suddenly speaking with the irritating pomposity of an Olympics commentator. "You will notice one little guy just achieved a rather smart front aerial with a half twist. On a scale of 10.0, I would give him high marks for effort and originality but he didn't follow through. The layout lacked the 180-degree twist. Regrettably, I can only give him a 9.3."

"Say what?" I said, looking over to make sure it was really my wife sitting there beside me at our little patio table in the dog park.

She started giggling, and reached over to tickle me in the ribs.

"See, you can dish it out but you can't stand it when I do it to you," she said, adding, "This is fun. I've got to do this more often."

We both started laughing. It was a fine morning, albeit slightly chilly. The sun was just starting to peep over the mountain. If the previous winter had found us discontented with the lack of moisture, this was the spring of our contentment. I was sipping a mug of steaming Earl Grey; Maureen had a cup of hot chocolate. Harpo and Waldo were making their morning rounds, making sure everything received a proper tinkle.

While the humanoids and canines in the park were still waking up, the squirrels were wide-eyed and bushy tailed. Although the count was difficult to nail down because they were popping up here and there, there appeared to be about a half dozen, all gold medal gymnasts. High in the sugar gum tree, one squirrel chased another around a large horizontal limb. I was concerned the one on the bottom of the limb would fall off but the aerial rodent ran under the limb as though it was a romp across a sofa. Others ran up an old pear tree standing more than thirty feet tall, and leaped through the air to race on the wooden highway provided by a limb extending from an adjacent apple tree. The nimble creatures bursting with surplus energy seemed to be everywhere at once. It exhausted me just to watch.

The aerial show also took a toll on Harpo. At first, he stood on his hind legs with his front paws on the trunk of the apple tree and barked up at the squirrels. Waldo studied them with his usual thoughtful manner. But Harpo lost interest and went back to watering plants. I did notice he wasn't hiking his leg up quite as high as he had been, a sure sign it had been a tiring morning. What with trotting back and forth to fill his bladder to make sure all the plants were watered and keeping an eye on the frisky gymnasts, he was tuckered out.

"Those definitely are not gray squirrels," I concluded as I finished my tea. "For one thing, they aren't gray with white bellies. And they are too small for fully-grown gray squirrels."

With the tails thrown in, the dark brown squirrels with light-tan bellies were barely a foot long. Nor do they bark like a gray squirrel. They emit a kind of cheerful chirp that seems to end with a question mark. But their most remarkable characteristic is their amazing acrobatics while traveling high in the forest canopy.

"What the heck are they?" I asked myself out loud.

"Whatever they are, they fly through the trees with the greatest of ease," Maureen offered. "Maybe we ought to call them 'Sterling Creek's Flying Circus.'"

"You are on a roll today, giving it the full monty," I told her. "Had he existed, I'm sure Monty Python would have been honored to be associated with a gang of squirrels."

Like the characters in the old Brit comedy show, they are fun to watch. But we have never been able to properly identify them, although we dubbed the longest one John Cleese. We

called several friends who are wildlife experts to see if they could hazard a guess without having seeing one of the furry acrobats. One suggested they could be northern flying squirrels, but others were skeptical. It could be they are one of several squirrel species introduced into the northwest, a wildlife biologist observed.

Whatever are squirrelly guests are, they don't seem to like cold weather. While they were plentiful during the summer and into the fall, we did not see them after Veterans Day, the first morning we awoke to a frost that year. Perhaps they stay close to their nest—known as a drey—during the chilly months. Or maybe they become totally nocturnal during that period.

But we missed the little chaps. We were glad to see the Sterling Creek Flying Circus return the following spring to train for the squirrel summer Olympics. The front aerial with a half twist is showing promise, according to the Olympics commentator of Gilson Gulch.

We never saw one large visitor which scared the bejabbers out of both of us. One evening just as night was falling we took Waldo and Harpo out to the dog park so they could make their rounds and conduct canine affairs. Suddenly there was the anguishing cry of an animal attacked in the woods just beyond the high fence. It was a piercing scream, almost like that of a child being harmed. That unsettling sound was followed by a thrashing noise made by an animal struggling to get free from whatever gripped it in its jaws.

"Oh my God! A cougar is killing a fawn!" Maureen whispered. "We've got to do something."

"What the hell can we do?" I retorted, angry at myself for feeling so helpless. I shined the flashlight into the trees in hopes of scaring off the predator. The dogs helped, growling and barking ferociously.

The trees blocked the shaft of light. We could see nothing in the woods.

Three deer ran out of the dark forest and into the open meadow at the bottom of the valley where the evening light lingered. They stopped and stared back at the forest. We could now hear what sounded like a doe calling for its fawn. It was a forlorn cry, one devoid of hope. There was the sound of something being dragged, more bleats of anguish from the doe, followed by a deep silence.

Waldo and Harpo stopped barking. They sat on their haunches as they looked toward the forest, periodically glancing up at us. It was as though they knew a natural event had just occurred. We also knew we had witnessed something that had been occurring since the reign of dinosaurs.

"It's sad to us but we have to look at it as nature's way," I told Maureen . "A cougar is now able to feed its starving cubs. One animal dies so that another may live."

"Right, and I intend to kill that son-of-a-bitch if I ever see it," said the sweet lady who just happens to be a decent shot.

"Yes, well, that is definitely another way to look at it," I said as we walked the dogs back to the house.

Of course, we don't know for sure if it was a cougar. It may have been a bear which sometimes preys on a young fawn. But chances are it was a panther.

While we have seen no cougars on the property, we did find a deer apparently killed by a mountain lion in the draw about 400 yards west of the cabin. It was a towhead, a young deer not yet wise to the dangers lurking in the wild. There was also a large pile of bear scat near the remains. The bear, an opportunistic omnivore, probably found the dead deer and had a little venison snack. That would have left the cougar wondering who ate his porridge.

Maureen did encounter a cougar on the way to work. It was a June morning just about two miles shy of Jacksonville. The big fellow was loping across Sterling Creek Road, probably heading to the historic hamlet to bag a tourist. Too bad. Dining on a tourist could cause a sour stomach.

But the strangest animal encounter at our cabin didn't come from the wild, although it could be mighty ferocious if ticked off. This big boy was a gentle 150-pound Olde English mastiff owned by daughter Amy and

Denny, her significant other. A teacher by training, Amy had moved to Boulder from Oregon while Denny continued working in the building trade in southern Oregon. Like many young couples, they had some issues they were working out in their own unique way. Moose stayed with his buddy Denny who needed a dog sitter when he flew to Boulder to visit Amy. It seems the folks who normally watched the big bruiser were unavailable. Something about having moved, changed their names and leaving no forwarding address. Coincidentally, this occurred just one day after they last dog sat the huge fellow.

In addition to his enormous weight, he is about six feet long from the tip of his nose to the end of his tail. You need to watch out for his tail. A happy pooch, he often shows his good mood by swishing his tail back and forth like a giant horizontal metronome. When that tail slaps you on the posterior, it feels like you are being whipped by a large rope. It really smarts.

Everything about him is enormous. With his gaping maw, he could easily pick up a soccer ball, although those gleaming white fangs would make for a game-ending bite. A glance at him would have made the Baskervilles embarrassed over the fuss they made about their nocturnal visitor of the canine kind. When you muster up the courage to pat him on his head, your hand seems very small. In Alaska, it would be comparable to petting a grizzly. And his paws produce prints that are the size of the biggest wolf tracks I ever saw in the Far North. Stick antlers on him and Moose would be a moose.

The only thing small about him was his visit. He romped into our lives on a Wednesday morning and galloped out the following Tuesday afternoon. But it seemed longer. Much longer.

Don't get me wrong. Moose is as loveable a pooch as you will ever find in dogdom. He is a gentle giant who loves nothing more than to lie on his bed and have his ears licked by Mouse, our cat whose mission in life is to clean as many dog ears as she can find. As you can imagine, Moose has big ears. Our little Mouse nearly swooned when she beheld these huge acoustic organs that feel like velvet. She was in love.

What's more, Moose is funny in a way that only a dog can be funny. Like Harpo, he has perfected an Elvis lip that would have had the King all shook up. When he looks at you with that top lip curled up, you can't help but laugh.

He is also a mighty handsome dog. A brindle, he has a naturally camouflaged coat any designer of military commando gear would be wise to emulate. Despite his massive head, his big brown eyes are warm and friendly. He is the complete package when it comes to a fine-looking canine, proving you like them monster size.

There is one tiny problem with Moose. What we are talking about here is vast amounts of dog drool flung about. He is a furry slobber factory. The larger slimy stalagmites can dangle a foot or more. When he shakes his head, slime flies in every direction. If you have a weak stomach likes yours truly, the mere thought of his drool triggers a gag reflex.

"You are letting your imagination go wild," the wife said when I voiced concern about the drooling problem. "All you need to do is wipe his face with a paper towel when he starts doing it. So just buck up, bunky."

"That's very easy for you to say," I replied. "First, you have a cast iron stomach. Secondly, you will be fleeing to your shop during the week. Which reminds me, didn't you decide to visit your sister this weekend? That means I will be fending off the slobber machine alone."

Our cabin would be filled with more than 350 pounds of dog, not to mention another 150 pounds of cat, give or take. With Maureen suddenly finding countless reasons to be out of the cabin for much of the next six days, that would mean about 185 pounds of a gagging droolaphobe against some 500 pounds of furry creatures.

"You can handle them," Maureen said as she was ready to dash out the door on the morning Denny was to truck the brute over. "Just remember that animals can sense fear."

What hurt most was hearing the wife's maniacal laughter all the way down the driveway as she left for town. Her excuse was that she had to go to work. Likely story.

Moose had been to our place before, but only for a short supervised visit with drool handlers Amy and Denny standing at the ready with towels. These were large towels, mind you, the kind you take to the beach.

"You probably should have a scoop shovel handy," Amy casually tossed out at the time. "He does produce some hefty poop."

I laughed off what I figured was a little levity by Ames to reduce my shock of what he would leave in his wake.

"When it comes to fecal matter, I'll have you know that Harpo and Waldo hold up their end very well," I countered, figuring a foul pun was needed.

The conversation occurred while Moose was throwing Denny around in the dog park. He is a strong young man but he was being tossed about like a rag doll during his romp with the Moose. Denny was huffing and puffing in the man-against-dog tussle. He was still gasping for breath when he brought the mastiff back to their pickup truck for the ride home. The truck groaned when Moose leaped into the back. The huge dog looked down at me. A particularly large drool hung from his jowls. But a shake of his head sent it flying over my head to slap up against a nearby flowering plum tree. I'm sure it was no coincidence the tree fell over the following winter. Maureen blamed the heavy snow but I suspect it was the victim of the slobber attack.

I noticed on the day of Moose's first visit that Denny had apparently started using hair mousse. Only it hadn't stayed in his hair. It appeared to have been slathered on the side of his face. One forearm glistened with the stuff. A glob hung on his knee.

"No offense but your dog seemed to have messed up your hair mousse," I told him, thinking it wasn't something you would expect someone in the building trade to wear.

"It's not mousse—it's Moose," he said with a grin as he began using a towel Amy had handed him to wipe off the Moose hair gel. "He drools more when he gets excited. Sort of flings it around."

Later, after they had left, I reluctantly picked up the scoop shovel and went hunting for Moose leavings. Now, in Alaska, moose poop are nothing but droppings, each barely larger than your average marble. Our Moose could have been an Oregon logger, one who produced his own logs. One glance at the mountain of poo and a bear would scat. Fortunately, I'm made of sterner stuff than your average grizzly.

But I couldn't shake that memory of Moose's early visit when Denny pulled in on day one of the dog sit. The pooch, who filled the back end of the truck, was grinning down at me with an Elvis leer. I made a mental note not to get the front end of the slobber mill excited. As for the back end, Amy's advice to keep a scoop shovel handy would be heeded. If our scoop shovel wasn't up to the task, we had a large snow shovel as back up.

"You'll need this," Denny said, handing me what looked like a small metal bath tub. It was pink.

"Uh, I don't think I'll be giving him a bath," I said. "Besides, it's a bit small."

"That's his water bowl," Denny explained. "The high walls help control the splash when he drinks."

I didn't even want to think about a dog water tsunami across the cabin's concrete floor. Contemplating puddles of dog drool was a slippery slope I didn't want to start down. Next came his dog bed, complete with two large throw pillows. A pachyderm would have been comfortable in his spacious bed.

"And here is his food," Denny said as he lugged a bag of dog foot into the cabin. "It should last him until I get back."

It wasn't the mountain of food that concerned me. But the fact everything would be headed south to the land of scoop shovels was worrisome.

"Have fun, guys," Denny said as he hopped into his truck and made good his escape. At least he had the decency to hold his laughter until he got out of ear shot and onto the blue highway.

I slowly walked back into the cabin with Moose in tow. Undoubtedly the largest dog to ever enter the cottage, he seemed happy to be on another adventure. He was prancing, eager to check out his new digs. I dragged my feet like a condemned man on the way to the gallows. Gallows humor helps when the straits get dire, incidentally.

"OK, everything is copacetic," I informed all the waiting hairy creatures when we entered the cabin. "We are going to get through this just fine. But there will be no playing grab ass and definitely no fighting. We are going to live in harmony."

Moose leered at me with his goofy grin. The other twelve cabin inmates were not grinning, save for Mouse. She was purring, eager to start working on the big fellow's ears.

To make sure everything was indeed copacetic in their dog-eat-dog world, the three pooches immediately took turns sniffing each other's rear ends. I'm happy to report that whatever they were checking out was apparently just fine.

Having accepted the cabin as his new big dog house, Moose strode over to Harpo and Waldo's water dish and lapped. Never mind his bath tub of a watering hole stood nearby, already filled with a reflecting pool of cold, clear water. Sadly, the bowl was not deep enough to contain the drool flung forth from the huge tongue. Had you been standing on the other side of the bowl from Moose, you would have had a very disgusting shower. Half a roll of paper towels later, the slimy mess, along with Moose's dripping mug, was wiped up. I made a mental note to call Maureen and ask her to pick up a case of paper towels. Giant size.

Before I had the chance to clean the bowl and refill it, Harpo came over for a drink. He stopped short when he saw some floating goblets. He looked up at me, his lower lips drooping in disgust. It was the first time I had seen a dog look like he was going to hurl because of something he saw. I gave him fresh water and patted him on the head.

"It's just for six days, buddy," I said. "It'll be fun. You'll see."

There is something about lying to your best friend that leaves a bad taste. Worse yet, one glance into Harpo's expressive eyes told me he knew I was fibbing. I felt like a cur.

Before heading upstairs to write, I sat down at the dining room table to consider the situation. Waldo wasn't at all bothered by the scenario. He lapped up some water and nonchalantly trotted over to his doggy bed for a long nap. Harpo plopped down at my feet and laid his head on his paws. For him and his master, it was going to be a long six days.

Moose came over and laid his head on the table. At the other end, his hairy metronome whipped dangerously.

"Head off the table, Moose," I said. He left behind a sizable wet spot, one I made disappear with two paper towels. Another mental note: disinfect table to avoid coming down with some horrible dog disease.

But I couldn't help but notice he was a bright dog who obviously wanted to please. "Come here, Moose," I told him. He came over and sat down next to me. Harpo snorted in disgust.

As I petted Moose, he leaned against me, eating up the attention. He pushed the back of his head and neck up against my face. His fur smelled like what I suspect would be the last odor you would take in if you buried your nose in the back of a grizzly's neck. This particularly grizz would have found ecstasy in rolling around in carrion as well as dead salmon along a river bank. I pushed him away in an effort to inhale cabin air that was relatively fresh. Apparently thinking I wanted to play, he whirled around and stuck his mug up against mine, letting out a wolfish bay of pure joy. It was at that precise moment in time I fully understood the meaning of fetid breath. The dog spittle? There was probably some but I was too busy gagging to notice.

Thus ended the first happy hour of that dog day afternoon.

Feeding time at the Sterling Creek zoo that evening was memorable. To keep peace in the valley, I had to feed Moose first, otherwise Harpo would have wolfed down his food and gone after the mastiff's meal. I don't even want to think about that scenario. Moose may have been easy going but taking a bite out of his dish might be going too far. So I put Harpo and Waldo in our bedroom and fed our monster guest first. I then fed our two boys, making sure to close the door. With our pooches eating, I hooked Moose to a leash and cajoled him to drag me out to the dog park where he could do his business. By then, Harpo had finished his meal and was howling mad. He knew I was two-timing him with Moose. He is the only dog I know whose bark sounds like "It's not fair!" But the big guy finished his business in short odor, er, order and was ready to go back to the cabin. I let him in and hooked up our two mutts for their turn in the dog park. Like I said, copacetic.

For me, these moments of outfoxing canines are cherished. Too often have I been outwitted by the wily creatures. Chock one up for the humanoids.

After all the animals were taken care of, their pillows fluffed and beds made to their liking, we humanoids hit the sack. Everything was going smoothly.

But I awoke around midnight to a growling noise. It sounded like a bear was in the bedroom, one which was mighty cranky. Why weren't the three fierce watch dogs awake? I tried to wipe the cobwebs from my brain. The growling continued, and yet no dog seemed to notice. Something wasn't right. The growl rose and fell. It was Moose snoring. I turned on my side and covered my ears with a pillow. Maureen? She was sleeping quite nicely.

But the pillow provided no protection to the loud whine filling the cabin at 3:00 a.m. Bleary eyed and stumbling, I went out to the kitchen where Moose was sitting at the door, all but crossing his back legs. Obviously, the poor fellow had to tinkle. After putting on some slippers and a coat, I harnessed him and led him out the door to a tree which needed a good soaking. Steam rose. I made a mental note not to water the tree anytime soon. With our nocturnal watering done, the dog returned to the cabin with the sleepy man in tow.

If Sasquatch had been standing in the forest watching the strange goings-on that night, it would have looked like a man had led a horse out of the cabin to take a leak. The great ape would have wondered just what kind of bipeds inhabited Gilson Gulch.

"Well, that wasn't so bad—I slept well," Maureen said the next morning. "Everybody seems to be getting along fine. I think Moose likes it here."

"Grumphh," I muttered into my coffee cup.

But she was right. Moose enjoyed his stay. And once he trained me to his habits, we got along fine. I was his newest best friend. The gentle giant took to sitting or laying down by me, although he did not climb the stairs to my loft. That was just as well. The upstairs couch would have been too small for the Moose.

"He is a wonderful dog," Maureen said as she patted his massive head. "He is so easy going."

"If we ever decide to try our hand at horse logging, we could use him to pull logs down the mountain," I said. "We could always grease the skids with slobber."

I missed the big lug after he was gone. Were it not for the enormous creature's drooling ways, I would have dognapped him.

TWENTY-FIVE

Chainsaws and Tree Rings

S OME TWO DECADES BEFORE JAMES STERLING BEGAN whooping it up down on Sterling Creek after discovering gold in the spring of 1854, a tiny Douglas fir seed sprouted on the forest floor at the upper end of Gilson Gulch. A tendril of green began poking its head up out of the duff, seemingly taking a timid peek at its new world.

It likely dropped as a seed from a cone hanging high in its mother tree the previous fall. Perhaps it landed only a few feet from its parent's trunk. Or a wind gust beneath its single wing may have lifted it high overhead, sending it hundreds of feet over the forest before it drifted down. It could have also been carried in the cheek of a gray squirrel to a seed stash whose location was later lost to the forgetful fellow whose ilk are notorious for overloading their memory banks with one too many caches.

Always a little high strung as witnessed by constantly switching bushy tails and never-ending chatter, these colorful characters' excitations over the loss of their nutty treasures incite the forest's feathered community. Turkeys start running around in circles and gibbering gobbledygook, nattering jays hop nervously from limb to limb and a squadron of croaking ravens fly sorties overhead. All this clatter because of a few lost nuts.

Unlike most of its other sibling seeds gobbled up by squirrels, shrews and mice, not to mention all manner of birds which pluck them straight out of the cone, the small seed survived. The leaves that drifted down from the oak trees scattered amidst the largely conifer forest formed a protective winter blanket over the little capsule of life. Moistened by the life-giving Oregon rain, the tender pip began to stir in the forest duff.

But even with its roots beginning to spread, it was still not out of the woods yet. It had to compete with other trees and brush for sunlight, water and soil nutrients. Moreover, there were now predator browsers to withstand, including deer and rabbits who love snacking on young green things. Even after it reached several feet high, it could still be nibbled on by a hungry porcupine or savaged by a buck needing a rubbing post to remove velvet from its antlers come spring. Indeed, when it came to survival, a gambler playing the long shot had better odds than the lone fir seedling.

But survive it did. By the time the Civil War began in 1861, the young fir had already weathered hard times, judging from the tale told by its growth rings. For the fir tree challenged, each ring reflects a year's growth, much of which occurs in the spring and summer. Beginning around its twentieth year, the tree rings are extremely tight, indicating it was experiencing a challenging period. It could be a drought provided little water to the thirsty young tree. Or it may have been that other large trees towering overhead left little moisture and nutrients for the spindly conifer. But it appeared to enjoy fat times around the end of the 1800s when Teddy Roosevelt was leading the Rough Riders up Cuba's San Juan Hill in 1898 during the short-lived Spanish-American War. The story of the rings tell us lean years returned about the time the U.S. entered World War I in 1917 but it was growing well when the Great Depression began shortly after the stock market crash in 1929. Another set of tight rings reflected tough times during World War II right up to the birth of rock n' roll in the late 1950s. Although fat rings indicated it thrived into the early 1960s, the tree possibly died in the middle of that decade, about the time the U.S. was getting ready to step in it in a country called Vietnam.

It's anyone's guess what caused its death. If memory serves, the early

'60s, highlighted by the devastating December '64 flood, brought ample precipitation to southern Oregon so death was caused by drought. It may have succumbed to an insect infestation. We found several hollow areas in the rounds split for firewood where wood-burrowing insects had feasted. The tree had been used as a post for a barbed wire fence years ago but that wouldn't have caused its demise. Maybe it died of a broken heart after pining for a particularly comely pine in the distance, knowing its love could never be consummated. But we'll leave the sex lives of conifers to OSU forestry graduates who ponder such matters.

One fact solid as its dense interior wood is that it obviously lived for more than a century. After the old snag was felled for firewood in early November of 2015, the ring count near its stump indicated the tree was at least 130 years old when it died. But it was a little older since the rings in the epidermis immediately under the inch-thick bark had rotted away.

Measured on the ground, the trunk was 111 feet long. To put it into perspective for you urbanites, it was around eleven stories tall when it stood with its wooden feet firmly planted in the ground. The stump is nearly three feet in diameter. By any measurement, it was a wooden colossus, although neither the largest nor oldest fir on the property.

Exactly when the tree died is open to conjecture since dating a dead snag is tricky business. But we know the old wooden sentinel was long dead when we bought the property fifteen years earlier. Add another thirty-five years, a conservative estimate since fir snags can stand around for a very long time, and you have a tree dead for half a century. Throw in the 130 growth rings and that takes you back to 1835, the same birth year as Samuel Langhorne Clemens, alias Mark Twain. In essence, young Twain and our juvenile tree were roughing it at the same time. If the tree time table is in error, it is surely because the fir took root before the famous writer was born. But for argument's sake, lets agree the fir sprouted well before Mr. Sterling discovered gold in the stream which would bear his name.

While it was living, it was obvious the tree did not subscribe to the old saw that a straight line is the shortest route to journey's end. Something, a large rotting log perhaps, blocked it from growing straight up during its woody adolescence. For the first ten feet, the tree curved dramatically to the east before resuming its vertical quest. At that point, it grew truly vertical for another thirty feet before making a slight easterly detour for the remainder of its upward journey. Perhaps it veered as it grew to avoid the sun shadow of a taller tree that once stood nearby. Then again, it may have been contrary by nature like some humanoids.

While we had observed it from afar for the first decade and a half we were on the land, it was not until we were realigning the old fence to match the western property line in the summer of 2015 that we stood directly under it.

"That's one gnarly tree," I observed while gawping up at the wooden behemoth. "There's a lot of good firewood in it but this guy is going to be a bear to fall. It's hard to tell where it leans. It's all over the map."

Listening, or at least politely pretending to take in my verbal nuggets of wisdom, was Pat Earle, an old high school buddy. He had come up from the Reno area to lend a hand in the fence-building project. Maureen had been helping me on her days off but handed off the responsibility of keeping an eye on me to the former Marine and retired police officer turned arborist. The former gendarme had dealt with plenty of miscreants so Maureen figured he would keep her hubby from pulling some harebrained scheme. As a product of the southern Oregon woods, Pat also knew his way around trees before going arboreal. He had toiled in the woods in his youth, cutting firewood and logging a bit. He is as woods wise as an old owl.

"That one is damn dangerous," he said in a voice that sounds like gravel sliding off a metal roof. "You don't know how rotten it is. It could go any direction. Even an experienced timber faller would hesitate to tackle that one. Whoever cuts it down needs to know what he is doing."

Then he gave me THE look. You never strayed from the straight and narrow in elementary school so you don't know about the look I'm talking about. Suffice it to say it's the kind of glare a battle-weary teacher gets upon telling, for the umpteenth time, an immature pupil known for doing bad deeds to straighten up. The look invariably includes a dark frown and a laser-like glare that would sear pork chops at fifty paces. For good measure, a pedagogue with a master's in disciplining wayward urchins always throws in an upper lip curl with a silent snarl. I would have been a foot taller if I hadn't had to suffer such withering looks from teachers throughout my childhood. Stunts your growth when you are continually slinking down in your desk as a kid, hoping you won't get caught, you see.

"So don't get a wild hair and go lunatic on me," Pat growled. He may have meant "hare" but we'll let it go at that.

"Fine, in this one and only instance, you may be on to something," I said as I continued to study the firry mammoth. "But we'll save the debate about cutting that tree for another day. Right now, we are out to prove that Robert Frost's neighbor was right."

"Ah, yes—good fences make good neighbors," Pat said. "That fellow should have been arrested for being stubbornly obtuse."

"Obtuse? We certainly wouldn't want to obfuscate the obvious, old buddy," I told him, knowing full well he had thrown out a word seldom heard in the Oregon woods just to poke fun at my penchant for occasionally using a $10 word when a five-center would do the job just fine. I tell my wife it is to keep the words alive in my head but she doesn't buy it either. OK, maybe it might be to try to impress folks, although it doesn't seem to be working.

So I resorted to an old Kerbyism. "Maroon," I muttered to Pat.

"Moron," he fired back.

Like an old pair of cozy shoes, childhood friendships are comfortable. Out on the fence line, we slipped easily back into our friendly verbal sparring that began more than half a century ago. When he chided me for using words that would have caused a fight back in Kerby, I made sure to continue to throw them out to irk him. Although both of us wrestled for four years in high school, neither of us were in shape for grappling with anything other than words while on the fence line.

At the time, Pat had not yet fully recovered from a hip replacement in Reno's VA hospital and he was undergoing therapy for a shoulder injury. The attentive reader already knows about my challenging locomotion and lack of dexterity in my right arm. Although his physical challenges were impressive, I like to believe my gimpiness would have taken his impairments in two out of three rounds. Of course, he would be able to walk away from his temporary gimp, returning to the hearty soul I've known since childhood. I should have charged him for the physical therapy provided by the fence work but sometimes I'm just too magnanimous for my own good.

The bottom fence line was that we were an army of two crips taking on a dug-in barbed wire battalion stretching for a quarter mile. Unfair? Not really: we agreed to take it easy on our steel foe.

What prompted our Sterling Creek version of Frost's "Mending Wall" was a survey Maureen and I had done on the property in 2012. As witnessed by the barbed wire embedded in the ancient fir snag, the old fence purportedly marking the property boundary meandered a bit from tree to tree through the woods, although steel posts were used when a tree wasn't handy. In several areas, one old fence ran parallel two to three feet from another old fence. Perhaps fence builders of old found it easier to erect an adjacent fence instead of repairing one that fell down. Or maybe bovines of yesteryear were hoofed Houdinis requiring two fences to keep them corralled.

What we knew for sure was that we wanted the fence aligned with the property line, in part to make sure all the firewood we cut was on our property. Like rustling cattle, pilfering firewood in the Applegate country is not tolerated. I'm not sure what the penalty is but, having already broken my neck once, I'm not about to see if it's a hanging offense. As you can well imagine, snapping one's neck tends to smart. Once satisfied my curiosity, particularly if you're talking about a severe rope burn to boot.

The survey determined the old fence along the west side of our property—there is 1,333 feet of it—was 75 to 100 feet east of the boundary onto our property. But even before our survey, our western neighbor Pete had told us the fence wasn't faithful to the property line. He observed the U.S. Bureau of Land Management, which administers public land to our immediate north and is also his neighbor to the east, had surveyed its boundaries a few years earlier and planted a metal survey marker nearly 100 feet west of the old fence line.

When our survey confirmed Uncle Sam's determination the fence was that far off in the corner as well as off the beam all along western property line, Pete responded in his laconic fashion. "What's right is right," he said. "That fence needs to be put on the property line."

Of course, the octogenarian, a former logger no doubt as tough in his day as anyone who ever lived in Sterlingville or its environs, was physically past rebuilding fences. He chuckled when told I would be working on the fence that summer.

"You be careful out there," he said. "Hardly any of that ground is level."

Being a kindly fellow, he wasn't about to suggest I wasn't up to the task. He was merely observing that building a fence in this country was difficult. But he must have wondered, given my unreliable leg and equally untrustworthy right arm, how I would fare.

In my head, I went out there and pulled it off perfectly. The Romans who built Hadrian's Wall in England would have been ashamed of themselves if they had seen the fence I built in my mind. An arrow never flew as straight and true. Never has a builder of fences been so clever, so quick on his feet. But when the daydreaming stopped and my boots were on the ground, reality proved a little messy. In addition to being up and down as Pete observed, the uneven ground is a mine field of ground squirrel holes, jutting broken limbs and cast aside old wire, all of which conspired to trip me. But I didn't need any help. Mostly I pitched forward, although sometimes, just for a little variety, I fell backwards or sideways. As noted early on in this tome, I am an expert at falling down.

"That Fattig, he is no Shakespeare but nobody can touch him when it comes to tripping and falling," writing acquaintances will tell you. "You mark a dotted line on the ground and he will sign it with his signature fall. But continually landing on his head has left the poor fellow permanently wandering and wondering. God knows how many readers are wandering around out there, lost in one of his digressions." When it comes to feasting on one of its own, well seasoned cannibals are cowardly pettifogs compared to those who espouse to write, you understand.

Sure enough, within five minutes of arriving at the job site with Pat on our very first day working together, I tumbled headlong. A malevolent root grabbed my foot, gleefully pitching me down the hill. Fortunately, a sympathetic stump was there to catch my face, breaking my fall. Stupefied, I groped around for my glasses, hoping not to goose a sleeping rattlesnake by mistake. Snoozing buzz worms can be very cranky when rudely fondled.

"Not bad," Pat commented. "You still need to work on your landing. However, leading with your head is smart since you can't damage anything useful."

"I appreciate your heartfelt words of sympathy but it's just a little flesh wound," I said, wincing as I rubbed the end of my nose where a little blood oozed from a minor scratch. A quick pat down of my lower extremities reassured me there were no compound fractures with broken bones jutting out of the flesh.

"I always land like a cat," I said as I stood up on unsteady legs like a drunk after a bad night.

"A cat with three legs, blind in one eye and eight lives very badly misspent," he said, shaking his head. "You'll live, marine. Let's get on with it."

Despite the verbal jousting, the fence building progressed fairly well. Not only did the fence grow, albeit slowly, but the work provided excellent opportunities for trying out challenging falling techniques. I became quite adept at difficult landings in which clinging vines keep you from getting your arms out front to break your fall. Although I had plenty of practice, I never quite developed the knack for avoiding facial lacerations. After a few days my mug, never a thing of beauty, would have scared the bejabbers out of the bride of Frankenstein.

Building a fence on uneven, brushy ground can be entertaining in a masochistic fashion. Any self-mutilator would delight in being slashed by rusty barbed wire, giggle at jabs in the face by dead limbs and look forward to hours of scratching after falling into a patch of poison oak. While I didn't find it particularly amusing, it was an interesting diversion from sitting in my writing loft for hours on end.

To clear the way for the fence, we cut and piled brush in hopes of slowing a wildfire should one come our way some summer. Even before starting the fence work, I cut weeds and grass on the access road that had been carved out by a bulldozer when the area was logged some thirty years earlier. Actually, it is more of a goat trail but serviceable for us in our old four-wheel-drive pickup, providing you aren't squeamish about hurling along a skid trail with iffy brakes.

Once we entered fire season, the vegetation along the road would turn into so much kindling. It would be very inconvenient if our old pickup truck ignited a blaze in the dry grass. Under state law, anyone starting a wild fire through acts of irresponsible stupidity during fire season can be made to pay for the suppression costs. Driving Old Sparky up there after the fire season is lit would certainly fall under a dumb deed covered by the law. After the state of Oregon reamed us financially, our neighbors would have made shunning by the Amish seem like friendly greeters sent out by the local chamber of commerce. Best to avoid the gaffe altogether.

When it came to thinning a fire-prone forest of underbrush and debris, the swath along the bucking property line on the western edge of the old Gilson Ranch forestland wasn't our first rodeo. A few years earlier, with memories of the Squires Peak fire still on our minds, we asked the Oregon Department of Forestry for advice on reducing the threat of a wild fire around the cabin. While I know my way about the woods, I figured it wouldn't hurt to get a refresher course on reducing wildfire threat from those who do it for a living. Maureen hoped it would at least reduce the chances of me getting hurt. After all, the cost of reattaching limbs is rather steep these days, not to mention the messy business of trying to find the missing part in the brush.

While our ODF visitor was too professional to indelicately suggest that razing the cabin and its adjacent junk piles would noticeably improve our property value, he suggested we remove as much flammable material as possible from around the cabin. Too bad the stained toilet wasn't still sitting in the yard. The ODFers may be a polite bunch but the old commode would have gotten a derisive rise out of even them. It is a curious fact that many of us who live in the country are hoarders. But hoards of old flammable stuff piled near a home can become the dreaded ladder fuel firefighters warn you about when a wildfire looks for something to climb so it can peek in your windows come July or August.

In addition to removing flammable material around our home, we thinned the forest in a three-acre swath on the steep side of the valley immediately south of the cabin, a goal laid out for us by the ODF. In theory, you should thin tall trees near a home so the canopies are not touching but we felt would have made the forest look like it had been butchered. So we took a butcher-light approach on the big fellows. But we took no prisoners when it came to the toddlers in the forest kindergarten, mowing them down left and right.

We were also getting into shape by climbing the hillside while lugging a chain saw, ax, pruning shears and pole saw. Thinning a forest is somewhat like weeding the garden, albeit on a larger scale with tools that are both bigger and infinitely more dangerous than a hoe.

When I told a photojournalist friend about a new chainsaw we bought for thinning the forest around the cabin, his response was less than enthusiastic.

"No offense, Paul, but I don't want to be around when you are running a chainsaw," he said. "Isn't that a little dangerous for you? What if you trip?"

Although he was saying something that most folks would think but too polite to utter, I took no offense. He was simply concerned about my walking-challenged ways, apparently picturing me running through the woods while revving the chainsaw, leaving a trail of victims looking woefully at their severed body parts and spurting stumps.

"I don't run with a revving chainsaw," I told him. "Actually, I can't run at all. But I also don't lurch with one, either. Hate to be responsible for Oregon's version of the *Texas Chainsaw Massacre*, particularly if it left photog's body parts scattered about."

I've never seen the horror movie classic but understand it involves a chainsaw-carrying killer chasing really slow people. You have to wonder why it is the horror movie victims are invariably dumber than your proverbial fence post. Maybe that's what got the chainsaw murderer fired up in the first place.

But the intellect of folks living along Sterling Creek is like that of the offspring of Lake Woebegone inhabitants: they are all above average. And all nearby critters—humanoids, coyotes, rattlesnakes—are smart enough to get out of the way when I fire up the saw. Hopeful turkey vultures gather overhead, optimistic that a delectable body part might be severed and lunch served.

While a reliable chainsaw, sharp ax and a pole saw are all necessary tools for thinning a forest, we can't forget the other big dog in the tool box. What we're talking about here is the ability to employ blue words. Fortunately, as a youngster in the Illinois Valley, I was blessed with a remarkable uncle with a swearing ability that was legendary. That speaks volumes since this was a region where the cussing competition was mighty fierce back in the day.

But my late Uncle Ed could string together sinfully delicious adjectives into a thing of beauty that would have impressed even my Marine Corps drill instructors. God knows they were no slouches when it came to barking out a sailor's blessing. Uncle Ed was a poet of the profane, a Billy Sunday of expletives who delivered swearing sermons with evangelical power and conviction. For him, cussing was an art form to be carefully crafted.

Yet he did not swear as a matter of coarse conversation or to produce highvolume vulgarity. I never once heard him toss out an F-bomb or blaspheme in vain. His six-cornered oaths were well aimed. They were simply his way of beseeching a higher power to bring hell fire and damnation down on whatever was bedeviling him.

I can still see him casting curses at his fishing fly snagged in tree branches overhanging Sucker Creek in the early 1960s. I remember him driving expletives into a chunk of wood reluctant to surrender to his splitting ax. As an impressionable kid, I concluded his verbal venting somehow helped him conquer his foe. Having learned from the master blaster, I came to respect blue words as select tools not to be abused. Like any dangerous tool, they needed to be handled carefully.

Small wonder I sometimes employ those underutilized verbal instruments when cutting brush on our property. Incidentally, I go for the root ball to ensure the brush doesn't grow back. As a result, it often takes numerous hefty whacks strengthened by wellchosen swear words to cut the tough root down to size.

"You really should get a grip," Maureen told me one day when I was battering a root ball with an ax and swear words. "When you are wildly swinging an ax while questioning the parentage of brush at the top of your lungs, it makes me a tad nervous. Besides, you are scaring the dogs."

"The profanity helps," I panted in protest.

But my wife did have a point. Our large mutts Harpo and Waldo were huddled together down in the dog park. The cowardly curs were whimpering with their paws over their ears. Man's best friends? Hah.

We'll save the debate over whether dogs swear for another time, although Harpo does utter three sharp barks at Waldo when he has a bone to pick with him. It sounds disturbingly like he is referring to his mutt mate as the son of a female dog. While that description is apt in dogdom, it grates on the ears of some humanoids. Maureen has been talking to Harpo about his potty mouth.

She is most assuredly not a swearer, even though I have been patiently giving her execration lessons over the years. Like a former journalistic coworker whose best attempt at swearing was "drat nabbit," Maureen seldom goes there. She is a much nicer person than her spouse.

However, thinning a forest does have a way of whacking the hell out of such social niceties, so to speak.

So after chopping away at the monstrous root wad, only to have my ax and curses bounce repeatedly off it, I threw down the ax and flopped on the hillside for a rest. Maureen promptly dropped her pruning shears and picked up the ax.

"Watch and learn, sweetie," she said.

She swung. The ax bounced off. Again she struck. Again it bounced off. She swung again and again. Each time the ax bounced back. I started to ask for the ax back but there was a look in her eyes warning me to back off.

She lifted the ax overhead and brought it down with all her might. The ax might as well have been made of rubber.

That's when the dam burst, flooding everything within earshot with words seldom heard in a house of prayer.

"You dirty, rotten jerk," she suddenly shouted as she continued to flail away. "You dunginfested, lowlife piece of garbage. Damn you!" With that, she threw down the ax and plopped down beside me. "Not one peep," she snarled at me. I'm talking about a real snarl here, the kind with her incisor showing on the left side where her lip curled up. There was also what could be described as a low growl. I uttered nary a peep.

Sure, it was a mite pedestrian in its delivery, perhaps even a bit redundant. She certainly could have reached a little deeper into the bucket of blue words. But it was a wonderful break through. I like to think that somewhere Uncle Ed was smiling.

Thus, armed with ample swear words, murderous tools and experience of having thinned three acres near the cabin, we were well prepared for whatever faced us in thinning the forest and installing the fence on the western property line. Yet there are always things that can catch you by surprise out in the woods.

One early summer morning while walking up the hill with Maureen en route to fight with the barbed wire, I was telling her one of the tall tales of my misspent youth. Just as I got to the point where I was about to grab a mountain lion by the tail, something in my lower periphery caught my eye. It seemed vaguely familiar. I glanced down at my feet.

"Waaaa!" I yelled as I jump-lurched off the jeep trail, trying in vain to defy gravity by keeping all body parts off the ground. "Errrgaahhh!"

A rattlesnake was stretched out on the road. His head pointing toward my right foot, the one that had stepped near what would have been his shoulder if a buzz worm had a shoulder. I clinched my teeth, bracing for the imminent sting caused by two viper needles sinking into my calf.

Only he didn't move. He was dead. His soul had slithered on to whatever place it is that serpentine spirits coil up in the afterlife and wait for victims. It appears I had unknowingly run over the buzz worm with the pickup truck one morning en route to fence building before fire season began. It wasn't a large snake, only about eighteen inches long. But his fangs were plenty long enough to pierce footwear, let alone a cotton pants leg containing a nice, fat calf.

Expired though he was, the rattler rattled me. Up to that point, we had only seen vipers down in the valley. Now we knew they also lurked in the higher forest. From that moment on, I was dead certain they were waiting under every log and bush I stepped over for the remainder of the fence-building summer.

"Geez, calm down," Maureen told me after I shrieked later that day after an alligator lizard crawled out from under a log to see what we were up to. "It's just a lizard. Besides, you've always told me that rattlesnakes aren't aggressive. You said they just want to be left alone."

"That was when they were after you," I said after I regained my composure. "When they are after me, they are aggressive. They are still ticked off at me for having killed so many of their brethren when I was a kid. Rattlers hand their grudges off to each succeeding generation with instructions to get even. They are like my Scottish highlander ancestors. Their grudges live on forever until the family is avenged."

"I'll bear a grudge if you don't stop jumping around and talking weird," she said. "The rattlesnake was dead, for crimony's sakes. So just calm down."

While I remained a little antsy, we continued to extend the fence along the property line. But we did not finish that stretch before we had to stop to focus our energy on cutting firewood for the winter. Because we cut dead or down trees, we usually harvest firewood in the autumn when the weather is cooler and the winter rains have not yet started. The wood in a snag is already well seasoned, made bone dry by Mother Nature. Even in the dead of winter, a fir snag will provide dry firewood.

One autumn weekend found us cutting up a wind-blown downed fir no more than thirty feet from the huge snag which loomed over the beginning of this chapter. The downed wood was a little pulpy but it would serve. I bucked it up and we quickly filled up the back of the old pickup.

As I leaned against the bed of the pickup, I looked up at the massive snag, trying to figure out which way gravity was pulling for it to fall. But its twists and turns made it difficult to determine how it leaned. If the snag were a politician, it would have been despised by liberals and conservatives alike for appearing to lean neither left nor right.

"I'd really like to take down that big one today," I told Maureen. "There is no wind. With the firewood we already have, that tree would provide enough wood for the rest of the winter."

"Not a good idea," she replied. "We've already got a load of wood and you are tired. No offense, but that tree should also be cut down by someone with a little more experience. It's too dangerous."

As you may have noticed, I tend to have blinders on when I start focusing on something. It's a useful trait if you are writing a book or pulling a hay wagon, two activities that are more alike than most writers are willing to admit. While blinders can be helpful on draft horses and in first drafts, but they are foolhardy when falling big trees, especially snags. I blithely ignored my wife's wise words.

"We would have to move the truck," I said as I walked toward the snag, continuing to size it up. "It's only about eighty feet from the tree. The truck could be smashed flat where it is."

"It could also smash you flat," Maureen continued. "Like Pat said, you can't tell where it might land."

I walked up to the trunk of the snag and looked up. It looked even more dangerous when you are standing under the tree with its huge, wayward trunk. Some three feet in diameter at the base, it curved up in an odd twist the first ten feet, then decided to grow toward the west for another forty feet, and veered eastward for the remainder of its life. Understand that trees grow from the top so it spent the last century of its upward journey exploring the forest canopy. As a result, it was all over the map. Standing at its base, it was difficult to determine which way it wanted to fall if it decided to on its own volition. The tree scared me, although I didn't have the pluck to admit it.

The bluster I had mustered fled back down the hill. I meekly followed. Had I a tail, it would have been tucked between my legs.

"Yeah, maybe I'm a little too tired to fall it today," I fibbed to Maureen. "We'll get him next time."

"It's not going anywhere," she said. "Besides, there are plenty of other snags out there."

I drove slowly down the hill, the truck creaking from its load of firewood. I glanced in the rearview mirror at the old snag. It stood there, silently taunting me. The test of wills between a bullheaded male of the humanoid species and a horrid old hag had begun. I am still referring to the tree, by the way.

Veteran timber fallers have told me they don't like falling big snags because the old behemoths often do what they damn well please when it comes to crashing down. They can also break off in route, sending down a rain of deadly wooden missiles, they add.

With the snag in mind, I consulted an expert in the form of my oldest sibling, Jim, who is nearly four years my senior and a longtime timber faller, having worked in that dangerous profession for half a century. Among loggers, a timber faller is elite, top of the line.

However, in our youth, I never quite saw eye to eye with the future timber faller, and that sibling rivalry has never faded. Even with both of us now well into geezerdom, neither places much credence in what the other says, especially when it involves politics or religion, topics which seem to be one and the same these days. But I would be the first to acknowledge he knows of what he speaks when it comes to cutting trees. Not only was he a well-regarded timber faller, but he routinely hired fallers in his day. He also fired those who didn't measure up.

"Usually you always have to fall them with the lean," he explained of cutting dead snags. "If you try to wedge or jack them any other direction the vibration can cause parts of the tree to fall on you. The wood around the hinge is usually decayed enough that the tree can break off and go in a different direction."

To illustrate his point that falling snags is dangerous work, he noted that a fellow he had grown up with in the Illinois Valley had been killed while cutting a snag.

"I think the top broke out and hit him," he added. "He couldn't have had much experience because he was on one of my tree planting crews just a couple of years before and at that time he had never fell a tree."

Jim was once hit on his notoriously hard head by a heavy limb snapped off by a tree he was falling. Having been temporarily knocked cold, he spent the night in the hospital. The limb? Poor thing splintered into so much kindling.

During our brief communication via e-mail, the logger who takes pride in his work took the high road. But the idea that a recovering journalist, let alone someone who spends more time falling on his face than walking upright in the woods, would dishonor a stately tree by cutting it down must have galled him. In his world, journalists were little more than the fungus found between a hairy logger's toes. The fact I have a college degree only reinforces that belief.

Yet I knew his words of caution were spot on, echoing what other timber fallers had told me over the years.

"When it comes to a snag, I make a good undercut, start cutting on the back side until the trunk starts to move, then run like hell," one once told me. "You can never tell what those bastards are going to do. The top could break and knock your head off. Or the trunk may break right above your head and you'll get squished like a little bug."

I knew he was pulling my leg a mite because you want to keep your eyes on the falling tree, not running blindly away from it. No one could outrun a falling tree. But he was dead serious about a falling snag being fraught with danger. As brother Jim observed, the tops do break off and have been known to kill fallers. Felling a big tree invariably poses danger. A big snag enhances that danger.

It doesn't make any sense but I couldn't get the thought out of my mind that I had let myself and Maureen down by not felling the snag. Never mind it was an inanimate object. The snag nagged me. I couldn't see it from my writing loft but I could look up the valley and see the forest where it stood. My grudge match with the big snag had me silently hyperventilating.

Four days after we had cut the firewood, I could stand it no longer. It may have been midmorning but it was my High Noon. I got out the chainsaw and filled it with gas and oil. I ran a finger along the chain. The teeth were sharp. Maureen was away at work. It was time for me to follow suit.

I drove slowly up the hill to the humongous fir snag, careful to park some 200 feet away. It was bad enough there was a chance I was going to get "squished like a little bug." No need for the old truck that had served us so faithfully over the years to suffer that indignity as well.

For nearly a half hour, I studied the snag towering above me. Using other trees as guides, I could see where, if you craned your neck just right, it appeared the tree was leaning slightly. There were also more limbs on that side which would add additional pull in that direction.

Still, common sense told me to turn around and go back down the hill. But, as I have done countless times in my life, I ignored that irritating little nagger. I was out to prove that men in their mid-sixties can be just as stubbornly stupid as teeny bobbers. OK, not all men in their mid-sixties. Just the ones who don't heed the wife, friends and big brother's sage advice.

There was a very good chance the tree could sit back on itself when I cut into it, smashing the new fence and making me feel like a real Bozo. As my brother had said, no jack or wedge could direct the fall if the wood just under the thick bark is conky.

I was also reminded that size counts in the logging woods. My saw's bar is two feet long but the snag at the base was nearly three feet in diameter. That meant I would start the undercut on one side of the trunk, but have to cross over to the other side of the tree to complete the undercut. Not a good scenario since an old snag with even a partial undercut is a mighty dangerous creature.

I looked around. There was a tree nearby which I could hide behind should the falling snag launch wooden missiles my way. I made sure there were no vines or debris between me and the shelter tree.

To be candid, I was half hoping the saw would not start. It sometimes refuses to work, apparently hung over or just lazy. But it let me down, roaring to life at the first pull.

There was no one else out in the woods to witness whether I felled the tree or not. I could turn the saw off and slink away with no one the wiser. But there was no going back. Call it pride or self esteem. Something bigger than me was pushing me to kneel at the base of the snag and begin the undercut. I had the same butterflies in my gut I had back in high school wrestling when taking on a foe I knew to be stronger, quicker and tougher than me.

Taking a deep breath, I began cutting into what would be the largest undercut I had ever undertaken. I started a few inches above the ground, careful to avoid the area where barbed wire stuck out of the thick bark. Nothing like metal on metal to dull a chain.

At first, the sawdust spitting out from under the heavy bark was dark brown, indicating the epidermis was rotten. Not a promising indicator. A few beads of sweat trickled down my forehead.

But the chain's teeth quickly bit into solid wood as demonstrated by light-colored solid wood chips being spat out. A good sign, it indicated the bulk of the trunk was largely dense wood. At least it wasn't likely to crumple straight down, leaving little more than a temporary messy stain where I was. Moreover, the solid chips revealed the tree would produce excellent firewood.

Now, if I could get it to fall down a path where it wouldn't squash either live trees or the live biped operating the saw. With the undercut completed on one side, I quickly scooted to the other side and began slicing the wooden wedge from that angle. The saw ate swiftly through the wood, making short work of the rest the undercut. I pulled the huge wedge out and looked up. The tree had not budged.

Next came the acid test. I knelt behind the tree on the opposite side of the undercut and began cutting across the back, careful to begin on the side nearest me and slowly pushing the bar away to cut across the entire backside. As it did with the undercut, the teeth initially spewed brown sawdust at first, followed by a stream of solid bright chips. Yet I was halfway to the center and there was still no indication from the tree that it had any desire to fall. I continued sawing, frequently glancing up to see if the snag was beginning to have second thoughts. I certainly did.

That was when a telltale gap, albeit small at first, began to appear between the flat side of the bar and the trunk above. The snag was beginning to make its plunge toward earth. What's more, it was falling in the direction I intended it to go. An undercut in the form of a grin spread across my face. The new fence was safe.

But the stubborn fellow cutting the snag was still in harm's way. The tree could kick back or break apart above me, dropping wooden bombs weighing several hundred pounds. When the falling trunk began gaining momentum, I yanked the saw away, shut it off and retreated. The big snag must have made a tremendous wallop when it hit the ground. But I didn't hear it. I was too busy scrambling off to one side to hide behind my sanctuary tree. I did hear a neighbor half a mile away honk his car horn twice. Either he was giving me an "Atta boy!" for bringing down the tree or was angry at me for killing a dead tree.

The top thirty feet of the tree broke off, creating a log more than a foot in diameter at the thickest point, landing about fifty feet downhill from the stump. I couldn't help but wonder if the forest monarch would have made a sound if it had squished the fellow who brought it down. I am dead certain the fellow would have become incontinent and made a whimpering sound seconds before his light blinked out.

Having slain the mighty monarch that had been silently challenging my manhood, I packed up my saw and gas can and climbed back into my rig. Loggers drive rigs, you see. I returned to the cabin, changed back into my writing garb of slothful clothes and climbed up to my loft.

But I was feeling too keyed up to write. I called the wife to tell her of my amazing feat.

"You what?" she asked. "Are you out of your mind?"

She stepped out of her shop and began reading me the riot act.

"Promise me you will never again up there by yourself and fall a tree, particularly one as dangerous as that," she concluded. "It's too dangerous. You could have been killed. And if you had, I would have never, ever forgiven you for being so irresponsible."

The dressing down could have been worse. Yes, she was right on every point and I was better for the sobering reminder. Yet a little smugness remained. I had faced my fear. So I called my old buddy Pat, informing him of my impressive accomplishment.

For a moment, there was silence on the phone, followed by a deep sigh.

"That was not wise, my friend," Pat said. "You could have been one of those people whose body they find out in the woods. That was a dangerous tree to fall. Yet you go out there by yourself. There is no one to warn you that tree was doing above your head. Not smart at all, young man."

My first thought was "*Et tu, Brutus?*" Then it hit me how utterly insensitive I had been. You see, his father was cutting timber in the Illinois Valley in 1952 when Pat's paternal grandfather, visiting from Los Angeles, came out one day to watch his logger son in action. When the tree fell, it struck a nearby snag which also crashed down, instantly killing Pat's grandfather. In fact, Pat was there that day, albeit only as an infant held in his mother's arms. It was obviously a horrible day for the family.

In the months that have elapsed since I cut down the old snag, I still feel betwixt and between. The feeling is not unlike the one I felt after I shot the big buck in my youth: thrilled about having the venison and the bragging rights but silently wishing the majestic stag was still walking in the woods. Before bucking the tree up for firewood, Maureen and I measured it at 111 feet, including the thirty-foot portion which had broken off. As indicated at the outset of this chapter, it had at least 130 growth rings. A logger who swears, of which there are a few, would have described it as a big mother and thrown in a coarse acronym to boot.

As expected, the snag was dense and dry, making it ideal for firewood. But it seemed like an ignominious end to a once noble tree, one whose roots preceded Sterlingville. Even now, I feel a little pang when I see the open space in the forest canopy where the big fir snag had reigned for so long. I'm also reminded of Pat's pithy words: Not smart, young man.

UP STERLING CREEK WITHOUT A PADDLE

TWENTY-SIX

Weird Stuff Happens
in the Country

W HEN YOU LIVE IN A RURAL AREA, STRANGE THINGS sometimes occur for which there is neither rhyme nor reason. OK, they may happen because there are times when I don't think things out before taking action. A less generous assessment would conclude that is because there are times when I'm as thick as two planks. But that's a little harsh. One plank, maybe. Besides, the freaky episodes do make interesting learning experiences, although ones that you never, ever want to repeat. Some are even a little funny, albeit not until years later and after you've had a couple of glasses of wine. Unfortunately, others can make you fear for your very life.

We'll start with funny, then take a deep breath and venture into the night of terror. For some reason, these things always seem to happen at night.

Like most moronic moments of mine, the night of March 3, 2003, began with innocence as pure as the driven snow. Actually, there was no snow but it was a frosty night. The ground crunched underfoot.

We had arrived home from work well after dark. After bringing the dogs in from the kennel, I fed them. While they were happily munching, I started a crackling fire in the woodstove to warm the house. We both changed into comfortable clothes and Maureen fixed a quick but tasty dinner of leftovers.

That's when I suggested we take the mutts for a quick walk.

"Better grab our coats," said Maureen who was dressed in a light sweat suit and clogs.

"Pshaw," I replied in my t-shirt, jeans and tennis shoes. "We'll be back in a jiff."

She led the furry procession out into the brisk night. The stars twinkled like ice crystals. The pooches trotted happily at our heels.

Remember, we had just recently moved into the cabin from the trailer house from hell. The cabin had newly installed doors with door handles that lock automatically unless the center dohickie is turned to the vertical position. The last fellow out the door forgot to make sure the center dohickie was vertical.

It was a sad sound, the cold click of the door locking behind me.

"Uh, you got keys?" I asked my wife.

"You've got to be kidding," she replied. "I don't even have pockets."

"No problem," I said, hoping to convey this was just a temporary setback. "I'll just grab the pair of spare keys I stashed outside."

Fetching the spare keys, I inserted one into the door handle. It didn't work. I jiggled it. Still noting. I tried the other key. More jiggling. Nada.

"You got to be kidding," Maureen said. By now she was starting to stomp her feet in an effort to keep warm.

"Pshaw," I said again, trying not to let her know I was now becoming a little concerned this was no little hiccup. "We'll just try another door," I said.

I tried the other three outside doors. The keys either fit the deadbolt or the door handle but not both. There was no door-opening combination. The spare keys refused to do their job.

Pressing my now rosy-red nose up against the frosty pane, I could see the cats lounging around the woodstove, basking in front of the rosy-red fire. They were warm and sleepy. One of them got up and stretched, then moved a little farther from the stove and flopped down. Poor thing was too warm.

Shivering, I checked to see if a window was unlocked. No luck. They were all burglar proof. As a burglar, I was a bungler.

By now, the dogs were staring, puzzled by the sight of their teeth-rattling master in short-sleeves frantically shaking doors and trying windows. Ally, the alpha mutt who would mutter and call me names when she grew impatient with my shenanigans, became very impatient. She wanted to go sprawl out in front of the stove.

"Mmmmorrrrron!" she yowled into the nippy night.

But that was nothing compared to Maureen's mutterings, much of which I hadn't heard since the Marine Corps.

"Pshaw, we'll just go with Plan B," I mumbled, no longer trying to sound cavalier.

"If that includes whimpering and whining, you've already tried that," Maureen offered. It was one of the few times in my life when I saw her without a smile.

Ah, but a cunning plan was starting to jell in my chilled brain. Granted, some of the details were as shaky as my cold fingers. But anything was better than breaking down a door, freezing to death or being chased down the dark driveway by a very mad woman and three equally mad dogs.

The plan was to get the eighteen-foot extension ladder and lug it around to the side of the house where we would then have access to a large triangular-shaped vent located on the second level. The vent is covered with a thin wire mesh.

The problem was the ladder had to be placed at the same angle as the metal roof. To accomplish that, we placed the foot of the ladder on the hillside overlooking the cabin, creating a bridge between the land and the roof.

I was glad it was dark. If it had been during the day, I would have been too scared to try the idiotic plan. My numb fingers were only slightly warmer than the metal rungs as I crawled across the chasm. I reached the roof, and crawled up the ladder which ended about two feet shy of the vent.

But I managed to reach the vent, remove the mesh and tumble inside the dark attic. Maureen in her clogs followed suit.

Now came the really tricky part. To get into the main house, some brave soul had to remove the trap door and drop onto the floor some eight feet below.

It was just after midnight that my wife, alias Nadia Comaneci, swung down through the trap door and landed lightly with both feet on the floor. It was as though she had been training for the performance that night.

Unfortunately, my wisenheimer mouth wasn't yet frozen shut.

"The discount was well executed, but you didn't quite plant the landing," I told her as I peered down from the trap door. "I'd judge that about 8.6."

There was silence down below.

"Uh, are you going to get a ladder for me?" I asked.

"Pshaw," came the distant reply as she opened the door to let in the chilly dogs.

En route to plopping down by the warm stove, Ally stopped, looked up at her shivering master and barked one last comment. "Mmmorrron!"

Later, after climbing down the ladder that Maureen did bring to my rescue and both of us were sitting by the fire with mugs of hot chocolate in our still cold hands, I reflected on the night's lessons. First, I made a mental not to make sure the spare keys actually work. And two? Always give your rescuer a break. She may not have stuck her landing properly but she did have good form and execution. In retrospect, I should have given her a 9.2.

When it came to sticking a landing, I like to think she would have given me a perfect 10 a decade later on Dec. 6, 2013. But in all fairness a pickup truck is not usually used in gymnastics.

The incident happened during a driving snow storm on the night of Dec. 6, 2013. Now, as one whose snow-driving skills were finely honed while living in Alaska, I'm not particularly concerned when roads turn to ice rinks. Even the sloppy, slick snow of my native southwest Oregon have never proven to be much of an obstacle.

You simply slow down, feather your brakes and avoid folks intent on playing bumper cars. Of course, this is all predicated on the fact you have a reliable vehicle with the traction needed to claw its way along in severe weather.

Still, the best option is to stay home unless you absolutely have to be out on the road when the snow flies. God knows road crews and those who respond to emergencies have enough on their hands without having to contend with another yo-yo stuck in the snow.

But I was confident that we would stay out of harms way that dark and stormy night. I had gotten up in the predawn to write for a couple of hours. Later that morning I took Maureen to work.

"Thanks for taking me today, sweetie," she said when I dropped her off. "I'd rather have you drive when it starts snowing. But be careful. This could be a bad storm."

"Hey, you are talking to an old snow dog who has yet to meet his match when it comes to snow," I replied. Yes, those are words I will be eating for the remainder of my days.

I headed back to our Sterling Creek cabin, noticing the clouds were darkening.

It reminded me of Alaska when a big snow storm is brewing. After feeding our hairy crew of dogs and cats, I happily went back to my writing loft to work. By mid-afternoon a few dry flakes were beginning to drift down outside. The predicted snow storm had arrived.

Recalling Robert Service's immortal words that a promise made is a debt unpaid, I quit writing to fulfill my pledge to Maureen. I did my dreaded household chores, even washing the dishes and firing up the cursed, whiny vacuum cleaner to hunt down a couple of evasive dust bunnies. My plan was to pick up her up at 6:00 p.m., come home to our warm cabin and make tacos, one of the few edible meals I'm capable of preparing. The furry creatures were fed again, and I took the pooches out for a romp just before dark.

That's when I noticed our little valley looked remarkably like the deep winter setting in which Doctor Zhivago holed up in his epic Russian struggle. We were flocked.

I called Maureen who warned that snow was also falling heavily in Medford, a rare occurrence. I decided to drive our four-wheel-drive pickup truck equipped with snow tires instead of the all-wheel drive wagon I had driven that morning. I thought about throwing in the snow chains but figured it would be just a quick trip into town.

When I left our cheerful little cabin, the fierce creatures were gathered around the stove like moths to a light. Although tired from rising early I knew we'd soon be back, enveloped in the warm arms of our mountain home where a cheery fire crackled in the stove. Life was good.

However, the unplowed road to Jacksonville proved a bit more challenging than anticipated. The frozen pavement was covered with powdered snow, creating slippery conditions reminiscent of the Far North. When the road isn't slippery and there are no traffic snarls cause by deep snow to block my path, it normally takes less than a half hour to reach Maureen's shop. But I had to inch along in four-wheel low, stopping periodically to turn around and take an alternative route to avoid the fender-bending bumper cars. It took one hour and forty-five minutes to make the twelve-mile trip.

When Maureen climbed into the truck, I told her that both main routes from Jacksonville to Sterling Creek Road were blocked by traffic jams. We headed out Poorman Creek Road, only to find its link to Sterling Creek Road also blocked.

"We can still take Griffin Lane," I told her as I turned the truck around in the snow. "Guarantee you no one will be on it to block our way."

"No one in their right mind will be on it," she countered. "That road is bad enough in the summer. Too steep. too remote. Let's just wait until the other roads are cleared."

"It's not like we're going into the wilderness," I insisted. "We'll be home safe and sound in a half hour. Remember, you are talking to an old snow dog."

For good measure, I reminded her that Chris and his wife Lorie, medical doctors who live near us, routinely take that road en route to their medical offices in Medford. "Chris is our doctor and I trust his judgment completely," I told Maureen. Somehow, the little niggling fact they don't take that route in bad weather must have slipped my mind, what with all the slick snow and all.

She protested a bit more but the thought of being home sooner than later tipped the scales in favor of trying Griffin Lane. Sadly, her usually steadfast common sense that serves as a firewall when I get an idiotic idea failed us that night.

Griffin Lane didn't seem too bad at first. But then we left the warm glow of lights from the rural houses, venturing beyond the point where the road was maintained. The incline grew steeper, the snow deeper. Russian Cassocks in sleighs jingling down the road would not have surprised.

It was about halfway home at a point where the road makes an awkward hairpin turn on a very steep grade that it happened. Just as we got around the turn, our forward motion stopped. Our tired tires simply gave up the fight. We began sliding back from whence we came.

For thrill seekers, I suppose it doesn't get much better than flying backwards down a mountain road in the dark of night. But I'm not partial to it. It was like the nightmare you are always relieved to wake from, only there was no waking from this one.

"Brace yourself we're going over," I yelled. Maureen didn't say a word

Unfortunately, I was right for the first time that night. The truck seemed to have a mind of its own. Where the road turned, it continued straight, ignoring my manic efforts with the brakes and steering wheel. We shot over the bank into the darkness, streaking backwards towards the trees below. A fiery crash seemed imminent

For a fleeting moment, there was a free-falling sensation. If you've ever been in a car crash, you know that things seem to go in slow motion at times. This was one of those moments. It gave me time to contemplate what might happen when we slammed into the trees below. Having survived one near-deadly crash, I figured I was a goner. I just hoped Maureen would not be hurt.

But there was no fiery explosion. There was bouncing, horrible grating noises and a final violent thud. Our heads snapped back into our head rests. We were dead stopped but apparently not dead. The headlights were pointing straight up. Big snowflakes were drifting down through the limbs illuminated by the headlights. It was beautiful, actually.

First, there was relief over the fact we were alive, that there were no missing body parts or bones jutting out. There was no blood flowing. Of course, there was a brief fear on my part that my wife's still-working fingers were about to close around my throat. A jury of her peers would have been lenient. "For taking that route in the snow, the yo-yo deserved worse," they would quickly conclude. Six months probation. Suspended.

Having gotten ourselves into this mess, I was determined to get us out without calling 911. If it became a life-threatening situation, that would be my last resort. We weren't there yet, albeit only the width of a snowflake away.

After turning off the engine and the lights, I used the cell phone to call AAA Oregon. After determining that we were unhurt, the spokeswoman indicated they were only able to respond to dire emergencies at that point because of the numbers of calls they were receiving statewide. I told her our situation wasn't quite dire. She couldn't promise a tow truck that night. A call to a taxi service in Medford determined that they were snowed in.

The gas tank was full but we didn't want to run it since we didn't know if there was a leak. Besides, we didn't want to stay in the truck. We had no idea whether it would suddenly break away from its perch and plunge on down the mountain.

That's when I remembered that our heavy coats were back in the car. There was a light rain jacket in the truck, a small flashlight and my hiking stick. We also had a cache of tools in the back but nothing that would help us out of this jam. I had on a thin U of O sweatshirt, a heavy leather vest, jeans and boots. Maureen was wearing a light sweater, slacks and sandals. She put on the vest and a pair of mittens she found in the vest pockets. I donned the rain jacket. It was like pulling on a sheet of ice.

Our goal was to climb some thirty feet up to the road, then walk down to where someone could pick us up. After a half hour of trying, of grabbing brush and branches, Maureen was finally able to reach the road. However, because of limited mobility on my right side, I couldn't make it up to that point. But I knew the road snaked around below us after making a U-turn. Giving up on trying to climb the bank, I slid and fell downhill until I came to the road below. Maureen was able to walk down the road.

We began walking back toward civilization. It was now close to 8:00 p.m. The temperature was in the high teens, possibly low twenties. Tops.

With Maureen lurching along in her sandals and me dragging my right leg, we must have looked like the Frankenstein monster and his bride. Either that or a pair of ax murderers heading out on the graveyard shift. We periodically slipped on the ice, landing hard on the concrete-like surface. We would help each other up, then trudge on. There were no other vehicles. Just as Maureen had predicted, no one was crazy enough to try it. Save one, of course.

We hiked slowly for about three hours, making any Marine Corps march I've ever made seem like a stroll in the park. Maureen never faltered, never whined, although the sweet lady may have muttered something about the world's biggest "__hole" at one point. It was hard for me to hear, what with the rain jacket hood pulled over my head. But I had to agree. It was quite an ice hole.

Fortunately, the cavalry arrived in the form of friend John Decker and his son, Jesse, who braved the dangerous conditions to pick us up at a point some three miles from the crash. Both being gentlemen of decorum, neither commented on my lamebrain decision to try to make it home via Griffin Lane that night.

They took us straight to Maureen's shop, dropping us off just before midnight. We spent a memorable night trying to catch a few hours sleeping in reclining shampoo chairs. In the words of the great Patrick McManus, it was the finest of miseries.

Come daylight on Dec. 7, we were back on the phone, checking with AAA and local tow truck companies to see when a towing crew could take a little ride out on Griffin Lane. Just before noon, a tow truck from Medford arrived to pick me up. When I warned crew members Ed and Phil that it would be a challenge, they cheerfully responded they had yet to be defeated when it came to retrieving a vehicle.

Yet they seemed favorably impressed with the challenge when they saw our pickup truck some thirty feet down the embankment and the road's steep incline. They quickly determined they could extract the vehicle by using an ingenious method which involved anchoring their truck with a cable to the base of a large madrone tree farther up the mountain. Apparently in the towing game, it's bad form to have your tow truck slide over the edge to crush the customer's vehicle.

However, before they could put their plan into action, a four-wheel rig came down the road, only to lose control at the sharp turn. The driver hit the brakes, stopping with the front tires clinging precariously on the edge of the bank just above our vehicle. A young woman passenger jumped out, reached in and grabbed a screaming toddler, then quickly retreated to a safe location. That vehicle was then carefully pulled back from the brink.

I spent the next couple of hours farther up the road, standing guard to warn drivers of the danger ahead. Using a winch, Ed and Phil carefully began inching our pickup up to the road.

When I came back down the road, our truck was parked on the side of the road, it's engine purring contentedly with the heater warming up the cab. Amazingly, there was absolutely no damage. Ed and Phil had extricated it with nary a scratch. I would like to take credit for not having slammed into a tree but I had no control after the vehicle went over the edge that night. It was sheer luck.

We arrived home exactly twenty-three hours after I had left. The pooches were happy to see us, and equally eager to race outside to relieve themselves after holding it all that time. The long-awaited taco dinner— our first meal since noon the previous day—was excellent, by the way.

As for this old snow dog, he was learned one new trick when it comes to icy roads: don't go off the beaten path.

TWENTY-SEVEN

Strangers in the Night

T HE INSISTENT TAPPING JUST BEYOND OUR CHAMBER door at precisely 2:30 a.m. in the spring of 2014 would have caused Edgar Allen Poe to sit bolt upright in bed and blast away with a musket. At the very least he would have made a startled large black bird take flight, thus depriving the world of a wonderful poem.

But it was no raven croaking "nevermore," causing the insistent rapping and rudely rousting us from our dreams of forgotten lore. The sound was coming from the outside metal door off the kitchen, well beyond our chamber door. I only heard the tapping for a few seconds before Harpo and Waldo stopped chasing cats in their snoring slumbers and erupted into snarling growls and barks. More than 220 pounds of fanged canine were immediately bent on breaking down the door to get at the rapper. Being sensible dogs, they are not fans of rapping of any sort, be it on the door or in a music video. And they were exceedingly cranky to hear rapping at this hour. We share their opinion of both rapping music and the uncivilized early hour. Besides, I had just hooked a large trout in a very pleasant dream and wanted to sleep a few more minutes in order to reel it in. He was a lunker.

Dressed in pajamas—I had taken to wearing them after we moved into the cabin to help ease the shock of slipping between cold sheets—I stumbled toward the growing kerfuffle in the kitchen. Harpo was standing on his hind legs, his massive black head pressed against the door while Waldo stood bowlegged beside him, both letting our visitor know with each rabid bark that they were eager for a pound of flesh.

I flipped on the outside light after cautioning Maureen to leave all the inside lights off. We needed to be able to see outside and not let the would-be ax murderer see the bleary-eyed, confused homeowners stumbling about within.

The person outside didn't appear to have much promise as a murderess, although they probably learn in Ax Murderer 101 not to dress in a threatening manner. It was a slim young lady with blonde hair in her early twenties. She was dressed in clean jeans, a sensible shirt and short jacket. Very nice attire, I thought, although Maureen felt the ensemble lacked sophistication. Our visitor's car was also running, poor strategy for an evil doer bent on a sneak attack. The headlights illuminated our pump house. Not for the first time I noticed we had yet to put the finishing touches on the pump house, giving it a proper covering of red cedar planks to match the cabin. The weeds were also growing a bit high around the pump house door. And it occurred to me that I probably should coil up the water hose onto the hose reel when I get a moment.

But the uninvited nocturnal guest apparently didn't drop by to talk about the pump house appearance. At least she had the good taste and propriety not to mention it was a little untidy. That was where her sense of decency took flight. She didn't introduce herself or apologize for the late hour. Or early hour, depending on your perspective.

"Where is Jacksonville?" she demanded. "I'm lost and almost out of gas. Tell me where Jacksonville is."

The question baffled me for a moment. In my sleep-addled mind, my first thought was that something had happened to Jacksonville. Could it be it was no longer located at its assigned place on the map? All those poor people living there no longer had a place to call home. Very sad, that. I hoped the beautiful old brick courthouse at least had survived whatever calamity had befallen the historic little town.

However, I was starting to grasp reality, such as it is at 2:30 a.m. when rudely awakened from a pleasant dream.

"It should be in the same place we left it about eight hours ago," I replied, by now getting a little rankled at her snotty attitude. "You just go back down our driveway, turn left and follow the road. It'll take you to Jacksonville and Medford just beyond."

"Well, how far is it?" she said. For someone who had rapped on our door at zero dark thirty, she was mighty persnickety.

"It's about a dozen miles to Medford, the only place locally where a gas station will be open at 2:30 in the morning," I said, now fully awake and nearly as cranky as the dogs. "For some odd reason, they seldom stay up past midnight, particularly if they have to go to work early in the morning. It's very rude of them but there you are. Some people are ill mannered like that.

My snide words didn't faze her. Perhaps that was because I was speaking through a metal door and the words failed to reach their intended target.

"Do you have any gas I could put into my car so I can get back to civilization?" she asked. "I was out here visiting some friends and got lost. All I want is to get back into town."

"No, no gas," I said. "We just gave our last gallon to the fellow who was here at midnight."

OK, that was a lie, at least the part about the previous visitor. We do have several gas cans but they are invariably empty since they are quickly consumed by our various machines which include a riding mower, weed beater, rototiller and the old pickup truck we use for hauling wood on the property.

"Figures," she said. "So what am I going to do?"

Beyond being feloniously grumpy, she didn't seem to be a threat. She wasn't armed, at least there was no gun or ax visible on her person. Of course, there could be an assistant ax murderer lurking on either side of the door. Or another one creeping up on our deck on the other side of the cabine, getting ready to plunge the double-bitted weapon through the wood and greet us with a resounding "Here's Johnny!"

By now, Maureen had pulled the pooches away from the door and retreated back into the dark recesses of the cabin. They had calmed down, although they were still uttering intermittent growls punctuated with an occasional baritone bark to let the intruder know they remained ready to conduct business.

I opened the door a few inches so we could communicate above the din of the muttering mutts.

"I'm sorry but we really don't have any gas," I said, then peeked around at her vehicle. It was a late model small car, the kind that sips gas as though it's served in a martini glass. "Is your fuel emergency light on? If it isn't, you have at least one gallon left. You can get to Medford on that with no problem."

She allowed her fuel light was not on. But she was still not sure we were bright enough to understand that she didn't know where she was.

"So I just go back down to the road, and turn left?" she asked. "There are no forks in the road or anything? Are you sure?"

"Of that, we are very sure," I replied, then asked, "Are you sure you are OK to drive?"

She appeared to be sober but I didn't want to contribute to a drunk driver crash. As rude and annoying as our early, early morning guest was, she didn't deserve to be in a wreck, injuring herself or anyone else.

"Yeah, I'm fine," she said as she started to walk back to her car. But she wasn't quite through with us yet, having one last comment to throw over her shoulder. "This place is real creepy," she concluded.

I certainly had no argument with that assessment. Fortunately, the creepiness left when she pulled out of our driveway and headed back to her version of the civilized world where 2:30 a.m. surprise visits were apparently the norm. We staggered back to bed where I found the fish were no longer biting. After staring at the ceiling awhile, I got up and wrote a bit about a rude nocturnal visitor.

Three weeks later on a Sunday night we were taking the dogs out, heading to the dog park where they could see a man about a horse or conduct whatever other hopefully brief nocturnal activities they had planned. We were looking forward to retiring early after a long weekend of working around the old place.

It was a little after 10:00 p.m.

I stifled a yawn as Harpo pulled me along behind him, apparently impatient to get on with the horse transaction. He fancies himself as a past master at horse trading. If the ability to lift a rear leg above his back is any indicator, he is an equine expert. He certainly is very adept at horsing around.

"Let's just hope no one shows up at 2:30 tonight asking for gas," laughed Maureen whose leash was attached to a polite and prancing Waldo. "I'm really not up for something like that again tonight. You know, we might think about keeping some gas aside for emergencies like that."

"I don't think it would be a good idea to be known as the place where you can get free gas," I replied, yawning yet again. "Pretty soon they would want us to check the oil and squeegee the windshield. Besides, that was just one of those weird things that happens once in a lifetime."

Just then—I kid you not—a voice hailed us from down the long driveway.

"Do you have any gas we can borrow?" a male voice yelled out of the darkness. "We ran out of gas. And our cell phone doesn't get any service out here."

At least that seemed to be the gist of what he was saying. It was difficult to hear precisely, what with Harpo and Waldo throwing snarling hissy fits and digging in with their four-wheel-drive paws in an attempt to reach the disembodied voice from down the driveway. Waldo was snorting like a wildebeast. Harpo joined in with his foghorn bark that would have sent Sasquatch sprinting for the deep woods.

After finally reining Harpo in, I shined the flashlight down the driveway where the beam revealed two young men. One was sitting in the driveway. The other was standing by him, holding a small red gas can and carrying a syphon hose.

"Do your dogs bite?" asked the fellow sitting down.

"They rip and tear their victims more than bite, although the results are pretty much the same," I answered. "Better stay there until we get these brutes back in their reinforced cages."

In truth, they have never sunk their teeth into any biped. Nor did they have cages. I wanted to keep the strangers in the dark as to the canine corps' watchdog capabilities. Harpo and Waldo are actually both big babies who loved to be scratched behind the ears. But there is no doubt in my mind they would give their all for us if we were ever in harm's way.

We alternately pushed and pulled the dogs into the house where Maureen stayed with them. I walked down the driveway with the flashlight to chat with our visitors. Fortunately, I had yet to slip into my pajamas for the night.

They were in their early twenties. One was short and stocky; the other tall and lanky. Both were polite, unlike their ill-mannered predecessor three weeks earlier.

"We were helping our friend John who has a cabin on Yale Creek over the weekend and borrowed his rig to go into town," Stocky explained. "But we ran out of gas about two miles down the road. We saw your lights and wondered if you could help us."

Yale Creek is a tributary to the Little Applegate River half a dozen miles south of us. There are cabins in the area so their story was conceivably true. But the siphon hose was a little problematic. If yours is the same make and model as my naturally suspicious brain, you may suspect there was at least a passing notion on their part of making a gas withdrawal from a vehicle without the owner's knowledge.

They asked to use our telephone to call a lady friend in Medford to come pick them up. We still have a land line because our cell phone service refuses to serve within six miles or so of the cabin. Maureen says a cell tower would fix that but I think the cell phone just doesn't want to be bothered when it is home. In any case, we both agree that a cell tower would be butt ugly. So we live with two phone services. The landline includes a mobile phone which is good up to 100 feet of the house. I brought it out so Stocky could call his friend. Judging from Stocky's continued cajoling, the friend was less than thrilled about driving out to the wilds of Sterling Creek in the dark. I could hear her protestations. Like our 2:30 a.m. visitor, maybe she thought it was creepy. In fact, maybe it was the same young lady who visited three weeks earlier. Naw, couldn't be.

"She said she could head out here in an hour or so," Stocky said after thanking me for the use of the phone. "We can just wait at the end of the driveway if that's OK."

"That's fine," I said. "I wish I had some gas to give you. I just poured the last of it into our rototiller this afternoon."

I had emptied the contents of three nearly empty gas cans into the noisy machine so I could till the garden but hadn't gotten around to working in the soil. I was saving that task for the next day.

The two seemed harmless enough but I still didn't feel comfortable with inviting them inside. For all we knew, the somewhat awkward telephone conversation could have been with a parole officer.

That's when Lanky, the fellow who had been sitting on the driveway, spoke again.

"Is there any way you could take us to a store or something?" he asked. "We would really appreciate it. If she doesn't show up, then we'll have to walk into town. That would take all night. And I am really, really tired. If we had any money, we'd pay you to take us."

Figuring it would be better to take them to J'ville rather than have them waiting at the end of our driveway for an iffy ride, I decided giving them a ride was the most sensible solution. If their intentions were for ill, I wanted them away from our house. I also had a feeling they would be more likely to be rapping on our door after midnight than be picked up by Stocky's lady friend anytime in the next couple of hours.

"I'll give you a lift into Jacksonville," I said. "The gas station is still open. You can call your friend from there. She can pick you up at the station."

I told them I didn't want any money, that they could do someone else a favor down the line. "I'd buy you some gas but I'm afraid I'm also broke," I added. This squared with the facts. Since retiring at the end of the previous year, I was still adjusting to my new life which didn't require I have money on me. My self-imposed routine is to write in the early morning hours, then work outside in the afternoons. Maureen takes me shopping with her on weekends, providing I shower and promise not to leer at the natives or engage them in scary conversation. I didn't think my little chat about soup with the elderly lady with the walker was scary at all, although there was an awkward moment when I realized I was standing in front of the prophylactic display. But perhaps Maureen is right. It may have been a touch of cabin fever. A walker could give one a feeling of confinement. Poor lady.

With Stocky and Lanky, I wanted them to know I wasn't carrying wads of money. Like our gas, our cash seems to be quickly consumed by various demands.

"Yep, poor as a church mouse," I said. "We were waiting for our ship to come in but we gave up. We think it sank with no survivors."

When I stepped into the cabin to tell Maureen, she was not happy to learn I was about to drive off into the dark of night with two strangers.

"What if they try to rob you and you get hurt?" she asked. "Maybe they just want our pickup. This is not safe. Don't do it. I don't like it."

"It'll be OK," I assured her. "They seem harmless enough. They are certainly polite. I'll go straight into Jacksonville, drop them off, then come right back. Besides, it's a pretty pathetic world if you can't help someone just because you don't know them. I'd rather take a chance on someone than live in fear that everyone is just waiting to rob you."

"Yeah, well, Ted Bundy had manners," she said, repeating, "I don't like you doing this. Please be very careful."

I did ask her to lock the door when I left. Just in case.

I was taking our "new" truck. It is a dozen years old but a mere youngster compared to our decidedly old truck we keep for farm work. Lanky squeezed into the back to perch on a little jump seat while Stocky hopped up front to ride shotgun which, as far as I could see, he didn't have.

I sped out of the driveway and onto Sterling Creek Road, all but squealing the tires when we hit the pavement. My plan was to drive fast. Real fast. If they tried something, they would have no doubt in their minds that we would crash and that they would not be walking away from the mangled wreckage. The flaw, of course, is that the chances were good that I would also not be walking away. But it was the best idea I could come up with at the time.

I also figured I could keep them off balance with an endless line of bull.

"The reason I've driving fast is that my wife says I have exactly fifteen minutes before she calls the cops," I said. "So hang on because it is about fifteen minutes away. I'll call her as soon as I get there. She is a little distrusting of her fellow human beings. Comes from her mom, the parole officer."

I was hoping that my mother-in-law would forgive me for that little fib.

By this time trees were zipping past. There was no other traffic to worry about so I cut corners a mite. I hoped no deer would come sauntering out onto the road at the last second. Nor did I care to meet up with the large black bear I had seen on the road a few times in recent years. A black bear on a dark night doesn't exactly stand out. And this big fellow would definitely total the truck.

"This is where I've seen a big black bear crossing the road a few times," I told my passengers as we raced through a forested area where he hung out. "I'd hate to have to walk through here at night. He probably weighs around 400 pounds."

That was sticking my verbal toe on the weight scale a bit to enlarge the bruin but I wanted them to know it was not a good place to stop.

In the corner of my eye, Stocky scrunched down into his seat as we threw a little gravel while rounding a corner on the steep downgrade. Lanky was frantically searching for a seat belt. The pickup may have fishtailed just a hair.

"Jesus!" Stocky exclaimed.

"Christ!' Lanky echoed from the jump seat behind him.

Now, it could be they were very religious fellows but I'm doubtful. Probably just impressed by my driving skills.

"Not much of a super there—fishtailing a bit," I observed. "The back end is a little light. But we'll be there in a jiffy."

I continued to chat away as the road writhed like a snake under the speeding tires. My passengers may have been impressed by my glibness, but they weren't in the mood to banter. Tired from their walk, no doubt.

I slowed but did not make a full stop at the one stop sign between our home and Jacksonville. Normally, I am not a scofflaw when it comes to the rules of the road. I also pride myself in driving safely. But this was an unusual night.

My captive audience was clearly happy to see the lights of Jacksonville. They immediately hopped out when I pulled into the gas station which was still open.

"Thanks for the ride," Stocky said as he quickly walked away.

"Yeah, thanks," Lanky said, then added to his chum as they walked away, "good God, I'd rather take my chances with the bear than his driving. I thought we were goners back there."

While making a mental note to add another 100 pounds to give the bear more heft to bolster future scare tactics, I turned around and headed back towards our cabin. I was nearly halfway home when I remembered I was supposed to call Maureen to let her know everything was kosher.

When I pulled up the driveway, all the exterior lights were in a blaze of glory. Inside, it was dark. The only sound was the deep barking of the canine crew.

I walked up the stone path to the door and called out. An interior light flicked on. Maureen was standing there, holding a rifle at the ready. Knowing her, I presumed it was locked and loaded.

"You scared me," she said. "You were supposed to call me. I didn't think there was any way you could have driven to Jacksonville and back. So I thought they had taken the truck and came back here to rob the place. You couldn't have possibly made it there that fast."

"I could and I did," I said as I stepped in and gently pushed the muzzle down toward floor. "I'm sorry I forgot to call. By the time I remembered I was already in the no-call zone."

"But I hope you realize that most people don't shoot burglars breaking into their homes," I said. "Mostly they end up shooting family members. It would really put a damper on this otherwise fine night if you winged me."

"I wouldn't have winged you, honey," she said, obviously still a little heated from the fact I hadn't been considerate enough to call to relieve her of worrying. "I'm a better shot than that."

Although I wasn't sure of what she meant, I let it go. Sometimes it's better not to know.

The next morning I got up early to write and help Maureen get ready for work, including making her lunch. I returned to my loft in the cabin and continued writing until early afternoon. After grabbing a quick lunch, I went out to till the garden.

There is something about tilling a garden that I enjoy. Since we have worked the soil for several years, the tilling is easy. It's relaxing and you inhale the earthy smell of newly churned soil. It also gives me a chance to add to our square nail collection since we continue to harvest them.

I checked the depth of the gas. It appeared I had enough to do the job, providing I didn't lollygag. A warm but not too hot sun had risen overhead. Life was good.

I set the choke and was just about to pull on the starter cord when a disembodied voice invaded my peaceful garden reverie.

"Excuse me, but do you have a gallon of gas I could buy from you?" a man shouted from the road. It was a casual, friendly request, not an impolite demand.

A gray-haired fellow was standing on the road near the end of the driveway. He was carrying a gallon gas can in one hand. Alongside him on a leash was a little pug, the kind of pooch who spoke volumes in the *Men In Black* flick. The pug let the man do the talking that day.

"My truck is down the road—out of gas," he said. "All I need is enough to get into town."

"Sorry, but I just put the last gas I had into the tiller," I said, although I was nearly speechless that yet another person had shown up in less than twenty-four hours to request some gas. Never mind no one had stopped to ask for gas in the dozen years since we bought the place. Now we were being inundated by gas seekers. Perhaps Maureen was right about keeping a little extra handy. Better yet, maybe we ought to open our own station, considering the spate of recent customers.

"No problem—you have a good one," he replied before picking up his dog to continue walking toward town. "Nice weather for gardening. It's sure beautiful out here today."

He resumed his journey, his happy mood unaltered by the fact he had a long uphill walk ahead of him. I turned back to the tiller, grabbed the cord again and started to give it a yank.

Instead, I let it drop. I strode into the cabin, grabbed the keys to our Subaru wagon and called Harpo and Waldo.

"We're going for a little ride, boys," I told them as they joyfully piled into the back of the car. Each had a big grin as I rolled down the back windows to give them—and me—plenty of air. When they get excited, they sometimes emit a little flatulence, hence the need for a steady supply of air that hasn't been filtered through a dog's digestive system. Heaven to the pooches is lolling a long pink tongue out a window on a warm spring day, flinging gobs of dog drool in their wake and tooting.

By now, the man and his dog had disappeared around the corner. I pulled over next to them when we saw them and rolled down the front passenger window.

"I don't have any gas but I can give you a ride to Jacksonville," I said. "That's quite a walk, particularly if you are carrying a dog."

"That's mighty kind of you," he said as he climbed into the car. "But I don't need to go that far. I'm heading to a friend's place just a couple of miles from here."

He reached back to give Harpo and Waldo a rub behind the ears. The bug-eyed pug sat in his lap. He probably would have joined in the conversation but was a little intimidated by the big mutts grinning down at him from the back seat. No doubt they looked as fearsome as any alien on MIB.

"You live around here?" I asked.

"No, I'm from Talent," he said of a bedroom community to Medford. "But I have a cabin on Yale Creek. I was over there doing some work on it."

"You wouldn't have had two young guys out there helping you, would you?" I asked. "One real stocky, the other tall and lanky?"

He confirmed such was the case.

"How would you know that?" he asked, a little startled. For a second, I started to tell him about a lifelong clairvoyance but for once common sense overrode the urge to spoof someone.

"They stopped at our place last night after running out of gas," I said. "They said they were helping a fellow who had a cabin on Yale Creek. They borrowed his truck but ran out of gas. I took them into Jacksonville. So you must be the guy with the cabin."

He started chuckling.

"Yes, they wanted to go into town but the truck must have been too low on gas for them to make it," he said, noting the gas gauge is faulty. When they didn't return, he figured they had run out of gas and decided to walk into town or hitch a ride. He found his truck parked along the road a few miles short of our place.

"I hope they were polite," he said. "Sometimes young people today forget their manners. They need to be reminded to treat folks right. But they are good kids."

I told him they were very polite, although they did give us a start when they called out in the dark. We chatted for awhile. Turns out he had also been in the Marine Corps, then came to Oregon from his native California shortly after his discharge for a change of scenery. When I dropped him off at his friend's place, we shook hands.

"Thanks for the lift, my friend," he said. His pug remained silent, his buggy eyes still warily watching the big boys leering down at him.

Out of curiosity, I drove past our cabin to check out his vehicle. Sure enough, just two miles beyond our place was a well-kept pickup truck parked alongside the highway. Its presence corroborated both their stories.

I went back home and put Harpo and Waldo in the dog park, and returned to the garden to begin tilling.

The odd thing about tilling is that while the machine is going nuts as the tines chomp into the soil, you have a sense the world has slowed down as you play an earthy lento. Tilling provides one with a fine opportunity to think and observe. About an hour into tilling, I noticed the earlier stalled truck passing by, driven by the fellow I had given the lift. The pug stood with his front paws on the dash, seeming to be chatting away. All was right with their world.

TWENTY-EIGHT

'Tempus Fugit' on Sterling Creek

W HEN WE BOUGHT THE AGED CABIN ON STERLING CREEK, our nation
had just embarked on its longest war. It would take a dozen years
for the Iraq war to start winding down, albeit remains a messy quagmire
whose legacy appears to be that of helping unleash religious fanatics upon
the world. But peace came to us the moment we stepped onto the old
Gilson ranch property. We had found a tranquility we had been searching
for on this sometimes hostile sphere.

As I write this, we have lived on the land for more than fifteen years,
the longest either of us have inhabited the same abode. Like weary feet
slipping into a pair of comfortable old shoes, we feel secure and relaxed in
the restored cabin. On a cold winter's night when frost covers the deck, we
bathe in the glow of the woodstove, slipping off our shoes and wiggling
our toes in its cheerful warmth. It is for those wonderful moments we
worked hard to rehabilitate the old place. Although it remains a work in
progress, the cabin is home.

I have this urge to get a little board from the recycle pile of left-over
cabin wood, pulling out my Leatherman and carving on it, "*Hic habitas*

felicitas." I once saw the phrase painted on one of those cute little signs in a theme park garden. You've seen those signs, the kind miscreants stomp when the gardener in residence is looking the other way. This particular gardener was a cultured nerd who smugly informed me the Latin phrase means, "Here dwells happiness." This was after he overheard me telling Maureen the phrase warned visitors they were about to enter an area where cats frequently take dumps. He seemed taken aback when I challenged his reading, informing him that's not what we were taught back at Kerby U. From his frown, it was obvious he had never heard of that particular institution of higher learning. Probably went to private school. I wanted to hang around the garden until the cultured nerd looked the other way but Maureen quickly marched me out to the car like an exasperated teacher taking a misbehaving brat to the principal's office.

As snug and comfortable as the cabin is inside, providing you appreciate sharing a rustic dwelling with a slumbering pet herd emitting purrs, satisfied snorts and flatulence in the form of cheerful toots now and then, its thick walls do not protect us from the harsh world outside. Since moving to Sterling Creek, we have lost loved ones, including my mom, both of Maureen's parents, nephew Blair, along with several uncles and cousins. Although the memories remain, it seems that each time someone you care about dies, a little bit of yourself fades with them into the ages.

In fact, we started out 2016 by attending the Jan. 2nd funeral of my first cousin Dale, one of the finest people I've ever met. We were a little late for Dale's funeral because of a hummingbird emergency at the cabin, an admittedly very strange reason but one he would have understood. The problem, you see, was that Maureen insisted we couldn't leave that morning until we could safely put out the hummingbird feeder without freezing the little guys' life-giving elixir. Two hummingbirds, no bigger than my little finger, had decided to hang around the cabin for the winter instead of flying south with the smarter feather brains.

"Not to be picayune but the funeral begins at 11:00 a.m. and it will take at least five hours to get to the church on time," I told her. "Remember, the roads will be icy and the most direct route has been closed by a landslide."

"Do you really want to be known as a hummingbird murderer?" she asked her worry wart of a husband. Without waiting for me to answer, she made an executive decision for the both of us. "We are waiting until daylight to leave," she decided.

Maureen knew she had me with the hummingbird homicide comment. Unless we provided food for them, they would surely perish. Dale's wonderful wife, Eleanor, a retired elementary school teacher who passed in 2003, would surely have had Maureen's back on the hummingbird issue. Like I said, Dale would have understood my dilemma.

We had been bringing the feeder in every night it was likely to freeze, returning it at daybreak so the spoiled little guys could sip a warm breakfast before I stumble into the kitchen to boil water for a cup of Earl Grey. My bird book informs me the hummers are likely Anna's hummingbirds, given the iridescent red on their heads and coat of greenish feathers. It also says the hardy little fellows often stay in our area over the winter, although it doesn't explain where they spend those cold nights. Do they shiver the night away, peering with longing at the warm lights in the cabin, their tiny beaks chattering from the cold? We don't know the answers to what has become an annual phenomenon. All I know is that I have two cheeky hummingbirds on my back and that Maureen has happily adopted them as airborne pets. It's worrisome.

But on Sterling Creek we have witnessed that within any entity, be it biped or birch, dwells a strong desire to live. That lesson came from an ancient apple tree standing just south of the garden. When we bought the place, the tree looked like it was not long for this world. The trunk, once some two feet thick at the base, was literally a half shell of its former self. All of the inner wood was gone save for a two-inch thick bark and dermis on one side. Since all the deciduous trees had already dropped their leaves when we moved onto the property that first year, it appeared the tree was dead. But the skeleton tree came to life in the spring, leafing out in dark green foliage, followed by a beautiful array of pink and white blossoms. That August, small apples hung by the dozens like little red

Christmas balls on a Charlie Brown tree. Each ensuing year it has followed suit.

One fall day while living with us during his convalesce from a stroke, my twin brother looked at the tree and made one of his black-and-white snap judgments that don't brook disagreement.

"Cut that down—it looks like death warmed over," he growled.

"That old tree looks better than we do on a good day," I countered.

"God, you make my ass ache," he grumped back and walked off to bark at the dogs or hiss at the cats.

Honestly, it wasn't merely because I am my twin's contrarian that I told him it had earned the right to dawdle away the autumn of its years. Oregon may be the nation's first right-to-die state but the decision to leave this mortal coil rests with the one contemplating making the exit. I figure the tree had a right to live, and had declared loud and clear its intentions by its tenacity to cling to life. Besides, I like the thought of it persevering long after the peculiar bipeds living in the cabin, as well as one's equally eccentric twin, had departed for the great beyond.

Like the apple tree that refuses to die, we are heeding poet Dylan Thomas's remonstration not to go gentle into that good night. Maureen still maintains her shop in town while I doggedly persist in mangling the English language at home. But I'm not addicted to the news like I once was. I now follow the threads of long-term trends in an effort to better understand developments on this odd little planet. That idea comes from having read in college about a fellow who made a point of not poring over a newspaper until a week after the ink dried. He felt it was healthier to digest the news, allowing everything to settle out before worrying about it. Now, of course, it is difficult to escape the twenty-four-hour news cycle, what with everyone connected to the world's pulse via computers. Obviously, ours is a digital future, one I find promising yet potentially troublesome.

What got me pondering its negative ramifications was an article in the February 2015 issue of the *Smithsonian* magazine. In the article, a very smart fellow named Yuval Noah Harari, the author of the just-released book, *Sapiens: A Brief History of Humankind*, envisaged humankind disappearing in a century or two. Harari explained that we will simply upgrade ourselves. Hmmm. I'm not sure what the upgrading will entail, although I'm assuming this will involve artificial parts along with artificial intelligence. With the steel plate in my left leg and wiring in my neck, both of which periodically cause a dull but persistent pain, I could do without additional artificial parts. Granted, I could use all the additional intelligence I can muster, artificial or otherwise. I just don't much like the idea of lighting up like a cyborg.

Besides, the thought of having a robot clanking about our cabin is unsettling. Sure, it could chop firewood all day without breaking into a sweat but it wouldn't appreciate discovering a square nail or watching a golden eagle soar over Gilson Gulch the way we do. It wouldn't look forward to the March daffodils or planting tomatoes after the last frost.

But, at the risk of ticking off the Borg by adjusting their mantra a bit, resistance to change is futile. Change is indeed inevitable, both inside the cabin and beyond the bounds of earth. For instance, after living comfortably for half a century with the certain knowledge there were nine planets orbiting the sun, I awoke one morning in 2006 to discover one had vanished. Poof. But it wasn't because of some cataclysmic explosion in the solar system. Pluto had simply been downsized to dwarf planet status by the scientific powers that be. It seems the far away real estate didn't measure up to strict planetary standards established by the folks in the white laboratory coats. However, in January of 2016 two California university brianiacs in white lab coats announced there might be a ninth planet in our solar system after all. But it was not Pluto. Although the ninth planet hasn't been physically seen, the astronomers have spotted circumstantial evidence that its gravitational pull is herding the orbit of half a dozen small bodies beyond Neptune. This solar system stranger would be about 4,500 times larger than Pluto with an orbit that takes more than 10,000 Earth years to orbit the sun, they reported. But the astronomic jury is still out as I write this. It could be an "Aha!" scientific moment or yet another "Oh, never mind." Those who quote the bible cite Eccelesiastes when they insist there is nothing new under the sun. We'll leave that for others to hash out but even the most devout must accept there are and always will be new things to discover.

Back on earth, like the fellow who read newspapers after the news had a chance to age, I have come to cherish the time I have to think long thoughts. But I sometimes wonder if I am becoming a misanthrope by living and working in the cabin while my wife daily travels to work in town where she communicates with other humanoids. Some folks made of less sterner stuff than I would certainly suffer from cabin fever after living in the confined space for such as extended period. But I'm doing just fine, aside from the sobbing outbursts, frequent claustrophobic panics and arguing with the pesky voices constantly whispering behind my back.

With the life we have chosen, we will never become old codgers who stare at television all our waking hours, filled with a growing panic and paranoia created by unfair and unbalanced bilge. We have too much work to do, too many things books to read, too many trails to hike, too many places to see and too many future friends to meet.

Admittedly, not watching television does leave you a few steps behind when it comes to social mores. Consider what happened a few years ago when we dropped in one autumn weekend to visit my mother-in-law Wilma whose cable TV offered a zillion stations. The screen was about the size of a drive-in theater. While Maureen and her mom were busy working on a quilt they were making for a grandchild due late in 2014, I sat down on the couch and picked up the remote to see what was on at the drive-in. I was hoping to catch a Duck football game but my timing was off. Unable to find anything worth watching, I began scrolling through the channels. A political extremist in the midst of a diatribe filled the screen, his face beet red as flecks of spittle sprayed toward the camera. Following that was a religious fanatic, also all but frothing at the mouth as he warned of hellfire and damnation unless viewers dipped deep into their pockets to purportedly help save souls. He would have made a snake oil salesman blush. Popping up next was an infomercial hawking a wicked-looking gadget guaranteed to make slicing tomatoes, carrots and fingers as easy as pie. And so it went.

Wilma came in to chat just as I clicked on to a channel featuring a man and woman going to town. Only they weren't going to town, if you get my drift. I frantically clicked away to change the station but my fumbling only managed to increase the sound of passionate moans filling the room. I slid down into the coach, trying to disappear among the cushions.

You would have thought Wilma would be the one more uncomfortable, being an octogenarian at the time. But you would be wrong. She was an old hand at separating the TV wheat from the chaff.

"Oh, they show that stupid stuff all the time now," she told me, waving a hand at the moaning couple as though swatting at a fly buzzing past. "It's such a silly show."

Seemingly coming to my rescue was a commercial featuring a studious looking middle-aged man resembling a mild-mannered minister about to give a pleasant discourse on the merits of helping others. I sat up, silently giving thanks at having found salvation. Until he started preaching the virtues of Viagra which he swore performed a miracle by saving his marriage, that is. It left this viewer wondering if the marriage was worth saving and whether he should take up quilting.

Not watching TV has given me ample time to contemplate this world of ours. As a lifelong wonderer, I have developed a knack for pondering things that normal people with a life don't give a rat's patootie about. Consider, if you don't find it too disgusting, the problem of old men and their sagging pants. While it may be fashionable among some younger segments of society to show the crack of their ass, it's even more repulsive for those entering geezerdom to follow suit.

Oddly enough, it was Maureen who brought it up the other day. She wasn't pondering but merely making an observation, presenting it in a much more tasteful way than yours truly would have.

"No offense, honey, but your pants are starting to sag a tiny bit," she said. "Your derriere seems to be shrinking a little. Perhaps it is time to get a pair of suspenders."

I must admit it hurt a little, coming from the love of my life. Still, I couldn't let a comment like that go without a, well, smartass retort. Never mind I had also noticed I had been hitching my pants up more and more of late.

"It may be a half-assed excuse but I've been working my ass off since I retired," I told her, causing her to roll her eyes while a grin was growing on her pretty face.

Unlike a fine wine, my humor does not improve with age. It just gets a bit more peculiar. But our friend Stuart who is only a year or so behind— so to speak—has a witty answer to the saggy-ass phenomenon among men of a certain refined age. "I just tell people I went into real estate and lost my ass," quipped the recent retiree. Compared to mine, his humor has aged well.

But Maureen has a more diplomatic assessment on the fact a man's posterior goes south as he seasons.

"Men tend to lose a little weight in that area as they get older," she said. "It's a natural progression. Your body is just redistributing itself a little. And there is nothing wrong with wearing suspenders. You don't have a pot belly or anything. You are still adorable to me."

I know she threw that last part in to soften the news but I bought it, nonetheless. After all, when I look at her, I still see the sixteen-year-old who forever stole my heart. I'm just glad she didn't point out that I'm also developing jowls that would be the envy of a prize hog at the Oregon State Fair.

But there is no question gravity is pulling a little harder these days in Gilson Gulch. I feel it when I climb the stairs or take a walk up the valley, wearing my new suspenders. As the hitch in my gait becomes a little more acute, I rely more on a walking stick when we take a stroll. But I'm not the only one aging in dog years: Waldo is also sagging here and there, although I'm way ahead of him in the jowl competition.

Nor is gravity the only thing gaining ground on Sterling Creek. There is the fact my hair is turning from salt and pepper to a silvery gray. It is quite obvious the salt is reproducing faster than the pepper on my thatch.

"It makes you look distinguished," Maureen assured me, knowing full well a large white lie is easier to live with than the truth when you are dealing with the aging of a significant other.

"I suppose it does distinguish me from those pushing up daises," I grumped.

Like me, the cabin is feeling its age as it nears the century mark. When a snowstorm just before Christmas 2015 left us temporarily without power, we were reminded the cabin had no electricity when it was built. Like my grandparents when they first homesteaded in the Applegate Valley, those who lived in our cabin made do with kerosene lamps and a wood stove. Unless it was Sunday, they weren't going to take a bath. Makes one wonder how my grandparents ended up having five children but let's not go there. Thinking about your grandparents copulating is even grosser than the spectacle of old men in sagging pants. So let's get back to the weather.

I'm guessing that, like me, they loved to look outside at the gently falling snow, providing they didn't have to go anywhere, there was plenty of firewood, the farm animals were taken care of and the fodder was in the shock. Even back then, the sight of falling snow must have given them a secure feeling of being safely shut off from the craziness of the rest of the world.

That's not to say all snow encounters are warm and fuzzy, as demonstrated by our wild ride down the mountainside that December night in 2013. No doubt there were plenty of snow-bound hardships in my grandparents' day. Members of the Donner party certainly never felt all that cozy in the snow, not even when discussing proper cannibal etiquette while passing around the leg bone of a recently departed friend to gnaw on.

Some things, of course, never change. When a large black bear ran across a field by his house in August of 2012, our friend Pete, like good neighbors of old, warned us of our approaching visitor. But he did cheat by using the phone.

"He's a big one—just wanted you to know because he's probably headed for your apple trees," Pete said in his usual cheerful voice.

A week after the bear advisory we got a call from Bjorn Everson, a neighbor a bit farther to the south. The former teacher called to invite us over for a classic music recital by members of the Rogue Valley Symphony at their comfortable home. His wife, Cecile, is a classically-trained pianist. The evening was memorable, especially for a Kerby product who doesn't know Schubert about Bach or Beethoven. Even after a couple of years, the soothing sounds of the cello still resonate in my memory. I like to think there was a big bear sitting with his back up against a large fir in the woods above Sterling Creek that wonderful evening, tapping his hairy toes as he listened to the soft strains of the music. His tummy full of our apples, no doubt.

Bears and cellos are an odd mix but in our neck of the woods they reflect today's unique harmonious balance. Of course, when it comes to bears and cellists, there are more bruins than players of big string instruments in our 'hood. Not long afterwards a large bear scampered across the road one evening as I was driving home from work. I have yet to see a cellist scamper across the road, morning or evening. Doubtless it would be difficult to scamper while lugging a cello, although Bigfoot could pull it off.

While winter and summer have had their pleasant moments on Sterling Creek, it is the spring, a time when the land is fat and full of green promises, that invariably causes us to do handsprings, at least in our minds. The infectious sense of optimism can be heard in the songs of the birds and the humming of the bees. That is a time of year when we take our steaming mugs out to the dog park in the morning to see the latest blossoms and watch the sun rise over the mountains. Harpo and Waldo go for a romp while the cats hop into our laps.

Spring invariably offers reassuring sights of the cycle of life. This spring, a pair of robins took up a homestead in one of the branches of the old fir towering over the tack shed. I spotted it when one robin, likely the father, flew into a dense section of a lower branch where a chorus of chirps erupted. Two youngsters, each in gawky adolescence, had their beaks open, demanding the fast food. He dropped off two bugs, and flew to the meadow near the pump house. He stood for a moment on the ground, looking back at the nest before returning to his endless spring hunt for insects. I thought he looked tired.

But we never tire of the sights and sounds on Sterling Creek. Some folks would look askance at our work in progress but we are in our element. Its challenges continue to provide a source of inspiration. In fact, the next big project calls for building a barn, a red one with a gambrel roof. It was Maureen's idea, one she hatched after a daughter announced that, if she ever gets married, she wants to tie the knot in a barn in the Applegate Valley.

"It won't be real big, but large enough to house all our larger tools and other equipment," Maureen said. "The tool shed we built has grown too small. In the barn, we'll have a storage area upstairs. And, of course, there will be room for a marriage ceremony on the ground floor. It'll be fun. We need to keep our eyes out for a weathervane with a bride and groom on it."

No pressure on the would-be real life bride and groom, of course. But it would certainly let them know which way the matrimonial wind is blowing.

"Well, you are right about the tool shed," I said. "It does seem to be growing smaller. In fact, I was thinking about taking the shovels out before the handles snap. The walls are definitely closing in."

I said that out of habit, knowing she expected a smart aleck remark before seriously pondering her latest plan involving hard labor. Initially, I had a few niggling little concerns, including dealing with a county building department which hires only those who have had their sense of humor surgically removed, not to mention the thought of climbing up a shaky ladder to the top of a barn roof to affix the weathervane. But I was excited after she noted we would hire a builder.

"It will be our magnum opus—our great work," I said. "All the livestock in the Applegate Valley will want to hang out in our barn. It will be the Mecca for rodents within a dozen miles. Barn owls will become impatient when they see it going up."

"You are going over the top again, honey," she said, laughing. "It'll just be a solid old-fashioned barn that will be practical for us to use. It will be our contributing legacy to the land after we are gone. And that will be good enough, especially if we get to use the wedding arbor again."

Her plan calls for the barn to stand near a huge and healthy old apple tree some 150 feet west of the cabin. The red barn with a green roof will be within an apple's throw of what had been the Gilson barn on the north side of the gulch bearing their name.

ABOUT THE AUTHOR

C ONTRARY TO WHAT HE SOMETIMES tell folks with tongue held firmly in cheek, Paul wasn't actually raised by wolves. But it is true his grandparents homesteaded in the beautiful Applegate Valley, and that he, like his siblings and his father before him, was born and reared in Southwestern Oregon where they all ran rampant in the mountains, making wolves exceedingly nervous. After a less than stellar scholastic career, he managed to graduate from the University of Oregon, majoring in journalism. Over the subsequent decades, he was able to convince more than a dozen newspaper editors from Alaska to California to hire him, decisions which he hopes did not leave a long-lasting blemish on their careers. Upon retiring to become a recovering journalist, he immediately fell off the wagon and started writing books. He lives happily with his wife, Maureen, in their restored but still rustic Sterling Creek cabin with assorted fierce creatures, including a few which she insists don't bite all that much. His second non-fiction book, *Madstone*, scheduled to be published in the spring of 2017, will take the reader farther into the Oregon wilds with two World War I draft evaders, both of whom were Paul's uncles.

hellgatepress.com

CPSIA information can be obtained
at www.ICGtesting.com
Printed in the USA
FSOW02n1320071217
42165FS